MACROMEDIA

MISSION, MESSAGE, and MORALITY

RALPH L. LOWENSTEIN

University of Florida

JOHN C. MERRILL

Louisiana State University

Longman

New York & London

To Earl F. English, Dean Emeritus, School of Journalism,
University of Missouri—Columbia
whose devotion to the mass media and to journalism education
has been an inspiration to students of all ages

*P
90
.L69
1990
150283
nw.1990*

Macromedia: Mission, Message, and Morality

Copyright © 1990 by Longman

Longman, 95 Church Street, White Plains, N.Y. 10601

Associated companies:
Longman Group Ltd., London
Longman Cheshire Pty., Melbourne
Longman Paul Pty., Auckland
Copp Clark Pitman, Toronto

Executive editor: Gordon T. R. Anderson
Production editor: Marie-Josée A. Schorp
Cover design: Michael Jung
Text art: Fine Line
Production supervisor: Kathleen M. Ryan

Library of Congress Cataloging in Publication Data

Lowenstein, Ralph Lynn, 1930–
    Macromedia—mission, message, and morality/Ralph L. Lowenstein,
    John C. Merrill.
        p.   cm.
    Includes bibliographical references.
    ISBN 0-8013-0471-7
    1. Mass media.   I. Merrill, John Calhoun, 1924–   . II. Title.
    P90.L69   1990   89-48306
    302.23—dc20   CIP

ABCDEFGHIJ-DO-99 98 97 96 95 94 93 92 91 90 89

Contents

Preface   *ix*

Part 1   Foundations   **1**

Chapter 1   "Everybody's Talkin' at Me":
             The Puzzling Process   3

             A Flood of Messages   4
             What Is Communication?   5
             The Elements of Communication   6
             Communication Types   8
             Defining Mass Communication   9
             Barriers to Communication   11
             Caution: Entropy at Work   13
             Overcoming Noise and Entropy   14
             Afterthoughts   *15*

Chapter 2   Characteristics of Mass Media:
             Pieces of the Puzzle   16

             Reproduction: Cloning the Message   18
             Circulation: Being There   19
             Feedback: Two-Way Conversation   21

Support: Singing for Your Supper	23
Other Pieces	25
Drifting in a Sea of Words	28
Afterthoughts	*30*

Chapter 3   A Natural Law of Media Development   31

Elite Media: Programming for the Few	31
Popular: The Common Denominator	33
Specialized Media: Into the Twenty-First Century	34
Borrowing a Foreign Language	38
Afterthoughts	*41*

Chapter 4   Print Media: Changing for the Twenty-First Century   42

Why Some Choose Print	45
Print Media around the World	47
Understanding National Patterns in the Print Media	50
Magazines	53
Books	53
Newspapers	54
Afterthoughts	*59*

Chapter 5   Electronic Revolution and Counterrevolution   60

The Regulated Medium	61
Entertainment and News Compete	63
The Identity of Television	64
The Star System	65
The Importance of "Footage"	66
Are Channels Still Limited?	69
Audience Ambivalence	70
Afterthoughts	*71*

Chapter 6   Advertising: Benefactor or Intruder?   73

Who Pays for the Product?	75
The Audience *Likes* Advertising	76
How Does Advertising Influence Content?	77
Advertising as a Political Animal	79
Who's Responsible?	80
Afterthoughts	*83*

Part 2   Participants   **85**

Chapter 7   Institutions   87

Institutions as Functions of Complexity   88
Institutions as Collectivizing Bodies   89
Concept and Structure   90
Press System Concepts in America   92
Foreign Concepts   94
Pluralism: Key to the American Concept   95
Journalistic Orientations   96
Afterthoughts   *99*

Chapter 8   Communicators: Origin of the Species   100

The Four Ages of Journalism   100
Who Become Reporters?   103
Credibility and Involvement: Who Watches the
    Gate?   105
An Unlicensed Profession   107
Training: Journalism or Liberal Arts—or Neither?   109
Afterthoughts   *111*

Chapter 9   Audiences: The Elusive Targets   112

Two Mass Audiences Types   113
Characteristics of Audiences   115
Three Attitudinal Subgroups   116
Audience Behavior and Motivation   121
Conclusion   123
Afterthoughts   *124*

Chapter 10   Critics: Appraising the Media   125

Media Systems Under Attack   126
Criticisms of Individual Media   128
Who Should Appraise the Media?   129
A Problem of Context?   131
Criteria of Evaluation   133
Criteria for "Free" Newspapers   136
Criteria for "Controlled" Newspapers   138
Afterthoughts   *139*

Chapter 11   Media Effects: Myth and Reality   141

        Problems in Communications Research   143
        To the Children's Rescue   147
        Do Polls Sway Elections?   148
        The Denmark Case Study   151
        Afterthoughts   *153*

Part 3   Freedom and Responsibility   **155**

Chapter 12   Beyond Four Theories: Media and Government   157

        Away from Democracy   159
        Trusting the Masses   160
        The "Four Theories" Concept   163
        Defining the System   166
        Afterthoughts   *173*

Chapter 13   Historical Perspectives on Liberty   174

        The Spirit of Reason   175
        Discordant Voices   176
        John Stuart Mill   178
        Early American Perspectives   179
        Jefferson and Madison   180
        Recent American Voices   181
        The Trend toward "Responsible" Freedom   183
        Afterthoughts   *185*

Chapter 14   Ethical Perspectives   186

        Needed: An Ethical Concern   187
        A TUFF Ethical Formula   187
        Two Basic Journalistic Orientations   188
        Reason and Ethics   189
        Ethical Theories   190
        A Dialectical Typology   192
        Journalistic Ethics: A Middle Way?   195
        Afterthoughts   *197*

Chapter 15   External Restraints   199

    Punishing the Press   201
    Keeping the Press Out   205
    Chilling the Press   209
    The Positive Approach   212
    Afterthoughts   *213*

Chapter 16   "Marketplace" Media: An Appraisal   215

    Sources of the Marketplace Model   216
    Assumptions of the Model   216
    Problems with the Model   218
    Questions for the Marketplace Model   220
    Afterthoughts   *223*

Chapter 17   Are the Media Machiavellian?   224

    Succeed by Any Means   225
    An Amoral Philosophy   226
    Arrogance and Expediency   227
    An Interview with Machiavelli   229
    Afterthoughts   *232*

Part 4   Media and Society   **233**

Chapter 18   Credibility: A State of Mind   235

    Traditional Credibility Problems   236
    Recent Factors Diminishing Credibility   238
    Closing the Credibility Gap   241
    Afterthoughts   *243*

Chapter 19   Media and Propaganda   244

    Media-Related Propaganda   245
    Toward a Definition of Propaganda   246
    Journalism and Propaganda   247
    Propaganda Techniques   250
    The Propagandistic Journalist   251
    Afterthoughts   *256*

Chapter 20 Letting the People Know   257

    Full-Disclosure Reporting   257
    What about "Fairness"?   258
    And What about the "Right to Know"?   259
    The Story's Integrity   260
    Reporter or Moralist?   262
    Remaining Questions   263
    Afterthoughts   *265*

Chapter 21 Semantics and Objectivity   266

    The General Semantics Perspective   266
    Objectivity Revisited   269
    The Subjectivist or Advocacy Position   271
    The Objectivist or Neutralist Position   273
    What Does It All Mean?   275
    Afterthoughts   *276*

Chapter 22 For the Mass Media, the Future Is Now   277

    The Word Is "Digitize"   278
    Twenty-First-Century Media   279
    The Quandary of Regulation   281
    Afterthoughts   *282*

Selected Annotated Bibliography   **285**

Index   **299**

Preface

This book is designed as a catalyst to thought. It is not the typical survey of mass communication which tries to provide a little of everything—historical perspective, media statistics, career advice—for the information-hungry student. Rather it is intended to get students (and faculty) thinking about mass communication, considering the mass media from an analytical perspective rather than a purely substantive one. To be sure, the book provides many facts, names, and formalized concepts and theories, but these are ushered into the pages unobtrusively and only as foundation stones, points of departure for critical thinking and reflection.

We have called this book *Macromedia: Mission, Message, and Morality* for several reasons. First, it deals with the "big picture" of the expansive quantity of media, as well as with big (or mass) media. Second, it contains within it an echo of our earlier (1979) book title, *Media, Messages, and Men,* also published by Longman. Third, this new book stresses media morality or ethics far more than did the earlier work.

We are here again trying to provide a distinctive text, one that should at least begin to involve the reader in thoughtful consideration of basic *issues* in mass communication. Such a book should have a special appeal in today's academic atmosphere where faculty and students are increasingly imbued with a healthy desire to challenge sacred cows, debunk traditional and unanalyzed clichés, and get directly to core questions and first principles.

Most curricula of journalism schools and departments—although maybe not in all mass communications and speech communication programs—give overriding attention to practical, professional, or techniques courses. The reader looking for an exposition of media practices and techniques (how to write headlines, edit tapes, write editorials, etc.), a restatement of historical media highlights and data, and the like, will be disappointed by what follows. We have instead been guided by our feeling that an "idea" or thought-oriented book is essential somewhere in the student's communication education. Increasingly, concerns such as those taken up in this book are being dealt with on many campuses; we are pleased to note this trend and hope that this book will fill a need there.

At any rate, we have tried to provide an eclectic, heuristic book, one that will invite the reader to argue with us and with each other, to read further about the various issues and problems facing society as the macromedia impose their influence through mass-oriented messages in ever more sophisticated ways.

Footnotes have been kept to a minimum since the book is largely a catalytic work, but related readings are suggested in the Annotated Bibliography at the end of the book. At the end of each chapter the reader will find questions ("Afterthoughts") designed to stimulate further thinking.

Authorship is divided as follows: Lowenstein wrote Chapters 2, 3, 4, 5, 6, 8, 11, 15, 18, and 22; Merrill, Chapters 1, 7, 9, 10, 13, 14, 16, 17, 19, 20, and 21, and both authors, Chapter 12. Not only do we realize that not all students and professors, and certainly not all media practitioners, will agree with all our viewpoints, interpretations, opinions, and ideas, we in fact welcome such disagreement. We are not trying to gain proselytes for our concepts; we are attempting to get people concerned with issues and problems related to mass communication and society. When teachers using this book disagree with a viewpoint, they will undoubtedly present their position in class, thereby adding to the pluralism of perspectives. If we are able to stimulate thinking, discussion, argument, and further reading by what we say in these pages, we shall have our reward.

R. L. L. and J. C. M.

PART 1

Foundations

CHAPTER 1

"Everybody's Talkin' at Me": The Puzzling Process

Before dealing with media problems *per se,* we should think briefly about the process of communications itself. Without a doubt, this is a complex and puzzling process. It is more than a linear (A *sends* a message to B) event, for often the message seems to develop in B's mind in a form substantially different from A's original message. In other words, it would seem that B brings as much to the message as does A, thereby showing that personal values, interpretations, and biases affect the sender's message.

In spite of all the research done, the communication process is still enshrouded in mystery, raising all kinds of questions. A basic one, evolving from the awareness of the multifaceted nature of communication, serves as an illustration: Is any given act of communication *always* partial or incomplete? We are frustrated by such uncertainties and imprecision, because we *do* know firmly and clearly how extremely important communication is in our personal and social lives.

Everyone appears to be concerned about the communicative act, about understanding and misunderstanding, about human involvement and human response. Spoken and printed words proliferate on the subject of languages, symbols, and signs—on the whole matter of a person speaking to another person, people speaking to people, and institutionalized persons (that is, spokespersons for an entity larger than themselves) speaking to specialized and mass audiences. Language about language, communication about communication—*metalanguage* and *metacommunication*—are in vogue.

Concern about communication is understandable. Certainly communication has been, is, and will be a fundamental—essential—process in human activity and society, because in social living people must share, at least to some degree, their desires, knowledge, experiences, and thoughts. It is only because of communication that societies exist. But in spite of all the benefits we might attribute to communication, it would be well for us to consider the possibility that there is *too much* communication—that moderation in all things, including communication, is the most sensible position. And surely no person, at least in an "advanced" nation, can believe we are moderate in our communication activities.

A FLOOD OF MESSAGES

Messages are flooding in upon us from all sides in tidal waves. A "concern" with communication has increased the total number of messages in geometric proportions since the late 1950s, paralleling the advance of communication technology, heralded by the advent of television in our homes. The entire social and intellectual environment may well be undergoing a communication pollution that will threaten our social fabric with chaos and frustration and disrupt the functioning of our interpersonal civilizing ecology. For the more communications we receive, the less each is taken seriously. In a sense, we are experiencing a period of communication inflation in which messages become "cheaper" (of less value) as they become more numerous.

Many readers will think these words too harsh or pessimistic. It may be that they are, but surely we are increasingly aware of verbal pollutants stretching endlessly before our eyes and droning ever more loudly in our ears. Fortunately for us and our sanity, we are able to screen out most of these messages: we are able to select and reject, to "tune out" much of the communication content that daily inundates us.

But the greater the number of messages, the greater the bulk of trivia and destructive material that fights for our attention. One research study has shown that the average American is exposed to 1,600 advertising messages each day but is moved pro or con by no more than 15 of them. Another study by the Batten, Barton, Durstine and Osborne advertising agency included only those messages disseminated by mass media and outdoor advertising; its findings show that the average American male is exposed to 285 advertising messages a day: 35 television commercials, 38 radio commercials, 15 magazine ads, 185 newspaper ads, and 12 outdoor messages. A 1988 *Sports Illustrated* article reported that the average American child sees 10,000 commercials for beer between the ages of 2 and 18.

Undoubtedly there is also an increase in total quality, but this seems obscured in the repetitions, jargonized gush of pap and prattle. No wonder there is a "credibility gap." What should be believe? Which of the many viewpoints or versions we are exposed to is the correct one? Does the mushrooming of information really help us live better lives, react more humanely toward other persons, or understand better the world around us?

Little wonder that sensitive persons increasingly detach themselves as much as possible from the world of communication. Having too much information may be a dangerous thing. Ignorance perhaps *is* really bliss, and a kind of "ostrich complex" may prove the sanest stance for a human being to take today.

Of course, it is impossible for a person to escape entirely the pervasive impact of communication. For, as national populations explode throughout the world, additional millions of people are talking and writing—thrusting their opinions and ideas on one another with growing intensity. Physically we cannot escape the communication explosion; we must learn to live with it. Nevertheless, if our psychological shelters are not constructed quickly and well, we and our children will certainly suffer serious and lasting damage from the intellectually and emotionally debilitating fallout.

WHAT IS COMMUNICATION?

Such inveighing will not generally find favor with modern students of, and apologists for, communication. It is fashionable to see communication not only as social cement but as the hope for a troubled world. If we could only communicate with one another, we could solve many of our problems, go a long way toward eliminating friction, and usher in a new day in which understanding has replaced misunderstanding; this understanding, we are told, would result in social harmony, interpersonal brotherhood, and peace. But persons who have such faith in communication—and there are many—should take a closer look at this miraculous but not always well-understood process of communication.

The word "communication" comes from the Latin *communis* (common) or *communicare* (to establish a community or commonness, to share), so the occurrence of communication implies a sharing—the achievement, or at least the seeking, of an understanding. Communication, then, as a process, is a two-way street; messages flow both ways, resulting in participation, in shared responses. It should be emphasized that we are considering communication as a *process,* not as a synonym for *message.* One may speak of "a communication" as equivalent to the message communicated; in that sense there may be a communication without there being a receiver of the message. But when we speak of the process of communication, there must be both sender (communicator) and receiver (communicatee).

Communication is basically a social process. Not only with a spoken and written language do we communicate, but also with a wide variety of actions (kinesic communication): with smiles, frowns, gestures, nods, handshakes, shrugs, embraces, pushes, blows, and so on. Actions do indeed speak louder than (or as loud as) words in interpersonal communication, as well as in communication between nations. In addition to gesture—tactile, and action "language"—we also communicate in innumerable subtle ways, such as modes of dress and social formalities. We constantly create misunderstandings with our nonverbal "language" as well as with our verbal language. As Edward T. Hall says in *The Silent Language,* an excellent discourse on nonverbal communication, enormous distortions exist among people trying to communicate with each other. "The job of achieving understanding and insight into the mental processes of others," Dr. Hall says, "is much more difficult and the situation more serious than most of us care to admit."

THE ELEMENTS OF COMMUNICATION

Various students of communication look at the communication process in different ways. Colin Cherry in his *On Human Communication* has called communication essentially a "relationship" formed by what he refers to as the "transmission of stimuli and the evocation of responses." Probably the most common way to look systematically at the communication process is to resort to the well-known paradigm of Harold Lasswell: *Who says what, in which channel, to whom, with what effect?* So we can say that in every communication situation there is a *source* generating a *message* that is transmitted through a *channel* to an *audience*. And then, theoretically, there is some kind of *response* on the part of the audience. José Aranguren, a highly respected Spanish philosopher and student of communication, has said that communication may be defined as any transmission of information by (a) the emission, (b) the conduction, and (c) the reception of (d) a message. Most writers would probably add an (e) to Aranguren's paradigm: the response by the receiver.

It is conceivable, however, that a speaker speaks but has no audience, though the speaker may not know this. The *response* in this case would take place within the speaker himself. Actually this is a very real possibility in communication; most of us "talk to ourselves" more often than we care to admit.

Taking into consideration all the many ways to look at the communication process, it is probably safe to say that communication always requires four factors: a *source,* a *message,* a *channel,* and a *destination.* When the communicator (source) has translated his or her mental message into symbolic stimuli (constituting the message), he or she sends it to the communicatee (destination) in some manner, that is, via a medium or channel. If these stimuli reach and are understood by the communicatee, then the communication process is concluded. Most likely, if the communicatee does respond to the message overtly, this response will actually be the first step in another communicative process: it will constitute a new stimulus or message directed toward somebody else.

Many communication scholars are insistent that really we do not communicate "messages" but merely physically transmit signals or signs —visible, audible, or tactile. Colin Cherry takes the interesting position that the mere transmission and reception of a physical signal does not bring about communication. It stimulates the "message" *in* the recipient who perceives it. In other words, the signal has the potential for triggering or selecting responses in the recipient. Messages, from this point of view, are really no more than "triggering" mechanisms; they have no actual *content.* As Cherry has said, the information content of a message is simply the property or *potential* of the signals to elicit a response in the receiver.

In the process of communication there are participants who interact. The *encoder* (formulator of the message) either sends the message him or herself or entrusts it to another (the communicator) to send. Most often the encoder and the communicator are the same person. The message is sent to a person who translates the symbols of the message into his or her own meaning context; this receiver–translator is called the decoder of the message; he or she can also be called the communicatee, the receiver, the recipient, the receptor, the audience, or the destination. When this communicatee reacts or responds overtly to the message received, he or she becomes the encoder (communicator) of a new message, which goes back to the original communicator or to someone else. In other words, the decoder becomes an encoder, usually of a return message.

This return message, sent by a receiver back to the sender, is usually referred to as *feedback.* The feedback or response may be either immediate or delayed in reaching the original sender. (In some circumstances, the original sender may "sense" or "infer" a response on the part of the receiver when there really is no evidence of it; this type of feedback is sometimes called *inferential feedback* and is certainly not highly reliable.)

Immediate feedback occurs in small-group dialogue or in person-to-person communication where a conversation necessitates give-and-take. It may occur in any communication situation where a speaker may be interrupted by a question or comment. In face-to-face communication (in our sense, any direct communication, including those via telephone or computer) the communicator can see or sense immediately (simultaneously with the message or very soon thereafter) how he or she is doing. If need be, the message can be revamped or repeated until misunderstandings have been eliminated. Immediate feedback basically answers this question for the communicator: "How am I doing?" *Delayed feedback*, on the other hand, answers the question, "How did I do?"

Delayed feedback can occur in various situations, but most often it involves *mass* communication. For instance, a newspaper reader might write a letter to the editor about something in the paper, or a television viewer might phone a station about some remark just heard or about a program watched the day before.

Mass communication delayed feedback, of course, is highly selective, and the communicator gets an insight into how only a minuscule portion of the audience feels about the message. It is also likely that those members of a mass audience who provide feedback are *atypical;* therefore the communicator cannot assume very much on the basis of their delayed feedback.

COMMUNICATION TYPES

Communication can be classified in many ways. One way is to talk of *intrapersonal* and *interpersonal* communication. *Intra*personal communication, of course, simply means the process that goes on *within* a single person whereby he or she thinks and reacts to this thinking. The study of this kind of communication is mainly a concern of the psychologist and neurologist and does not interest us here except as the process of thinking interests all of us. *Inter*personal communication, however—the process of communication going on between or among persons—is of paramount importance to anyone concerned with humans as a social beings.

The journalist especially is constantly concerned with the various aspects of interpersonal communication—from the time he or she seeks to get information through an interview or through observation of an event until the message is encoded for transmission via a mass medium. Mass communications is itself a kind of interpersonal communication. Since mass communicators (institutionalized persons) are endeavoring to communicate with a mass audience, they find themselves in a most difficult and often frustrating situation. Before looking more closely at mass communication, however, let us consider a typology for classifying interpersonal communication generally. Four main types of interpersonal communication exist: (1) person-to-person, face-to-face; (2) small-group, face-to-face; (3) large-group, crowd; and (4) mass.

The first of these is the most personal, informal, and unstructured, and

the relationship between the two participants (or the very few participants), who are in immediate proximity, is one in which a very great degree
of dialogue and empathy can take place and where immediate feedback is a
normal, unconscious part of the communication situation. Theoretically,
all other factors being equal, this person-to-person communication situation has the best chance for success of the four types. That is, the message
can be effectively channeled to the destination.

The second type, the small group, is what Aranguren has called a
microgroup situation. Examples are a conference, discussion group, forum or round-table discussion, board meeting, or seminar. Ample opportunity is provided for the participants to talk and respond, but the situation
is more formal and more structured than is the person-to-person situation.

The third type of communication situation is the rally or crowd-
oriented gathering, which Aranguren calls a *macrogroup*. Members in this
situation can, and do, react with one another or with some others in largely
an emotional manner. Here, by and large, everyone is a part of the audience. One or a very few persons do the primary message sending. Here,
for example, might be Hitler addressing a vast audience in the stadium at
Nuremberg, Billy Graham preaching to an overflow crowd in Madison
Square Garden, or a rock music group performing before thousands of
young people on a hillside. In this kind of situation there is the potential for
a kind of infectious exaltation, a sort of mass hysteria or collective hypno-
sis that will affect thought and action.

The fourth type of communication is mass communication. The media
or means of mass communication have been set up to act *as* (or *for*)
persons; they are, in effect, artificial or institutionalized channels—
generally newspapers and magazines, radio, television, films, and books.
These mass communication media have an advantage over large gather-
ings: they rule out pathological crowd phenomena, collective hysteria, and
loss of self-control. Audience members, in other words, usually react
individually to messages from mass media.

DEFINING MASS COMMUNICATION

The mass (or institutionalized) communicator is much like the bird hunter
who fires his shotgun into a clump of trees that he knows contains a large
number of different types of birds. He aims at no one bird in any one tree.
He does not even see the individual trees or birds. He simply blasts away
in scatter-shot fashion, having faith that he will have some success. And,
of course, he will—but to a limited degree. Many birds in the tree cluster
will not be hit by any of the pellets; others will be hit solidly with many
pellets, and others will receive only glancing shots having little or no effect

on them. The hunter may have a fairly good idea as to what kinds of birds are in the tree cluster but he is not sure, nor does he know the proportions of types. He knows that his blast (the mass communicator's message) is capable of achieving its purpose if it hits enough birds with sufficient impact.

Mass communicators, like hunters, know nothing very helpful about the mass audience—only that it is large, unseen, and heterogeneous. They know that their messages will reach some, and not others, of this audience. They know also, however, that their messages will reach other members of the audience *secondhand* (the bird-hunter analogy breaks down here), through opinion leaders and other *conveyer persons*. They know too that their messages will probably be distorted as they diffuse through various stages of conveyer persons. And what is more frustrating, they will never really know *how* their messages were understood by the mass audience or portions of it. All they can assume is that their messages reached *some* persons who selectively perceived them in many different ways.

When we talk about "mass communication," we immediately get into semantic trouble. We understand it to some extent, but not completely. So we say that a mass communicator is an "institutionalized person"—a person representing a disseminating medium—or we think of the institution *itself* as communicating *to* (seldom *with*) the mass audience. The complications really begin, however, when we start thinking about the mass audience. Sociologists tell us that it is large, anonymous, heterogeneous, ever changing, and scattered. They tell us more, but that is the gist of their definition. So we know that the mass audience is large. But how large? We do not really know. It is anonymous; by that we assume that its members are unknown to one another and to the mass communicator. It is heterogeneous; by that we assume that its members are of different sexes, ages, educational levels, religions, races, and so on. It is dynamic and scattered; by this we assume that audience members are tuning in and out and that they are not in one geographical location; they do not form a group. They cannot be addressed by the communicator in one place, in a face-to-face situation.

What about mass communication as a process? Some adjectives that characterize it are the following:

1. *Transient* or expendable, meaning that it is produced to be consumed immediately by audiences, without being made part of a permanent record (although modern technology, such as videocassette recorders (VCRs), tapes, and photocopying machines, may be changing this aspect somewhat)
2. *Public* and not private communication
3. *Pervasive,* in that messages are simultaneous and persistent, with the ability to reach members of large audiences at the same time

4. *Powerful*, in that large numbers of people are exposed to the same messages and there is no real fear of competition or feedback

And we can say with many critics that mass communication—largely because of its transient nature—is prone to emphasize haste (so as to be timely), sensationalism (so as to ensure big audiences and big profits), and superficiality (so as not to intimidate or bore those audiences).

What are the main purposes (and consequences) of mass communication? Harold Lasswell has suggested that the functions of mass communication are basically three: (1) surveillance of the environment (the news function), (2) correlation of the parts of the society (the news analysis and interpretation function), and (3) transmission of the social heritage from generation to generation (the educational function of all media messages, including advertising). One might certainly add *entertainment*.

Mass media are of three main types: (1) print media (newspapers, magazines, books, and the like); (2) film media (movies of various kinds); and (3) electronic media (radio, television, and recordings). These media are encountered almost everywhere in our daily lives. And they are big businesses, selling information and entertainment; they even refer to themselves as "industries."

Now, after saying all this, we still are not quite satisfied with a clear-cut definition of mass communication. There are still unanswered questions. We do have a generalized idea of what a mass audience is, but it is very fuzzy around the edges. It certainly is important to recognize how very difficult it is to communicate with it. How does the mass communicator make decisions about what this mass audience wants? How is impact evaluated? When should messages be changed (or stopped)? By intuition?

Of course, many mass communicators have access to surveys, polls, and selective delayed feedback that give them some sense of their audience, but generally they communicate intuitively or egoistically. On the basis of their own likes and dislikes, they sense what at least many in the mass audience will want. In effect, they project their own biases onto the mass audience. Contrary to many high-sounding rationales for message formulation and distribution, most day-to-day decisions are made in a self-projective, existential manner. And that is probably as good a way as any to handle messages going to this amorphous, ever-changing, almost mystical entity (or nonentity) called a mass audience.

BARRIERS TO COMMUNICATION

Effective communication implies communication wherein an understanding is established, where the message elicits in the receiver the response desired by the sender. In effective communication the message "gets through" to the communicatee, whose interpretation of it is very similar to that of the communicator. It is extremely difficult to achieve effective communication; in fact, many students of communication say it is impossible. But at least we can say that there are cases wherein participants achieve something that must pass for understanding—a similar sharing of meaning. Many barriers exist, however, to disrupt or frustrate communication. Probably the two most important are often referred to as "noise." They are (1) mechanical noise and (2) semantic noise—and they are at work in every type of communication situation.

Mechanical Noise

This is often referred to as physical or channel noise. It is in most respects what laymen think of as "noise," related to the electronic media of mass communication or to oral interpersonal communication. For example, mechanical noise that would disrupt communication would include static on the radio, "snow" or other screen distortion on television, hums in public-address systems, coughing or laughing by members of an audience. In the print media, examples of mechanical noise would be poor printing that results in illegibility; lines of type missing or upside down; missing paragraphs; torn, muddy, or wet pages; and story continuations to other pages.

Semantic Noise

This is, in a sense, not really noise at all. It is an interference with the message brought on by discordance or breakdown in the sharing of meaning. Semantic noise filters into a message through the language used. The more confusion there is among participants in the communication situation over the meaning of terms and concepts, the more semantic noise there is in the message. Semantic noise results in misunderstanding. The participants, in effect, interpret the language of the message in different ways; therefore, they have differing meanings in their minds. They may have received the message very clearly in a mechanical or phonetic sense— physically it got through loud and clear—but because of meaning difficulties (semantic noise) their communication has broken down.

What are some of the other barriers that tend to hinder or disrupt effective communication? Here are a few:

- Divergent backgrounds of the participants
- Differences in education, formal and informal
- Differences in interest in the message
- Differences in intelligence

- Differences in language levels and usages
- Lack of mutual respect among participants
- Differences in such factors as age, sex, race, and class
- Mental and/or physical stress at the time of communication
- Environmental conditions at the time of communication
- Little or no chance for "feedback" or interaction
- Little or no "experential overlap"—few, if any, common experiences
- Lack of skill on the part of the communicator (poor writer or speaker)
- Lack of skill on the part of the communicatee (poor reader or listener)
- Lack of information in the message ("empty" message)

CAUTION: ENTROPY AT WORK

All these hindrances or barriers to effective communication, and many others as well, tend to frustrate and complicate the process of communication and to alter messages during the process of transmission. Often this frustration of clear communication, this change brought about in the message by a multiplicity of barriers, is referred to by communications scholars as *entropy*.

Mathematicians and physicists use the term "entropy" to depict a tendency everywhere toward disintegration and chaos—an inclination to run down. Entropy might be considered a "measure of disorder"—the concept stemming from the Second Law of Thermodynamics, which says in essence that systems can proceed only to a state of increased disorder. In a journalistic sense, then, entropy could be seen as the natural tendency of a message to dissipate, diminish, change, or lose information or proper emphasis during the complex communication process. Just as Norbert Wiener sees overall society plagued with increasing confusion and disorientation (entropy), we can look at journalism or simply at one message or "story" and see a similar kind of entropy at work. Always in journalism there is a breaking down of reality, a tendency toward disorganization and disorientation, a loss of, or change in, primary or basic information, a tendency toward informational anarchy.

To give a simple example: A newspaper reporter goes out to "cover" an automobile accident and arrives on the scene *after the fact*. The reporter begins selecting data related to the accident, talking with certain persons, observing certain signs of the accident, and making certain references. In short, the reporter *selects* or *abstracts* a very few aspects of the accident from the *real* accident. The real accident, with its billions of simultaneous stimuli produced as the accident was taking place, has now been reduced to a few hastily selected impressions in the reporter's mind and notebook. The process of entropy—loss of information from the message—has begun.

Next the reporter returns to the office to write "the story" from notes and mental impressions. Selecting again from memory and scribbled notes, the reporter types out a story which is again a bare skeleton of the (selected) data collected at the scene of the accident. Then the story goes to copyreaders or editors who further tamper with the information, changing it in some way and often deleting portions of it. The message changes further, losing additional information. Then the story is sent to typesetters, who often distort the story further in some way. And if the story, after being set in type, is too long for the space available, it will be shortened until it fits. So the story loses still more information. At last the story of the accident is printed in the newspaper, hopefully with no lines missing or out of place.

Now we have the story of the automobile accident translated to some three or four inches of type in a narrow column, competing for readership with dozens of other "stories." The reader will finally add to the process of entropy by further selecting portions of the story to perceive—if he or she bothers to see the story at all. In other words, what finally filters into the consciousness of the reader is only a small part of the printed story, which was a small part of the reporter's total perception, which was only a small part of the actual event. So we have an example of message entropy in a journalistic situation. No wonder people are concerned about "communication gaps" and "credibility gaps." These gaps are intrinsic to the very process of communication and the mass media simply project them on a mass screen.

OVERCOMING NOISE AND ENTROPY

Entropy—the changing of message during the communication process—and "noise" (semantic and mechanical) pose great problems for the communicator, especially the media-related communicator. Although there is probably no way these problems can be fully resolved or overcome, there are certain things a communicator can do to minimize the impact of noise and of entropic tendencies.

First, the communicator can be aware of these problems and resolve to deal with them. Clear, unambiguous encoding is, of course, essential. At times doing this may require a certain amount of tautology or repetition, because redundancy—saying the same thing in a different way—is often a good way to minimize semantic noise.

Then there is the need to make clear what is meant by certain abstract terms, to explain exactly what the communicator means by them. The communicator may try to avoid using certain abstract terms altogether (like "progressive," "conservative," "liberal," "patriotic"), opting instead to describe actions and provide quotes. As for mechanical noise, the communicator will make every effort to have a good technological and physical environment, a well-designed venue, for the message.

But what can be done about message entropy? Something, to be sure, though never enough. First, the communicator will want to get as much information into the message as possible, recognizing the fact that much of it will be lost. Therefore the communicator must be a "message packer," providing the audience with the maximum amount of data from which to select. A certain redundancy is helpful here, too, for if datum A is dropped out in the process of transmission, datum Y, repetitive of datum A, may get through to the receiver.

These common-sense suggestions on overcoming barriers to communication are certainly not exhaustive. The communicator's knowledge of the subject being communicated, skill in communicating it, and familiarity with the intended audience will all help limit entropy. But even the conscientious, knowledgeable, and skillful communicator will only partially succeed. The puzzling communication process is simply too complex and filled with snares to permit complacency, satisfaction, or arrogance.

AFTERTHOUGHTS

1. Would successful communication imply that *all* persons in the communication situation receive the identical "message" (body of information? impression? conclusion?)?

2. Does a mass communicator in fact communicate to the members of a mass audience even if he or she never learns of the message's impact or effect? In other words, is feedback necessary for communication?

3. When Colin Cherry says that communication is a "transmission of stimuli and [an] evocation of responses," is he providing a useful definition of communication? For him, the communicator's intended meaning might be totally irrelevant to the act of communication. What would be an example of a stimulus–response situation devoid of any shared meaning?

4. What is the main implication of message entropy for the journalist who maintains that reportorial objectivity is possible? What are some of the ways a reporter can overcome some of the entropic barriers to communication?

5. What does laughter or applause from an audience indicate (if anything) about the process of communication?

CHAPTER 2

Characteristics
of Mass Media:
Pieces of the Puzzle

The various media are like old acquaintances. Some we avoid for reasons we know not why; others are as comfortable to be around as a favorite member of the family. Just as people have personalities made up of many parts, each mass medium has its own characteristics that together form an "image" of the medium. Radio, for example, offers an "atmosphere" that we can take with us wherever we go. Recordings offer us a seemingly limitless choice of entertainment. We can lose ourselves in the movies, shutting out the surrounding environment. Videotex is a stranger—a new medium just beginning to enter our media persona.

The late Marshall McLuhan declared that "the medium is the message." If he has done no more than force those involved in communications to take a closer look at the media—the physical media—he has done an important service. Perhaps the medium is not the message.[1] But the medium often *shapes* the message and sometimes influences the event that forms the basis of the message. It always affects the communicator and the audience.

This chapter contains a chart that looks at the physical and economic characteristics of the media from a slightly more analytical perspective. The "elements of mass media channels" listed there—reproduction, circulation, feedback, and financial support—are certainly not newly conceived ones. They are qualities that are familiar to everyone, but they can

---

[1] McLuhan, who also liked to mix humor and provocative insight with his fresh descriptions of the media, also referred to the medium as the "massage" and the "mess-age."

ELEMENTS OF MASS MEDIA CHANNELS

		Print Media				Sound Media		Motion Media	
		Books	Magazines	Newspapers	Videotex	Radio	Recordings	Movies	Television
elements of REPRODUCTION	Verbal Symbols	X	X	X	X			X	X
	Picture Symbols	X	X	X	X			X	X
	Color	X	X	X	X			X	X
	Sound					X	X	X	X
	Motion							X	X
elements of CIRCULATION	Portability	X	X	X		X	X	X	X
	Reviewability	X	X	X	X		X	X	X
	Simultaneity					X			X
elements of FEEDBACK	Verbal	X	X	X	X	X	X	X	X
	Nonverbal	X	X	X	X	X	X	X	X
elements of SUPPORT (U.S.)	Single Sales	X	X	X	X		X	X	X
	Subscriptions		X	X	X			X	X
	Advertising		X	X	X	X		X	X

be arranged in a pattern that allows us to compare the media with each other and gain new insights into the effect of the channel on the event, the communicator, the message, and the audience. Let's think together about each of these elements.

REPRODUCTION: CLONING THE MESSAGE

In the pre–mass communication period the ordinary individual depended upon others to record, interpret, and transmit messages, usually in a very personal way. The era of mass communication arrived when machinery could either substitute for the personal communicator or multiply the messages. The era of mass communication began with Gutenberg's development of movable type in the fifteenth century, and it continues today with message enhancements offered by computers, digital technology, satellites, and fiber optics. Humans have popularized machinery that can utilize all the elements of reproduction (see below). We stand only on the threshold, however, of an era of machinery sophisticated enough to produce maximum fidelity and maximum multiplication of the original message.

There are five elements of reproduction:

1. *Verbal symbols,* the use of ideographs or the phonetic alphabet to reproduce the spoken language
2. *Picture symbols,* the use of woodcuts, engravings, and similar devices (including photoelectric cells) to depict the original event
3. *Color,* processes utilized to highlight verbal symbols or give lifelike hues to picture symbols
4. *Sound,* the reproduction or transmission of voices, music, noises, and the like
5. *Motion,* the reproduction or transmission of animation

Three of the four print media (books, magazines, and newspapers) have utilized the three elements of reproduction to which they have been limited since the earliest days of printing. The Gutenberg Bible, for example, used color to highlight initial letters, and some books of the same era were color illustrated (illuminated). The challenge through the centuries has been to improve the fidelity of these elements through better-designed letters and reproduction processes, and to design machinery that would speed up the printing process itself. Videotex, a medium in which text and pictures can be transmitted electronically and appear as "print" on the home or business computer, is still in its infancy. It is capable of adding sound (although it does not yet do so) and motion (through still-primitive animation processes) to the print format.

Theoretically, the "motion" media should be more effective than the print and sound media, since movies and television can utilize all five basic elements of reproduction. Verbal symbols, for example, can be reproduced on film, and certainly television incorporates a radio, in a sense, since it can transmit sound in the same way that radio does. In fact, if the screen went "black," a television set could substitute for a radio set, and if a page of print were flashed on a TV screen, the screen could substitute for a newspaper.

Though motion media represent perhaps the ultimate in exploiting all the elements of reproduction, some of their advantages are potential rather than actual.

CIRCULATION: BEING THERE

Once embodied, a message must be circulated, in the sense of being dispersed or disseminated. (Indeed, the word "broadcast" originally meant to scatter seed.) Given a literate (in the case of print media) and moderately affluent audience, three basic elements are necessary to achieve maximum circulation:

1. *Portability,* the ability of the medium to reach members of the audience wherever they may be
2. *Reviewability,* the ability of the message to be received and/or reviewed at the audience's convenience
3. *Simultaneity,* the ability of the medium to deliver the message to the audience at the instant the message originates

Obviously, portability and reviewability are relative terms, whereas simultaneity is an absolute term. For example, radio has achieved real portability through the development of the transistorized and battery-operated set; record players made a breakthrough to portability years ago through the development of audio-cassette tape recorders. Although available for a number of years, hand-held, battery-operated television sets are just now approaching a price that puts them within reach of the average person. Until the last few years, the so-called "portable" television sets within a popular price range were still quite bulky when compared with miniature radios and tape recorders, and they were umbilically dependent on an external power supply. Toward the end of the 1980s, manufacturers were able to produce tiny portable TV sets with battery-supplied energy. But true "portability" for this medium is still potential rather than actual, because of the high cost of miniature sets. The practical "wristwatch" TV receiver depicted by cartoonist Chester Gould in his comic strip "Dick Tracy" in the 1940s is still slightly out of reach in the 1990s.

Only radio and television have achieved simultaneity. Through these media, the listener or viewer can make instantaneous contact with an event or message. With the other media there is always a time lag, newspapers experiencing the shortest and books and motion pictures perhaps the longest. (The ability of radio and television to "circulate" a message immediately has all but eliminated the tradition of newspaper "extras.") It should be noted, however, that paperback book publishers can, when the need arises, deliver a product to newsstands and booksellers within a week of receiving raw copy.

Reviewability, or on-demand access, is a relative term also, in that one could review a radio program if one chose to record it—but almost no one does. On the other hand, television has undoubtedly achieved "reviewability" as a result of the popularization of VCRs during the 1980s.

Reviewability also implies "previewability," the quality of permitting the audience to know ahead of time what they will find inside the message presentation. Books, magazines, and newspapers accomplish this with dust jackets, tables of contents, indexes, and headlines. Recordings, compact discs (CDs), and cassettes use liner notes, and some television and radio shows provide teasers just before or at the top of the program.

Movies provide an indication of how swiftly an advance in technology can transform an entire medium. Until about ten years ago, movies could not boast *any* of the three elements of circulation. That would seem to imply that movies did not "circulate" at all, but this, of course, was not true; movies simply had the most severe circulation handicaps. Messages on other channels could be consumed by the audience without the aid of a middleman, whereas a motion picture was of no benefit to the average viewer until it was projected by someone else onto a screen. And projection equipment has a markedly low degree of portability. People have to come *to* a projector under normal conditions, and even then a special, darkened room has to be provided or the film has to be shown at night. Movies, then, were not easily reviewable; viewers had to sit through an entire film again to review any part of the message (and in most cases they had to pay a second time in order to review it a second time).

The motion picture industry had been able to improve circulation by grafting its product onto the medium of television. Then along came the VCR, changing the nature of movie circulation forever. The VCR, first a means of recording television programs, quickly became a way of multiplying the circulation of movies. Video stores now proliferate in every modern city around the world. Movies, once a medium with virtually no portability or reviewability, now have a high degree of both.

FEEDBACK: TWO-WAY CONVERSATION

The channel is a major determinant of the nature and degree of feedback from the audience. A medium that encourages feedback is likely to adjust more rapidly to audience needs and involve its audience more in the process of mass communication. Conversely, a channel that restricts feedback is likely to lag behind audience tastes. Worse, such a medium contributes to audiences' (and society's) frustration.

Each medium receives two kinds of feedback, *verbal* and *nonverbal*. These are relative terms, however; to say that all media feedback is of the same quality and quantity would be far from the truth. Verbal feedback for books, recordings, and movies might consist of reviews by critics and direct suggestions by distributors. For television, it could mean reviews, actual criticism from viewers in the form of letters and telephone calls, or comments from advertisers (sponsors). For radio, it would consist primarily of phone calls to local stations. For magazines and newspapers, most verbal feedback would be in the form of letters to the editor, but it also includes letters and calls to various department editors and the circulation department.

In considering verbal feedback, we must recognize two subfactors, *proximity* and *participation*. It is usually simpler for a reader to transmit feedback to a local weekly newspaper, for example, than to one of the nation's major dailies: It seems closer, and the reader may know the personalities who manage and write for it. Also the chances of having a letter printed in it may be greater; perhaps there is less competition for space. The reader feels more closely linked with the newspaper's audience and encouraged to share opinions with it.

These subfactors of participation and proximity are extremely important because they concern the frustration level of the audience itself. A medium that carries noncontroversial material need worry little about feedback, but a medium that proposes to transmit controversy—and depends upon a sustaining audience for its economic existence—must open up reverse channels of feedback to risk frustrating its audience to the point of alienation.

Book publishers generally do not face this problem from the mass audience because they do not depend upon a sustaining audience, but rather upon single sales. Radio and television do depend upon a sustaining audience. Radio has created open-line or party-line programs at the local level to open channels for feedback. The entire programming day for some stations in major cities is devoted to "talk radio," where the host and listeners sound off on any subject, throwing inhibition to the wind.

This format is not as widespread in television, though for some talk shows and public information broadcasts the viewers, like the studio audience members, may present a question or comment for the guest's response. Some local stations have talk-back programs in which station representatives answer mailed and telephoned questions and complaints about programming selections and even the actual content of programming. News and magazine-format programs print (on the television screen) excerpts from letters sent in by viewers; some TV stations have equipment that records telephone "votes" from the audience on various issues of the day, and some stations air editorials as well as viewers' replies.

Each medium also receives some form of nonverbal feedback. This would consist primarily of sales in the case of print media, recordings, and movies, or audience size in the case of radio and television. In short, the audience can register its preferences by buying, subscribing, listening, or viewing. It can register its dislikes by canceling a subscription or turning off a set. Nonverbal feedback is perhaps far more important than verbal feedback, which is usually only the tip of the iceberg of audience reaction. Since books, recordings, and movies normally depend upon single sales, their audiences' purchases and admissions are the most important barometer of nonverbal reaction. Newspapers and magazines watch subscriptions and sales carefully but gain additional feedback through readership studies. Radio and television depend primarily upon rating services.

In some cases, the power of nonverbal feedback can be an illusion. To the argument that listeners or viewers can always turn off a set if they do not like what they hear or see, one critic responded, "People do not buy sets to turn them off." Many cities have a very small selection of TV stations, especially those producing local news and public affairs. Even in an era of plenty, where radio is concerned, there may be few radio stations with the same programming format. And there are few cities in the United States where newspaper monopoly is not the way of life. In such cases, listeners, viewers, and readers cannot simply "turn off," especially if they want a particular format, if they desire some local news, or if they want a variety of opinion. In such cases, broadcasters have a responsibility, if no longer a legal obligation, to be responsive to listener and viewer feedback. Editors in one-newspaper cities have a particular responsibility to provide an open forum somewhere in their columns, and not merely a selection of letters or columnists that represent an extension of the newspaper's editorial policy or the editor's personal political inclinations.

An increasing number of media critics are now pointing out that feedback is important for the welfare of society itself. The media, they say, must not only permit feedback but encourage it, and especially encourage the sort of feedback that can be shared with other members of the audience. Newspapers have responded by giving more attention to the Op-Ed page, making sure that it serves as a forum by printing a number of longer, more reasoned articles on public issues from nonstaffers. Feedback thus serves as a safety valve for the frustrations of society—and also as a means for minority groups to express their views in the mass media that we all consume.

SUPPORT: SINGING FOR YOUR SUPPER

There are four basic elements of support: *single sales, subscriptions, advertising,* and *subsidies.* In the United States, subsidy by government and nongovernment organizations is not yet a significant factor of support for the mass media as a whole. However, for an increasingly viable segment of American radio and television—public broadcasting—public subsidies are imperative. Justification for this type of government and nongovernment subsidy within the American free-enterprise philosophy comes from the perceived need to provide alternative, special-focus programming that would never be supported by advertising. In developing countries, Communist-bloc nations, and countries with both varied and vigorous political parties, this element becomes far more important.[2]

The kind and variety of support affect the content of the medium ("He who pays the piper calls the tune"). Obviously, sponsors on commercial television are reluctant to have their advertisements displayed alongside controversial programming, and this reluctance has undoubtedly been a factor in the disappearance of the hard-hitting documentaries that were seen in the early years of network television. Critics have also contended that corporate underwriters on public television also prefer noncontroversial programs, leading to the dominance in prime time of entertainment programming, as opposed to public affairs programs that explore in depth social and political issues. As contributions from individual viewers have become an increasingly important part of a public station's budget, rating "numbers" have become more important even for this medium. The result has been a trend toward popular-appeal programming, such as the British situation comedies, called "Britcoms." Thus, "ratings" are a factor for public broadcasting because people who don't watch are unlikely to make voluntary contributions.

In authoritarian countries, government support usually dictates the party line. In Western countries, efforts are made to insulate public broadcasting from the governmental funding source. In Great Britain, funding for the British Broadcasting Corporation (BBC) comes primarily from

---

[2] The subsidy in such cases is often outright payments. However, it may take more subtle forms: government advertising, government purchases of bulk copies of the publication, or government subsidy of programming.

annual fees applied to radio and television receivers, and BBC has its own independent board of directors. However, this arrangement could not insulate BBC from the Thatcher-government order prohibiting the network from airing interviews with members of the Irish Republican Army. In the United States the Public Broadcasting Service (PBS) and National Public Radio (NPR) have their own boards but derive their financing largely from the Corporation for Public Broadcasting (CPB), which in turn receives funds from Congress. This plan is supposed to insulate the two networks from politics, but it is more theory than fact, since members of the CPB board are political appointees, and the need for congressional funding involves CPB, PBS, and NPR in the political processes, including lobbying members of Congress.

Books, recordings, and movies, while relatively unaffected by their audiences' verbal feedback (as opposed to critics' feedback), receive almost immediate audience reaction to a product or type of product, via single sales. The verdict of single sales is swift and often merciless. And since the sometimes mercurial reaction of audiences can be measured most quickly by single sales, even magazines that depend on subscriptions for the great bulk of their circulation give extra weight to single sales in gauging current audience satisfaction with the publication—and so do advertisers.

One could hypothesize that those media having an even balance of income from single sales, subscriptions, and advertising would have distinct advantages over those media that do not. Support from the audience would then provide about two-thirds of the income of the medium, and this income would be produced by thousands of sources (members of the audience). In such a situation, single sales would be a finely tuned barometer of audience reaction, subscriptions would provide long-term financial stability, and advertising would enable the medium to provide better programming at a cheaper price.

Such a situation, of course, is utopian. Books and recordings sell at a relatively high price, since they depend upon single sales only. The risk is high for each book or record, because the audience awaiting each message is rather unpredictable. The same situation holds for movies, although at least one part of the channel (the local distributor) introduces advertising at the local level and subsidizes the operation by selling refreshments.[3]

---

[3] The moviegoing habit is so pronounced in Israel (which did not establish general television on a regular basis until 1969) that an Israeli equivalent to the Audit Bureau of Circulations (an American agency that provides advertisers with certified circulation figures for newspapers and magazines) actually measures movie audiences for purposes of setting advertising rates at major movie houses.

Popular magazines and newspapers in the United States are largely supported by advertising income, and the loss or gain of advertising lineage can alter the profit status of a publication much more rapidly than single sales and subscriptions. Radio and television are wholly supported by advertising, forcing these media to react more quickly to the exigencies of advertising than to their own good judgment about the needs of the audience and society.

Advertising's impact on media is primarily a result of its *concentrated* power: It provides more money from fewer people. Unlike the audience, it does not buy the message; rather it adds to the message, interrupts it—and sometimes alters it. It has a power not only for bad, but also, we would argue, for great good. The question of advertising will be considered in more detail in Chapter 6.

OTHER PIECES

Although reproduction, circulation, feedback, and support are the major elements determining media characteristics, additional factors also affect the efficiency and effect of each medium: (1) the number of channels within a medium, (2) the expense of operation, (3) the complexity of distribution, (4) the frequency of publication, (5) the flexibility of the channel, and (6) emphasis in the media.

Number of Channels

Print media, recordings, and movies theoretically can proliferate without limit. In fact, their numbers are limited by factors of competition and audience saturation. There is a limited spectrum of frequencies for both radio and television, and this fact initially invited government intervention as a "traffic cop" to assign and patrol frequencies. It also justified later intervention by the government to force the limited number of licensees to act in the "public interest, convenience, and necessity." However, technology and affluence are constantly expanding the spectrums of radio and television: frequency modulation (FM), shortwave, ultrahigh-frequency (UHF) television, and cable television, to name a few. The channels of television are opening even wider as a result of satellites, fiber optics, and VCRs. By 1990 the average television household had access to 28 channels. Cable television had 50 million subscribers—more than half of all the TV homes—with one-third of the subscribers signing up for one or more pay channels, such as Home Box Office. (For a further discussion of these technologies and their implications, see Chapter 22.)

Expense of Operation

Wide fluctuations in cost occur within each medium. Television is a highly expensive medium to establish and operate. Daily newspaper operations are expensive. Specialized weeklies can operate on a shoestring by doing all their layouts and pasteups themselves and taking the finished pages to an offset printer. Most magazine and book publishers do the same thing, though in a somewhat more sophisticated style. Few own their own presses any longer. Centralized presses handling many different publications utilize equipment at greater efficiency and reduce publication costs. Networks and corporate communicators "rent" uplink and transponder facilities from specialized companies. Radio stations can be started with relatively inexpensive equipment and can broadcast "canned" programming from satellites with minimal local personnel. Radio stations that are serious about news, on the other hand, must invest in expensive equipment and educated personnel.

Complexity of Distribution

The more middlemen, the more complex the process of distribution for each medium. Book publishers have to deal with a tangle of salespeople, distributors, book clubs, and retail outlets. Magazines must consider address changes, truckers, and mail schedules, among other things. Newspapers, if they were lucky, had fewer problems with truckers and the mails, but more with the paperboy who threw the paper into the puddle— or forgot to throw it at all. (To avoid this dependence on children as the final link in their distribution chain, most dailies have phased out the traditional paperboy in favor of adult vendors.) Radio and television have no middlemen (only a few middle machines) in the distribution process, although local stations frequently do not buy, and thus do not retransmit, the entire package of programs offered by the networks.

The complexity of distribution can result in a control just as severe as can a limitation on the number of channels. If it is too difficult to get a magazine or book to a retail outlet in a small town, for example, the publication will never be delivered there at all. As we discuss in Chapter 22, devices have already been developed that will create a revolution in the distribution process, leading to increasingly electronic transmission of the printed word—and probably, at some future date, to an end to paper as a necessary element in "mass" communication at all.

Frequency of Publication

The first newspaper in the American colonies, *Publick Occurrences Both Forreign and Domestick,* pledged to publish "once a moneth (or if any Glut of Occurrences happen, oftener)." Today magazines and newspapers are committed to regular publication, as are radio and television to regular broadcasting. Leo Rosten once referred to two deadly "curses" of the mass media: They are "committed to periodic and unalterable publication," and a "gargantuan amount of space" and time "*has* to be filled."[4] The more frequently a medium publishes or broadcasts, the more likely it is to transmit news and present it briefly. Conversely, the less frequently a medium publishes, the more likely it is to transmit interpretation and present it in detail. We move on a continuum from books (lengthy interpretation) to magazines (shorter interpretation) to newspapers (lengthy news) to television (brief news) to radio (headlines). These are oversimplifications, of course. There is sometimes news in books and often interpretation in radio.

Flexibility of the Channel

Print media can adjust their sizes to accommodate differing quantities of information and advertising. A Saturday afternoon newspaper is usually extremely thin, a Sunday paper normally quite fat. Unfortunately, advertising content, not the amount or importance of the news, is usually the key to size. Radio and television are cursed and imprisoned by time. They must operate a certain number of hours each day, and they have to fill up those hours. And when there is a "Glut of Occurrences" they cannot expand into another frequency or stretch the hours during which they operate. To present the extra material, they must encroach upon other time already allotted to entertainment or advertising. When they feel the need for more revenue, they tend to add more commercials rather than simply increase the price of a commercial minute, and to do this they must reduce the amount of time assigned to entertainment and information.

In emergencies, when the electronic media must present breaking news, they must preempt commercially sponsored time, at great financial cost to the networks and local stations. In borderline cases (of great national interest but not always involving breaking news)—such as the Army–McCarthy hearings in the 1950s, Senate Foreign Relations Committee hearings on Vietnam in the 1960s, the Watergate hearings that led to Nixon's resignation in the 1970s, and the Iran–Contras hearings in the 1980s—network executives are torn between public service and corporate loss. The decision is not always easy to make, especially when the financial loss to the networks can extend into the millions of dollars.

---

[4] Leo Rosten, "The Intellectual and the Mass Media," *Daedalus*, Spring 1960, p. 335.

Emphasis in the Media

Finally, note should be taken of the overall emphasis in each medium. Certainly the physical advantages and limitations of a medium largely determine whether emphasis will be on news, interpretation, or entertainment. Of all eight media, only newspapers and videotex emphasize news above interpretation and entertainment. Television has become the preeminent entertainment medium, while both magazines and books have moved in the direction of offering more interpretation and advice than they did in the past and less pure entertainment, especially in the form of fiction.

DRIFTING IN A SEA OF WORDS

Enumerating the elements of mass-media channels and describing them should provide more than an academic exercise. There is practical value in taking a hard look at the media with which we deal each day. Audiences are far more aware of what they *don't* like than of what they *would* like. It is up to media executives to anticipate audience needs and analyze their own competitive disadvantages, finding solutions if possible.

There are some areas, naturally, in which handicaps cannot be overcome. Except for videotex, the print media cannot incorporate sound and motion, for example, under any foreseeable circumstances. But books and newspapers can utilize color to better advantage than they have in the past. It is interesting to note that books, even when they use illustrations, rarely use color illustrations. It took a long time for newspapers to begin catching up with magazines in the area of color technology, and newspapers still have a distance to go. But with improved presses, newspapers have begun to offer more and better color in news and advertising columns. Some newspapers need to make a greater effort in this area and push ahead toward bolder use of color in cartoons, print, photographs, and layout design.

A more practical aspect of circulation (and competition) generally being neglected by newspapers and television is the element of reviewability and previewability. When newspapers were four or eight pages in size, it took no great effort to read through those pages and at least scan each story. In any case, it was difficult to miss a story. Today, with some urban dailies regularly producing newspapers with more than a hundred pages, it is sometimes difficult to *find* a story. Many newspapers run a simple index on page 1, indicating where special sections and certain regular features can be found. Most newspapers now follow the lead of the *New York Times* in running an index of all major stories on an inside page. However, few copy the *Times* in gathering all related stories, according to either geography or special interest, on the same and succeeding pages. As newspapers get larger, stories will be even harder to find, and many readers will not want to spend long periods of time scanning and rejecting hundreds of headlines in hopes of finding material in which they have a special interest.

Newspapers must do a better job of categorizing news—*and* advertising—*and* indexing them for readers. They must especially make the vast variety of news they present each day really previewable. It is time for newspapers to consider devoting a lower quarter of the front page to previewing in greater detail major items of interest inside the newspaper. With almost every daily newspaper, the reader is set adrift in a sea of headlines and copy without a simple compass.

Television generally does a sad job of previewing its own program schedule. *TV Guide* has built its gigantic circulation on the inability of newspapers and television to offer adequate indexes of daily television fare and content. Television, of course, has definite handicaps in this area, but it is within the realm of possibility for the medium to satisfy viewer curiosity better, and perhaps win larger audiences. At one point during each evening—perhaps just before the prime-time period—each network could devote two to five minutes to simply posting on the screen a printed schedule for the rest of the day's (and perhaps the next morning's) programs. The schedule could include the main stories and special features on the network news program, the regular programs for the evening with basic plots or guest stars, and a listing of guests for any evening talk programs and for the next morning's talk program.

Cable already has enough channels to devote at least one to previewing the day's fare in an intelligent, selective manner, but it is still too unsophisticated to recognize the advertising possibilites in doing so. Cable can, and one day will, provide a service of "highlights," "best choices," and reviews, all constantly updated for quick viewing by the confused viewer.

Media permeate our society and set the agenda for public affairs discussions and entertainment viewing. The newest medium on the scene, videotex, has the best capability for guiding readers toward the most beneficial use of media time, since it has optimum elements of rapid reviewability and can come very close to simultaneity, thus making immediate adjustments possible. For example, at some point in the future every household will have a two-way videotex (print) terminal next to the telephone, and probably one videotex TV channel. It will be a simple matter to determine the programming for the evening, a review of the programs available, and the reviewer's recommendations. News items scheduled for each network or local news program can be inserted into the videotex database with ease, as well as guests scheduled for various talk and interview programs. Indexes of articles appearing in weekly and monthly magazines will also probably be available in the database, along with the latest videotapes offered by video rental stores. We have a plethora of information and entertainment in our modern world, and a scarcity of sources telling us what it is, where it is, and whether it's worth our time to obtain. In the opinion of the authors, videotex will fill this void in the communication process.

AFTERTHOUGHTS

1. Why does videotex's lack of portability handicap its ability to provide preview-ability of television programming?
2. Is the lower half of a newspaper's front page too valuable as a medium for displaying news to devote to outlining the major stories inside the paper?
3. What changes in other media are likely to occur when TV and VCRs achieve true portability?
4. What changes would you like to see on your local newspaper's Op-Ed page? Do you think those changes would improve the newspaper's circulation?
5. If television is the only medium that offers all the elements of reproduction, circulation, feedback, and support, does this mean, *per se,* that television is the best medium?

CHAPTER 3

A Natural Law of Media Development

While the technology of each mass medium is available worldwide, economic, educational, and demographic factors specific to each country influence media growth patterns. By looking closely at these factors, one can explain the past growth of mass media in each nation and predict the rate and direction of its growth in the future as well.

Patterns of media progression generally follow the EPS curve: media in any nation grow from *elitist* to *popular* to *specialized* (Figure 3.1). In the elitist stage, the media appeal to and are consumed primarily by opinion leaders. In the popular stage, media appeal to and are consumed by the masses of a nation's population. In the specialized stage, the media appeal to and are consumed by fragmented, specialized segments of the total population. (It must be noted, however, that many countries do not fall clearly into one stage of this pattern; it is frequently possible for different media to be in different stages of the EPS pattern within the same country.)

ELITE MEDIA: PROGRAMMING FOR THE FEW

Illiteracy and poverty are daily facts of life in most nations. In such countries, only the elite are literate, and only the elite have the money to obtain messages from all media. In an underdeveloped country, the average person—even though literate—could not afford to purchase a daily newspaper regularly nor buy magazines and books. Even for the illiterate,

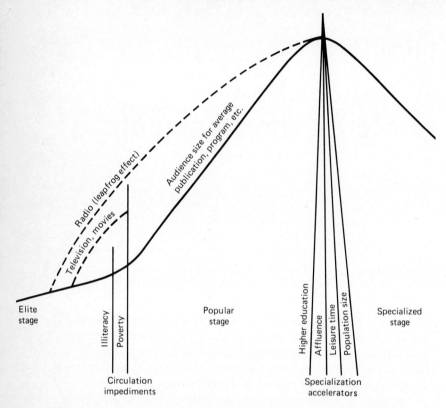

Figure 3.1. Elite-Popular-Specialized (EPS) Curve of Media Progression

a radio and television set are expenditures not to be taken lightly, with television especially being out of the reach of the average person.

The two rings of this set of handcuffs—*illiteracy* and *poverty*—also serve to restrict large geographical segments of a nonaffluent nation. The urban areas of such a nation may have all the mass media accessible to them; the vast rural areas have none, with the possible exception of radio. Newspapers need roads and literate customers in order to circulate outside of urban areas. Television receivers and motion picture projectors must have sources of electric power; otherwise they are unable to operate in rural villages.

Not surprisingly, elitist media have a general content quite a bit different from that of media in other stages of the EPS curve. Their content is aimed primarily at informing, but even the entertainment material is set at a higher cultural level. Income from circulation is higher than income from advertising, and the media themselves are relatively expensive to obtain.

Most of the nations of Africa and Asia fall within this stage of media development. In a typical African country, for example, there are only a few newspapers, and their readership is restricted to the elite. There may be no magazines, and such books as exist are imported from other countries. The audience for the print media is an urban as well as an elite audience. Television transmitters may not reach far beyond the urban areas; radio has reaching power but limited "receiving" power, and the nature of radio programming beamed into the rural areas is didactic.

India is an example of a nation whose media fall almost completely in the elitist stage. Although the second most populous nation in the world, the country suffers severely from both poverty and illiteracy. The media, reflecting this situation, are aimed primarily at the urban elite. A surprisingly large number of newspapers are published in English—the elitist language of the country—and these are also the circulation leaders in most urban areas.[1] India has only 3.0 radio receivers and .6 TV receivers for every 100 persons in the population (the United States has about 200 radio receivers and 58 TV receivers for every 100 persons), and programming directed at the rural areas has a heavy content of educational information.

POPULAR: THE COMMON DENOMINATOR

Once a nation breaks through the barriers of poverty and illiteracy, its media move into the *popular* stage. Circulations begin to rise as the media are able to reach larger groups of citizens who are able to read (in the case of print media) and can afford mass media. During this stage we see the dominance of the "mass-mass" media, those films, programs, and publications that appeal to a huge, heterogeneous audience. Content, in short, is designed to appeal to the great majority of the population. The "lowest common denominator" principle, which means the content is geared for the least sophisticated portion of the potential audience, is applicable in the popular stage because most of the potential audience is not far removed from the lowest common denominator. Of course, specialized publications and programs are also available in this stage of media development, but these could be said to be vestiges of the elitist stage and of an elitist

---

[1] An exception is the *Malayala Manorama*, printed in the Malayalam language, with a circulation of more than 300,000. However, the state in which it is published, Kerala, has a literacy rate of 92 percent, compared with India's average of 38 percent.

mentality in the country rather than a deliberate attempt to reach a highly fragmented audience.

The media in most of the developed countries of Europe and North America are squarely in this stage of the EPS curve, and so too are those of Japan, Israel, Australia, and New Zealand—along with the media in the large urban areas of many other countries throughout the world.

It must be noted here that the inexpensive transistor radio has permitted radio stations in fairly primitive countries to leapfrog across the barriers of illiteracy and poverty into the popular stage. Radio appeals to the masses in those countries, and indeed reaches the masses. In such countries, radio programming is more didactic and has a lower common denominator than the print media, which essentially remain in the elite category. Motion pictures and television are also able to leapfrog across the barrier of illiteracy, but at present are still restricted by the poverty barrier. Movie houses, equipment, and admissions are still costly in underdeveloped countries, and no cheap, battery-operated television set has yet appeared to put it in the same class as the transistor radio.

SPECIALIZED MEDIA:
INTO THE TWENTY-FIRST CENTURY

A fully developed country with a wide range of popular media is ready to move into the specialized stage—the third and final stage of the EPS curve—when four conditions obtain: widespread higher education, an affluent population, available leisure time, and significant population size. Like the transition from the elite to the popular stage, the evolution from popular to specialized media is gradual—perhaps so imperceptible, in fact, that many communicators themselves do not realize they have been left behind by a new audience quite different from the mass audience of the previous stage. A closer look at these four factors will explain why a population becomes receptive to more specialized media.

Higher Education

As people specialize professionally and/or intellectually, they have different intellectual and cultural tastes and interests. Elementary and high school education is largely uniform throughout a nation. When a sizable proportion of the population goes on to university education, individuals leave a homogeneous education path and begin to follow new trails. Specialized literacy, scientific, and professional interests are cultivated and developed. These new, individualized interests, furthermore, are not restricted to those who go on to university training. Urban and industrial societies demand job specialization, and those who specialize have a particular interest in publications that offer an opportunity to hear from and communicate with other persons with the same specialization.

Affluence

Specialized media can be obtained only by a population able to afford a variety of media; therefore, the population must have attained a high standard of living before this stage can be reached. This means that the average family must be able to afford not only a *variety* of media (one television set, one radio, one newspaper, and one or two magazines), but a variety of specialized units *within* each medium (several radios and television sets, various publications). Specialized media appeal to a fragmented audience, and this implies a fragmented family as well, because individual members of the family have different entertainment and intellectual interests. Children, for example, are often not interested in television programs that appeal to their parents; wives frequently are not interested in programs that attract their husbands.

Leisure Time

This factor is closely related to affluence, but it emphasizes that the population needs more than simply the money to buy the products of specialized media. It must have the free time away from work to pursue activities such as travel, hobbies, sports, and other special interests that whet the appetite for specialized media relating to these interests. And obviously it must have the leisure time in which to consume the media products (now available in greater variety) themselves. The 40-hour work week, the two-day weekend, regular holidays, annual vacations, and workdays ending by 5 P.M. are important elements of leisure time. Persons in developed countries take these for granted, not recognizing that leisure time as we know it is unknown in most Third World countries.

Population Size

A population must be large enough to support minimum circulations for media. A country with a small population can support publications and broadcasting operations with a wide appeal; it cannot support those with a very narrow appeal. The audience of any media unit must be large enough to justify the expenses of production and distribution, whether income is derived from advertising or subscriptions. Preliminary studies indicate that a country must have a minimum population of about 10 or 15 million before it can enter the specialized stage.

Some specialized media exist in small nations, of course, but the communications scene there is dominated by popular publications and programs. Theoretically, massive government subsidies could provide specialized programs and publications for a small nation that has otherwise achieved the other three conditions characterizing the specialized stage. In fact, however, the cost would be prohibitive, and there are other avenues by which most such nations can obtain specialized media, as we will see later.

Five countries—the United States, Great Britain, France, West Germany, and Japan—have reached the point where the four conditions coalesce, and all have now plunged into the specialized stage of the EPS curve. "Mass-mass" publications have virtually disappeared; popular programming in the electronic media has peaked. This statement could appear to be exaggerated until one takes a closer look at the individual media.

Books have been in the specialization stage longer than any other medium. With the huge population of the United States as a market, book publishers have been able to attract a substantial number of buyers from among select audiences—children, hobbyists, education specialists, and others. The era of the massive best-seller, such as *Gone with the Wind,* has itself gone with the wind. The mass-mass magazines, such as *Life* or *Look,* have breathed their last.[2] They were by their very nature too general for this era of specialization, a fact that advertisers noted before the publishers did. And newspapers, recordings, radio, and motion pictures now seek out specialized audiences to a far greater extent than they did three decades ago.

Television has been the last mass medium to make the full leap into the specialized stage. It still has vestiges of a nonspecialized, mass-mass medium, with the three major networks programming for a heterogeneous audience. Its slowness in moving into the specialized stage was caused by a scarcity of channels for expanded programming, the relative expense of receivers, and the expense of programming. When the possibilities of cable and satellite transmission opened the television spectrum from a handful of local channels to several dozen or more, the television medium made a belated leap into the specialized era.

Media may achieve specialization in one of two ways: by *unit specialization,* meaning that the entire publication or programming day appeals to a specific audience, or by *internal specialization,* meaning that parts of the publication or parts of the programming day appeal to different audiences.

---

[2] A few of the old mass-media magazines, such as *Life,* have now reappeared as regular publications. But they are now specialized magazines, aimed at a much smaller target audience. They do not try to be all things to all people, as they did in the past.

Reader's Digest, for example, is usually considered a mass-mass maga-zine, simply because it has one of the largest circulations of any periodical in the United States. But even though its total audience is heterogeneous, *Reader's Digest* is able to appeal to specialized audiences within this group by offering a variety of articles on widely different subjects. It therefore achieves internal specialization.

Ethnic stations and classical music stations in urban areas are exam-ples of unit specialization in radio—what is called "narrowcasting." The *Financial Times* in England and the *Wall Street Journal* in the United States are other examples of unit specialization. More typically, the aver-age daily newspaper in America is an example of internal specialization. Since it is usually the only game in town, it must appeal to a heterogeneous audience; however, it has evolved to a sectionalized product, attracting specialized audiences to the section rather than to the whole. Larger business and sports sections—even special business and sports inserts, such as "Business Monday" and "Sports Friday"—along with specific entertainment and lifestyle sections characterize today's daily. Major dail-ies customize the newspaper for different neighborhoods of the city, and there are predictions that the newspaper of the near future will be highly customized for the individual, through use of computers. For example, people who want more business news will receive an expanded business section, or perhaps even specialized types of business news.

Recordings and radio stations utilize unit specialization. There are no longer popular records or radio stations that appeal to all age groups in all segments of the population. Instead, we have hard rock, soft rock, country rock, regular country, religious, classical, golden oldie, blue grass, and soul records, to name only a few, and radio stations with the same format. Motion pictures select audiences by genre: children's, horror, sci-fi, ad-venture, comedy, drama. There are few movies that all members of the family can enjoy together, and most parents would not be comfortable watching many movies with their children sitting beside them.

Network television utilizes internal specialization, but to a lesser extent than any other medium in the United States. Specialized programs are confined mostly to the daytime hours, and even then the audience appeal is very broad—children or homemakers, for example. Evening (prime-time) programming is still directed toward an all-inclusive audi-ence. As ultrahigh-frequency (UHF) stations, satellite channels (CNN, TBS, Arts & Entertainment), and cable television chip away at the domi-nance of the networks, we are beginning to see television drift toward the same unit specialization that we have already seen in the radio medium in the United States.

As a country moves completely into the specialization stage, there is a withering away of the mass media as we know them today. "Mass" media cannot exist without a mass audience. Specialized tastes and abundant channels in every medium must result in an end to the age of the mass audience. Taking its place will be highly fragmented, specialized audiences.

BORROWING A FOREIGN LANGUAGE

What happens to those fully developed nations in which the factors of affluence, higher education, and leisure time have coalesced but in which there is a population smaller than, say, 10 million—or in which there are multiple languages, none of which is spoken by more than 10 million persons? Most such nations become "borrowers" of the specialized media of other nations, a fact that has important implications for international communication.

The ability to borrow assumes that the entire country or significantly large groups within the country have a familiarity with one of the four "technological languages"—English, French, German, and Russian. Technological languages are those languages in which most of the original scientific and technical articles and books are published and circulated worldwide. Spanish, Chinese, and Arabic, for example, although spoken by vast numbers of the world's people, would not qualify by this definition. Japanese, which has more than its share of scientific publications, is a language understood by few outside of Japan, so it also would not qualify. Thus a country like Switzerland could easily consume the specialized media of Germany and France (and, to a remarkable degree, those from English-speaking countries as well), the French-speaking portion of Belgium borrows the media of France, New Zealand borrows from other English-speaking countries, and so on.

This phenomenon indicates that fully developed but small-population nations that are not in the mainstream of a technological language must make a conscious effort as a matter of national priority to adopt or develop one as a second language or otherwise risk creating an ever-widening technology gap between themselves and the major modern nations of the world.[3]

There is evidence that some advanced nations are already making this effort. One indicator is the international distribution of newsmagazines, which can be considered specialized publications. Small nations are unable to provide enough subscribers to warrant establishment of a first-

---

[3] An interesting discussion of the serious disadvantages resulting from small population size can be found in Donald B. Keesing, "Small Population as a Political Handicap to National Development," *Political Science Quarterly,* March 1969, pp. 50–60.

TABLE 3.1. WORLD DISTRIBUTION OF *TIME* AND *NEWSWEEK* (CIRCULATION PER 1,000 OF POPULATION)

	Population (in millions)	Principal Languages	Per Capita Income	*Time* (per 1,000)	*Newsweek* (per 1,000)
United States	247.5	English	13,451	19.1	13.4
United Kingdom	56.6	English	7,216	.9	.5
Singapore	2.7	Chinese Malay	6,200	5.6	7.7
Israel	4.5	Hebrew Arabic	5,995	5.0	2.2
Norway	4.2	Norwegian	13,790	4.1	2.6
Switzerland	6.5	German French Italian	14,408	2.9	1.7
Sweden	8.4	Swedish	11,989	2.5	1.6
Finland	5.0	Finnish	11,007	2.3	2.2
Denmark	5.1	Danish	11,312	1.8	1.7
Netherlands	14.7	Dutch	13,065	1.8	.5

SOURCES: Circulation figures are from Magazine Publisher's Statement *from the Audit Bureau of Circulations, for period ending June 30, 1988 (mimeograph); population and per capita income statistics are from* The World Almanac and Book of Facts, 1989 *(New York: Newspaper Enterprise Association, 1988).*

rate newsmagazine with international coverage; they therefore become borrowers of such publications from other countries. Table 3.1 shows non-English-speaking countries in which *Time* and *Newsweek* have a substantial circulation.[4]

It is perhaps not surprising that most of the non-English-speaking countries appearing on the list are nations with a relatively high per capita income, a primary language unique to their own country, and an educational program that encourages the study of English even in elementary school. Exceptions to one or more of these factors are Singapore, which is isolated from Mainland China, its natural language link, and Switzerland, whose multilingual, cosmopolitan population subscribe to *Der Spiegel* and *L'Express* (German and French newsmagazines, respectively) in greater numbers than they subscribe to *Time* and *Newsweek*.

Similar studies would probably show that these same nations are

---

[4] Hebrew and, to a far lesser degree, Arabic are the primary languages of Israel, which has a high readership of *Time* and *Newsweek* for a non-English-speaking country. However, the study of English as a secondary language is mandatory, beginning in the fifth grade of elementary school. An Israeli who completes high school will have had eight years of English. No student who cannot show a high proficiency in this language is admitted to an Israeli university.

heavy borrowers of specialized English-language publications in fields such as medicine, science, the humanities, and social sciences. Small nations not in the mainstream of a technological language must demand that students seeking a university education first have familiarity with a mainstream language. Their libraries are filled with books and research papers in a language or languages other than the country's primary language. A nation of less than 10 to 15 million population is simply incapable of producing up-to-date textbooks for courses that will enroll perhaps fewer than one hundred students per semester. If they are to offer higher education worthy of the name, they must by necessity become borrowers from other countries, and their students must be prepared to do much of their research and reading in this second language.

The need to know a second language in such countries also extends to those who would seek out specialized information or entertainment (movies, books, recordings) of any kind, because a small nation usually will be unable to satisfy such appetites unless it is done at a prohibitive cost. American movies, for example, are usually not dubbed in the native languages of these countries, since the process is too expensive for such a small population. Movies in theaters and on television carry subtitles only. Thus children and adults in these countries are exposed to English much more than are the citizens of larger countries that import American movies.

Vast numbers of people live in countries that have large population size but that lack one or more of the remaining three factors necessary for the specialized stage. In these countries the elite, especially the scientific elite, usually learn a technological language and become individual borrowers from a lending nation offering specialized media. Unfortunately, this practice does not permit the underdeveloped nation to leapfrog into the specialized stage, nor does it do much to narrow the technological gap. However, it would seem that a conscious effort by such nations to impose the study of a second language during the earliest years of schooling would be an essential shortcut toward the goal of national development.

Obviously, there is a danger of language "imperialism." As English has become the predominant language of world trade and science, it has also intruded its vocabulary into other languages. Each nation has an urge to maintain the purity of its language for legitimate cultural reasons. But to discourage the use of technological languages because of nationalistic pride will in effect only bar citizens from the major sources of scientific knowledge. Nations must, as a matter of national imperative, seek a balance between protecting their culture and seeking intellectual nourishment from the outside world.

AFTERTHOUGHTS

1. In the United States will there always be a major audience for television networks that appeal to a heterogeneous audience, as opposed to specialized audiences?

2. In developing countries, can movies piggyback on VCRs to leap across the barrier of poverty in a way that they could not do in the absence of VCRs?

3. Which is more accurate: "The *New York Times* is a vestige of the elite stage of media progression" or "The *New York Times* is a product of the specialized stage of media progression"?

4. Assuming that Spanish is *not* a technological language, would it make sense for Mexico to follow Israel's lead and make English a mandatory language to be taught starting in the fifth grade?

5. In which stage of media progression would there tend to be more political harmony among the populace? Why?

CHAPTER 4

Print Media: Changing for the Twenty-First Century

We see ourselves in the middle of an unprecedented technological revolution, as one breakthrough in communications development follows hard upon another. Yet, it was in truth the invention of movable type in the fifteenth century that began the revolution that transformed European religion, economy, and culture. Gutenberg's invention moved power away from the Church into the hands of any person who could think and translate those thoughts into words. The Reformation followed and then the Counter-Reformation, as these words became the most powerful weapon against the Church in the sixteenth and seventeenth centuries. Mechanical words multiplied both ideas and literacy and were the tools for changing the nature of the State in the eighteenth, nineteenth, and twentieth centuries.

The print industry itself, far from maintaining the status quo that one associates with metallic presses and type, has undergone rapid changes in looks and appeal. It has not only spawned its own inventions—the steam-driven press, the Linotype, the halftone engraving—but quickly assimilated the inventions of others—the telegraph, telephone, computer, and satellites, to name only a few—and each time the products of the print industry have changed. The halftone, toward the end of the nineteenth century, offered as startling a new vision of the world as did the television set in the middle of the twentieth century. It enabled the print industry to become a picture medium as well as a word medium. It gave illiterates and marginal literates greater access to information than they had ever had before and served as a stepping-stone toward the goal of full literacy.

Technical developments, then, have altered the looks of the print media and refocused their appeal. But the philosophy of the press has undergone significant changes, too, as a result of stresses exerted by dynamic people and dynamic audiences. Urbanization and rising levels of literacy in the United States forced print media to evolve from a colonial press to a penny press to a specialized press. Similar historical changes have occurred in other modern countries.

This is not to say that print media have been unaffected by television, but it does emphasize that there had been significant traumas caused by developments inside and outside the press well before the invention of the cathode-ray tube. Even in the twentieth century, tabloid journalism left its imprint on newspaper personality, and the widening popularity of radio forced newspapers to relinquish a few of their traditional roles.

The worldwide effect of television on print media is difficult to assess. In many developing countries television, along with radio, has simply filled a communications void. In the more developed nations television has had a more profound effect on radio than it has had on the print media. Everywhere, publishers have feared that television would skim off their advertising revenues, but this has actually occurred only where the print media—magazines, primarily—had already lost the *audience* that advertisers wanted to reach. Otherwise, advertisers have expanded their budgets to purchase television commercials in addition to print media ads. Daily newspaper income from advertising in the United States, for example, has shown a steady rise almost every year since World War II.

Television seized a good portion of the audience (and advertising) of picture-oriented and general-audience-oriented magazines in the United States. But television also created the need for new magazines devoted to television schedules and criticism,[1] and it made the newspaper a necessity in some homes if only because the paper provides a schedule of the daily television fare.

Despite their inability to compete successfully with television for the public's time, the print media have still been able to retain the public's interest. Television has not caused a dissolution of the print industry, as some had feared. The production of books has increased (approximately 50,000 different books titles are currently published each year) and maga-

---

[1] One of the largest circulation magazines in the United States is *TV Guide* (about 17 million), which includes a variety of television commentary and criticism as well as program listings. It is the authors' opinion that the circulation of *TV Guide* in a particular community is in inverse ratio to the quality of the local newspaper's TV coverage. Most newspapers still give too little attention to the medium that engages the average American for more than four and a half hours every day of the week. Editors who seek to assess the effectiveness of their TV coverage, tables, previews, and reviews need only check the circulation of *TV Guide* in their cities relative to that magazine's circulation in other communities.

zine births far exceed magazine deaths. Weekly and Sunday newspapers have increased in total circulation. Although the United States had about 8.3 percent fewer weekly newspapers in 1987 than it had in 1960, total circulation increased 146 percent in those 27 years. The number of Sunday newspapers in the United States has increased by 65 percent since the end of World War II, and these newspapers have shown impressive circulation increases, especially in recent years.

The exception to this pattern of growth seems to be the daily newspaper, whose circulations in the United States have remained flat in recent years, lagging far behind population increases. The following statistics tell the puzzling story of the daily newspaper circulation doldrums: In 1946 there were 1,763 dailies with a total circulation of 50.9 million. By 1987 there were 1,645 dailies, a decrease of 6.7 percent, but total circulation had grown to 62.8 million, an increase of 23.4 percent. But at the same time, the adult population in the United States had grown by 80 percent. Between 1970 and 1987, daily newspaper circulation changed by only a fraction, while the U.S. adult population increased by about one-third.

What logical explanations are there for this phenomenon of flat circulations among U.S. dailies while other print media are doing so well?

1. *Competition from television.* In content, newspapers are more vulnerable to the competition of television than are books and magazines. Most people get their news first from television, and cable television offers all news networks such as CNN and CNN Headline News. In addition there are channels with constant updating of sports, weather, business, and entertainment information. In 1967, 73 percent of adults in the United States said they read a newspaper every day; by 1988, only 51 percent said they did so. A significant percentage of the population is obviously not finding the daily a necessity and is turning to weekly and Sunday papers. One sometimes hears the argument that busy Americans simply no longer have the time to read a daily newspaper, especially considering the higher incidence of working couples. However, these same busy Americans have found about four and a half hours to watch television each day, time that they were not spending on this medium prior to 1950.

2. *Adult illiteracy.* As we will see later in this chapter, literacy in the United States is pegged at "99 percent," according to *The World Almanac and Book of Facts, 1989.* However, the almanac also notes: "Literacy rates are usually based on the ability to read and write on a lower elementary school level. The concept of literacy is changing in the industrialized countries, where literacy is defined as the ability to read instructions necessary for a job or a license.

By these standards, illiteracy may be more common than present rates suggest.'' In fact, the U.S. Census reports on American literacy are notoriously flawed, as described in detail by Jonathan Kozol in his book *Literate America*. Kozol contends that 10 million adult Americans (almost 6 percent of the adult population) are ''absolute or nearly absolute illiterates'' and 60 million Americans —one-third of the adult population—are functionally illiterate or only marginally literate. Reg Murphy, publisher of the *Baltimore Sun,* reported to fellow newspaper executives in 1988 that 14 percent of adult Americans read below a fifth-grade level and 20 percent more read between a fifth- and eighth-grade level, while most newspapers in the United States require a minimum ninth-grade reading level.

3. *Inability to adapt to the specialized stage of media development.* Although the daily newspaper has adopted internal specialization to reach target audiences better, it is still a mass medium in an age of specialized audiences. The fact that it is unable to appeal strongly enough to some specialized interests within its circulation area probably accounts, in part, for its loss of audience. For example, it cannot devote enough space to business, entertainment, hobbies, even sports, to mention only a few subjects, to satisfy those who want or need more depth in these areas. Part of this problem is the inflexibility of the daily paper medium itself. But part is also probably due to a mind set that resists refashioning the newspaper to fit the needs of a changing era. In Canada, the United States's next-door neighbor with similar population characteristics, circulation of daily newspapers has kept pace with adult population increases, largely through the introduction of competitive tabloid newspapers.

The circulation problems of the daily newspaper aside, there are obvious reasons for the steady popularity of print media: the world literacy pool gets larger each year, more people are able to afford books and periodicals, and more people find books and periodicals a necessity in obtaining and maintaining professional competence.

WHY SOME CHOOSE PRINT

Beyond all this, however, print media have innate advantages over radio and television. These advantages accrue despite the overwhelming popularity of the electronic media and their ability to attract the ''mass-mass audience.'' The outstanding advantage of print media is *reviewability*. This factor of on-demand access was discussed in some detail in Chapter 2. The print media do not exist in "time" in the same manner as sound and motion media; they may be previewed, scanned, or reviewed at the convenience of the reader. One word, one chapter, one picture, or one advertisement can be examined and analyzed at the reader's leisure. The permanence of the written word and the accessibility of words on paper offer advantages that sound and motion media are so far unable to equal, even with the arrival of the age of electronic video recording.

Print media also offer a far larger selection than the other media; the United States alone produces about 20,000 magazine titles each year. The consumer of print media shops in a supermarket of ideas, entertainment, information, and advertisements. In a free country the number of individual publications may seem to range toward the infinite. True, the consumer of sound and motion media also has increasing choices, as a result of FM, cable television, UHF, TV, and video rentals, but the selection is still limited *relative to print*.

We speak of "selective perception" as the unconscious act of picking out information that we prefer to read or see—usually information that reinforces our own beliefs—and ignoring information in the same source that goes against our preconceived notions or beliefs. "Message choice" is the characteristic of print media that permits us to make a *conscious* selection. Headlines, chapter headings, and illustrations permit us to pick out, in a very convenient manner, information that we find interesting or useful. We spend a good deal of our newspaper reading time, for example, simply culling through headlines, quickly discarding stories and advertisements that we do not want to read and fixing upon those that are more attractive to us. Obviously, we also discard whole bundles of information that perhaps we *should* read—information that would be "good for us." But there is pleasure in this choosing; we are rarely offended by information that we don't read.

Electronic media, on the other hand, do not offer "message choice." "Selective perception," of course, is still at work, but even so the information that we find useless—or even offensive—is still pouring out in an unbroken stream that we can hardly avoid. Some broadcasters have said that members of the audience can correct this situation by simply switching off the set. However, doing this may be inconvenient for listeners or viewers, and in any event can better be described as "abstention" rather than "choice."

"Message choice" implies that the reader has the option to separate and choose. Many people in our society would rather not know about war, poverty, deficits, or catastrophes. From the point of society, the fact that radio and television feed them this information whether or not they want it is advantageous. From the point of view of the individual, it is disadvantageous. There is wasted time and traumatic shock in being fed information and commercials that one finds useless and even unwanted. It obviously leads to audience frustration and dissatisfaction.

PRINT MEDIA AROUND THE WORLD

The major world trend in the print media is toward monopoly ownership. In the United States more newspapers each year are purchased by chains or, as the proprietors prefer to call them, "newspaper groups." Reflecting this trend at a higher level is the expansion of "media conglomerates": huge corporations engaged in multimedia ownership, including books, magazines, newspapers, movies, radio, television, and cable. The Gannett Co. Inc., for example, owns more than 80 dailies and controls 10 percent of the total daily circulation in the United States, in addition to television stations, radio stations, weeklies, and outdoor advertising. The Time Inc./ Warner merger brought together a vast network of magazines, motion picture production, and cable systems. The trend toward monopoly is also apparent in other modern, developed countries throughout the world— where, if the government is not already the sole owner of media, the large, privately owned "national" newspapers are tending to swallow those of smaller circulation.

Big business is a fact of life in the developed countries. It is perhaps natural that this trend is reflected in the communication industry as well. The "mom and pop" corner grocery store is history. And increased competition from other media, especially television, has accelerated this trend toward chain ownership. "Party papers," newspapers supported largely by contributions from political parties, traditionally provided competition to privately owned newspapers in Western Europe, but these newspapers are now losing their fight for survival as well. Rising production costs, a failure to attract advertising because of limited circulation, and an inability to compete with the improved products and flexible editorial opinions of independent newspapers are some of the causes for the disappearance of party papers. In some Scandinavian countries indirect government subsidies are prolonging the lives of party papers. But the fact seems to remain: where the people have a free choice between party newspapers and independently owned papers, the latter emerge victorious.

The will to survive in the face of tougher competition from other newspapers and other media has forced some of the most traditionally minded newspapers to alter their character. Dependent more and more on advertising to compensate for rising labor and production costs, the "quality" newspapers are coming down from their pedestals and seeking a broader audience. Newspapers would thus seem to be moving counter to the specialization trend. On the contrary, they are becoming even more specialized, but it is an internal specialization. The paper as a unit appeals to a more heterogeneous audience, while individual parts of the paper appeal to specialized segments of the audience.

The trend toward monopoly ownership of the print media is not without both advantages and disadvantages. Concentrated ownership offers the press an increased amount of economic efficiency and therefore adds to the economic stability of press units within the group. But it also reduces, in theory, the variety of viewpoints offered by the press. This creates a dichotomy: the need for the press to be economically strong and independent on the one hand, and the need for the press to offer the ultimate range of views and analysis, on the other. The public is faced with an entirely different situation from that of concentrated ownership in industry. Monopolistic ownership of soap, for example, reduces consumer choice, but it still gives consumers the product they seek. Monopolistic ownership of the press threatens to remove from a democratic society the product itself—critical variety.

Fortunately, the trend toward concentrated ownership of newspapers in many Western countries has been accompanied by new means and methods of communication. Newsmagazines and other specialized magazines have proven to be new sources of interpretation and analysis. The electronic media, though highly restricted in the area of direct editorializing in many countries, have provided documentaries and commentaries that are, in effect, a source of political and social criticism. Paperbacks are still another source of opinion. And American newspapers, realizing their responsibility for providing a variety of viewpoints, now present more syndicated political columnists than ever before.

But there is evidence that although these sources have contributed supplementary perspectives on national government, they have not been able adequately to supplement the reduced variety of criticism on the local and regional levels.

Some critics have seen in group and conglomerate ownerships the potential power to mold public opinion on a vast scale. Others say that a more likely danger is that they will wield no power at all—that, becoming vulnerable to attack by government as a monopoly, they will recognize themselves as a public utility and assume a position of neutrality on political affairs, especially in those cities where their enterprises face no print opposition. In fact, there is already a move by the public and the government toward regulating print media as public utilities, in much the same way that electronic media are already regulated. Press laws, press councils, and press subsidies in nations outside the United States are part of this particular mosaic. In the United States the major step in this direction came in the mid-1940s when the courts ruled that the Associated

Press was subject to the nation's anti-trust laws, like any other big business, and therefore had to make its service available to virtually any newspaper that wanted it. Justice Felix Frankfurter, in the same case, *Associated Press* v. *United States (1945),* wrote that government had a compelling reason for attempting to control media activities that tended to restrain trade. In addition to being a commercial enterprise, he wrote, the press "has a relation to the public interest unlike that of any other enterprise pursued for profit." The most recent efforts toward regulating print media as public utilities in the United States are (1) a law that exempts certain newspapers from normal monopoly restrictions, on the grounds that a "combined operating agreement" between a failing newspaper and a strong one preserves pluralism of information and opinion; (2) regulations limiting the number of broadcasting properties a corporation can own and barring the license of a broadcasting property to a corporation already owning a daily newspaper in the same community; and (3) court rulings limiting the kinds of information services that telephone utilites can offer in competition with print, broadcasting, and cable industries.

The Print "Jet Set"

One often considers the modern age in terms of the wonders of message communication, from the wireless to the communications satellite, without considering the new changes in the transmission of correspondents and publications themselves. Jet aircraft travel has made it possible for a large newspaper, magazine, or news syndicate to place its best correspondents in almost any spot in the world in a matter of hours. This means of transportation has inaugurated the age of "mobile bureaus." It has reduced reliance on the major international news services and permitted publications to offer a more individualized product to their readers.

Beyond this, however, jet transportation now encourages elite newspapers to spread their messages beyond their native countries; it has given meaningful international communication an immediacy never before achieved. A subscriber in New York can receive European and Middle Eastern newspapers the day following publication; the *New York Times* and *USA Today* can be purchased at some European and Asian newsstands on the day of publication. The major newsmagazines (*Time, Newsweek, U.S. News & World Report, Der Spiegel,* and *L'Express*) are delivered to subscribers all over the world at approximately the same time as subscribers within the country of publication receive them, and there are many other weekly publications that could be added to this list.

The influence of these publications goes far beyond that of international broadcasts, primarily because they are generally privately owned and therefore viewed as more credible than is official output, they are purchased and therefore desired by their readers, and they are reviewable and therefore able to compete successfully with the media in the countries in which they are distributed.

UNDERSTANDING NATIONAL PATTERNS IN THE PRINT MEDIA

The vital statistics of every nation's press system are available in various sources. These statistics would include the number of morning and afternoon dailies and weeklies, the types of magazines available, the total number of book titles published each year, annual newsprint production and consumption, the names and number of news agencies, and so on. It is more interesting, however, to understand the nature of a country's print media by looking at these statistics in the light of three major factors: (1) population, (2) geography, and (3) politico-economic system.

Population

One must consider this factor in terms of population size, urbanization, languages spoken, education, and affluence. A large, literate population, highly urbanized and speaking one major language (Japan fits all these characteristics) has a high potential for large-circulation "quality" newspapers and specialized magazines. A lower degree of literacy, more people living in villages, and a multiplicity of languages (India, for example) obviously reduces the potential for print media, even with a large population. A highly literate but small population (Finland) may be able to support quality newspapers but not specialized magazines or a great variety of book titles in its own language.

If an urbanized, literate population is divided into language groups, the circulation potential for mass magazines and newspapers is greatly reduced, sometimes both quality and specialization being affected. Belgium, for example, is divided into two major groups, fragmenting a population of 10 million into essentially a population of 4.5 million French-speaking Belgians and 5.5 million Flemish-speaking Belgians. Although many Belgians are bilingual, it is safe to say that most are more comfortable in one language than in another and prefer—for political, cultural, and religious reasons as well—publications printed in that language. Neither the French-language nor the Flemish-language Belgian publications are noted for outstanding quality or large circulations. One reason is the availability of quality publications from nearby France and Holland. But what about tiny Finland and Israel, whose major languages are unique to their countries? Or compare the Swedish-speaking minority in Finland, who may subscribe to Swedish publications, with the Arabic-speaking minority in Israel, who can receive current periodicals from surrounding Arab countries only with great difficulty, since those countries refuse to send mail to the State of Israel.

Factors such as these help to explain why a particular country has few specialized magazines, why it may borrow heavily from the publications of other countries, or why it must subsidize its own publications and perhaps encourage the learning of a second language so its educated citizens can consume the specialized publications of larger countries.

Geography

The size of a country, the physical barriers to overland communication, and the location of major cities are important elements to consider in understanding aspects of the country's print media. The smaller a country and the fewer its physical barriers, the more likely it is to have strong "national" dailies that circulate throughout the country.[2] Large cities separated from each other by significant distances are able to nurture strong newspapers, since competition is kept to a minimum. Norway, for example, is not a large country, but the physical barriers of mountains, a serrated coastline, and winter snows have served to reduce the circulation territory of Oslo newspapers and strengthen the provincial press. Mexico City, a center of population, culture, and the arts, could be expected to dominate the daily newspaper picture in Mexico, but the mountain chain running north and south through the length of the country forms an impossible barrier to east–west overland communication; therefore, the provincial press in the western half of Mexico is extremely vigorous.

Politico-Economic System

Newspapers, especially, bear a close relationship to the politico-economic system in which they exist. It may appear obvious that the most independent newspapers are found in the most democratic countries. Less obvious, however, is the incidence of cooperatively owned papers in socialistic countries, newspaper chains in capitalistic nations, party-owned papers in multiparty systems, powerful religious newspapers in theocratic states, and so on. England was a traditionally private-enterprise economy into which socialism made heavy inroads, even though more than a few vestiges of the class system remain in the country. It is not pure coincidence

---

[2] There are exceptions to this, especially where governments can exert control to subsidize papers or regular circulation. The Soviet Union is a huge country, yet *Pravda* and *Izvestia* are "national" papers, published simultaneously at different plants throughout the nation.

that the most influential "popular" newspaper, the *Daily Mirror,* is a Labor daily, while the unofficial voice of the Tories is the "quality" daily, the *Times* of London. Communist countries can be expected to have state-owned newspapers with strong central direction.[3] In the "guided democracies" of the emerging African nations, the newspapers are also frequently "guided"—directly, if they are owned by government, and by more subtle means if they are owned by private corporations.

The number of variables lying within these three major factors alone (and certainly there are other many factors, such as culture and tradition) weave different print media patterns in every country. Taking only one country, the United States, as an example, we can understand how they offer important insights into media characteristics.[4]

The United States

Population

Size:	247 million
Urbanization:	80 percent
Languages:	English
Education:	Literacy, 99 percent (but see the discussion earlier in this chapter on probable error of this figure)
Affluence:	Per capita income, about $13,500

Geography

Size:	3.6 million square miles
Physical Barriers:	None of significance; overland communication excellent: Alaska and Hawaii not contiguous to mainland
Major Cities:	Scattered throughout country, with largest population centers in eastern U.S. and along West Coast
Neighbors:	Canada (English, French); Mexico (Spanish)

Politico-Economic

Political System:	Representative democracy with traditional two-party government
Economic System:	Free enterprise, with private ownership dominating

---

[3] In this, as in many other aspects of communist affairs, Yugoslavia is somewhat of an anomaly. Newspapers there are cooperative enterprises, more dependent on advertising and less responsible to central government than dailies in other Eastern-bloc nations.

[4] From *The World Almanac and Book of Facts* (New York: Newspaper Enterprise Association, 1988).

MAGAZINES

With the exception of China, the United States has the largest population in the world literate in a single language. This literacy, along with the affluence and educational level of the population, has provided an optimum audience for specialized publications. Advertiser interest in pinpointing their potential customers, the ability of the average American to buy an assortment of publications, and differences in reader tastes due to varying educational experiences and leisure-time pursuits have caused a sharp trend toward specialized publications.

At the beginning of the 1970s there were only two mass-mass magazines (*Life* and *Look*) remaining in the United States. Both had their highest circulations in history, largely due to vigorous subscription campaigns. But both were in deep trouble because of their inability to be all things to all people. Advertisers, realizing this limitation, were beginning to abandon ship, and the two magazines were producing a thinner product, since advertising accounts for about two-thirds of a mass magazine's income. *Look* ceased publication in 1971. *Life* could not change its content and image and appeal to a specialized rather than a general audience. It ceased publication at the end of 1972. After lying dormant for more than six years, the magazines were reborn as "specialized" publications in the late 1970s.

The two magazines with the highest circulations in the United States (*TV Guide* and *Reader's Digest*) were already specialized. *TV Guide* is an example of unit specialization, the entire publication appealing to an audience with a common interest, while *Reader's Digest* represents internal specialization, a publication offering a wide variety of articles from which a heterogeneous audience can select items of particular interest. Mass-mass magazines, of general interest, are likely to be found in a country of small population, or where the population has a common educational background, or where the average family can buy only a few publications. By the 1970s not one of these factors existed in the United States, and so the age of the mass-mass magazine came to an end.

BOOKS

Because of the same elements of population size, education, and affluence, the United States produces more than 30,000 book titles each year. The vast literate population provides sizable audiences for a wide array of specialized books. The sharpest increase in unit sales during recent years has been posted by university textbooks, reflecting the fact that more than 50 percent of all high school graduates enter colleges and universities.

University students are also large consumers of trade paperbacks (paper-bound editions of general market books that are traditionally hardbound and jacketed), frequently assigned in university courses as supplements to textbooks or (in increasing numbers) instead of textbooks. The compara-tively low price of pocket paperbacks has made them in many cases competitive with magazines, whose copy price has been on the rise.

Other nations, both English-speaking and non-English-speaking, have become borrowers of America's specialized book production. For exam-ple, a small or medium-sized nation cannot afford to print textbooks for advanced university courses that enroll fewer than several hundred students a year. This is particularly true of textbooks in science, technol-ogy, medicine, and management, which quickly become dated. Such countries must borrow textbooks from a larger country, usually the United States. Students in those countries therefore must have a fluency in En-glish. As a result of this acquired fluency (for educational purposes), they become potential consumers of other English-language trade (general-interest) books. Export sales of American books totaled more than $200 million in 1989.

NEWSPAPERS

The impressive statistics regarding the newspaper industry in the United States deserve the attention of any student of communications. We will approach those statistics from the back door, going first to the important data about America itself to see if the data explain *why* the newspaper industry exists in its present form.

Population Size

This is the most troubling factor affecting the present condition of the newspaper industry. In 1909 the United States had only about 90 million people but approximately 2,600 daily papers compared with about 1,650 today. The number has dropped by 100 in just the last fifteen years, as afternoon newspapers folded throughout the nation. Between 1970 and 1987, total daily circulation grew less than one percent while there was a 34.4 percent growth in the U.S. adult population and a 41.4 percent growth in the number of households. These figures indicate a growing preference for electronic sources of information daily and an interest in softer, more lasting news from newspapers (Sunday newspaper circulation grew 22.4 percent between 1970 and 1987). As more people enter the literacy pool, newspaper circulations should increase apace. The leveling of daily circu-lations even while the population continues to rise gives some indication of inroads other media have made in the average citizen's media consumption time.

Urbanization

Part of the urbanization pattern in the United States is "suburbanization," middle-class urbanites moving to their own homes in the suburbs. This shift accounts for the growth in weekly community papers. The proximity of suburbanites to large cities also accounts for the desire of metropolitan dailies (and their retail advertisers) to appeal to this audience in preference to the generally less affluent city dwellers.

Languages

About 8 million adult Americans speak Spanish in their homes, according to the 1980 Census. Although the Spanish-language press has grown because of recent immigration from Mexico, Puerto Rico, and Cuba, it is insignificant when compared with total newspaper circulation. Any foreign-language press has been temporal in the United States because of the domination of the English language and culture. For the same reason, the non-English-language periodical press of other countries makes virtually no inroads in domestic circulation; the general American reader is unfamiliar with any language other than English. A striking exception in the United States is the greater Miami area, where about half of the population of more than a million grew up speaking Spanish. The *Miami Herald* distributes the Spanish language *El Nuevo Herald,* along with the English-language newspaper, to any reader who requests it; in 1989, 100,000 readers were doing so on a daily basis. It remains to be seen whether *El Nuevo Herald* will go the way of the once-strong German and Yiddish press in the United States or will maintain circulation strength because of an undiluted ethnic, cultural, and language base in the Miami area.

Education

The relatively advanced education of the average American accounts for a weak tabloid press and the absence of sensationalism in American daily, weekly, and Sunday newspapers. There is no equivalent to *Bild Zeitung,* a sensational daily in West Germany, or *The People,* a sensational Sunday paper in England, both of which have massive circulations. In the 1920s the United States saw a brief outburst of tabloid sex and scandal. Although some critics of American culture refuse to recognize the fact, average Americans are now more educated and more sophisticated than their

European cousins. They are therefore a poor audience for sensational copy.

Affluence

Although Americans have a larger average disposable income (income remaining after the purchase of necessities) than the citizens of any other country in the world, they buy fewer newspapers per capita than the Swiss, English, Danes, Swedes, or Japanese. Indirectly, this is partly a result of American affluence. Americans have the money to spend and the means of getting to large department, grocery, and specialty stores in the central city and shopping centers. The stores must reach them by retail advertising in newspapers, and such advertising provides the largest part of an average paper's income. But retail advertisers are reluctant to buy space in competing papers with overlapping circulation. They prefer the newspaper with the largest circulation, thus speeding up the process of natural selection among papers. The average American therefore buys fewer newspapers because he or she has fewer from which to choose. (Only about 20 U.S. cities now have head-on competition between two independent newspapers.)

This discussion far oversimplifies the reason for newspaper monopolies in America; geography, economics, and politics also play a role in this phenomenon, as we will see shortly. But it does suggest that at a certain level of newspaper development within a nation affluence becomes a negative rather than a positive factor.

Geographical Size

For many years, the sheer size of the country precluded the development of a "national" newspaper in America. The *Wall Street Journal,* originally published in different locations with the aid of telephone transmission, was once the nearest thing to a national newspaper, but it was and is a specialized publication appealing to a select audience. The *National Observer,* produced by the same parent company, tried to become a national weekly, but from the point of view of content it bore more similarity to a newsmagazine than to a daily newspaper. The death of the *National Observer* in 1977 was probably less a result of the geographical size of the United States than of the inability of the publication to define its image clearly, either as a newspaper, a newsmagazine, or a specialized feature periodical. In 1983 *USA TODAY* utilized satellite transmission to publish duplicate editions at multiple sites, thus overcoming geographical barriers to give America its first truly national newspaper.[5] The *New York Times* achieves the same daily feat via satellite, but on a smaller scale.

With these exceptions, the geographical size of the United States explains why morning papers represent only 31 percent of the total number of daily papers yet account for 62 percent of the daily circulation. Metropolitan morning newspapers are able to travel between midnight and dawn to surrounding areas and arrive at the breakfast table with news as fresh as that in a local product. Metropolitan afternoon papers are unable to offer the same service to regional customers; their deadlines must be earlier or their deliveries later than those of their local competitors. Thus, if a small town near a major city had only one newspaper, it was likely to be an afternoon newspaper; it could not compete on even terms with a nearby morning daily. As the United States neared the twenty-first century, however, there was an interesting trend toward conversion of afternoon newspapers in one-newspaper cities to morning publication. This phenomenon was caused by two factors: (1) the ability of small-city newspapers to compete with big-city morning papers for circulation by offering local citizens more relevant local news and advertising content, and (2) a growing dependence by the public on early evening television news for the day's breaking information, thus making the daily newspaper an all-day paper that, though published in the morning, can be read at any time of day. As the newspaper has become an all-day paper, it has moved from a hard news to a soft news publication, including many feature stories and special-interest stories not tied closely to a time peg.

Physical Barriers

Since overland communication is excellent throughout the United States, this is not a factor affecting the nature of American papers.

Major Cities

The fairly even distribution of large cities throughout the United States has caused the evolution of regional newspapers, metropolitan dailies (usually morning papers) that aim editions at surrounding areas. Such editions emphasize stories of statewide and regional interest. In a sense, these perform the function of a national newspaper for more limited regional

---

[5] For an interesting narrative on the planning and development of this innovative newspaper, read *The Making of McPaper: The Inside Story of USA TODAY,* by Peter Prichard (Kansas City: Andrews, McMeel, and Parker, 1987).

areas. Small-town and community dailies and weeklies are satellites within the gravitational field of these papers.

Neighboring Countries

To a minor extent, Americans of Mexican descent are borrowers of Spanish-language newspapers published in the larger border cities of Mexico. This situation does not exist on the Canadian border, since there are no French-speaking communities of significant size on the American side. Canadians, for their part, have long been concerned about "cultural imperialism" because of the proximity of U.S. media, and they spend considerable amounts of government funds to encourage indigenous Canadian programming on television to counter this effect.

Politico-Economic System

A two-party system in a country as large in area and population as the United States implies that within each party there are heterogeneous groups with conflicting regional and ideological interests. This is especially true when there are negligible differences in the philosophies of the two parties, especially concerning the economic structure of the country. American newspapers reflect this politico-economic situation in the following ways:

1. Newspapers are generally uncommitted to a specific political party; because of their private enterprise nature, however, they tend toward conservatism in political and economic outlook.
2. Reflecting the all-inclusiveness of political parties, newspapers generally admit competing ideas and opinions into their syndicated columns and letters sections in order to attract a wide spectrum of readers, a practice that also reduces the demand for competing papers.
3. Believing in minimal restrictions to business competition, the private enterprise system is receptive to chains, conglomerates, and limited monopolies; newspaper groups control about 82 percent of daily circulation, while only 20 cities have two or more dailies that are completely independent of each other.

This survey should demonstrate that the nature of a country's population, geography, and politico-economic system goes a long way toward explaining the characteristics of its press. Although all three factors exert nearly equal influence on the structure of the press in the United States, this may not be so in the case of other countries. In the Soviet Union, for example, central authority is powerful enough to emphasize the politico-economic factor, diminishing the influence of geography and population. In some developing countries, the factors of geography and population might overshadow the influence of the politico-economic system.

AFTERTHOUGHTS

1. Examine the coverage of television in your local newspaper. In your opinion, would this coverage lead to higher or lower circulation of *TV Guide* magazine in your community? If you were designing this coverage, given the limited space in the newspaper, what changes would you suggest?

2. If you were the publisher or editor of the daily newspaper in your city, what changes would you make in design or content to increase circulation? Invite the local editor or publisher into one of your class periods to discuss these suggestions.

3. The authors state that average Americans are a "poor audience" for sensational copy. Does the popularity of such media fare as the *National Inquirer* contradict this statement? What other magazines, television programs, newspapers, or motion picture genres would you also call "sensational"?

4. There may be many reasons why Sunday newspaper circulation is rising at a much higher rate than daily newspaper circulation. Try to determine all the possible explanations.

5. Do "national" newspapers pose a threat to local dailies, in the long run? What effect are they likely to have on the content and focus of local dailies?

CHAPTER 5

Electronic Revolution and Counterrevolution

The electronic revolution will be perhaps the defining characteristic of the twenty-first century. Radio, unheard of in the nineteenth century, roared upon the scene in the twentieth to give the world true *message saturation* —the ability to distribute a single message to a total mass audience. Because of limitations on production, distribution, affluence, and literacy, the print media even today can achieve only a low degree of message saturation.

In the electronic revolution, a relatively short time elapsed between the invention of radio and television and their attainment of a high degree of message saturation. The electronic media did not have to reproduce a separate message for each member of the audience (everyone could "read" the same electronic "newspaper"), and distribution was a minor problem since transmission was dependent largely on the air. The nature of the audience was also different than previously. At the beginning of the electronic revolution, only part of the audience was affluent enough to avail themselves quickly of the sets necessary for receiving the message. With the development of the transistor radio, the nonaffluent could receive the message also. Radio, then, is within the reach of all; television is on the threshold of being so. And literacy, for its part, has never been essential for access to the electronic media.

The electronic media's ability to leapfrog across regions and con-tinents, and especially across the barriers of illiteracy and poverty, has made them a much more important political weapon than print. In the words of Gamal Abdel Nasser, the late president of the United Arab Republic:[1]

> It is true most of our people are still illiterate. But politically that counts for far less than it did 20 years ago.
>
> Literacy and intelligence are not the same thing. Radio has changed everything. Once the villages had no knowledge of what was happening in the capital. Government was run by small coteries of people who did not need to take account of the reactions of the people, who never saw a newspaper or could not read if they did.
>
> Today people in the most remote villages hear of what is happening everywhere and form their opinions. Leaders cannot govern as they once did. We live in a new world.

The electronic revolution is not without its ironies and dichotomies. On the one hand it has the power to teach; radio and television can penetrate a whole society and reach the young even in their first moments of awareness. On the other hand, the electronic media may perpetuate illiteracy by making it possible to receive meaningful communications without knowing how to read. Communication is the highest order of priority in an underdeveloped country. By permitting communication without literacy, the electronic media may help deprive a population of the skills necessary for attaining a higher level of development.

And though the electronic media have great potential as multipliers of democracy, at the same time they exist as powerful instruments for authoritarian control. Modern revolutionaries understand that if they would overthrow a government they must first control the radio and television stations. In some countries, stations and their transmitters are guarded like Fort Knox.

In dealing with the issues raised by electronic media, one must first keep in mind two broad propositions that deeply affect them: (1) radio and television are highly susceptible to government control; and (2) radio and television are basically entertainment media.

THE REGULATED MEDIUM

Outside the Western Hemisphere, radio and television were usually established as government-owned or public-owned instruments. In some cases, government attempted to ensure the independence of the two media by

---

[1] Quoted in Daniel Lerner, "Communication Systems and Social Systems: A Statistical Exploration in History and Policy." *Behavioral Science*, October 1957, p. 274.

setting up separate corporations to administer them. In other cases, government control was absolute and the media functioned directly as an arm of the government.

In the Western Hemisphere, with the exception of Canada,[2] radio and television stations were primarily privately owned. However, this did not mean that they were free of government control. For one thing, to prevent chaos, frequencies and channels had to be assigned by the government. In the United States the Radio Act of 1927 provided a system for allocation of frequencies, including a provision that stations must serve the "public interest, convenience, and necessity." This licensing process initially led to the "franchise" concept of electronic media, which implies that the station owner virtually has a permanent lease on a frequency in the absence of *negative* conduct. This concept has evolved over the years until owners of the electronic media in the United States are now recognized as "fiduciaries."[3] Under this concept, station owners hold only temporary title to their frequencies; in order to renew their licenses, they must show that they have acted *positively* in the public interest.

Two cases in 1969 confirmed that the courts in the United States now support the fiduciary principle. In one case involving a Jackson, Mississippi, television station, Warren Burger—later to become chief justice of the U.S. Supreme Court—ruled:

> The infinite potential of broadcasting to influence American life renders somewhat irrelevant the semantics of whether broadcasting is or is not to be described as a public utility. By whatever name or classification, broadcasters are temporary permittees—fiduciaries—of a great public resource, and they must meet the highest standards which are embraced in the public interest concept.

In the second case—one involving a Red Lion, Pennsylvania, radio station—Justice Byron White wrote for a Supreme Court majority:

> As far as the First Amendment is concerned, those who are licensed stand no better than those to whom licenses are refused . . . there is nothing in the First Amendment which prevents the government from requiring a licensee to share his frequency with others and to conduct himself as a proxy or fiduciary with obligations to present those views and voices which are representative of his community and which would otherwise, by necessity, be barred from the airwaves.

---

[2] Privately owned radio and television stations exist side by side with the publicly owned Canadian Broadcasting Corporation's radio and TV networks.

[3] In legal terminology, a "fiduciary" is a person to whom property is entrusted to hold, control, or manage for another—in this case, the public.

It is the purpose of the First Amendment to preserve an uninhibited marketplace of ideas, in which truth will ultimately prevail, rather than to countenance monopolization of that market, whether it be by the government itself or by a private licensee. It is the right of the public to receive suitable access to social, political, esthetic, moral, and other ideas and experiences. . . .

Electronic media, then, even when operating under private ownership, are more bridled than print media because of government regulation to prevent "negative" conduct and government surveillance to assure "positive" conduct.

During the Reagan administration, the Federal Communications Commission (FCC) moved to deregulate radio and television as much as possible. We will look at some of the ramifications of this trend. Although the theory of regulation of these media remained in effect, there was less monitoring of the performance of radio and television stations and a strong move to extend to the electronic media the same First Amendment freedoms already enjoyed by the print media.

ENTERTAINMENT AND NEWS COMPETE

Because of their special appeal to the eye and the ear, television and radio are primarily entertainment media. "All-news" radio stations and television networks exist, of course, but taken as a whole, the overwhelming proportion of broadcast programming is given over to entertainment, not information. Radio Cairo is the most influential station in the Arab world, not simply because Egypt is the largest country or has the most to say; its influence rests on its ability to present the top entertainment stars in the Arab Middle East. But Egyptian *information* broadcasts directed to neighboring countries thereby gain a captive audience.

In democratic countries the entertainment function is so dominant that it tends to smother the information and education potential of the medium. This dominant role of entertainment is not opposed by the average viewer or listener—or even by those who are above average. A national survey reported in *The People Look at Television,* by Gary A. Steiner,[4] showed that the more highly educated, higher-income viewer turns to television primarily for relaxation and entertainment. The survey

---

[4] Although Steiner's study was conducted in 1960, it remains the most comprehensive survey ever made of the U.S. television audience. Steiner's findings were supported by a follow-up survey conducted by Robert T. Bower a decade later. See Robert T. Bower, *Television and the Public* (New York: Holt, Rinehart & Winston, 1973).

also showed that although these above-average Americans *said* that television should offer more education and information, they did not take advantage of such programs when they were offered.

This desire by most segments of the audience for entertainment, almost to the exclusion of all but the daily news programs, is reflected in the total content of television. It is also at the heart of many of the problems faced by television news executives trying to obtain the proper time and format for news and documentary programs. In the words of the late Edward R. Murrow:

> One of the basic troubles with radio and television news is that both instruments have grown up as an incompatible combination of show business, advertising, and news. Each of the three is a rather bizarre and demanding profession. And when you get all three under one roof, the dust never settles.

In the case of newspapers, entertainment is a guest in what is essentially a news medium. In the case of the electronic media, news is a guest in what are essentially entertainment media. This fact of life has implications not only for the style and content of news programs, but also for the *attitude* with which audiences approach such programs. For example, the news on television may be preceded by a syndicated rerun and followed by a situation comedy. The news items themselves, often of the most serious nature, are interspersed with commercials of the most trivial nature.

Broadcasters have indeed pointed out that there are also trivial advertisements in the most serious newspapers. But obviously the audience option to avoid such ads is quite different in each medium.

Keeping in mind these important influences—government control and the entertainment emphasis—we can now turn to a brief examination of the basic characteristics of the television medium and their effects on the aspects of the communication process explored in Chapter 1: the *communicator,* the *message,* the *channel,* and the *audience.*

THE IDENTITY OF TELEVISION

As a medium of mass communication in the United States, television itself (outside of the impact of VCRs on television viewing) has the following basic characteristics:

1. *It has an audiovisual medium.* It appeals to the eye and ear. It is therefore able to present not only words, but noises and music and inflections of voice. It is able to present not only pictures, but

motion pictures, including nuances of body movement and facial expression (kinesics).

2. *It is a time-locked medium.* It exists in time, rather than in space. For example, a commercial exists for one minute, with the slow reader/viewer being given no more time to absorb it than the fast reader/viewer. Because a television program exists in time, viewers have no opportunity to select out specific portions or review the material seen. If two similar programs are telecast at the same time, they cannot compare them, unless they use a videocassette recorder.

3. *It has a limited number of channels.* Part of this problem is due to the development of very-high-frequency (VHF) before ultrahigh-frequency (UHF) broadcasting. Licensing of more UHF stations and expansion of cable television are increasing the number of channels available to the average American.

4. *It is a highly complex and expensive medium to operate.* Cameras, videotape, transmission equipment, and other paraphernalia require numerous specialists in addition to the reporter or host. The costs associated with operating the medium are accordingly high. The extensive credits at the end of most television programs give some indication of the tremendous costs in personnel alone.

5. *It depends on advertising as the single major source of income.* This factor may be only a temporary one in the United States, but it is a factor that has existed since the establishment of television and it still prevails. Public broadcasting and pay television have not yet made major inroads into the American tradition of commercial broadcasting.

Television as a news medium in the United States has evolved to its present state because of the these characteristics, and as these characteristics change, television news will evolve even further. The following pages, however, attempt to show how the various communication processes of television have been affected by characteristics as they currently exist.

THE STAR SYSTEM

As television became more of a mass-mass medium, attracting huge audiences for its news programs as well as for its entertainment programs, it began to attract quality newspersons. They came from other media and also directly out of school. Because television is an audiovisual medium, those who appeared on the air had to have certain qualities of voice and looks. Because television is supported by advertising, and advertisers are interested in ratings, television networks and stations encouraged the "star system"—featured personalities who attract a regular audience.

In network television there are implications of the star system that bear more examination than they have so far received. First, in order to become a star, one must receive exposure. In order for correspondents to get exposure, their stories must be selected for use on a news program. Since competition for the limited amount of time on a news program is usually severe, correspondents are sometimes tempted to help their own cause by emphasizing the sensational aspects of a story.

Or consider network anchors. Their voices and faces are more a part of the average American's life than are the voice and face of the President of the United States. And while Presidents come and go every four or eight years, television anchors stay on, speaking to their public night after night, year after year. Belief in a favorite anchor may exceed a viewer's belief in any other personality or institution in the United States. Walter Cronkite retired from his anchor spot on CBS News in 1981. Five years later a Times Mirror Co. poll found him still to be the "most believable" personality in the United States, with a score of 92 percent on a 100 percent scale. At the same time, President Reagan scored 68 percent, below Peter Jennings, David Brinkley, Dan Rather, Ted Koppel, Tom Brokaw, and Sam Donaldson.

The necessity to utilize a handful of proven stars rather than a much broader corps of specialized reporters and commentators has also served to blur the distinction between news and commentary. On one night a television newsperson may be doing a straight reporting job; on the next he or she may be called upon to analyze a political situation. Sometimes there is confusion in viewers' minds about whether they are hearing news or analysis. Because television reporters are stars, highly paid and usually highly qualified on the basis of experience, there is the danger that they will tend to think of themselves as omniscient, there to make assessments rather than to report the news.

THE IMPORTANCE OF "FOOTAGE"

Messages on television are often quite different from messages in newspapers. In television news the emphasis usually is upon what can be pictured. As one American broadcast executive described it, television is more likely to emphasize the "goings and comings" of diplomats than the issues that they are discussing. At the very least, good "footage" of a trivial nature will probably receive inordinately more air time than important news for which footage is unavailable. A veteran BBC public affairs reporter and program producer, Robin Day, has pointed out that this emphasis on pictures has caused television news to adopt the "tabloid vices of sensationalism and superficiality." He added:

> . . . the fact is that television's dependence on pictures (and the most vivid pictures) makes it not only a *powerful* means of communication, but a *crude* one which tends to strike at the emotions rather than at the intellect. For TV journalism this means a dangerous and increasing concentration on action (usually violent and bloody) rather than thought, on happenings rather than issues, on shock rather than explanation, on personalities rather than ideas.

The visual nature of the medium has also forced television away from the "inverted pyramid" style of news presentation used by newspapers for a hundred years and, with modifications, by radio for more than half a century. Moving pictures do not lend themselves to a style of identifying the most important facts first; rather, they accommodate a chronological order of narration traditionally associated with the feature story. Stylistically, then, the anchor on a news program is the straight news reporter; the correspondent in the field is the feature writer. Sometimes a "news" story will have both elements, the anchor introducing the story in a straight news fashion and then switching to the correspondent in the field for feature commentary.

Television has also added "feature" devices to the store of news presentation. Two devices used are the "speculative indefinite" (What he would do if the union rejects the agreement, he did not say . . .) and the "editorial fade" (Death lurks in the coal mines near this mountain community, but the state has a history of ignoring the danger until it is too late. . .).

The fact that television is a time-locked medium also means that many important stories of the day will never be presented on network news and other important stories will be reduced to a few lines. A half-hour newscast, since it exists in time, cannot be stretched. The total amount of news delivered over a network news program on an average night would, if set in type, hardly fill the front page of a daily newspaper. Such limits, of course, are manufactured; a nightly network news program could be an hour or even two hours long. But the "need" or possible interest of the audience is, in any case, secondary to the network's inability to preempt this time from local stations, which can derive greater advertising revenue from local news or syndicated programs.

The complexities and attendant high cost of the medium further reduce the range of stories available to television. It is expensive (and sometimes physically impractical) for camera crews to accompany reporters on all assignments. Further, authoritarian regimes can restrict the movement of equipment and censor tape more easly than they can restrict the movement of individual reporters or censor their notes when they are departing the country. This does not mean that information thus missed by the television crew does not get on the air. But its chances of receiving air time commensurate with its importance are reduced. It also means that television is likely to give far more attention to the problems of democracies than it is to the problems of authoritarian states, resulting in a comparative "public relations" advantage to the authoritarian regimes.

The Reluctance to Editorialize

Because of the limited number of frequencies in the early days of radio, Section 315 of the Communications Act of 1934 included the "equal time" doctrine: if free time is available to one political candidate during a campaign, equal time must be made available to all other candidates for that office. (In 1959, Section 315 was amended to exclude from the "equal time" provision certain types of news programs on which candidates might appear.)

In 1941 the Federal Communications Commission ruled that broadcast editorializing was illegal. The FCC reversed itself in 1949 and again permitted editorializing, with the proviso that stations also "provide the listening public with a fair and balanced presentation of differing viewpoints. . . ." The "fairness doctrine" was thus established. It was later extended to force broadcasters to give a reasonable amount of rebuttal time to opponents of any controversial ideas aired on radio or television.

Thus the limited number of frequencies and channels during the formative period of radio and television had the effect of virtually eliminating overt, meaningful editorial messages from the two media. Most stations were reluctant to offer the air time and personnel time necessary to bring in sometimes not one but many opposing opinions to a strong editorial stand. In effect, many stations did not editorialize at all; others that did editorialize did not take the forceful stands that one would see in the daily newspaper editorial page. To avoid the fairness doctrine, both radio and television news resorted to "commentators," who made editorial judgments as individuals rather than as spokespersons for the station. This substitute for station editorializing apparently brought few demands for rebuttal within the spirit of the FCC's 1949 ruling.

The FCC eliminated the fairness doctrine in 1987 as part of its general deregulation effort. The Commission said that doctrine no longer served the public interest and was unconstitutional on the basis of the First Amendment.[5] However, "equal time" (which still exists) and the fairness

---

[5] In 1989 a federal court upheld the FCC's right to repeal the fairness doctrine. The court did not rule, however, on the constitutionality of the doctrine.

doctrine had already served to subdue most overt editorializing in the broadcasting industry, and there was no rush to take advantage of the new ruling. Few stations editorialize; many are reluctant to grapple with controversial subjects unless they can accord clinically even "balance" to all sides. Government regulation, rationalized on the grounds of limited channels, thus largely removed from the electronic media one of the basic functions of the press: criticism clearly labeled as the management's editorial stand. Although there is little direct station editorializing, television newspersons editorialize in more subtle ways, often unwittingly. Because of the audiovisual nature of television, the personality of the anchor or correspondent is bound to color the message; the newscaster appears physically between the message and the viewer. The anchor typically bridges two news items with an editorial comment ("Meanwhile, in another action fraught with danger, the prime minister . . ."), and correspondents end their reports from the field with an editorial conclusion ("State police escorted the candidate to his car and away from the violence that has been the signature of his campaign . . .").

Television news reports are themselves frequently highly interpretative, often without being identified as analysis. The result has been to confuse fact and opinion, in contrast to the newspaper tradition of clearly separating the two.

ARE CHANNELS STILL LIMITED?

The electronic media encounter special government regulation because of the limited number of frequencies and channels, but many broadcasters have argued that these regulations should be relaxed and electronic media given the same First Amendment rights as the print media. They point out that they can hardly be called a monopoly when there are more television and radio stations in most cities than there are newspapers; in fact, there are seven times more radio and TV stations than daily newspapers in the nation. The courts have held that numbers in the electronic media, especially in the case of television, are deceptive. Because of the expense of programming, most stations must affiliate with one of the major networks and carry network programs for almost all of the television day. In practice, then, a monopoly exists and entry is restricted, since those stations that were able to obtain a network affiliation in the early years of televison traditionally occupied a preferred position. Each year this monopoly is being significantly diminished, however, by independent stations and cable. By 1989 the three major networks' share of the television audience had dropped to 66 percent, a decrease of four percentage points from just the year before.

As a result of the nature of broadcast transmission, local stations occupy a position quite different from that of independent newspapers. Dailies are able to exercise a gatekeeping function vis-à-vis wire service and syndicate copy, which they can "pick up" (print) or not, in whole or in part. Local television stations, however, are unable to edit any part of the regular network news programs. They are simply "paperboys" in the transmission of such programs. And since the news programs frequently carry interpretative material closely akin to editorial opinion, the local stations are in the ambiguous position of transmitting opinions for which they are legally, but not editorially, responsible.

It is ironic that newspapers in the United States have a dual tradition of political advocacy and objectivity while television stations are apolitical but less objective. Part of this contrasting situation is due to the nature of the medium and government regulation. But one is left with the impression that network news has a lower degree of objectivity than newspapers for two other reasons: television correspondents are given more leeway to interpret the news than are newspaper reporters, and television does a poorer job of separating and identifying news and opinion.

AUDIENCE AMBIVALENCE

The audiovisual nature of television news, and possibly even the fact that it is tightly compressed and therefore more easily absorbed, make the daily network programs a favorite with the mass audience. A majority of Americans now consider television their primary source of news. The majority also find it the most credible source of news. This is probably so because of their belief in the integrity of familiar and favorite anchors, because of their feeling that television is editorially neutral, and because of their conviction that "seeing is believing."

At the same time, there are sizable numbers of viewers who are disgruntled about the presentation of network television news. Broadcasters credit this reaction to the desire to "kill the messenger that bears bad news." Undoubtedly this is part of the explanation, but not all of it. The point is that television has a vast, heterogeneous audience and only a tiny selection of networks. Consider this contrast: The early evening news programs of the three major television networks reach about 40 million Americans daily; 1,650 daily newspapers reach a little more than 62 million subscribers each day. It is true that the average subscriber has even less choice of newspapers in his or her hometown than networks. However, the newspaper probably comes closer to appealing to readers' political and sectional prejudices than does network news. And whereas readers can avoid the "bad news" in the newspaper and ignore its editorial opinions, they can do neither of these with television; they must take all the news, the good and the bad, the straight and the interpretative. Given such conditions and such a varied audience, large numbers are bound to react adversely to news that, in their own minds, is presented unfairly.

Network correspondents undoubtedly are able to insert more editorial comment into their stories than their print colleagues, for reasons we have touched on. For one, their comments cannot be edited out of the footage without the entire story being destroyed, and their "editors," in any case, are frequently on a lower rung of the pecking order than the TV "stars" themselves and probably have less authority to edit for content. Furthermore, their comments appear in an audiovisual form and lack the permanence of print. The viewer is sometimes uneasy about what he or she has heard, but is never quite sure. Television reports are so ephemeral that viewers frequently call up and complain about comments that have never been made, or they call the wrong network.

Basically, however, the structure of television news itself is the chief culprit. The chronological narrative style is a storytelling format: There is a beginning, a middle, and an end. If a story has an "end," that end is a means for tying the entire report together with a little blue ribbon. It will be either a punch line, an exit line, or a succinct summarization with a purported insight.

When all the nations of the world met in Geneva early in 1989 to consider a ban on the manufacture of chemical weapons, a CBS television correspondent ended his report with this comment: "None of the nations that pushed for this conference is arriving with totally clean hands." Whether true or false, that is commentary, and it would find no place in a straight news article in a newspaper.

It is the authors' observation that at least one out of every three news stories on network television concludes with an editorial comment, a result of the qualities of the medium itself that make television news presentation quite different from that of its newspaper cousins.

AFTERTHOUGHTS

1. Now that the "fairness doctrine" has been eliminated, why have television stations generally not moved to editorialize in a vigorous manner?
2. If, as the authors believe, television news is less objective than newspaper stories on the same subject, why do newspapers usually receive more adverse feedback than television stations and networks?
3. Compare and analyze a story on the same subject reported by a newspaper and by a television station or network.

4. Watch local and network news for one night or one week, and analyze the closing statements of the correspondents for (subtle or unacknowledged) editorial opinion.

5. At a time when radio frequencies are so numerous, and so many television channels are available to the viewer, does the "fiduciary" concept of radio and television ownership have any real justification?

CHAPTER 6

Advertising:
Benefactor or Intruder?

In Western societies, our lives are surrounded by advertising: billboards, point-of-sales posters, packages, even labels on the outside of blouses, pants, and shoes. Advertising becomes most controversial, however, in its relationship to the mass media, because here it is not only selling its own product but in some ways determining the nature of another product: the content of the media we read, hear, and see. The student of mass media has to think about the role of advertising as both a promoter and gatekeeper within the process of communication. The following three quotations provide a good basis for beginning that consideration:

> The function of advertising . . . is to stimulate demand, develop and shape consumer behavior and provide the seller of a product with a measure of certainty as to sales, an assurance that if not available could be financially disastrous. . . . the past tendency to put the advertising industry outside the realm of responsible economic thought and discussion is inexcusable.[1]

> A modern economy requires the generation of a vast amount of information on the identity and location of sellers, on types and changes in product, and on prices and other terms of sale. It is not surprising, therefore—and certainly not to be deplored—that there is a vast amount

---

[1] John Kenneth Galbraith, Harvard University economist, *Advertising Age*, Nov 9, 1988.

of advertising: a practical alternative, not involving economic stagnation, is not immediately evident.[2]

[The] phenomenon of American advertising . . . has been permitted to dominate and exploit the entire process of public communication in our country. It is to me positively inconceivable that the whole great, infinitely responsible function of mass communication, including very important phases of the educational process, should be farmed out—as something to be mined for whatever profit there may be in it—to people whose function and responsibility have nothing to do with the truth— whose function and responsibility, in fact, are concerned with the peddling of what is, by definition, untruth, and the peddling of it in trivial, inane forms that are positively debauching in their effect on the human understanding. After the heedless destruction of natural environment, I regard this—not advertising as such, but the consignment to the advertiser of the entire mass communication process, as a concession to be exploited by it for commercial gain—as probably the greatest evil of our national life. We will not, I think, have a healthy intellectual climate in this country, a successful system of education, a sound press, or a proper vitality of artistic and recreational life, until advertising is rigorously separated from every form of legitimate cultural and intellectual communication.[3]

The first two statements taken together appear to contradict the third statement. Actually they are not contradictory, although the Kennan passage surely exaggerates and oversimplifies advertising's effects. Galbraith and Posner are saying, "Advertising is necessary to the proper functioning of the American economic and social system." Kennan is answering, "Possibly so, but it corrupts the media and therefore should be eliminated from them." Galbraith and Posner would undoubtedly be content to have the media exist without advertising, if such were possible. Kennan would be satisfied to let advertising live if it were separated from the media.

Advertising is a salesperson substitute, and salespersons are necessary in our competitive, free-enterprise society. In an economy of mass production, mass distribution, and mass consumption, we need salespeople substitutes to tell us the benefits of different products, their prices, and where they can be purchased. The problem with advertising vis-à-vis the mass media is this: Should the salesperson's role extend beyond selling the product?

Critics of advertising make an analogy between advertising and ency-

---

[2] Richard A. Posner, Stanford University law professor who served on a presidential task force on productivity and competition, *Advertising Age*, June 23, 1969.

[3] George F. Kennan, former U.S. ambassador to Russia and a presidential adviser, *Democracy and the Student Left* (New York: Bantam Books, 1968), pp. 201–2.

clopedia sales representatives. The encyclopedia sales representatives may offer us a free gift to get into our home, but once in our home, do they have the right to stay as long as they like, interrupt our activities at will, and determine the subject of our conversations?

Like encyclopedia sales representatives, advertising is allowed into our homes because it brings us free gifts—print media, which it subsidizes, and free television. However, we are then bothered to find that advertising dominates space in the print media, takes an inordinate amount of time on the television screen, interrupts the message in most of the media, and, above all, apparently determines the content of popular publications and television.

One may gain a deeper insight into these allegations by attempting to answer the following questions: Does advertising really give the media audience a free gift? Does the media audience want advertising? Does advertising determine the content of the media?

WHO PAYS FOR THE PRODUCT?

Although some media manage to survive without advertising—notably books, recordings, and movies—advertising subsidies provide television programming free and reduce the cost of magazines and newspapers. Just how much cheaper magazines and newspapers are as a result of advertising is not to be found in the balance sheets released by publishing enterprises. For example, income from circulation is slightly less than one-third of daily newspaper revenue, while income from advertising is slightly more than two-thirds. But from 55 to 75 percent of the average daily is devoted to advertising. Readers thus pay only one-third the cost of a newspaper but are also getting only one-third or less of the space.

Many of the expenses incurred by newspapers and magazines are directly attributable to their advertising function: paper, printing costs, business staff, and so on. This is not to say that a newspaper or magazine could do just as well, and sell as inexpensive a product, without advertisements. Some have tried—and failed. But one must remember that part of the "cost" of a publication or program being partially or fully supported by advertising is the cost of running (and procuring) the advertising itself. In addition, one can add the larger mailing costs required by advertising-swelled publications and the additional local fees and taxes required for disposal of the newspapers and magazines (largely composed of advertising) once they become waste paper.

The proliferation of advertisements also costs the reader something in wasted time and annoyance. Because of the ads, and the additional pages to accommodate them, the reader frequently has difficulty finding a story, and related stories may be in scattered pages or even different sections because of the scarcity of news space on a given page.

As for television, viewers must "pay" for free programs by devoting 15 to 20 percent of their viewing time to commercials. If average Americans watch television about thirty hours a week, this means that they spend about five or six hours each week watching commercials. It should be noted that in survey after survey Americans have said that it is worth spending this time viewing commercials in order to receive the return gift of free television.

THE AUDIENCE *LIKES* ADVERTISING

Advertising is a message, albeit a paid message. As a message, it is either news, information, or entertainment, and sometimes all three. Readers' or viewers' desire for an advertising message is therefore related to their need for the product, the information and/or entertainment value of the advertisement itself, and the unobtrusiveness of the presentation.[4]

Readers undoubtedly do have a strong desire for the retail ads in newspapers and for many advertisements in specialized publications. For example, the grocery ad in the daily paper may be more interesting to persons who run households than anything else in the publication: It gives them news of special sale items. A reader of a camera magazine may find the ads as interesting as the articles, because they are directly related to his or her specialized interest. Few print media ads are obtrusive, since the reader can largely control selection.

The media audience probably least desires the commercials that appear on network television. Their entertainment value is usually high, and in that sense they certainly appeal to the viewer, but the viewer has little need for the specific brand being advertised. About 80 percent of the networks' commercial income is derived from what one advertising executive called "economic pipsqueaks": deodorants, cosmetics, beverages (alcoholic and nonalcoholic), soap, toothpaste, hair preparations, patent medicines, breakfast foods, and the like. Above all, television commercials are obtrusive. Viewers can hardly avoid them, though most of the ads may not remotely relate to their individual interests. In that sense, and in the sense that commercials interrupt the message, viewers find them unappealing. The extent to which broadcasters permit—and advertisers demand—insertion of commercials in the middle of entertainment and

---

[4] These factors relate to the reader's *desire,* not particularly to the effectiveness of the advertisement. From the point of view of the advertiser, an obtrusive ad may be more effective than an unobtrusive one.

news programs reflects their estimation of viewer desire for such messages in and of themselves. During a network television re-run of *The Ten Commandments,* starring Charlton Heston, in March 1989, the movie was interrupted nine times between 9:05 P.M. and 10:58 P.M. by the network and by the local Ohio station with 76 different commercials, station breaks, and program promos. Remember, obtrusive may be effective.

From the point of view of the audience, the optimum ad is the one to be found in the classified section of a newspaper. It is categorized so readers can easily find it, yet it may also be easly avoided if they so desire. The entertainment value is low, but the information and news value is high, and the ads readers seek out relate specifically to their own special interests. Compared with classifieds, all other print advertisements and electronic commercials decline on a continuum of desirableness, perhaps hitting rock bottom with the underarm deodorant commercial that interrupts a news program and ends with the husband in the commercial skit coming very close to smelling his wife's armpit.

Advertising can, indeed, reach into the living room and become an unwanted, if not obnoxious, guest. A survey by *Advertising Age* reported in 1988 that the most disliked television commercials were those dealing with women's personal hygiene products. This finding did not indicate that the commercials were bad or even unuseful, but rather that viewers did not want a discussion of these products in their living rooms—presumably in mixed company. On the other hand, at least one major corporation includes advertising in its monthly newspaper mailed to employees and their families because the inclusion of advertising makes the publication look more credible. A publication without advertising seems to the average American either abnormal in appearance or so valueless that it could not attract advertising support.

HOW DOES ADVERTISING INFLUENCE CONTENT?

The late Howard L. Gossage, who was a San Francisco advertising executive, contended that advertising "will tend to shape all the contents of any communications medium that it dominates economically, and in our society that is very nearly the lot." He added that this control is "not by intent, but through the simple ability of advertising to bestow or withhold favors."

The popular notion of advertising influence sees the advertiser as telling a publisher to print or not to print a specific story in the paper; it sees the advertiser as a censor over the material to be included in a program that the advertiser sponsors. This overt interference does occasionally occur, but to a much rarer degree than the average reader or viewer suspects.

The more closely an advertiser's product name is associated with editorial or program material, the more concerned the advertiser is about presenting material that will win friends, not alienate potential customers. This is natural. But when Gossage spoke about advertiser control of "contents," he was referring to the overall character of the publication or programming day, not the specific message.

In the print media, where advertisements are rarely associated with (or blamed for) the editorial content, advertisers are concerned with *audiences,* not *messages.* The advertiser wants to know how many people read the publication and how they rank according to criteria such as age, education, income, and number of children. Indirectly, advertisers control the content of the print media they subsidize, since the publications attempt to attract an audience that will be most satisfactory to current and potential advertisers. For a general magazine, the articles may consciously be aimed at young, high-income urbanites because that is the audience most advertisers want.

For a newspaper, the content may be geared to middle-class citizens, largely urban and suburban, because *this* is what advertisers want. The charge has been made that newspaper content unwittingly ignores the inner-city poor and their problems on a day-to-day basis, because this is an audience that advertisers are little interested in reaching. In the words of former British press lord Cecil King, "The sobering truth remains that the survival of the daily newspapers depends not on their social indispensability, but on their ability to attract advertising." Paradoxically, it is this advertising concern with *audiences* that has played the largest role in the trends toward monopoly of the daily newspaper and proliferation of the specialized magazine.[5]

In the electronic media, especially television, the advertiser is concerned with the audience *and* the message. Unlike the print media, television depends on the individual program to attract an audience. The content of the program is important to the advertiser because that determines what sort of audience will be attracted and whether the audience will have a favorable or unfavorable impression of the product so closely associated with the programming itself. In the early days of television, advertisers carefully selected the programs they would sponsor and in some cases had veto power over content. The expense of commercial time is so great today, however, that few advertisers sponsor an entire program. Rather, they notify the network that they want a certain number of "rating points" (representing the number of people who will be exposed to the commercials) over a certain period of time addressed to specific audience demo-

---

[5] Advertising influence on these two trends is discussed in Chapter 4.

graphics (such as age groups, male or female, or economic and educational levels). They can also specify the kinds of programs that they prefer or want to avoid. NBC, for example, had a difficult time finding sponsors for its 1989 TV movie "Roe v. Wade," which involved the controversy over abortion.

The need for rating points and sponsor satisfaction encourages network television to produce programming that is attractive to the mass-mass audience, and so noncontroversial that the sponsor's product will incur no backlash. Entertainment programming is obviously more likely to fit these two criteria than public affairs programs or hard-hitting documentaries.

Even entertainment programs can incur the wrath of viewers, with the fallout on the sponsor's product. Terry Rakolta, a Michigan mother, started a one-woman campaign in 1989 against what she called the "blatant expoitation of women, sex, and anti-family attitudes" in the popular situation comedy "Married . . . With Children." She wrote hundreds of letters to the advertisers on the program, and several either withdrew their advertising or said they would take a closer look at the individual programs before committing more advertising (the Fox network later asked the producers of the program to tone down the scripts). In the same year, Domino's Pizza, Ralston Purina, and General Mills cancelled advertising on "Saturday Night Live" because of complaints by individuals and by groups such as Christian Leaders for Responsible Television, a coalition that threatens one-year boycotts of sponsors of programs it finds offensive.

Sponsors do not often act in a deliberate manner to censor programming material, as is commonly thought. Rather, their influence is one of "avoidance" where controversial or small-audience programming is concerned. The effect is the same. This "avoidance" factor ensures that such programs will not be shown frequently. The television medium is unsurpassed in its ability to present live coverage and analysis during times of national and international debate and crisis. Yet television networks, except in dramatic emergencies, hesitate to preempt entertainment programs and forfeit their advertising revenues. In the words of one of CBS's pioneer newsmen, Alexander Kendrick, "It is not required for television to be a marketplace of ideas, only a marketplace."

ADVERTISING AS A POLITICAL ANIMAL

A distinct advantage of advertising has always been that it provides a vehicle for the expression of political views that might be downplayed or ignored by the managers of news and editorial opinion. In recent political campaigns, however, political advertising, especially on television, has raised troubling problems.

Negative advertising in a national election raised its ugly head for the first time in 1964, when an advertising agency hired by Lyndon Johnson painted Barry Goldwater the color reckless in a series of television commercials. The most famous, aired only once because of the swell of protests that immediately followed, showed a young girl pulling petals from a daisy in time with the countdown for the launching of a nuclear missile.

With television now entering 98 percent of American homes, political advertisers recognize that with massive amounts of money they can bypass the normal gatekeepers—the print and the electronic press—and select the issues on the basis of which voters will make their decisions. This selection is made in 30-second and 10-second commercials, fed in repetitive fashion in key regions or districts through spot purchases. In 1988, Republicans used this method with devastating effect. The presidential campaign never seemed to rise above the issues of the Pledge of Allegiance and prison furloughs. Dr. Kathleen Hall Jamieson, widely known in the field of political advertising, said in 1988 that advertising had now begun to damage the ability of the American electorate "to get information that it requires to become informed and to make intelligent voting decisions." She said she was particularly concerned about "the deflective power of advertising—the ability of advertising to take important issues off the national stage and put trivial issues in their place, and the ability of advertising to invite false inferences."

There may be no workable answer to this problem, other than to hope that *all* opponents will henceforth use so much negative advertising that there will be a neutral effect. This assumes, however, that all candidates have an equal amount of money to spend on television commercials— which, of course, is rarely the case.

Another answer might be to copy the model of some European countries, which bar all political advertising on television but make an equal amount of time available for each political party or candidate. This time may be used only within a specific time period—no earlier, say, than six weeks before the election; it may be used only by the candidate in person or by a party leader (no film stars, no fancy animation or graphics); and it may be used only in specific blocks of time, none shorter than three minutes.

WHO'S RESPONSIBLE?

In many ways, the difficulties in extracting advertising's advantages while barring its disadvantages derive from the advertising industry's similarity to the press. The press is relatively unregulated by government and has only minimal self-regulation, since it is not a profession and consists of thousands of independent units. But there is an important difference between advertising and the press: a newspaper or television station is a medium and bears responsibility for the content of its total product (e.g., the whole newspaper or the whole magazine). Advertising is not a medium; it is a message. As such, it is responsible only for the content of the advertising message and not for the magazine or programming day in which the advertising message appears. It is therefore far more concerned with an advertisement's effect on the audience than with its effect on the medium.

To repeat this in a slightly different way, advertisers are neither responsible nor irresponsible where overall content of the publication is concerned. They are "a-responsible"; that is, they take no responsibility at all. They are responsible for *their* message, not the message of the publication. In television, advertisers involve themselves, to some extent, with the message of the program they sponsor because they are closely associated with this program in the viewer's mind. However, it is significant that even here advertisers are primarily concerned with the effect of the program's message on their product, not with the effect of their commercial message on the program.

The content of advertising messages is controlled to some minimal extent by the Federal Trade Commission and, in the case of certain products, the Food and Drug Administration. In addition, there are various advertising codes and the National Advertising Review Board, which offers guidelines for responsible advertising. But according to Kim B. Rotzoll, head of the Department of Advertising at the University of Illinois, advertising is governed by utilitarian thinking (whatever works is probably good, or it would be rejected by the audience) and a deontological philosophy (sort of a loose Golden Rule that depends on the individual advertising firm's sense of moral rectitude). Dr. Rotzoll sees the need for an ethical ombudsman within each advertising agency who "could essentially represent the consumer in the advertising transaction, introducing the arguably missing dimension of fairness in some persistent way."[6]

In the final analysis, it is the medium that must regulate advertising. For example, daily newspapers ordinarily do not sell space on their front pages for display ads. That is a method of controlling advertising. Television networks have time after time increased the number of commercial minutes per hour instead of adequately raising the advertising rates for existing commercial minutes. That is a failure to control advertising.

---

[6] Kim B. Rotzoll, "Advertising and Ethics—Observations on the Dimensions of a Cluttered Battleground," Advertising Working Paper Number 23, University of Illinois, January 1989.

The problem of control is compounded by the fact that huge amounts of money are involved. For example, virtually everyone with an ability to read or to understand news reports on radio or television knows, and has known for a very long time, that cigarette smoking is dangerous to one's health. Broadcasters, however, did not voluntarily eliminate this advertising from their networks or stations; it was eliminated by an act of Congress in 1969. This lost advertising resulted in a windfall for the print media. The tobacco industry now spends about $250 million a year on newspaper advertising alone. Newspaper publishers, like average Americans, understand the dangers in smoking; yet only seven dailies (out of 1,650) have barred cigarette advertising from their publications. The newspaper industry gives three major reasons for not voluntarily eliminating this kind of advertising: (1) tobacco is still a legal product to manufacture, (2) every ad is labeled with a prominent health warning, and (3) readers have a right to read various views, including those expressed in advertising, and make up their own minds.

Perhaps we can bring the problem of advertising and the mass media into better focus by asking and answering these two simple questions:

- *Should advertising be included in the mass media?* Yes. The audience has a need for the news and information content of advertisements; the advertiser has a legitimate right to distribute messages in the most economical and effective manner; and the publisher or broadcaster has an obligation to provide a periodical or program at the lowest possible cost to the consumer. In addition, advertisements provide an avenue for the expression of minority attitudes, opinions, and grievances; for the transmission of political messages; and for the conveyance of public service messages by industry and government. In this respect, individuals or groups can become their own publishers for a limited period at a relatively low cost.
- *Should advertising be regulated in the mass media?* Yes. Government agencies must regulate misleading and unfair practices. The media must regulate *position* (placement of advertisements and commercials) and *taste* (offensive advertisements and commercials).

In an era of increasingly specialized media, advertising plays a role that is much more positive than negative. The goals of media and advertising are the same: to reach an increasingly select audience. In this atmosphere, advertising plays a diminished role in influencing content. Rather, it is the specialized audience that determines the content, while advertising seeks that audience. The audience now has the opportunity for the first time to select channels supported by subscription or individual payment rather than by advertising. Even so, most members of the audience still seek the advertising-supported publications and channels, obviously finding that advertising provides worthwhile information, produces only minor interruptions and delivers entertainment or news worth whatever encumbrance it adds.

AFTERTHOUGHTS

1. George Kennan says that advertising, by definition, is "untruth." What untruth, if any, have you ever seen in a commercial? Is this typical?
2. Tobacco advertising provides only about one percent of the advertising income of the average newspaper. Do you believe this income is the reason newspapers decline to ban tobacco advertising?
3. "Advertising makes you buy things you don't want or need and forces you to pay higher prices." Do you agree or disagree?
4. "Get me $6 million and I can get a brick elected." Comment.
5. Would it make practical sense to initiate in the United States the European model for political campaigning on television? Could negative advertising then be successfully transferred to print media, just as was cigarette advertising?

PART 2
Participants

CHAPTER 7

Institutions

Mass media are social institutions. They are *social* because they are in the business of providing services for the society, or portions of it—that is, for general or specialized publics. They are organized, structured, and often bureaucratic *institutions* which are designed to make profits for the owners from fufilling this "service" function. Movies, radio and television stations and networks, record companies, magazines, newspapers, and books offer the society (in a sense, "sell") a wide assortment of "merchandise." Some media provide mainly entertainment and vicarious escapism, whereas the mainly journalistic media stress news and information and its analysis and interpretation.

But all media, as we saw in Chapter 1, are "institutionalized persons," acting and reacting in a social setting of other institutions in much the same way that an individual person acts and reacts in a less complex interpersonal group situation. Take the press of an entire country, for example. It can be thought of in a collective sense as being a social institution ("the press"); or each individual unit or medium (such as *The Chicago Tribune* or Ted Turner's Cable News Network) can be considered a social institution. So we can speak of "the press" as an institution in American society, or we can speak of a particular newspaper, radio station, or magazine as a social institution.

INSTITUTIONS AS FUNCTIONS
OF COMPLEXITY

Institutions, like persons, are difficult to generalize about, since they come in so many kinds and sizes. But there are certain commonalities among them, and it might be well to look at some of these in a general way before discussing the press specifically as a social institution.

Sociologists, of course, are most interested in institutions, for they see the whole process of socialization, the weaving of orderly and functional social relationships on communal and national levels, as essentially a process of institutionalization. That is, organized groups can accomplish certain things that individual persons cannot accomplish. In the face of overwhelming social complexities, individual tasks are therefore assumed by social organizations or institutions. Hence, it is quite obvious that as societies become more complex, as populations grow and specialization is more in demand, institutions themselves proliferate and become more complex. In a very advanced nation, for example, it is not uncommon for many *sub*institutions to spring up within a parent institution.

How does this phenomenon impact on media? Simple societies, underdeveloped or "new" nations, have a minimum of institutionalization and a maximum of individual freedom. In the realm of communication, then, we naturally find few if any institutionalized media attempting to reach the masses of a simple society. People speak to people more or less directly, person to person, in an unstructured way. It is not a very efficient system, though it has the virtue of not being monolithic either. Very few citizens of an underdeveloped or transitional nation understand what their government is doing; there is no institutionalized press system to tell them. They get their news and views in bits and pieces, and in an *unsimultaneous* fashion. The splintered nature of the society is reflected in the splintered, almost chaotic, manner in which a very small portion of the population receives its social information.

Complex, highly institutionalized press systems are found in highly developed, highly complex nations. Even when the press institutions (media, units) are multifarious, they form a well-organized part of a total national press institution that in some meaningful way synchronizes the diversity into a unified or functional whole. In other words, a highly developed press system, at least in a Western democracy such as the United States, might be considered the embodiment of institutionalized pluralism.

Social institutions are by nature conservative. They are set up in the first place, by and large, to conserve the social heritage and to achieve, through a kind of social conformity, some goal. They have a very large measure of social control vested in them, and they struggle to retain and exercise whatever control they have acquired and to extend it if possible. There is a natural tendency for social institutions to become inflexible, reactionary, and decadent. And there is a tendency for them to become dominated by conservative—even reactionary—administrators. This is not really strange, for the very nature of the institution actually dictates that this be so. What has just been said does not mean that institutions do not change; certainly they grow, progress, and adapt, but their adaptability usually follows the society in which they function.

INSTITUTIONS AS COLLECTIVIZING BODIES

Always there is a tendency toward institutionalization, and as this takes place the individual person tends to become a mere cog in the social machine. The person has, in a sense, been forced by social complexity to sell more and more individuality and independence of action in order to continue to exist and function in a mass, institutionalized world. As individuals become ever more institutionalized, they progressively become adaptable personalities who think more and more about the "collective," the society, and the institutions that subsume them.[1]

So institutions, organizations formed to serve a social function, not only act in society as "institutionalized persons," but function as social organisms that drain individuality and personality from individuals. And we would argue that they are also the primary building blocks of a collective society: institutions are extensions of personal needs or are like individuals functioning collectively as the persons who make them up would want to function individually. Some readers may not like the implications of such statements, may feel they are subjective, even biased. There is no doubt that some views—such as seeing institutions as building blocks of a cooperationist, or simply collectivist, society—contain considerable subjectivity. But we believe this situation follows logically from the most basic principle of institutionalization. If institutions come into being to systematize and organize activities so as to be socially functional, then it follows that institutions are based on *social* goals, not on individual goals. Social goal achievement, that is, institutionalization, assumes some form of collective or cooperative activity.

Even so-called capitalistic institutions lead to more social conformity, more mass-oriented activity, and ultimately a more monolithic society. As institutionalization increases, *in whatever kind of political or economic*

---

[1] Very good discussions of the forces in man that contribute to his collectivizing and institutionalizing are found in C. G. Jung, *The Undiscovered Self* (Boston: Little, Brown, 1957), and Erich Fromm, *Escape from Freedom* (New York: Holt, Rinehart & Winston, 1941).

context, one will find individual decision making decreasing and group-related decision making increasing. Therefore, without passing judgment on the ultimate implications of institutionalization at this point, we feel we can safely say that the process is a form of depersonalizing and social standardizing.

CONCEPT AND STRUCTURE

There are other, subtler aspects of institutions. Sociologists tells us that a social institution must have a *concept* and a *structure.* The concept is the purpose to be served, the social aim or objective—the idea, notion, doctrine, interest, or philosophy embedded in the institution. The concept, in other words, is the *why* of the institution. The *structure,* on the other hand, is the *means* used to bring about the concept—the *how.* It comprises the framework or apparatus designed to realize the purpose of the institution, including not only the *physical* apparatus (such as buildings or printing presses) but also the *human* apparatus (reporters, editors, printers)—in short, the persons or functionaries who cooperate in prescribed ways to achieve the goals.

In order for an institution to change, the concept or goal must first change. Then the structure, being dependent on the concept, usually changes slowly as the concept is modified. When the structure is so well adapted to the concept that the goal is reached, then what is called *institutional equilibrium* is achieved. It may well be that this equilibrium is not very often reached in many of our institutions. It is particularly absent in our press. Why is this so? Very simply, because the press's structure is generally very advanced but it has developed largely divorced from the concept. Said another way, the structure is well developed and the concept is, as we shall see, undeveloped or underdeveloped.

Technical facilities, buildings, and organized functionaries dominate the mass communications scene. What is rather strange is that this press structure has risen like an imposing monument on a weak conceptual foundation—and the daily pounding of its mechanical heart appears to keep the press's institutionalized body functioning. In fact, one might say that the structure of the press is large and vital enough to obscure the fuzziness of its institutional concept.

It is certainly easy to see, on visiting any of the great newspapers, magazines, or television stations across the country, where the emphasis is. A visitor would do well simply to gaze on the costly equipment and impressive buildings and observe the complex inner workings of the staff, asking questions about circulation, production problems, and hiring practices and not inquiring into the philosophy of the mass medium—its purposes and values, its *concept*. It appears to us that in the case of mass media as institutions, the structure has developed independently of any concept, or *in spite of* a vague concept. A gigantic mechanism, a complex structure, has come into being that manages to do rather haphazardly a large number of things without particular reference to any rationale. So in this respect we do not have institutional equilibrium, in that the structure is not designed to realize the concept. But we do have something institutionalized that works. It may well be that the fact that there is no single goal (concept) in the American press is the reason so-called professional schools of journalism often appear to be thrashing about wildly in the academic woods trying to cover all bases in the absence of any kind of unified goal, ethic, or body of professional lore.

Now, this is not to say that there is not some kind of extremely general (and vague) *concept of the press* in any society. In the United States, for instance, one could say that the press has as its main social functions (its concept) basically to *inform,* to *interpret* and *lead,* and to *entertain.* When we have said this, however, we have said very little. Obviously the press's concept is more profound than that. What is the overriding concept of the press, philosophically speaking, in the United States? The point we are making is that journalists do not appear to be sure; they have not really agreed on a basic press concept. Some might say that the basic function is free expression; others might say profit or incentive to the total economy; others might say political guidance; others might say support of the social and political status quo; others might say social change.

In other words, there is probably no one concept of the press, in a collective sense, in this country. Or if there is, we know of no student of the press who has isolated it. It is quite possible that in a country like the United States the main characteristic of the press is that there *is* no goal or aim of journalism. Philosophically, one can understand why in our type of pluralistic society there is no one concept understood and accepted by all press people and media. It is a little more difficult to understand why individual media or units of the national press system do not have institutional concepts. No doubt many press people would say that their respective media do have concepts, generally understood and worked toward by the functionaries in these individual media. A newspaper publisher may have a credo. This is something different from a "concept," agreed upon by all the workers. Where, indeed is the mass medium in which all personnel ever get together and even discuss the medium's function or concept, much less agree on it?

What does this newspaper stand for? Where is it going? What overriding objective does it have? How does it go about determining its concept, if it does at all? Does every functionary even think about a concept, or does he or she in fact simply work, producing his or her little isolated bit which is fed into the total product *without any meaning* being attached to it? Many persons would equate the newspaper's concept with the philosophy or ideology of the *publisher* of the newspaper. But how could this be when most newspaper personnel do not have the slightest idea *what* the publisher considers the aim or objective of the paper? If the publisher represents the newspaper's workers, it is only in the same way that the President of the United States represents the people of the country; and certainly we cannot say that the President by definition represents the people *conceptually*—philosophically or ideologically. In fact, it may well be that this very atypicality of our leaders is at the root of much social discord and rebelliousness. And, it may well be that functionaries in our mass media will increasingly (they have already begun) demand a voice in the day-to-day policies and activities of their institutions.

In spite of what has just been said about the absence of, or vagueness of, a basic overriding press concept in the United States, it is safe to say that there are some functions of the institutionalized press system that are accepted by various sectors. Let us briefly look at these, which are derived from our American tradition.

PRESS SYSTEM CONCEPTS IN AMERICA

One of the basic functions of the press in this country is that of presenting news and presenting it *objectively*. For most of our journalistic history we have heard that news stories must be "objective." The term "objectivity" is, of course, a very difficult one to define, but generally journalists have considered objective reporting to be that which is free (or virtually so) of bias, reporting that is factual—and that could be verified. The problems of objectivity in journalism will be discussed in more detail in Chapters 14 and 15.

A second concept or objective of the press in the United States is that of *fairness*. Most journalists in the country would not hesitate to say that their aim is to be fair. This, like most traditional concepts, is a glittering generality—vague but virtuous—and leaves us with many questions. One of the most important is: Fair to whom? For often we know that when we try to be "fair" to one party, the result is unfairness to another. Usually American journalists relate the concept of fairness to that of balance—to "equal time" and other ambiguous and fuzzy ideals.

A third traditionally held function of the American press is that of community and national *leadership*. It is a generally accepted journalistic premise that a mass medium should exert influence, should affect people's opinions and actions. Although most media probably would extol the leadership function unreservedly, it might strike most observers that media generally reflect and follow rather than striking out in new directions or going beyond the typical thinking of their communities.

A fourth concept quite common in this country is that of the press as a *seeker and defender of freedom.* The press normally presents itself as being for an "open society," with the restraining doors of secrecy being everywhere pounded down by the freedom-loving functionaries of the mass media. Most journalists would probably look upon themselves as libertarians concerned with the existence of a free marketplace of ideas and information. They would insist that they are against would-be and actual restricters and censors of information that they feel the public has a right to know.

Few journalists seem to realize that there is something amiss here, that the concept of *freedom seeker and defender* tends to lose meaning when it comes up against the very nature of the press as a social institution. Institutionalization, as we have seen, implies systematic ways of doing things—of having a kind of sanctioned mode of behavior, a socialized prescription for action. In reality, then, any institution is diametrically opposed to freedom. As we institutionalize, as we define social roles, we are really *losing* freedom and acquiescing in its loss.

Related to this freedom-seeker concept is the idea that the press is a check on the power structure, a kind of anti-Establishment watchdog. Most traditional textbooks in American journalism speak of the press as a public servant, a critic of government, a defender of the people's right to know, a "fourth branch of government." It is only recently that astute observers and critics have recognized that this "watchdog" itself needs some watching, that this Establishment critic has in effect become an Establishment, that this crusader for the people's right to know has itself become a withholder and manager of information. Some people have begun asking: If the press is in fact the fourth branch of government, how then can a "branch of government" criticize government dispassionately? Others are asking if it is true that government is further removed from the people in our democracy than is the press. Why should the people support the press in its *anti*government stance when, at least in theory, the government is we the people. Who among the people elected journalists to be watchdogs on anything?

A fifth traditional press concept in this country is that of a *forum for the people.* We are told that the press exists so that a democratic people can express themselves, argue issues, make themselves heard. This idea, of course, is compatible with notions of pluralism and free expression—with the vision of an open society characterized by the free clash of ideas. Everyone must have access to the press, we are now being told by those who would even legally force media to publish certain information. Pluralism, then, is being carried to the limit of *forced* pluralism. Forcing anything into the media is, of course, contrary to freedom of the press and reactionary in nature, but this point is seemingly overlooked by some of those who would try to reconcile their type of *guided* journalism with an unrestricted, freely operating press. Here is one case where concepts—the right of a mass medium to make its own free decisions versus the right of the people to use the press as a forum—tend to cancel one another out.

What is probably happening, albeit slowly, in the United States and in most countries is that press concepts are increasingly minimizing the desirability of *freedom* and emphasizing the importance of *guidance* in the name of social responsibility. Even those journalists who continue to extol the virtues of freedom would place controls and guiding hands upon the press so that it might be "free" in *their* sense of the term. Today there are many people who seem to believe that freedom to control the press is as important as, or more important than, freedom of the press.

Many readers will wonder why so much emphasis is being placed here on the concept of freedom in a discussion about the press as an institution. In our opinion, the concept of freedom is basic to a discussion of institutionalization; it begs to be dealt with. And although we plan to examine it in far more depth in later chapters, some attention must be given to it here.

Actually, the concept of freedom is so important that it is possible to say that in all the world there are but two *fundamental* press concepts: (1) the concept of a press integrated into government itself so as to ensure ideological agreement, social progress, and stability, and (2) the concept of a press that considers itself, and is considered, to be outside government completely, free from all external restraints, and with no obligation to support the government.

The first of these two fundamental concepts is related to a press system that is a *supporter* of government, either because it is actually a part of the governing apparatus or because it sees itself in a role of support and not antagonism. The second of these basic concepts relates to a press system that sees itself generally in a role of *antagonist* to and critic of the governing apparatus.

FOREIGN CONCEPTS

In spite of substantial differences from place to place, all media concepts obviously have some common denominators. For instance, all media desire to provide information. All provide considerable entertainment. And whether they publicize the fact or not, they are interested (even if for selfish reasons) in national progress and development. In other words, the fact that they are *mass media* means that they share certain purposes and objectives or concepts.

We can place the press systems of the world in a continuum from supporter to antagonist. In many, probably most, of the so-called Third World or developing countries media are more than the supporters just cited; they are in a real sense "partners" with government in campaigns of national advancement. And most countries with Marxist media systems see their chief conceptual objective as supporting party/government policy and, thereby, social stability. It is media in the First World (the economically advanced capitalist world), in countries such as Japan, West Germany, and the United States, who see their foundational institutional role or concept as entailing either *neutrality* vis-à-vis government or an *antagonistic* or adversarial posture.

Concepts or *raisons d'être* also differ globally relative to media *support*—such as advertising, which supports capitalist media systems; socialist media systems are largely (or completely) government supported. It is not feasible to draw neat parallels, however. Some media systems extol entertainment, providing a minimum of informational content; others stress directive messages along with motivational stories and speeches. Others are largely propagandistic, rallying the society against a "common enemy." And still others stress information or "news" and try to provide a variety of perspectives and viewpoints. Despite various emphases, no national media system is conceptually pure; *all of them are to some degree mixed in their conceptual aspirations.*

PLURALISM: KEY
TO THE AMERICAN CONCEPT

Let us look more closely at the American mass media as institutions. We might say that the *concept* of the newspaper press is that of observer and critic of government and protector of "pluralism," defender of the coexistence of diverse viewpoints and systems. This is about as much as we can say (and some will disagree even with this) about the institutionalized press concept in this country.

The *pluralism* built into this concept is what really keeps the overall newspaper *system* of this country from having any more discernible image of its purpose.[2] Different newspapers seem to have different concepts; or at least we can say they appear to disagree on many fundamentals, such as the very foundation of journalism: What news is. Also, there is no gener-

---

[2] In the U.S. we can talk about journalistic pluralism in two main ways: (2) context, and (b) type. For example, we can talk of pluralism on a national, regional, or local scale; and we can talk about types or kinds of pluralism, such as media or unit, ownership, communicator, and message.

ally accepted understanding among American newspapers as to the desirability of fairness or balance in the treatment of minority groups, coverage of issues, or kinds of content (e.g., politics, economics, sports, society, comic strips). Even opinions relative to support or criticism of government seem ambiguous and fuzzy when scrutinized closely. Most newspaper people in the United States, if they actually have tried to ascertain an overriding goal for journalism, would probably agree that newspapers in this country have no *concept* beyond pluralism and, of course, beyond making money.

When we said that pluralism is the newspaper press *concept* of the country, we did not really say very much about the *system's* objectives, aims, purposes, or goals. We only said, in effect, that these objectives and goals are somehow intrinsic in the concept of pluralism and will in due course work themselves out in some kind of mystical manner. Newspaper people in this country have traditionally maintained that pluralism leads to a free encounter of information and ideas and that somehow out of this battle of ideas Truth will emerge. Pluralism has been conceptually enthroned in our press—and in fact, in our entire media system. There have always been persons, of course, who have challenged this concept. Why should Truth automatically emerge out of a clash of opposing opinions, ideas, or sets of facts? It would appear, many critics contend, that what might actually emerge would be confusion and frustration. In theory, perhaps, Truth might emerge in the sense of being evident to some persons receiving some messages at some times in some situations. But even then, those persons would probably not recognize what they had as Truth. What is more likely is that in a conflict of ideas, some persons come away with some of the ideas and other persons come away with others—more than likely, those compatible with their predispositions. People are basically looking for supportive messages—facts and opinions—rather than for Truth.

By and large a pluralistic press system has been firmly established in this country. A wide variety of information and a fantastically broad range of ideas and opinions flood us today from a multitude of sources. But how close to the Truth about anything are we? Or, said another way, if we are close to it, do we ever realize that we are? Pluralism may well make for a more interesting or exciting media system, but just how much truth we get from it is difficult to tell.

JOURNALISTIC ORIENTATIONS

Although it is next to impossible to discuss concepts in journalism as they relate to a whole media system as an institution, it is possible to talk about orientations as they relate to individual media or to individual journalists who are part of the institutionalized press. Media or journalists can be classified in many ways as to their basic orientations, inclinations, or concepts. It seems to us that a simple ternary typology is helpful in describing these basic orientations. Each mass medium and each journalist, we think, is predominantly inclined to accept one of these three concepts: (1) neutral or reflective, (2) ambiguous or multirole, (3) leadership or directive.

It may be difficult to assign any one of these roles or concepts to an entire mass medium, such as the *New York Times,* but we do believe that in a kind of generalized, overall way every mass medium does basically adhere to one of them. It is somewhat easier to describe individual journalists as accepting one of the three orientations. Each journalist, we believe, has an individualized concept or role of journalism; he or she may work with others who have differing concepts, and his or her own concept may undergo change, but at any time a journalist is inclined to accept one of these three conceptual orientations:

1. *Neutral.* Journalists accepting this basic concept are believers in "objective" journalism, a journalism of noninvolvement and non-advocacy. They think journalism should be concerned essentially with reflecting the world, not changing or directing it. They are basically reportorial, monpartisan journalists who try to keep themselves and their biases out of their work. They are dispassionate and nonjudgmental, concerned with fairness and balance. These journalists stand aside, apart from the turmoil of an event, and try to transmit the reality of the event, untarnished by distortion, to their readers, listeners, and viewers. They see themselves as neither critic nor supporter of government or the "Establishment."

2. *Ambiguous.* Journalists accepting this middle-area concept might be called multirole persons. They assume many roles, none of which really dominates. At times they advocate; at times they provide facts. They too believe in objective reporting, but they are willing to experiment with interpretive reporting replete with all of its judgmental overtones. They are sometimes passionate, sometimes dispassionate. They try to lead public opinion, as well as follow it; they see themselves as both critics and supporters of government or the "Establishment." They generally consider themselves open-minded journalists capable of flexibility and change.

3. *Leadership.* Journalists who are inclined toward this concept are as convinced of journalism's leadership or directive role as the neutralist is of journalism's "objective" role. Any journalism worth its name, they believe, must be advocative, judgmental,

catalytic. Journalism must lead, not follow. It must be subjective. There is no such thing as objective journalism, they believe, although many cowardly, spineless journalists try to act as if there is. Leadership journalism might be considered propagandistic. Such journalists have a belief or program which they are systematically trying to implant in others. In a real sense such journalists are elitist, believing that they have the answers for the masses. They use their journalism to try to spread their values, to foist their ideology on others. They are passionate, personal, and forceful; they are involved and, to varying degrees, radicalized. They are usually inclined to be critical of government or the "Establishment" but a leadership or directive journalist may just as passionately support the "Establishment." The common denominator is forcefulness of stance.

In addition to these three main attitudinal orientations, let us consider four other professional orientations that tend to characterize media practitioners. Many media people, we could say, are inclined toward the *neutral presentation* of information; others gravitate to media where they can be primarily *entertainers*. Still others seek out media where their talents as *polemicists and editorialists* can have full ventilation. Finally, there are others who seek media that will give them a chance to indulge in calm, dispassionate *analysis and interpretation*.

There are also print-oriented media people versus those who feel at home before a camera or a microphone, the tools of electronic media. There are those who are comfortable addressing small, segmented, specialized audiences and those who like the stimulation of massive audiences. And, of course, there are business-oriented media people, who have no real concern with the content of media messages, as opposed to marketing-oriented professionals, in advertising, promotion, and public relations, who are interested in image making and profit making as basic supports for the media institution.

In the next chapter, media communicators will be considered in different terms, from a different perspective, but it is well that we have begun an analysis of mass communicators by looking at the broad concepts or role definitions that they bring to the mass media system. So, as we leave this discussion of media as institutions, we should realize that institutional complexity comes about when an institutional "concept" is defined. And since a concept, to the degree that it exists at all, is generated and crystalized by persons in the media, it is natural that we turn next to an analytical discussion of these persons—these *communicators*.

AFTERTHOUGHTS

1. The media, as a collective social institution, are said to be essential for a society. Is this really true, and if so, to what extent?
2. Is there a common "concept" governing the press in the United States? Can you name at least three functions or purposes that all of the media have in common? Are a few common functions enough to warrant talking about a particular *media concept* prevailing in the United States?
3. Would you say the American media concept (if there is one) is significantly different from other media concepts throughout the world? If so, how?
4. Media workers are classified according to several orientations in this chapter. Are these types realistic, in your opinion? How would you design a better typology?
5. If you were the editor of a magazine that had too ambitious a *concept* for the limited *structure* involved, what would you do? What would be the easiest thing to do?

CHAPTER 8

Communicators: Origin of the Species

Journalism history is usually a rather dry narrative of chronological events, featuring forceful, even flamboyant, individuals who march across the printed and electronic page. When one looks at the sweep of journalistic history in the United States, however, one is struck by the incidence of *similar types of people* appearing on the scene at the same periods of time and then, with notable exceptions, disappearing from prominence. This phenomenon raises the hypothesis that inventions and social forces have played as prominent a role as individuals in shaping the content and nature of mass communication throughout U.S. history.

Thus we could describe the history of news in America in terms of the kinds of individuals created by conditions of the press and society at four specific periods: *publisher-printer* (eighteenth to mid-nineteenth centuries), *publisher-editor* (mid–nineteenth century to 1900), *institutional editor* (1900 to mid–twentieth century), and *reporter-personality* (mid–twentieth century to present).

THE FOUR AGES OF JOURNALISM

During the era of the *publisher-printer,* proprietors of the press were essentially servants of a hand-operated press. They were skilled craftsmen, but their inability to achieve high circulations because of the primitive state of press mechanics meant that their staffs were small and that they could not free themselves from duties such as writing some, if not all, of the news copy in addition to setting type and operating the presses. The "job-shop" nature of their operations and the extremely limited circulation meant that *publisher-printers* were likely to accept material from outside "contributing editors" and to cater to the political tastes of select groups of readers.

In such circumstances, the newspapers of that period often became vehicles for political and literary essays (many of them reprinted from other newspapers in this country and abroad) as well as for news and editorial items. Publishers had to stand responsible for the sometimes controversial content, although they were not always totally involved in its creation. Toward the latter part of the period, coincidental with the rise of political parties, newspapers became more partisan, and the contributing editors moved into the more formal position of functioning editors.

This situation provided a bridge from the period of the *publisher-printer* to the period of the *publisher-editor*. Inventions such as the steam-driven rotary press, coupled with the social phenomenon of public education, allowed publishers for the first time to reach a mass audience. Newspapers could now maintain larger production and reporting staffs, emancipating publisher-editors from everyday involvement in the details of both the printing and news operations. For the first time, they could afford their own division of labor; as publishers, they gave more attention to the editorial page. The publisher-editor was personally responsible for the editorial tone and position of the paper, and in the reader's mind the paper itself was closely associated with the personality of the publisher-editor. The period began with such memorable personalities as Benjamin Day, the James Gordon Bennetts, and Horace Greeley; it ended with men of similar force: Joseph Pulitzer and William Randolph Hearst.

Adolph Ochs's purchase of the *New York Times* in 1896 inaugurated the third period. In assimilating the technological innovations of the late nineteenth century, newspapers had become costly and complex machines dispensing news and advertisements. The newspaper industry now called for publishers who were first and foremost business-minded persons, although well grounded in the total functions of the press. These publishers set overall policy but were generally dissociated from the news operation and all but the basic tone of the editorial page. Having focused their attention on the business side of the newspaper operation, they delegated editorial supervision to *institutional editors,* supervisors of the production of reporters, wire services, and syndicated feature services (material produced by writers and cartoonists outside the newspaper staff and made available to a large number of papers). The newspaper achieved a rather bland balance of straight news and not-too-controversial editorial opinion.

This was a period in which the newspaper as an institution achieved greater recognition than individual publishers or editors. The inception and full flowering of the newsmagazine during this period epitomized the virtual anonymity of the communicators themselves. Highly skilled publishers amalgamated and forged newspaper groups. Equally skilled editors managed the glut of news. The volume of news and its credibility reached new heights. But the editorial page lost its punch, for it had begun to represent institutions rather than human beings with whom the reader could identify. Names of publishing families and groups stand out during this period: Sulzberger, Scripps-Howard, Annenberg, Newhouse, Gannett, Knight, Chandler. The names of great editors come less slowly to the surface of recognition.

Although reporters of the caliber of Henry M. Stanley, Arthur Brisbane, and Richard Harding Davis achieved fame throughout the nineteenth and twentieth centuries, and outstanding columnists and commentators—Walter Lippmann, Arthur Krock, and Edward R. Murrow, to name only a few—cast their giant shadows prior to the mid-twentieth century, these were the exceptions to the typical subordination of the reporter to the publisher-editor and later to the institutional editor. Television was the catalyst that, for the first time, permitted the *reporter-personality* to dominate the news scene in the United States. Radio had given reporters a voice. Television gave them a face, and it put this face in living rooms each weekday night. The immediacy and brevity of television news, however, gave newspapers an opportunity to compete by offering perspective and detail. The resulting interpretative stories and opinion columns emphasized the personalities and names of their authors.

Television was only one factor associated with the arrival of the reporter-personality. By the mid–twentieth century, daily newspaper monopolies existed in all but a few American cities. The newspaper had a dilemma: how to fulfill its function of offering a variety of controversial opinion without antagonizing large segments of its heterogeneous audience. The answer was syndicated columnists, who wrote under their own by-line and spoke for themselves rather than for the newspaper in which they appeared. The number of syndicated columnists has mushroomed, as has the number of syndicate services, and newspapers today are likely to regularly run four or more political columnists covering a broad spectrum of political opinion.

It may well be that we are still barely into the era of the reporter-personality. But most observers would agree that this type of newsperson has captured the imagination and interest of the American audience. It is the reporter-personality who draws the premium salary, especially if he or she is syndicated or in network television. Reporters, rather than editors or publishers, run for elective office. And television anchors "on location" at political rallies or conventions are apt to draw larger crowds than are major political candidates.

Some media units, of course, still operate under the institutional editor philosophy, and one could find a few magazines and newspapers, generally of small circulation, that even today are publisher-printer or publisher-editor operations. The development of offset printing made it comparatively simple for a person with something to say, or something to sell, to become a newspaper publisher. As a result, suburban weeklies have proliferated in recent years. Generally, in the early years of publication they are publisher-editor operations. The few that survive find it necessary to fill more space and offer a wider variety of content to their readers; as this occurs, they are likely to undergo a change to a reporter-personality orientation.

WHO BECOME REPORTERS?

Gay Talese, in his book about the *New York Times,* observes:

> Not only on *The Times,* but on other newspapers, the news staffs were largely populated by products of the lower middle class—by liberal Jews and less liberal Irish-Catholics from the North, by progressive Protestants from the South and Midwest, and, not unexpectedly, by relatively few Italo-Americans. The immigrants from Italy took longer to become familiar with the English language and its literature, as did other ethnic groups to whom the English language was difficult; they did not produce many newspaper reporters.[1]

Talese contends that only those from the lower middle class had the "drive, patience, and persistence to succeed as reporters." Journalism, he explains, provided people from this group with a vehicle for upward mobility. Whether one finds Talese's generalizations about the sources of reportorial manpower superficial or not does not alter the fact that he touches upon two important points that deserve amplification: the exclusion of certain groups from journalistic professions, and the belief that the profession is dominated by liberal, as opposed to conservative, personalities.

Too few reporters come from the racial and ethnic minorities in today's United States. This situation has often been attributed solely to discrimination by the mass media. Although media in all sections of the United States were guilty in the past of racist hiring practices, there are factors in addition to outright bias that have perpetuated this situation. As Talese implies, language is an important qualification for journalists, and a

---

[1] *The Kingdom and the Power* (New York and Cleveland: World Publishing, 1969), p. 326.

facility with English has always been a prerequisite for entrance into the print media. Until the mid-1950s, blacks in America attended schools of inferior quality relative to those in white sections. Even after school integration, many predominantly black public schools lacked some of the training facilities, such as school newspapers, that were available to schools in more affluent areas. In addition, the grammar of textbooks was almost a different language from that spoken in the inner city. Language has also been a problem, obviously, for those students from bilingual communities where, say, Spanish is the language of the home and neighborhood and English is the language of instruction.

Two additional factors have retarded the entrance of minorities into the print media: they are accustomed to seeing fewer newspapers and magazines in their homes, because of the lower level of income and/or education of the average minority family, and they are used to seeing fewer of their own racial or ethnic group as role models in the mass media. Fortunately, improved educational opportunities and active recruiting by the media are helping to correct the existing imbalance.

Talese also declares that those who enter the ranks of reporting tend to be "liberals" rather than "conservatives." This is a widely held view but is open to some question. It is true that writers are, in a sense, word "performers," and radio and television communicators are working on the fringes of show business itself. Like other creative personalities, they are more sensitive to the social ills that they observe and describe in the course of their professional work. It would be surprising if the average reporter were not more liberal than conservative, just as it would be surprising if the average trainee in banking were not more conservative than liberal. The real question is whether, as is commonly thought, reporters are *more liberal than the average American* and thus out of step with the audience for whom they are writing.

In *The American Journalist,*[2] authors David H. Weaver and G. Cleveland Wilhoit presented the results of an extensive survey conducted in 1982–1983 among American newspaper, newsmagazine, broadcasting, and news service newspeople. They found that "about the same proportion of journalists claimed to lean left as did the U.S. population in a 1982 Gallup Poll (21 percent), but considerably fewer journalists said they leaned to the right than did the general public, and substantially more journalists claimed to be middle-of-the-road than did the general public." As a group, then, journalists were about as liberal as the American public (22.1 percent to 21 percent), more middle-of-the-road (57.5 percent to 37 percent), and only about half as conservative (17.9 percent to 32 percent).

Those staffers working for "prestige" news media, mostly in the

[2] Bloomington, IN: Indiana University Press, 1986.

Northeast, were only slightly more liberal than the American public (24.8 percent to 21 percent), more middle-of-the-road, like the average journalist (58.7 percent to 37 percent), and half as conservative (16.5 percent to 32 percent). Weaver and Wilhoit reported that fewer journalists identified themselves as Democrats than did the population as a whole (38.5 percent to 45 percent), more as independents (39.1 percent to 30 percent), and fewer as Republicans (18.8 percent to 25 percent). They also found that in 1982–1983 about one-third of newspeople were women, and more than half of all newspeople in the United States were under the age of 35.

CREDIBILITY AND INVOLVEMENT: WHO WATCHES THE GATE?

In the days when publishers or editors fully controlled the content of newspapers, it was the publication's responsibility to see that some order of fairness in reporting the news was maintained. Today, in a time of newspaper complexity and size, and of high technology in the electronic media, the burden has shifted downward, to lower-level editors and to reporters themselves. The editor in many cases is a budget and personnel manager, able only to review the fairness of the newspaper *after* publication rather than before. Fairness in the news columns or editorial page might be in the hands of a copy editor, photo editor, or section editor. Ben H. Bagdikian studied editorial pages in the 1960s and discovered that in newspapers with conservative editorial policies most syndicated columnists were conservative, while in newspapers with liberal editorial policies most syndicated columnists were liberal. In the 1990s newspapers have theoretically opened their editorial and op-ed pages to a more balanced range of columnists. But there is still opportunity for an editorial page editor or that editor's assistants to express a personal prejudice on certain issues through selection of columnists (most newspapers have a large number to choose from each day) and choice of letters-to-the-editor, graphics, and headlines.

It is difficult for a news director at the network level to ensure fairness. As was discussed in Chapter 5, the format of the TV correspondent's report is usually chronological, making it more like a feature story. A videotaped story submitted on deadline pressure is difficult to edit for bias, and a live report from the field cannot be edited at all. Under such conditions, the reporter has a heavy responsibility to acknowledge the possibility of bias and try to avoid it.

Earlier in this book, in discussing the problem of press monopoly, we compared it with the problem of monopoly in the soap industry. We pointed out that a soap monopoly would still offer the product that consumers want, whereas monopoly of the press threatens to remove the product itself—variety of criticism. In a similar fashion, we can say that there are many professions whose practitioners can involve themselves completely in the problems of individuals or society as a whole without damaging the service they perform. But in the case of a reporter working for a truly mass medium, involvement threatens to destroy the reporter's product—a factual report arrived at by professional newsgathering methods.

This example is sometimes given: press photographers or television camera crews observe a man preparing to fire a pistol at the head of another man. Do they stand their ground and take their pictures, or do they rush to the aid of the intended victim? If they record the scene for their newspapers or television stations, these pictures may have significant effects on the minds of their audience. If they don't take the pictures, perhaps they will be able to save a man's life. Under a circumstance like this, we would hope that the photographers would instinctively act to save a man's life, a human life being worth more than a photograph or videotape under any conditions. But unfortunately, the lines are not always so clearly drawn or dramatically presented. In most cases, reporters have to determine consciously whether to serve their readers or serve a cause, and when they try to do both simultaneously it is usually the readers that are shortchanged.

Communicators who by dress or action identify themselves with a controversial cause damage their own credibility or impartiality. Some sources who properly identify them will withhold all or part of the information needed to produce a factual story. Some members of the audience who properly identify them will doubt the credibility of their reports, and some of this doubt will be transferred to the publication or broadcasting station that employs them. If the doubt becomes strong enough, many readers or viewers will turn to what they consider a more credible source, or they will (in the case of electronic media) demand government intervention to ensure fairness.

It is the responsibility of individuals, of course, to make their own decisions abut personal involvement, but they must remember that their decision affects the credibility of their publication or station also. Reporters who believe that they must become personally involved in political or controversial causes have other alternatives they should consider. These include asking that they not be assigned to a story in which they have a personal involvement, taking a leave of absence from their publication or station in order to work for the cause, or going to work for a publication that is clearly identified as an organ of opinion.

Several *Washington Post* reporters participated in a Pro-Choice parade in Washington, DC, in 1989. Shortly afterwards, Managing Editor Leonard Downie, Jr., sent a memo to the staff reminding them that this activity had been contrary to *Post* policy and barring anyone who had marched in the parade from covering stories on the abortion issue. He later held meetings with *Post* newsroom personnel to review the newspaper's long-held statement on standards and ethics, one sentence of which reads: "We avoid active involvement in any partisan causes—politics, community affairs, social action, demonstrations—that could compromise or seem to compromise our ability to report and edit fairly."

Network news personalities have traditionally avoided involvement with controversial causes, since their private personalities could not be dissociated from their professional personalities. During the Reagan administration it was revealed that George Will, a prominent Sunday morning news program panelist and syndicated columnist, had secretly counseled the President, prior to a press conference, on how to respond to certain questions. The revelation, which Will admitted, damaged his credibility, because he had also been in the potential position as a news commentator of critiquing the press conference, and certainly was in the position continually of critiquing the Reagan presidency on an ongoing basis. The term "mass" media implies that publications or broadcasts have audiences that range across wide political, economic, and social strata. Each city, no matter how large, has relatively few television news programs and usually only one newspaper. The news produced by these outlets must be believed to be fair so the audience can, among other things, utilize the information to make intelligent decisions at the ballot box. Those reporters who persist in identifying themselves, their reports, and their medium with a partisan cause on the grounds that doing so is the proper function of mass media in a free society harm the credibility of their medium and adversely affect the process of a democratic system.

AN UNLICENSED PROFESSION

With the individual reporter, columnist, and commentator playing a more important role in the communication process than ever before, some critics have suggested that communicators be held personally accountable for the quality of their product. A physician even wrote in his county medical bulletin that, considering newsmen's "tremendous, almost unlimited power in shaping public opinion," they should be licensed. A newsman, the doctor wrote, should be required to show proof of ability, training, and qualifications before being allowed to practice his profession, and he added:

> Almost all professions and even most skilled and some unskilled trades are so regulated. There seems to be no justification for the exclusion of news reporting, a profession, from identical regulation. This would not

limit free speech and would give at least minimal assurance as to ability, reliability, and veracity.

What the doctor failed to note is that, aside from the clergy, journalism is the only profession open to all under the guarantee of an amendment to the U.S. Constitution. Most trades and professions that license practitioners do so for one of two reasons: to limit artificially the number of persons who can engage in that work, or to protect the lives and property of those who purchase their skills or services. Journalistic reports rarely threaten the lives and property of readers and viewers,[3] and any effort to limit entrance into the profession would undoubtedly be declared unconstitutional. On the other hand, if a license were automatically issued to any literate person who wanted to write for a publication or work in broadcasting, it would be meaningless. As in so many other cases where the press is concerned, a gain in "responsibility" means a loss in freedom.

Few in the journalistic profession have ever seriously called for licensing of newsmen. The closest the profession has ever come to enforcing a standard among its practitioners was a famous episode involving the American Society of Newspaper Editors and its "Canons of Journalism." The ASNE adopted the Canons, a code of ethics, shortly after the founding of the organization in 1922, but the first effort to enforce the Canons was shattered when it ran against the figure of Frederick G. Bonfils, editor and co-publisher of the *Denver Post*. The case concerned Bonfils' involvement in the famous Teapot Dome scandal, which rocked the Harding administration. The principle was one of basic journalistic ethics—Bonfils had apparently accepted money in return for suppressing advance information about the scandal. The ASNE moved to toss him out of the society. Bonfils threatened to sue each member of the Board of Directors if that occurred. The ASNE did not expel Bonfils (he later resigned from the organization) and never again attempted to expel a member for violation of professional ethics. Some members of the society contended at the time that, reprehensible though Bonfils's action was, any effort to make a pariah out of him by expelling him would in itself be a violation of the spirit of the First Amendment. In the words of Benjamin Franklin, "Abuses of freedom of speech ought to be repressed, but to whom dare we commit the power of doing it?"

Codes of ethics can be found in many newsrooms, on the walls of most journalism schools, and in the annals of state press associations through-

---

[3] During the student uprising in China in 1989, TV reporters discovered with shock that their reports were taped by the Chinese authorities, and these videotapes were used to identify and punish dissidents. From that point on, reporters tried to disguise the features of persons interviewed.

out the land. But those who have created and adopted them would agree with Benjamin M. McKelway, former editorial chairman of the *Washington Star,* who said: "Codes and canons may be helpful outlines of desirable conduct, like the Sermon on the Mount. But a vital characteristic of a free press is the guarantee of freedom for what may be regarded as the worst, as well as the best, among its practitioners."

Along these lines, the *New York Times* recognized the potentially chilling effect of a national press council that moved beyond codes to pass judgment on the way newspapers or networks handled news stories. Publisher Arthur O. Sulzberger informed the National News Council, when it was founded in 1963, that the *Times* would not participate in any of its proceedings, and he ordered his editors and reporters not to respond to National News Council inquiries. When the National News Council was dissolved in 1984, the opposition of the *Times* and other news organizations was given as one of the primary reasons for the council's lack of effectiveness.

TRAINING: JOURNALISM OR LIBERAL ARTS—OR NEITHER?

Journalism education, pioneered in the United States, is now available in some form in every developed country of the world. In America, courses in all aspects of mass communication have been incorporated into the curriculum of most colleges and universities. The purpose of the undergraduate curriculum remains much the same as that foreseen by University of Missouri President A. Ross Hill during its School of Journalism's first year of operation in 1908: "I believe it is possible for this school to give dignity to the profession of journalism, to anticipate to some extent the difficulties that journalism must meet and to prepare its graduates to overcome them, to give prospective journalists a professional spirit and high ideals of service, to discover those with real talent for the work and discourage those who are likely to prove failures in the profession, and to give the state better newspapers and newspapermen and a better citizenship."[4]

The lack of a journalism degree, however, does not bar any college graduate from employment in the mass media. Indeed, there are numerous editors who prefer that beginning reporters have a degree in some other field, and still others who do not require educational qualifications beyond the high school level.

---

[4] Quoted in Walter Williams, *Twenty Years of Education for Journalism* (Columbia, MO: E. W. Stephens Publishing, 1929), p. 25.

Often, those editors who disdain journalism degrees are those who do not have them themselves. Self-made men and women usually feel that the best avenue to success is the one that they themselves followed. If medicine and the law were unlicensed professions—if "reading for the law" or learning medicine by practicing with an established physician were still as popular as they were a hundred years ago—similar attitudes would exist in those professions too. In the sense that no uniform educational standards prevail for entrance to the profession, journalism is anachronistic. But the severe demands of the First Amendment, permitting access to all, perpetuate this anachronism, and in the long run this is a benefit to society.

The American Journalist, the Weaver and Wilhoit book mentioned earlier in this chapter, reported that in 1982–1983, 40 percent of all journalists were journalism program graduates, and among those with a college education more than 50 percent were journalism graduates. Surveys in the late 1980s showed that of all new hires by newspapers (that is, persons without previous professional experience) about 85 percent were journalism graduates.

Journalism offers students complete freedom of choice in shaping their own education. If students choose to go the route of an accredited school or department of journalism, only about a quarter of their courses will be in the communication curriculum, and a number of these will be more akin to classes in the social sciences than to "nuts and bolts" technique courses. In effect, they will have "majored" in journalism in the same way that other students major in history or sociology. At the end of their college course work they should have an education as broad as those who majored in another field in liberal arts colleges, and at the same time they should be equipped to produce higher-quality work than beginning communicators with nonjournalism degrees.

Where journalism schools and departments do not exist, talented students who might best serve humanity in the profession of journalism are attracted to other fields of learning for which there *are* courses and dedicated professors. It must be noted that some private universities that do not offer journalism education on either the undergraduate or graduate level traditionally produce outstanding communicators who have learned journalistic techniques through work on university publications and broadcasting stations. But these schools also furnish fewer people to the mass communications fields than they should, and fewer people than the country needs, simply because they do not offer a full range of scholastic incentives.

Those students who do leave the university with journalism degrees should have an awareness that goes beyond a facility in journalistic skills. They should have a broad knowledge of the liberal arts, an understanding of media ethics, a recognition of the relationship between press freedom and political democracy, and a commitment to the role of journalism in a free society.

AFTERTHOUGHTS

1. Does the *reporter-personality* era also presage a permanent movement away from objective reporting, or are the two compatible?

2. If minorities are underrepresented in a newsroom, what is likely to be the effect on the coverage of news? Does this pose any serious problems for either the newspaper or the city in which it exists?

3. Journalists are less "conservative" than the population as a whole. Need newspapers or radio and television stations compensate for this leaning in some way? If so, how?

4. In your opinion, would students who are communications majors be likely to bring a different professional attitude to their first job than persons who had not majored in communications?

5. Granted, licensing reporters would be a violation of the First Amendment, but would it make sense for a professional journalism society, similar to the American Bar Association, to "accredit" reporters so that prospective employers would know whether individuals were qualified to work in a newsroom?

CHAPTER 9

Audiences:
The Elusive Targets

As smug and self-assured (even arrogant) as many communicators are, they are totally dependent on their audiences. "I think I'm a good communicator" is not enough. What is equally important is this: "I hope my audience members are interested, attentive, and receptive to my message."

Communicators who talk with friends, family, or homogeneous small groups can usually know a great deal about the interest, attentiveness, and receptiveness of these audiences. If we want to describe the persons sitting in an auditorium listening to a lecture, we can do so with some degree of success. We can at least count them and observe their reactions to the message and to the communicator; immediate feedback is possible. And if we are so inclined, we can get their names and do various in-depth studies in which a substantial body of data will be gathered. We can, then, say that it is possible to know this type of audience very well.

The situation is far more complicated for the *mass* communicator, however. Mass audiences are amorphous, transitory, and fickle; they constantly pose a mystery for the mass communicator. In spite of intuitions and studies, their real nature is virtually unknown. In the mass communication process they are the big question mark.

The term "audience" is very difficult to deal with analytically, especially when we are talking about mass audiences. Since these audiences are scattered, fluid, anonymous, unseen, and heterogeneous, it is impossible for us to know very much about them. The very nature of a mass audience defies careful analysis. Most generalizations that can be made about mass audiences must stem mainly from intuition; in other words, our ideas about mass audiences must be formed by a rather unscientific method of limited observation and inadequate induction. What most mass communicators do is project their own likes and dislikes onto their audiences.

TWO MASS AUDIENCE TYPES

In spite of the imprecision with which we must necessarily discuss mass audiences, it is possible to suggest several possibilities of classification that might prove beneficial in analyzing them. For instance, it appears reasonable to say that there are two main kinds of mass audiences. One would be the very broad, completely heterogeneous, and anonymous audience that is often referred to as the "general public." The other type of mass audience would be a more specialized audience formed out of some common interest among its members. In other words, it is rather homogenous in at least one important aspect. Let us look a little more closely at these two basic types.

The General Public Audience

Although some writers think this general mass audience is really mythical,[1] it does seem to have some meaning and is probably the type of audience to which most people refer when they talk about "mass" audiences. When we say that television (at least in its network programming aspect) is a mass medium, we are implying that it reaches, or has the potential of reaching, a very broad, heterogeneous *general* audience. Certain programs on television may be aimed primarily at specific segments of this broad audience, but television itself—or its message output *in toto*—is not specialized, but general.

Members of this amorphous, general, heterogeneous audience have *no sense of relationship with other members*. They have nothing (that they are aware of) really in common with them; they are, in fact, exposing themselves to the mass media in an atomized, individual way. They have no sense of camaraderie with others of like mind or interest. They do not think of themselves as part of a group of any type. Members of the general public audience, then, react independently to mass media messages. In one sense, therefore, they are really more *independent* or *individualistic* in

---

[1] Robert C. O'Hara in his *Media for the Millions* (New York: Random House; 1961), for example, contends that the concept of a mass audience is "one of the great fallacies of mass communication"; despite its having been discredited, he says, it still persists (pp. 35–36).

their exposure and response to the mass media than are members of the second type of mass media audience.

The Specialized Audience

This type of mass audience, although scattered, basically anonymous, and in most ways heterogeneous, is made up of individuals who have a *common interest or orientation* that causes them to be members of the same audience.[2] This type of audience is, in many ways, quite similar to what Gustave Le Bon refers to as a "psychological crowd"—not necessarily in one place, perhaps comprising thousands of isolated persons. For example, people with a certain interest or concern subscribe to the *Wall Street Journal;* usually they are homogeneous so far as economic interest is concerned. Not that they are all wealthy, but they are interested in finance and economic matters, and more than likely they are members of the upper-middle and upper classes. So this audience is specialized in the sense of interest in economics; it is also homogeneous in that this manifest interest in financial matters is a common bond and probably evidences a homogeneity in many other areas—for example, in social and political ideologies, values, and general lifestyle.

The readers of *The Nation,* without personally knowing each other, can assume that a kind of intellectual cohesion exists among them. They can, in effect, know a considerable amount about one another, and the, publisher, editors, and writers for the magazine can assume much about their audience members. One thing that can be assumed about the readers is that they are vitally interested in serious social problems, in politics, in war and peace, in international issues. It can also be assumed that they consider themselves "liberals," whatever such a term may really mean. That is, they are probably to the left politically, concerned with civil and minority rights, with what they see as exploitation of other nations, with injustices in the legal system, with excesses by the police, with tendencies against militarism and the allocation of an inordinate proportion of the national wealth to war and war-related enterprises. These are a few of the basic concerns that bring audience members to *The Nation* and similarly oriented publications. The audience of the conservative *National Review,* obviously, would be politically homogeneous also but would reflect a quite different political profile than that of *The Nation.*

It should be pointed out, however, that although the two publications named above may attract different types of audiences, they draw readers who have something in common. For example, readers of both magazines

---

[2] See Le Bon's classic work, *The Crowd* (1895); *The Crowd: A Study of the Popular Mind* (many editions).

are concerned with *issues* and are basically *political* persons. The two audiences are not concerned with issues in the same way or for the same reasons, of course, but they share a certain passion and intellectual curiosity. In this sense the specialized audiences of "liberals" and "conservatives" are very much alike.

Audiences, then, can be "mass" and at the same time can be united or specialized in one way or around one main interest. We can think of audiences that seek out media that will feed such common interests as politics, economics, country and western music, hunting and fishing, boating, stamp collecting, gardening, sex, and so on and on. And in a mass society such as that of the United States there are enough persons who have such special interests in common that communications media can afford to exist to satisfy these extremely sizable specialized audiences.

CHARACTERISTICS OF AUDIENCES

Before turning to the more specific types of audiences—subgroups of the all-inclusive mass audience—it might be well to say a few things that apply to audiences generally. Audiences vary in at least four essential ways: *size, composition, degree of homogeneity,* and *longevity.*

Every mass media audience is large, but when we have said this we have not said very much. "Large," "medium-sized" and "small"mass audiences evidently exist, but in a kind of fuzzy, undefined way. At any rate, it is safe to say that mass audiences vary in size. Different numbers of persons at different times are exposed to (become audiences of) various mass media.

Although there is undoubtedly some overlap among audience members making up mass audiences, we can say that each audience differs in composition. The makeup of every audience is fundamentally unique, with each audience having within it not only different individuals but often quite different *types* of persons.

The degree of homogeneity varies considerably between or among audiences. Usually, but not always, the larger the audience the less the degree of homogeneity; smaller subaudiences tend to become more specialized and thereby more homogeneous.

Finally, audiences vary according to the length of time they stay "in tune with" the particular mass medium and message. This factor might be called "exposure cohesion." In one sense, *no* audience remains completely cohesive or intact during the entire communication of message. Audience members are continually tuning in and out mentally and they are physically coming to and going from the message. *All* audiences, then, are in a constant state of flux, but putting that aside, we can say that audiences differ from one another more significantly in the matter of longevity: Some audiences essentially stay together or adhere without major change much longer than do other audiences. Therefore we can refer to audiences of short exposure and audiences of long exposure, though we may not be able to say precisely what "short" and "long" exposures are. On television, for example, the audience watching a football game differs considerably in exposure cohesion from the audience watching a half-hour network newscast. In the print media, the audience reading articles in *The New Yorker* is presumably quite different with respect to exposure cohesion from the audience reading articles in *Reader's Digest* or in a local newspaper.

THREE ATTITUDINAL SUBGROUPS

The kind of audience member a person is depends largely on his or her attitude, values, desires, and philosophy of life—what the Germans call the *Weltanschauung*. It is important for journalists to recognize the basic types of persons making up the mass general audience so they can aim at a specific type of person who, in a way, symbolizes a sizable segment of the public. Of course, these audience segments may be classified in many ways, but a fairly simple and useful one is a ternary typology of "illiterates," pragmatists, and intellectuals.

"Illiterates"

The reason we use quotation marks is that many of these persons can read and write. That is, this segment includes those who *can* read but are not inclined to do so, along with true illiterates who do not read but do expose themselves to picture publications, movies, television, and radio. Thus "illiterate" audience members are either truly illiterate or attitudinally illiterate. At least they are not *word oriented*. Their adherence to the mass media is superficial in nature; they expose themselves to the most superficial and action-filled media messages. They are entertainment seekers.

Illiterate audience members want excitement from their media messages. They may read light fiction that gratifies their emotional appetites; they may read captions with pictures; they may read headlines and certain action-type stories in the newspaper—*but basically they do not like to read*. They expose themselves to picture media so that they can expend a minimum of effort as they receive messages.

They are not idea oriented. In fact, it is safe to say that they are primarily self-gratification-oriented. To some extent they are "thing"-oriented, but often they evidence disdain for material possessions except those of a very simple type that will give them momentary satisfaction.

Basically, this type of audience member is mentally lazy. That is why such a person is a "looker" and not a reader, or is satisfied with a superficial picture of the world and not with a full interpretation or under-standing of events and issues.

"Illiterate" audience members are unimpressed with participation in political and social activities. In a sense they are loners, at least in the sense of involvement in the workings of the larger social world outside their own family or neighborhood. They feel that they can have little or no impact on major decisions of any type, and so they largely retire from the main currents of human activity.

Their communication world is thus turned inward. Since they are not concerned with social involvement, they are naturally not interested in any mass communication that attempts to activize them, to get them to partici-pate, to consider problems and issues, to think, to discuss, to become concerned. What the "illiterate" audience members take in from the mass media, they keep within themselves; they absorb messages for their own emotional benefit and to escape from the routine world of existing.

Socioeconomically, illiterates are generally found at the poverty or near-poverty level. Nevertheless, it is important to note that they exist in rather large numbers in the lower-middle classes as well; it should be remembered that their communication activities stem largely from their existing interests. Many financially well-off people too are "illiterates," because they focus on reading, viewing, and listening to messages that will give them personal and immediate enjoyment. However, since socioeco-nomic status does have a considerable impact on education and thereby on interests, one might conclude that most of these attitudinal "illiterates" would fall in the lower income levels of society.

A person's native intelligence (IQ) is also a related, but peripheral, factor in determining such "illiteracy." Many people have great mental capacities, great intellectual potential, but do not have the motivation, the interests, or the energy to make the effort to use them. One can only speculate as to the number of persons with extremely high IQs who go through life being satisfied with only superficial messages of a self-gratification nature, designed to erase their boredom momentarily.

There is no way to know what percentage of the total audience is made up of this "illiterate" group, but it is probably safe to estimate that it consists of at least 60 percent of all readers, listeners, and viewers. It is surely the largest of the three segments of the general mass audience of the United States. Let us turn now to the next largest, and probably the most important to the mass communicator: the *practical* audience.

Pragmatists

Probably 30 percent of the total mass audience can be found in this
important middle group, which has been referred to as the *pragmatic* or
practical audience. These pragmatists are social beings in that they like to
involve themselves in the machinery of their society. They participate.
They work. They campaign. They vote. They belong to organizations.
They have hobbies. They travel. They build homes. They buy automo-
biles. They watch television. They read newspapers and magazines. They
buy recordings and listen to radio.

Practical audience members, therefore, are not lazy, either mentally
or physically. They want to be accepted by others. They are ambitious;
they want promotions and salary increases. They want to keep up with, or
get ahead of, the Joneses. By and large, they are the ones who exercise
social power today.[3] They are interested in *status,* and since material
possessions are symbols of status in our society, they are interested in
accumulating possessions.

Pragmatists, since they may basically be characterized in the terms
used above, form the primary target for a commercially oriented mass
media system. Their concern with status and their ambitions cause them to
be great consumers of mass messages. Advertisers, and by projection all of
our commercial mass media, love them and try to satisfy their desires.
Since these practical audience members want to advance, and since they
are pragmatic in that they want to know *how* to do things that will help
them get ahead, they feed regularly at the troughs of expository journalism. How to live more meaningful lives. How to get the most out of a trip to
Europe. How to win friends and influence the boss. How to build your own
patio and save money. How to be stimulating and knowledgeable at the
company party. How to live a satisfying life. These are the kinds of
concerns that practical audience members have.

Unlike "illiterate" audience members, pragmatists are seeking information that will help them advance, get on better with others, and involve
themselves more usefully in their community and nation. They have a
practical reason for their communication habits: They are essentially *social* persons who are actually lonely and restless when not with others.
They are, in a way, snobs, but not seclusive; they are, as it were, involved
snobs—snobs on the basis of their activities, their accomplishments, their
possessions, their neighborhood, their title, their circle of friends and
associates. They are snobbish, then, toward the *inactive,* toward unin-

---

[3] See José Ortega y Gasset, *The Revolt of the Masses* (New York: W. W. Norton, 1932), for a
look at these middle-class pragmatists, these typical "mass men" who dominate in society.
For a more recent analysis of these persons from a U.S. perspective, cf. William H. Whyte,
Jr., *The Organization Man* (New York: Simon & Schuster, 1956).

volved persons who do not appear to be ambitious and who seemingly make no real contributions toward the ongoing life of the country.

Pragmatists are much *like* the "illiterates" in that they do not really like ideas. They are essentially thing-oriented persons. They do not like to think, to contemplate and philosophize, to analyze and scrutinize, to play with concepts. They often accept serious, thoughtful messages in the course of media exposure, however, because they know that they *might be expected* to know something about their subjects. They must at least *appear* interested in ideas and issues, not because they really are but because they feel it will pay off in the long run. In effect they are interested in issues and ideas for a very practical reason.

Intellectuals

Intellectuals—and this term should really be in quotation marks because it indicates their attitude (rather than a judgmental label)—make up the smallest segment of the mass general audience, probably no more than 10 percent. Intellectuals are concerned with issues, esthetic matters, philosophical problems, and concepts. They take "serious" things seriously.[4] They are not thing-oriented persons; in fact, they are prone to disdain material values and to enthrone *ideas* as something to be concerned about. Again, it is a matter of concern, a matter of priorities, of what is most important to a human being, of being rational and thoughtful. Intellectuals are concerned with the broad strokes of human existence, with the more nonpractical aspects of life (from the point of view of material success). They are practicing humanists; they are the thinking, conceptualizing individuals, the creative persons. Or so they see themselves.

Intellectuals are not so much antisocial as nonsocial. They are usually self-centered or clannish, generally introverted, and prone to gravitate to those nonconformists who fit their image of the intellectual. They conform, then, to their own kind of nonconformity.

The intellectual, the "thinker," is a person who basically is against the whole *mass* concept. Fundamentally suspicious of the intellectually "unwashed" hoi polloi, they are antidemocratic in basic orientation, although they would probably deny this fact. They are elitists—would-be directors of society, sure of their own "insights" and suspicious of institutionalized or group decision making. They are cultural aristocrats, ideological autocrats, and, as they see it, the saving remnant of humanity; they are

---

[4] Ayn Rand, in *For the New Intellectual* (New York: Random House, 1961), describes intellectuals as "all those whose professions deal with the "humanities" and require a firm philosophical base." Her entire book is a forceful description of intellectuals as persons guided by *intellect*—not by "feelings, instincts, urges, wishes, whims, or revelations."

those who are not simply living in this world but are concerned about it philosophically—who are seeking, through intellectual exploration and argument, a better world for tomorrow.

Since intellectuals care little for mass society, they naturally care little for the mass media. *Mass* communication, they say, is necessarily low-level, aiming its superficial and bland pabulum at a fundamentally naive, uncaring, mechanistic, self-seeking audience. Intellectuals feel that the mass media, giving the masses what the masses appear to want, are leveling society and do not recognize their important responsibility to raise the thoughts and aspirations of the general public. Intellectuals, since they take serious things seriously, would like the mass media to do the same. One might doubt the sincerity of intellectuals in this respect, however, for if the mass media were really to make intellectuals of the members of the mass audience, those elitists who now enjoy the status of their minority position would find themselves lost in the mass again—and this, to the intellectual, is the worst of all possible fates.

Whereas "illiterates" read adventure-and-sex fiction and comic strips, and pragmatists glean their informational diet from *Reader's Digest, Time,* the local newspaper, and the *Wall Street Journal,* intellectual audience members read journals such as *Harper's, The Atlantic,* and their particular brand of political journal. Of course, to many intellectuals such magazines are always in danger of becoming "middlebrow" as the number of intellectuals continues to grow and the circulations of those journals increase. So the avant-garde intellectuals are always pushing further and further out, seeking magazines, newspapers, recordings, and books that are "different," so as to isolate themselves more securely from the encroaching mediocrity.

And whereas pragmatists embrace serious material because they think it will help them progress in the practical world, intellectuals embrace such material for its own sake. They imbibe thought-provoking information because they want to think and enjoy thinking. They like being stimulated mentally; they need esthetic and catalytic communication in the same way pragmatists need directive and normative communication. (Of course, there are "fakes"—pseudo-intellectuals who have no genuine desire to think and create but have joined the intellectual world for some *pragmatic* reason, but we will not deal with these persons. It is enough to say simply that they are intellectual "leeches," sucking the elitist blood from the intellectual community so as to pass for something that they are really not.)

One type of intellectual, really different from the pseudo-intellectual, is the *ideologue.* Ideologues are intellectuals gone wild on one subject, dedicated crusaders for a particular cause. Usually they begin as balanced intellectuals, truth-seeking and open-minded, but slowly one particular idea takes precedence. They increasingly focus on one area of interest, one political orientation, one concept, one research methodology, one intellectual concern. They become obsessed with one idea, which becomes a consuming interest, leading them to a kind of monolithic world-view that in their eyes is the panacea for all problems. They are intellectual crusaders, who become ever more dedicated to their "program" until they become biased, extreme, and intolerant of dissenting positions. Ideologues, often extremely intelligent and articulate, make good propagandists. Usually persuasive and well informed (at least in one area), they are essentailly missionaries out to convert others.

Many writers seem to feel that most intellectuals are *at times* ideologues. It does seem that the passionate concern most intellectuals have for ideas often tends to turn them into polemic zealots of almost fanatical fervor. If one had to differentiate, one could say true intellectuals have no greater mission than speculation, contemplation, and meditation. They are not trying to impose their ideas on others. But ideologues think *in order to* persuade, crusade, campaign. True intellectuals like to think and create, if for no other reason than their own satisfaction. Not so ideologues; they must be pushing their concepts and ideology on others.[5]

AUDIENCE BEHAVIOR AND MOTIVATION

Now that we have looked at three types of audiences to which mass media must appeal, let us turn briefly to a more general view of the mass audience as a whole. Why do members of the audience make media selections and message selections from the media in the way they do? Why do they accept the offerings of some media and not others, and why do they accept certain offerings of one medium and not other offerings? A large number of factors affect the selections an audience member makes from among and within the mass media. Certainly two of the most important are (1) the availability of the message and (2) the potential for personal gain.

The first of these general principles states that audience members take the path of least effort, that they naturally tend to read, view, and listen to media and messages that are most accessible. The second principle assumes that audience members expose themselves to messages that will give them the greatest reward. Of course, it should be said that, in a sense, all messages offer some degree of reward, even if it is a kind of escapism or momentary enjoyment. It should also be noted that audience members are seeking, often unconsciously, messages that reinforce their opinions, pre-

---

[5] See Eric Hoffer, *The True Believer* (New York: Harper, 1951), for a fascinating discussion of ideologues and mass movements. Cf. Gustave Le Bon, *The Crowd*.

conceptions, and biases. They take in those messages compatible with their mental and psychological predispositions—messages that will cause them no "pain" because they tend to substantiate their beliefs. A person's past experiences and philosophy of life play important parts in determining which media and messages he or she will select. This factor in message receiving is usually called *selective perception*.

In addition to these factors, there are others related to a person's reading a certain newspaper, watching a particular television program, subscribing to a certain magazine, or selecting certain messages from any of these. Leisure time availability, state of health, political orientation, media availability at the time, special interests, finances, and habit—all these contribute in varying degrees to media and message selection.

Now that we have looked briefly at factors influencing selection of media and messages, let us consider some reasons why audiences turn to the mass media in the first place. What motivates them? Although motivation differs with the person, there does seem to be a basic core of relevant motivational factors, any one of which would explain the attraction of the media.

Three main motivational factors suggest themselves:

1. *Loneliness*. People are basically lonely. They do not like to find themselves unoccupied or detached from others. Such detachment gives them a sense of social estrangement, frustration, and anxiety. The next best thing to being with other persons is being with a mass medium of communication. In fact, for many persons it is *more satisfying* to be with a mass medium than with other persons; mass media make no social or conversational demands on them. Television, especially, satisfies the longing for companionship; the TV set becomes a friend helping to fill the time with pictures and sounds, and asking very little in return. The print media are friendly time consumers and companions, too, but perhaps to a lesser degree. At any rate, loneliness is a very powerful motivating factor that pushes people into the presence of the mass media.

2. *Curiosity*. People are basically curious. They are interested in what is happening around them—what others are doing, saying, and thinking. Outside their immediate surroundings, there is no way really to satisfy this curiosity other than by turning to the mass media. People are curious about a myriad of things, and not only those things that will affect them in a direct way. Curiosity, in fact, is probably the prime factor impelling people to the mass media. What is happening? Who is involved in it? Why is it happening? And, of course, in many cases: How might it affect me? A person's curiosity appears practically insatiable; the mass media can depend

on audiences' continuing to consume vast quantities of material about isolated happenings, quirks of nature, and eccentric persons and groups, along with all kinds of gossip and rumor. Curiosity may have killed the cat, as the old saying goes, but it has proved the very lifeblood of mass communication.

3. *Self-aggrandizement.* Human beings are basically selfish. They desire information that will help them achieve their individual ideas of success and happiness. They want help in their idealistic and realistic pursuits. They seek substantiation of their prejudices and biases. They want philosophical and religious reassurance and guidance. They want practical messages that will be of personal service to them, and information that will be of immediate, and also of long-range, value. They want messages that will help them make decisions, purchase products, and derive rewards from their activities. They also want to be humored, cajoled, and entertained. In short, they want their practical, philosophical, and religious needs all served by the mass media.

CONCLUSION

It might be well to reiterate what was said at the beginning of this chapter: It is very difficult to discuss and analyze mass media audiences. Yet in spite of the extreme complexity of this subject, it should be dealt with more often. Most books on mass communication give audiences little or no attention, concentrating on communicators and on the media themselves. This emphasis is understandable, of course, since most persons tend to place major importance on the *sending* rather than the *receiving* of messages.

Also, the sender—the mass communicator or the mass medium—is a person or institution that can quite easily be observed and described. Mass audiences, on the other hand, are basically nebulous, fluid, and unobservable—"distributed" or dispersed entities without real structure and basically inaccessible to empirical depth study.

If there is any aspect of the mass communication process that cries out for systematic study, it is the mass media audience or audiences. Just what (or who) are they? Does their fluidity have a pattern? What kind of commonality of message perception exists among their members? How do mass media messages affect them collectively and their members individually?

These and other questions admit of no easy answers. But we do know that audiences are important. They are the consumers of media—and so, the real *raison d'être* for their existence and for the communicators who speak to them.

AFTERTHOUGHTS

1. Is it really possible to talk meaningfully about a "mass audience"? Is there any way to analyze such an audience?

2. Are the two main audience types—general and specialized—discussed in the chapter meaningful and realistic? Do they not often overlap? If they do, how does this overlapping harm the validity of the typology?

3. If, as Robert O'Hara contends, the mass audience is one of mass communication's greatest fallacies, should we cease using the term and thinking about such an audience? What alternative term or terms might we use?

4. The attitudinal ternary typology suggested for audiences—"illiterate," pragmatic, and intellectual—has some inherent problems. What are they? Do you see any value for media managers in such a typology?

5. We have said that loneliness especially causes people to expose themselves to the mass media. Do you see any reason to believe that loneliness is diminished by increased media exposure?

CHAPTER 10

Critics: Appraising the Media

Media criticism is, indeed, a subjective and personal enterprise. Evaluating or appraising media quality and performance has become a popular enterprise for laypersons, academicians, and media people themselves. What makes a good newspaper, or TV program or magazine? "It's just a matter of opinion," we hear. All right, but only a fool would think that all opinions are equal, that all appraisals warrant the same respect.

Off-the-cuff critiques, hasty opinions expressed with no real supporting evidence, generalized statements of evaluation based on one or two incidents—all of these are common today. And such critical offerings issue not only from uninformed citizens, but from so-called professional media critics as well. Readers or hearers of such criticism often find themselves wondering about the qualifications of the critics.

Appraising the media is a mammoth enterprise in today's society. Nonmedia people, especially intellectuals and politicians, are articulating their opinions about the mass media more often, more loudly, and more assuredly. It has been a short step, indeed, from the critical appraisal of the press offered by the controversial Hutchins Commission in the 1940s[1] to the many sorties into the area of media criticism undertaken by a whole series of disgruntled politicians, from Spiro Agnew to Gary Hart.

---

[1] Its formal name was the Commission on Freedom of the Press, a group of 13 men who studied the U.S. press in the 1940s and submitted its report in form of a book, *A Free and Responsible Press* (1947). The commission's chairman was Dr. Robert M. Hutchins, then Chancellor of the University of Chicago.

Voices are heard from other quarters as well. In the late 1980s the Reverend Jerry Falwell lambasted the press for its "trashy" content and its "liberal bias," Jim and Tammy Bakker bemoaned the press's dedication to "undermining" their ministry, and the Reverend Jimmy Swaggart maintained his vendetta against a press which he saw as destructive to religious values. And there is no paucity of critical remarks about media bias and excesses from special-interest groups, minorities, and various and sundry concerned, or offended, individuals.

The academic world is also spawning a torrent of media criticism, generally of a political or ideological nature. Another strain of criticism (labeled neo-Marxist) suggests that the American media are corrupted principally by wealthy media entrepreneurs who think more of profits and worker exploitation than they do about individual rights, dignity, and welfare. Other appraisers of the media point to their sleazy nature, their negativism, their sensationalism, their catering to the lowest common denominator, and their callousness and general lack of ethics.

MEDIA SYSTEMS UNDER ATTACK

Certain consistent themes emerge from the general appraisal of the mass media in America. One of the most common is that media owners are too concerned with their own interests, too interested in making money, and not interested enough in public service. Some believe that advertisers are wielding too much influence on the media, or that a single socioeconomic class (the upper class) controls the mass media and that the media are therefore basically conservative and tend to perpetuate the status quo (which favors the wealthy). A related criticism is that media owners are "in bed with" the political leadership of the country and thus pull their punches when it comes to promoting any real change in American society.

Another criticism is that there is not enough diversity or competition in the mass media and that a monopolistic trend toward group or chain ownership, coupled with the high cost of getting into the media business, is exacerbating this problem. Average citizens and certain minority groups simply do not have proper access to the media for the airing of their opinions and perspectives, say many contemporary media appraisers. There are even some critics who believe that such media "disenfranchisement" is tantamount to a repudiation of the concept of press freedom, strange as that opinion might seem to others.

Another common criticism of the media is that atypical, eccentric, and destructive persons and groups are given too much emphasis and that trivia, sensation, sex, and violence are getting undue, disproportionate, and unrealistic attention. And while some observers of the media contend that they expose *too much* sensitive information about government, others maintain that the media are too timid and cautious in divulging information to the public.

If "the people have a right to know," just *what* does this concept entail divulging? Everything? Including details of a personal or private nature? Only those things related to a person's job, or to the "public" business? Some critics call for more care with respect to invasion-of-privacy issues; others want more information revealed about almost every aspect of life. The "right to know" *what*—if there is any such right at all—is a critical question and one that has not been answered satisfactorily.

What function(s) should the media perform in a society? In a free society, should any responsibilities or obligations be imposed on the media? Who should impose them? These are vital and persistent questions.

The Hutchins Commission, in their 1947 report, posited five main requirements for the mass media and, after judging American media by these standards, concluded that they were not really socially responsible.[2] The Commission maintained that the media should do the following:

1. Present a "truthful, comprehensive and intelligent account of the day's events in a context which gives them meaning"
2. Provide a "forum for the exchange of comment and criticism"
3. Project a "representative picture of the constituent groups in the society"
4. Present and clarify "the goals and values of the society"
5. Give "full access to the day's intelligence"

Given these largely unachievable standards (at least all but the second one are overly idealistic), it is little wonder that the Commission's verdict was that the American press was not responsible. This whole concept of "social responsibility" and journalistic ethics will be taken up in Part Three of this book; at present it is enough to say that anyone vaguely familiar with the intrinsic problems of the mass media will know that these

---

[2] See Chapter 2 ("The Requirements") in *A Free and Responsible Press* (Chicago: University of Chicago Press, 1947), pp. 20–29. An excellent discussion of more recent criticisms of the press and a reappraisal of the Hutchins Commission can be found in these three books: Bernard Rubin, *Media, Politics, and Democracy* (New York: Oxford University Press, 1977), esp. Chapter 3; J. Herbert Altschull, *Agents of Power: The Role of the News Media in Human Affairs* (White Plains, NY: Longman, 1984), Chapter 8; and a book appraising (unfavorably) the American media's coverage of a presidential administration: Mark Hertsgaard, *On Bended Knee: The Press and the Reagan Presidency* (New York: Farrar, Straus, Giroux, 1988).

"responsibilities" as set forth by the Hutchins Commission are unrealizable fantasies of impractical intellectuals.

CRITICISMS OF INDIVIDUAL MEDIA

When we come down from the mountaintop and begin looking at individual media in a direct, specific way, many less monumental and imposing criticisms suggest themselves. For instance, most media are careless with basics—spelling, punctuation, pronunciation and enunciation, names, quotations, statistics, and so on.

Look carefully at any newspaper. Consider its superficiality—in its selection of stories and pictures, in the way it handles each story. Glance down and across the columns; notice the haphazard fashion in which unrelated stories and pictures are presented. Is there an unsynthesized mishmash of bits and pieces of news and views? Look again and you will see that probably close to two-thirds of the total space is taken up by advertising, scattered meaninglessly throughout the pages.[3]

Notice a particular headline: Does it reflect what the story below it says? It may say just the opposite. Take a closer look at all that white space around the type and headlines, at those large, space-consuming headlines themselves,[4] at the typographical ornaments and borders. Ask yourself why the headlines and many of the pictures have to be so large, why there is so much white space here and there. Is it because the reader demands it? Do *you* demand it? How many additional stories and pictures could be in that newspaper if headline and picture size was scaled down?

One might be led to think that many newspaper editors are not as concerned about your knowing what is going on as they pretend; it appears they may be more interested in typographical experimentation and aesthetic appeal than in publishing news and views in as large amounts as possible. Take a close, careful look at any of the individual media and you will find similar aspects to criticize. There is no shortage of faults in any of the mass media.

---

[3] Why not put all advertising in a separate section of the newspaper? And why not classify it (even the display ads) for easy reference? We know the old reply: Advertisers want their ads adjacent to editorial matter so readers will see the ad whether they want to or not. But isn't this somewhat contradictory to another advertising dictum: that advertising is as sought after and popular with the reader as news?

[4] The great majority of newspaper copies are home delivered or sent through the mails. There is no need for large, eye-catching headlines on most papers, and there is no evidence that readers demand them.

WHO SHOULD APPRAISE THE MEDIA?

Since there is plenty to criticize in the media, the next question that presents itself is this: *Who* is really qualified to appraise the media? Professionals in the media generally think that nonmedia people know too little about the problems of the media, about its intrinsic weaknesses and specialized procedures, to offer meaningful and valid evaluations. Why, ask the media people, should a lawyer or doctor claim to know any more about the mass media than a journalist knows about medicine or law? Is it not presumptuous for a physics teacher or a state senator to tell media workers what they should or should not do? These are pertinent questions and they are being heard more every year as the mass media, by touching the lives of increasing numbers of citizens, are inviting a growing torrent of criticism.

One of the main faults that press people found with the Hutchins Commission's evaluation of the press in 1947 was that none of the commissioners was a journalist or media person. Therefore, many editors and journalists said, they could not take the criticism very seriously—it was uninformed, unrealistic, and impractical, and it tilted with journalistic windmills that professional press people would have known really did not exist.

The press has long considered *itself* a social critic—the "fourth estate," the "watchdog on government," or some such sobriquet—but it has been particularly sensitive when any outside person or group has dared criticize *it* or evaluate *its* performance. Newspapers traditionally evaluate and criticize—but seldom do they criticize or evaluate themselves or one another. Throughout the history of world journalism, newspapers have found it easy enough to point out all sorts of weaknesses in every other social institution; they bludgeon this man, that party, this group, that law. But when someone points out the derelictions of these same newspapers, newsprint is filled with indignant screams. Television commentators can regularly evaluate politicians—even Presidents—but pity the poor person who scores a telling criticism against one of these television sages!

The same media that insist that it is impossible to evaluate in a valid way the performance of the press or to rank newspapers as to quality proceed daily to evaluate politicians, colleges, universities, libraries, books, and any number of persons, places, and things. It is rather strange that they often appear to think that only communication media have the expertise to make intelligent, valid, and worthwhile value judgments.

All of this is not to denigrate the value of social criticism emanating from the mass media; we in the United States are extremely fortunate to have a critical journalism. And it is undeniably true, as newspaper apologists are quick to mention, that the Western democratic press serves as a check on government. But who, one should ask and keep on asking, is serving as a check on the press? Those who say there are no press excesses are blind indeed; and those who say that press excesses do exist but do not need to be brought to public attention have a peculiar ethical myopia. A nation's journalists are prone to cry in anguished tones about governmental secrecy, uncooperative sources, and unethical practices in various segments of their society, and all the while go their way in their own "closed societies," unexamined, uncriticized, and in all too many cases unchallenged. Informed and perceptive criticism of the media would seem to be the best check on the press in a libertarian system. But, alas, criticism of this type is rare indeed!

Pockets of criticism of the press, of course, exist in all countries; and individual voices cry out periodically against press irresponsibility. Various press councils and journalistic groups mouth their platitudes, publish their codes, deal in generalities, and hope. But this criticism is sporadic and too often isolated; too seldom is it specific; too seldom is it positive. And too seldom does it result from rigorous study and thought.

Back to the earlier question: Who is really qualified to criticize and appraise the press? Perhaps every person would have his or her own answer to this question, but one thing is certain: There is no reason to believe that informed, intelligent, helpful criticism and evaluation cannot come from persons who themselves are not part of any of the mass media. Mass communication is everybody's business. It is too public, too pervasive, too powerful to be left completely to the rather small group of media people who prepare and disseminate messages.

But we do not dare try to tell surgeons how to operate, the mass media apologists will declare. These media people, attempting to draw the protective cloak of professionalism about themselves, would have a difficult time drawing an analogy between their "profession" and that of a physician. Actually, journalism (one aspect of the media industry or trade), which comes closest to being a profession, has no clearly defined body of knowledge or professional lore; it has no licensing procedures that protect it and the public from corrupt, unscrupulous, or incompetent practioners; it has no generally agreed-upon code of ethics or guidelines for "correct" conduct. So it might be well if media people would divest themselves of the illusion that they belong to a profession and that their "professional expertise" makes them singularly qualified to criticize the mass media.

Although journalism is not a profession in the same sense that medicine and law are professions, the most prominent and serious of its practitioners agree pretty well on many of the fundamental aspects of what might be considered "good" journalism. For example, graphics people and page designers can agree pretty well as to what is good typography and page layout. Leading photographers can at least agree on what is *not* good photography. Journalists who take writing seriously and have concentrated on style and effectiveness generally agree as to what is good writing and what is not.

In other words, serious practitioners in the mass media do have a pretty good idea of what is quality and what is not. They do recognize a hierarchy of value; they do have standards. In spite of the high degree of subjectivity in journalism—as compared with medicine, for example—there does remain a rather large area where there are standards of quality. All is *not* relative in journalism. One person's opinion is *not* just as good as any other person's. Some media people *are* more effective than others; some stories *are* better written than others; some TV commercials *are* more artistic and effective. Some radio voices *are* superior to others. Some foreign correspondents *are* more accurate and perceptive than others; some headline writers *are* more skillful. And some photographers *are* more imaginative and technically proficient than others.

So it can be concluded that there are ways to evaluate media and discriminate among them and that both media people *and* nonmedia people can offer valuable criticism and evaluation of these media. What it takes is intelligence, interest, concern, systematic analysis, open-mindedness, and a desire to be fair and unbiased. Lawyers or biology teachers who criticize the media in this framework might actually, because of their more neutral stance, provide criticism and evaluation that is more valid than that of media persons, who stand too close to the object of their criticism.

A PROBLEM OF CONTEXT?

In this age of relativity, when special considerations have taken precedence over standards, it is easy to understand why many people say that it is unrealistic to rate this newspaper as good and that one as bad, to say that this page makeup is better than that one, that this television newscast is more reliable and better produced than another one. It is really impossible to evaluate a mass medium or a portion of its message, the relativists say, unless you know all the circumstances surrounding the medium and the specific context in which it exists. They would, in effect, make all media evaluation nothing more than a description of how well a particular medium is doing with what it has at a given place and time and under its specific circumstances.

The context is all important, they say. How can you possibly say that the *New York Times* is a better newspaper than, say, the *Wichita Eagle?* The *Eagle* in its context (Wichita and Kansas) may be just as good as the *Times* in its context. It is doubtful that many serious students of newspapers would accept this thesis, but the "context advocates" have a certain amount of logic to their argument, and such a position appeals to large numbers of people who see themselves as tolerant, progressive, and open-minded. Contextualists, if they took their concept far enough, would find themselves in the position of not being able to compare any mass medium with another as to quality; they would logically have to assert that every single medium ultimately exists *in its own context* and cannot, therefore, be compared with any other medium.

Context is, of course, extremely important when one is evaluating media and comparing one with another. No intelligent critic, for instance, would fault the *Podunk Weekly Gazette* for having only eight pages an issue in contrast to the *Washington Post*'s bulky edition. No critic would compare a television network's 30-minute newscast with a small independent station's coverage. No sensible critic would expect of *The New Republic* or the *National Review* what he or she would of *Time* or *Newsweek*. A person who would say that the *National Geographic* was a "better" magazine than *Esquire* could not be taken very seriously as a critic. So context *is* important for the media evaluator; the problem comes when the concept of context in criticism is taken too far—when the critic becomes like one who grows weeds around his house instead of roses because "in their own context" they are just as good.

A serious, educated person, in the media or out, will be discriminating and will reject, or at least question, the idea of qualitative relativity. He or she undoubtedly realizes that a large part of becoming educated is learning to see differences in quality, to pass judgments based on intelligent criteria, to discriminate and to tell the good product from the shoddy. As a person becomes better educated and more perceptive, he or she should become increasingly aware that all newspapers are not equal, that all communicators are not equally skilled, and that significant differences in quality exist everywhere. Those wishing to be critics or evaluators of the media will seriously seek to ascertain the most useful criteria that may be used for evaluation and criticism.

Certainly they will not forget the importance of context as they search for valid criteria of evaluation. For example, they must consider the theory or concept of the press under which a particular mass medium falls. One cannot evaluate a communist newspaper in the same way as a libertarian newspaper. The overall theoretical or ideological purpose, in other words, must be taken into consideration. And weeklies are compared with weeklies, medium-sized dailies with others of their own kind; likewise for big-city dailies and specialized dailies.

This, then, is a basic assumption of media criticism: criticize, evaluate, and compare only within contexts—or rough or broad contexts. Usually this is done by serious critics. But an interesting question arises: Is it not possible to say that one magazine (in context A) is better than another magazine (in context B)? Suppose the magazine in one context does almost everything in a more careful, professional, and discriminating manner than the other magazine does in its context? Is it not, then, a better magazine in a general, *non*contextual sense? Cannot the *New York Times* rationally be considered a better newspaper than some poorly printed, superficial weekly or daily in a small town, even though they are in different contexts? Obviously so. Therefore, we can assume that, although context is usually invoked in media criticism, it is possible to talk about quality across contexts also. In spite of the difficulty of evaluating and making distinctions among media, we believe that it can be done and done intelligently and meaningfully. Certain standards do exist. There are better and worse ways to do things journalistically; if not, then journalism education is a fraud and the student is wasting time and money.

There is a hierarchy of value or worth or quality in the mass media. Too long have media people, and others, evaded this issue; too long have they been reluctant to pass judgment on the media; too long have they timidly acted as if all newspapers were equally good (because *somebody* liked them and they fulfilled *some* purpose); too long have media people, and outsiders, been silent when they could have been saying loudly and clearly which media were good and which were bad and giving the reasons why. Let us now consider some of the criteria that can be used to evaluate the mass media of communication.

CRITERIA OF EVALUATION

Certain "common denominators" among evaluative criteria may be used in appraising a given medium in any context. Thus, there are certain factors that must be considered in judging *any* newspaper. And also, for example, if we are considering the quality of television newscasts—whether in the United States or in the Soviet Union—considerations such as pronunciation, enunciation, and voice resonance will always enter into the appraisal. These are examples of criteria that are useful regardless of the size or location of the medium; they might be called *noncontextual* criteria. For example, certain noncontextual evaluative criteria for newspapers may be applied to any newspaper, whether weekly or daily, communist or capitalist, large or small, urban or rural, general or specialized. A critic, of course, would not cite only one of these criteria in passing judgment; rather, he or she would attempt to invoke as many of them as possible.

First, there are at least eight *internal* criteria—referring only to the newspaper itself—that an evaluator would find useful in appraising or criticizing any newspaper.

1. *Good typography and makeup techniques.* There are typographic and design specialists in every country. They are the "experts" who, in a sense, define what is good typography and newspaper design. They know when typefaces clash; they know when blocks of type or pictures and type are juxtapositioned in such ways as to offend good taste or esthetic sensitivities. This criterion is, in a way, relativistic in that what offends esthetic sensitivities in one culture might not offend in another, but at least within a single culture this can be considered an objective criterion. Regardless of the language used, one does not crowd alphabetical units or space them so as to disrupt quick recognition; one does not transpose units or "mass" type; and one does not use different varieties of type in the same sentence—and probably not in the same story. So there are some common denominators of good typography, and typographic experts or "professionals" in all countries know them.

2. *Editing and proofreading care.* Regardless of where the newspaper is published, a universal criterion of evaluation is the care with which it is edited and proofread. Sloppy editing show up in any language, in any size newspaper, and in any nation, and it is considered undesirable. Poor proofreading, resulting in numerous errors, is also, obviously, a negative factor with respect to the quality of the newspaper product.

3. *Correct spelling, punctuation, grammar.* Although permissiveness appears to be growing in this area, there are still basic and generally standardized rules for spelling, punctuation, and grammar that educated persons in any country understand and respect. What constitutes "good" writing may be considerably subjective, but good (correct) grammar can be checked, as can spelling and punctuation. A newspaper that evidences care in such matters gives readers the feeling that they can have confidence in what the newspaper has to say. Carefulness in spelling and punctuation usually implies overall carefulness with respect to content.

4. *Picture reproduction and printing excellence.* Some newspapers have clearer picture reproduction than others. It is not difficult even for a layperson to judge quality in this area when studying a newspaper. In like manner, the general printing quality is obviously better on some newspapers than on others. Care in printing is an appropriate criterion to use regardless of what newspaper you are studying.

5. *Balance in editorial and news material.* When you are considering general newspapers, this is a useful criterion for evaluation. The assumption is that a good general newspaper will be balanced. It will not be overloaded with any one type of subject matter; for instance, it will not have two-thirds of its news pages filled with foreign news. Just what the proper balance is, of course, nobody is certain. But a reasonably bright person can tell when the balance is *not* proper.

6. *Concern with staff quality.* An evaluator of a newspaper can, by observing and interviewing, learn a great deal about the newspaper's concern with having a good staff—well-educated, skilled, and intelligent workers evidencing high morale. The evaluator can check into such things as salary levels, the number of specialists and foreign correspondents, training and other educational programs for staff members, job assignments and their correlation with special training and interests, and intra-staff communication.

7. *Concern with editorial policy.* The evaluator can check to see how much emphasis is given to editorial policy. Does the newspaper seems to have one? Do staff members know what it is? How well does the newspaper achieve this policy—or reach its goals?

8. *Concern with self-evaluation and outside criticism.* The assumption is that a good newspaper will evaluate its philosophy and practices regularly and will welcome criticism. The evaluator can very easily appraise the newspaper's activities in this respect.

There is another internal criterion: reliability or accuracy of reportage. Although quotations, facts, and, in a sense, whole stories can be verified by a careful and persistent critic, nevertheless it is very difficult to test factuality. That is, it is not a clearly evaluative criterion. Nevertheless, it is a possible criterion that may be used to ascertain the quality of any newspaper, regardless of its context.

Five other criteria might be called *external* since they involve measures of how highly a paper is regarded by its readers and users.

1. *Frequency of quotation and allusion.* This factor should be considered in evaluating a newspaper, although taken alone it is not very meaningful. When a newspaper is often used as a source in speeches, conversations, and academic lectures and by other publications and other media, this is an indication that the newspaper has a good reputation and that it is having some impact on opinion leaders and the people whose opinions they lead. One does not quote a newspaper unless one believes it has credibility.

2. *Number of library subscriptions.* Although it is quite true that many libraries subscribe to newspapers in a rather haphazard and thoughtless fashion, it may be assumed that libraries try to get newspapers that are the best representatives of their cities and nations. Certain newspapers, believed to be the most reliable for researchers, are commonly found in libraries around the world. A person can expect to find newspapers such as

Le Monde of France, *Neue Zürcher Zeitung* of Switzerland, *Die Zeit* of West Germany, *Asahi* of Japan, *Corriere della Sera* of Italy, the *Guardian* of England, *Pravda* of the Soviet Union, and the *New York Times* in almost every major library in any nation of the world. Their presence indicates something of their quality and value.

3. *Reputation among journalists and historians.* A good way to judge the quality of a newspaper is to find out what journalists think of it. Also it is well to ascertain the reliance historians place on it. Historians do use newspapers as sources—in spite of their constant criticism of the press generally—and it is useful to find out which newspapers they most frequently use, and why.

4. *Reputation in government.* Which newspapers do politicians, government officials, and diplomats take most seriously? Which ones do they read regularly to get what they feel is reliable and insightful information about their localities, states, and nations and about foreign countries? This is a key question when considering the quality of a newspaper.

5. *Reputation in academic circles.* College and university professors and administrators are among the most critical of mass media appraisers. When a significant segment of the academic world, including students, thinks a particular newspaper is good, there is reason to believe that it is.

The thirteen evaluative criteria above (eight internal and five external) are certainly not all the common denominators that might be considered, but we feel they form a useful core of determinants of quality and provide a systematic method by which a newspaper may be analyzed. An analyst using these guidelines can go a long way toward forming an intelligent and valid impression about the quality of a particular newspaper or can come to a rational conclusion about how one newspaper compares with another in quality.

Some may discount the value of such criteria and persist in their belief that "quality" is such a subjective and relative concept that newspapers (or other media) cannot be evaluated and compared in this way. Actually, in practice they do not accept the premise that it cannot be done, for they proceed to judge and compare regularly. So, it would appear valuable to have a systematic set of evaluative criteria, despite its limitations, that can be used to make criticism and evaluation more intelligent, complete, and valid.

CRITERIA FOR "FREE" NEWSPAPERS

The criteria for evaluation that have been briefly discussed above relate to *all* newspapers, regardless of what political or ideological context they may represent. They would apply to the Soviet Union's *Izvestia,* Spain's

ABC, or the *St. Louis Post-Dispatch* of the United States. What we need to consider now are a few other criteria that might help a student of the press evaluate a newspaper published in a free or libertarian nation. He or she could use the criteria just discussed and then supplement them with these others that are especially relevant to the libertarian press, which, as you will recall, advocates diversity of viewpoints.

1. *Concern for "the people's right to know."* How conscientious is the newspaper about informing the people, its readers, especially in the area of governmental affairs? The libertarian newspaper presumably is dedicated to letting the people know, to breaking down walls of secrecy, to exposing governmental corruption, to making people better informed voters. Is this just "talk," or does the newspaper evidence in its coverage that it is really dedicated to this concept?

2. *Concern for public service.* Here is another plank in the platform of the libertarian press. How seriously does the newspaper reflect such a concern? What does it do in the area of public service? "Public service" here must be defined by the newspaper as being something more than simply providing the public with something to read.

3. *Pluralism in news and views.* How well does the newspaper achieve a diversity of news and views on its pages? Is there an attempt to provide some kind of balance of argument in the opinion columns and a realistic range of viewpoints and subject matter in the news columns?

4. *Resistance to outside pressures.* A bedrock principle of a libertarian newspaper is editorial freedom. How well does the newspaper ward off outside pressures that might infringe on its decision making? What outside pressures are most dangerous to the newspaper and how are they dealt with?

5. *Separation of "news" and "views."* Traditionally in the libertarian press there is the concept of keeping facts and the reporters' opinions separate, clearly demarcated so that the reader knows what he or she is reading. Although this idea is beginning to erode as "interpretive reporting" and "advocacy journalism" make deeper penetrations into traditional libertarian journalism, it is still generally considered a firm principle. How well does a particular newspaper achieve this separation of reporting and analyzing/opinionating?

6. *Headline accuracy.* How well do the newspaper's headlines reflect the substance and tone of the stories beneath them? Do they give accurate information and impressions, or do they distort the story and deviate from its implications?

7. *Reliance on own staffers.* To what degree does the newspaper use its own staff members to report the news and write columns, features, and editorials?
8. *Economic stability.* In a libertarian press, it is very important that the newspaper be in good financial condition. This gives it an opportunity to improve its product, get better staffers, and ward off many pressures. How economically stable is the newspaper?

CRITERIA FOR "CONTROLLED" NEWSPAPERS

Are there not also criteria especially relevant to newspapers published in authoritarian or "controlled" societies, such as the Soviet Union, Paraguay, or Iran? Undoubtedly there are many, but a few will be suggested here. Some of these, you will discover, overlap criteria previously listed. All must be viewed from the perspective of the political philosophy of the authoritarian or totalitarian state, not ours.

1. *Understanding of, and achieving of, purpose or goal.* How well does the entire staff understand the purpose and goals of the newspaper and of the press generally? How well is the policy communicated internally, and how well are the goals achieved?
2. *Homogeneity of staff.* Is the staff dedicated to the purposes and goals of the newspaper? Is the staff unified in philosophy and journalistic activities? Do they, in other words, work together to achieve an end or do they often work at variance?
3. *Self-criticism and evaluation.* Does the newspaper have regular conferences for the purpose of self-criticism and discussion of press–government cooperation? Are there regular sessions where the total operation is scrutinized carefully and changes are made to permit the newspaper better to achieve its purpose?
4. *Dedication to staff improvement.* How much emphasis does the newspaper give to continuing education of the staff, to indoctrination, to critique sessions, to moving staffers from one job to another, to getting better people in every position?
5. *General media system cooperation.* How well does the newspaper integrate its activities with those of the whole media system? How much coordination is there with other newspapers, with television and radio, with news agencies, government, and various social institutions?
6. *Elimination of unstabilizing elements.* How well does the newspaper exclude information—stories, pictures, and the like—that will harm social stability and a sense of national unity or that will tend to undermine progress? Ideally, the whole editorial product

must eliminate discrepancies, contradictions, frustrations, puzzling questions, and negative criticisms that will destroy people's
confidence in their government and nation.

7. *Staff dedication and dependability.* Does the newspaper have staff
members who staunchly believe in the system and the paper's role
and who are not dedicated to "rocking the boat"? How dependable
are they? In other words, how little direct supervision do they need
in order to function? Every journalist must be dedicated to seeing
that the newspaper is harmonious with, not an irritant to, government policy and progress.

8. *Use of resource persons.* How often and how well does the newspaper make use of specialists and prominent persons outside journalism? The better newspapers will use such resource persons on a
regular basis to write guest articles of all kinds. In fact, the more
enlightened the newspaper, the more it will welcome to its pages
the contributions of nonstaffers. Resource persons, of the *right
kind* of course, are extremely important in the journalism of
a "controlled" press system. They are "safe" establishment
spokespersons who will reinforce government policy.

As we noted, many of the criteria for "controlled" newspapers given
above could also be applied to so-called "free" newspapers. Also it must
be said that in some ways all newspapers are controlled—by somebody.
We are simply suggesting some criteria that might be more appropriate for
media systems that are state controlled than those that are institutionally
controlled. Obviously when we call the former "controlled" and the latter
"free," we are exhibiting a certain cultural and ideological bias. But in the
context of Western terminology, we will probably not be misunderstood
by American readers.

One could, of course, point out many American control mechanisms
that impinge on freedom of the press here, and could at the same time point
to the lessening of controls (*glasnost*) in the Soviet Union as the media
system experiences some openness. Yet we believe that it is one thing to
appraise American media and quite another to appraise Soviet media, and
we cannot use identical criteria. The systems are still quite different, and
what makes *Pravda* a good newspaper is not what makes *The New York
Times* a good newspaper.

AFTERTHOUGHTS

1. What qualifications do you think are necessary for a media critic—one who
appraises or criticizes media? What is wrong with the above question?

2. No doubt many people would fault various media for many of their activities
and would even abolish certain of these activities if they had the power. How

can you reconcile a belief in press freedom with censorship of objectionable material?

3. Is it proper, in an appraisal of media, to compare one type of newspaper with another type—such as the *New York Times* with the *Wall Street Journal,* or one kind of magazine (e.g., *Playboy*) with another (e.g., *National Geographic*)? Or, for example, a small town weekly newspaper with a metropolitan daily?

4. If you were a judge for a contest that sought to recognize one television station for "best news coverage" in your city, what criteria would you use in your appraisal?

5. If you were appraising magazines primarily on the basis of "good writing," how would you determine whether it was present? Are you any better qualified at knowing "good writing" than the magazines' editors and writers?

CHAPTER 11

Media Effects: Myth and Reality

Communication research is a relatively young science. It is a science made especially difficult by the complexities of the human mind, the essential focus of much such research. Psychology, the basis on which part of communication research is built, is an inexact science that deals primarily with the individual. Communication researchers compound their task by focusing on the reactions of the *mass* audience.

The difficulties in this type of research, of course, do not stop here. Frequently, it is important to know the precise content of a message in order to evaluate its effect on an audience. With print media, doing this was relatively simple; the message could be carefully examined and the various parts of it catalogued in a process called *content analysis*.

Radio and television, however, have defied this kind of analysis. By their very nature, they are at this point impossible to review comprehensively. One would have to devise an acceptable system of cataloguing, with regard to radio, not only words but also voice inflections, background sounds, and pauses. In reviewing a television message, a researcher would have to code body movements, including facial expressions. Kinesics, the study of this body language, is now in its infancy, even though kinesicists estimate that most human communication is nonverbal rather than verbal. In that sense, television has returned human communication to its natural, preprint state by imparting qualities of sound and motion to the mass media.

Communication researchers, recognizing the near impossibility of coding the sound and motion messages of the mass media, have largely avoided any thorough analysis of this kind of communication. Cataloguing sound and motion bias remains a challenge. For example, researchers employed by one network gave the company's television news program a clean bill of health after carefully analyzing all the *scripts* for a specified period. This at a time when one observer has pointed out that the sentence "Did she buy two tickets to the play?" can be given at least seven different meanings by word emphasis alone. In an age when a majority of Americans consider television their primary source of information (so say Gallup polls), researchers have been churning out content analyses of magazines and newspapers, producing what one critic called a "plethora of definitive statements about the irrelevant and inconsequential."

Other researchers have bypassed the difficulties of coding radio and television message meaning by turning their analytical guns exclusively on the audience itself. Obviously an audience does not have to be aware of the precise content of a message in order to react in various ways. In fact, they may react as a result of receiving only part of the message. This phenomenon is especially true of electronic media audiences, as evidenced by the panic of those who missed the first part of the famous "War of the Worlds" radio broadcast in 1938.

It must also be added that a large part of the audience can be aware of the precise meaning of a message yet still disregard it. This type of response is in part due to the inundation of messages, which we examined in Chapter 1. It also stems from an independent spirit among receivers. A majority of the nation's newspapers of the time opposed the successful presidential candidacies of Thomas Jefferson, Andrew Jackson, Abraham Lincoln, Woodrow Wilson, Franklin D. Roosevelt, Harry S. Truman, and John F. Kennedy.

None of these observations is intended to denigrate the value of relevant communications research. Humans *are* affected by the messages they obtain from the mass media, and we need communication research to describe effective and ineffective messages and their positive and negative results. Students of mass communication should have an intellectual respect for research in the field, but they must also treat such research with healthy skepticism. They must be able to recognize the limitations of communication research; they must know that its findings are usually fragmentary, since researchers can delve only a tiny distance into the uncharted complexities of messages and the people exposed to them.

Practitioners in the media are sometimes critical of communication research though they have become dependent over the years on practical aspects of the discipline, such as readership and readability studies. Without communication researchers, the media would find it impossible to challenge the persistent charges that the mass media narcotize their audiences, produce conformity, weaken the nation's capacity for criticism, retard participatory democracy, and inculcate habits of violence and delinquency. Researchers, of course, are not able to prove or refute every charge made against the media, since the vast number of variables involved ensures that there will always be unanswered questions. But this situation poses a handicap for the critic, also. It is equally impossible to support many of the charges that are gratuitously flung in the direction of the mass media.

PROBLEMS IN COMMUNICATIONS RESEARCH

The criticisms directed at mass media are frequently unsupportable and the findings of mass communication research often contradictory for the following reasons:

The Messages of Mass Media Cannot Be Isolated from the Personality of the Receiver. Innumerable personal variables will cause the same message to have a different effect on two people. A person's health, religion, sex, economic status, education, race, prior experiences, and the like will affect his or her reaction to a message: What is "good" news for one person will be "bad" news for another. Yet, as was mentioned earlier, the mass communication researcher is usually interested in the reactions of the total audience rather than of any one individual in the audience.

Other personal variables involve the attitude of the receiver toward the source of the message, toward the communicator, and toward the medium itself. An accurate message coming from what the receiver believes to be an untrustworthy source, an unfair reporter, or an error-prone medium may be doubted or considered completely inaccurate. Inaccurate messages, on the other hand, may be completely credible if the receiver has a positive attitude toward the source, the communicator, or the medium.

That these multiple variables pose a severe handicap to the communication researcher has been demonstrated in studies on the effects of violence in the mass media, especially on children. Some psychologists have declared that even if an effect could be proved—that is, that violence in the media caused some children in the audience to become violent—it would be a minor factor when compared with the more dominant factors of the children's own individual personalities, their socioeconomic position, and the influence of their parents.

The best that researchers have been able to come up with in this area is that mass media violence may tend to trigger antisocial behavior in an abnormal child, or cause a potential delinquent to imitate aggressive actions depicted on television. Like adults, most *normal* children have an ability to separate aggression in the real world from aggression in the unreal world of drama or cartoons. One British study showed that children were less frightened by violent acts in television dramas than by scary background music. Mayhem on the screen upset them less than a mother and father arguing or a parent scolding a child in the same drama.

These examples suggest only a few of the complexities in this type of study. There are hundreds of other variables. For example, although violence in the media may have a more negative effect on abnormal than on normal children, it has also been determined that delinquent children read fewer books and magazines than normal children, and that aggressive children do not have the patience to watch as much television as do more passive normal children; yet one study has shown that delinquent children *perceive* more aggression in the media than do nondelinquent children. There are also indications that violence in the media may serve as a vicarious release (the safety-valve or catharsis effect) for certain violence-prone children. Even though virtually all researchers agree that violence in the media can be harmful for "some" children under "some" conditions, they disagree about the actual threat to the average child and whether violence in the real world of news—which cannot be easily excised—may not have a greater effect on the child than does violence in the unreal world of fiction and drama.

One Medium Cannot Easily Be Isolated from Other Media. People in a modern society are bombarded with messages from a variety of media. They may see or hear different versions of a message in newspapers, radio, television, and magazines. It is extremely difficult for them to remember precisely where they heard or saw a specific message; in fact, they may have received the information from a friend rather than from any mass medium.

There have been some outstanding examples of readers' inability to sort out the source of their information. One mass magazine, in a readership survey, gave interviewees a list of news events and asked which ones the magazine had covered with the greatest competence. Readers gave one of the highest scores to a story that the magazine had never covered at all.

Individuals in the audience not only confuse their sources of information, but they are also unable to recall accurately how much time they spend with a specific medium. For example, average Americans *admit* to watching less than three hours of television a day, but they actually watch about four and a half hours each day.

Surveys conducted by Roper Research Associates have shown that Americans consider television to be the most "believable" medium. But the unanswered questions in the surveys are these: How many respondents received virtually all of their news from television alone and therefore had no real basis for comparison? How many gave this answer as a justification for the time they spent watching television? How many believe in the accuracy of a televised event that they see with their own eyes but consider a newspaper "report" more accurate than a "report" by television correspondents or anchormen? How many are simply unable to recall clearly the source of what they considered information?

The Message Cannot Be Isolated from the Physical Conditions Surrounding the Receiver. The message transmitted by a medium is affected by certain characteristics of the medium itself. A book, magazine, or newspaper can easily be put aside while the reader is in the middle of a message. A television message is interrupted by commercials; a movie message is not. A television message is seen in lighted conditions, when the viewer is often accompanied by family members; a movie message is seen in darkened conditions, when the viewer is either alone or has the feeling of being alone. An individual may withdraw from a television message by changing channels or leaving the room temporarily; a moviegoer is tied more closely to the total message.

All these and many other factors surrounding reading and viewing play important roles in message impact. What happens, then, when communication researchers set up artificial conditions in order to conduct their tests more conveniently and more precisely? They may be getting reactions quite different from those that would be obtained under normal reading or viewing conditions. The dilemma for the researcher is this: Laboratory conditions are unreal and may seriously affect the results, yet results would be impossible to obtain under normal receiver conditions.

There Is Great Difficulty in Getting Representative Control Groups. When attorneys involved in a sensational murder case seek jurors who have read or seen nothing about the case, an observer is bound to wonder if a life-or-death decision will be made by a panel of idiots. A communication researcher seeking data about the acceptability of a specific advertisement might easily find one group that can be exposed to the ad and another group that can be isolated from it. But it is almost impossible to find representative control groups for research into problems that are of vital concern to society—problems involving obscenity, violence, racial coverage, or political bias, for example. The mass media penetrate and saturate the American environment. A person *not* exposed to information on these subjects is likely to be completely *un*representative of the important sectors of American society.

If researchers are attempting, say, to test the effects of television violence, how do they obtain a control group of normal children who are not exposed to regular television fare? And if they work the other way, attempting to select a control group of normal children and exposing them to concentrated television violence, then they are placing the children under abnormal laboratory conditions, if not running the additional risk of harming their psyches for the sake of science.

Obviously, good researchers are frequently able to obtain control groups under near normal conditions. However, because of the pervasiveness of mass communication, some problems defy accurate research.

There Is Difficulty in Determining Long-Range Effects. Under laboratory or normal conditions, television viewers may register startling reactions to a particular message: a half hour later they may have forgotten it. Other viewers may not have reacted so strongly, but this and similar messages may have a cumulative force that, in the long run, will affect them more severely.

It is virtually impossible for communication researchers to determine in any scientific way the cumulative effects of certain kinds of messages. Researchers cannot remain with the receiver for anything but a limited period of time, nor can they isolate the receiver from hundreds of other influences.

Some psychologists, for example, have said that constant exposure to violence in the mass media "conditions" children over a period of time until finally they feel less sympathy for victims of violence. Another observer complained about the impact of the "lone man" theme of many movie and television dramas. In these dramas, he said, the recurrent theme is of a brave little "good guy," surrounded by an indifferent or cowardly populace, who achieves his one great moment with an act of violence against a big "bad guy." These dramas had a cumulative effect, he said, on men like James Earl Ray and Sirhan Sirhan and resulted in the assassination of Martin Luther King, Jr., and Robert Kennedy, respectively.

Hypotheses such as these are offered by people who can give little supportive data. The inability of researchers to conduct controlled, long-term tests of communication effects opens the way, of course, to this kind of speculation, which may or may not be valid.

There Is Difficulty in Determining Whether the Message Is the Cause or the Effect. Is the audience being affected in a harmful way by certain messages of the mass media, or do the messages simply reflect the present state of the audience? Do the mass media force certain harmful messages upon the audience, or does the audience hunger for such messages and demand them? These are questions seemingly without answers, but they strongly affect the validity of accusations against the media and the validity of communication research.

To a certain extent, segments of the audience can avoid messages that are distasteful to them. By the same token, they can seek out those messages that particularly appeal to them. One study has shown that delinquents read more comic books and seek out more aggressive and exciting television programs than normal youths. One psychiatrist has remarked that the vast amount of violence on television is probably a reflection of the violent interests of viewers. It is a symptom, he said, not a cause, of the violence that exists in ourselves and in American society.

Whether the message is generated by the audience or by the communicator, there remains the tangential problem of control. How does one alter or censor messages in a free society, especially when the effects of phenomena such as violence, real and unreal, cannot be properly measured?

TO THE CHILDREN'S RESCUE

Some effects of mass communication can be proven; others cannot. But in certain cases, society would not be convinced even if the overwhelming results of communication research showed that a particular genre of message had no ill effects. For example, the majority of Americans are opposed to messages that they deem to be pornographic, especially if those messages are available to children. The fear of this ill effect could be called an effect itself, and even the Supreme Court has recognized this effect by upholding laws barring the sale of pornographic material to youths, despite contradictory evidence on the subject, as reported by the 1970 Commission on Obscenity and Pornography and the 1985 Attorney-General's Commission on Pornography.

In 1989 the Federal Communications Commission ordered a 24-hour-a-day ban on indecent programming on radio and television, following a Congressional mandate passed in 1988. There had been no proof that the broadcasting of "indecent" material had any harmful effect on children, particularly since an FCC ruling had already been in effect barring the broadcasting of such programming prior to 10:00 P.M. However, in making the new ruling, the FCC said that Congress had "the authority to protect children by prohibiting altogether the broadcast of indecent material," and that this was not a violation of the First Amendment.[1] In passing the legisla-

---

[1] *Broadcasting,* January 16, 1989, p. 98.

tion, Congress had determined that, practically speaking, there was no time when children were not in the TV and radio audience, since with VCRs and programmable tape decks they could record material broadcast at any hour and watch and listen to it later.

All the handicaps of communication research are multiplied when one attempts to pursue the effects of obscenity on children. One cannot imagine a researcher assembling a "control" group of children and bombarding them with concentrated doses of obscenity in order to measure the effects. And those children who are available for interviewing in this area are usually delinquent or deviant.

In the absence of empirical evidence, then, there is an abundance of speculation. Here, however, many psychologists who contend that pornography has no ill effects on adults believe that it might have ill effects on children. Children, they say, do not yet have the perspective to compare pornography with traditional views of sexual experience and are not yet mature enough to control sexual feelings once they have been aroused.

The overall problem of assessing mass communication effects can be exemplified by an examination of just two areas of recent communication research—the effects of political polls and the effects of pornography.

DO POLLS SWAY ELECTIONS?

A problem exists regarding the possible influence of political polls and election predictions. It is a problem that communication researchers have been able to study with beneficial results.

Political polls with a high degree of reliability have been on the American scene since the mid-1930s. Few people seriously question the relative accuracy of the major polls, although there are doubts about using polls for predictive purposes. With narrow margins allowed for error, surveys conducted by major polling organizations are accurate for the day or week in which the fieldwork took place. But people have a habit of changing their minds, and the findings of a poll may be quickly outdated.

Recent controversy has surrounded the possible effects of polls and—in the case of presidential elections in the United States—early election night predictions. In both cases, charges have been made that the information can have one of three effects: (1) the "stay-away" effect, causing voters to stay home and not bother voting in the belief that their candidate is an easy winner or doesn't have a chance; (2) the "bandwagon" effect, causing voters to choose or switch to the favored candidate in order to have the satisfaction of voting for a winner; or (3) the "underdog" effect, causing voters to choose or switch to the losing candidate out of sympathy or to make that person a closer contender and possible winner.

The potential effects of poll results have not been lost on the candidates themselves, who quickly release the favorable findings of polls that they have personally financed while withholding unfavorable results. Harry S. Truman contended during his 1948 campaign that the polls predicting a Dewey victory were "Republican polls" designed to keep Democrats away from the voting booths on election day. But the most convincing evidence of a stay-away effect came during the British parliamentary elections of 1970, when four out of five major polling organizations erroneously predicted a substantial Labor victory. Unlike the Gallup organization during the 1948 American presidential election, the British pollsters surveyed the electorate virtually up to the eve of election day, so they could not blame their mistake on a last-minute change of mind by voters. A few months before, favorable polls had convinced the Labor party to call an election in mid-1970. These earlier polls, widely publicized in the British mass media, apparently had a stay-away effect on many persons who had said they would be voting for the Labor party but in the end did not go to the polls to cast their ballots.

Scientific research is available on a similar problem in the United States—the fear that network predictions based on early election returns from the East Coast might strongly affect voting on the West Coast on the evening of presidential elections. Polls on the West coast, of course, had always closed three hours later, and in some sections four hours later, than polls on the East Coast, but by the time significant returns could be broadcast from the East Coast, polls were already closing on the other side of the country. Two developments changed this situation: (1) the establishment of the News Election Service, a cooperative of the three major networks and two major wire services designed to coordinate coverage of the 165,000 precincts in the country to make possible instant gathering of results, and (2) the programming of computers for analysis of early returns from key precincts and projection of final results in each state. In some cases, the broadcast networks could predict the final vote in major states on the East Coast when only a fraction of the vote was in, and this information could be broadcast to the West Coast hours before many of the West Coast polls closed.

Some congressmen proposed bills making it illegal to broadcast such predictions before all the polls had closed; others suggested a uniform voting day that would have polls open and close earlier on the West Coast to compensate for the time difference.

There were at least two major independent studies and three network-sponsored studies of this phenomenon during the 1964 presidential election. They combined random sampling of voters across the nation with depth interviews of those voters who cast their ballots after the polls had closed on the East Coast.[2] The surveys showed the following:

1. The great majority of voters on the West Coast had voted before the polls closed on the East Coast.
2. Only about one-fourth of the voters could have been influenced by election returns or projections from the East Coast, and less than half of these were in fact exposed to such electronic media reports.
3. Very few of the persons who had heard returns or projections changed their votes; in fact, a larger percentage among those who had *not* heard the returns and projections changed their minds on election day.

All the surveys generally agreed that early reports by the electronic media did not cause a significant stay-away, bandwagon, or underdog effect on the West Coast. The surveys further showed that even those who had heard the broadcasts were uncertain whether they had heard actual returns or network predictions, and there was evidence that they further confused the reports of opinion polls *prior* to election day with the whole lot.

The research showed that the overwhelming majority of the voters have too strong a commitment to their decision by election day to be influenced by early returns, even if they are in the small minority exposed to these broadcasts. Only in the very closest elections could forecasts broadcast by the media affect a national election. And in a very close election, it is unlikely that the networks could or would make clear-cut predictions so early.

More troublesome in the 1980s was the increasing use of "exit polling," whereby radio and television stations and afternoon newspapers sampled voters leaving the polls early in the day and predicted by midday or early afternoon how the election would turn out. Public and official fear of how this predictive device might affect the outcome of state and local elections led to threats of legislation and to voluntary restraints on the broadcasting of reports based on this polling procedure.

In nationwide elections the controversy died down, largely because of one-sided voting patterns in the presidential elections of 1980, 1984, and 1988. Even though early predictions would have made no difference in the outcome of the presidential races (they could have affected slightly the turnout for congressional races), the networks kept their word and volun-

---

[2] See Kurt Lang and Gladys Engel Lang, *Politics and Television* (Chicago: Quadrangle Books, 1970), pp. 250–88.

tarily refrained from broad predictions prior to the closing of polls in each state.

THE DENMARK CASE STUDY

Communication researchers are faced with a great number of variables when dealing with the relationship between pornography and sex crimes. Their findings, therefore, can never be as definitive as those of researchers investigating problems with more limited variables, such as the effect of election-day predictions on voter behavior.

Even so, there have been observers willing to draw hasty conclusions about the consequences of liberalizing obscenity laws. In 1965 the psychiatric department of Denmark's Council for Forensic Medicine reported that "no scientific experiments" could lead one to the assumption that pornography or obscene pictures and films contributed to the committing of sexual offenses by normal adults and youths.[3] In response to this report and substantial supporting sentiment in the country, the Danish parliament repealed legal prohibitions against written pronography in 1967. Two years later it ended film censorship for adults and legalized the sale of pornographic pictures and photographs to anyone over the age of 16. Sex crimes dropped sharply in the year following the 1967 government action and dropped again after the repeal of virtually all pornography laws affecting adults in 1969. Sales of pornographic material in Denmark have also shown a steep drop since the initial boom in sales in 1967.

Outside Denmark, persons who are opposed to obscenity laws have pointed to the Danish experience as proof that pornography does not contribute to antisocial behavior and, furthermore, that elimination of pornography laws actually leads to a decline in sexual crimes. They also contend that the sales drop in Denmark proves that most people are completely revolted by pornographic literature and films once such material becomes freely available.

Assuming that the statistical research on the Danish situation is valid, persons examining these reports should bear in mind the following relevant points:

---

[3] In the United States the Commission on Obscenity and Pornography transmitted a formal report in 1970 to the President and Congress with a similar finding: "Extensive empirical investigation, both by the Commission and by others, provides no evidence that exposure to or use of explicit sexual materials play a significant role in the causation of social or individual harms such as crime, delinquency, sexual or nonsexual deviancy, or severe emotional disturbances." See *The Report of the Commission on Obscenity and Pornography* (New York: Bantam Books, 1970), p. 58.

1. Any data concerning "sex crimes" should make some compensation for the revised definition of this term in Denmark. Prior to repeal, pornography itself was a crime; it no longer is.
2. Data should make adjustment for the increasingly permissive nature of Danish society, reflected also in police attitudes. Offenses that are perhaps still punishable by law are not prosecuted in many cases.
3. Data should also make a comparison of precise categories of sex crimes. There has been some evidence that while the number of trivial sex offenses (e.g., voyeurism) has diminished, the number of serious sex offenses (e.g., rape) has remained about the same.

Obviously, reliable data that showed no appreciable increase in sexual offenses would be a first step toward proving that the availability of pornography does not, in and of itself, cause unacceptable antisocial behavior. However, even this is still circumstantial evidence in the absence of a clear cause-and-effect relationship. Furthermore, communication researchers who are able to come up with significant findings regarding Denmark would probably be unhappy if their conclusions were lifted wholesale and applied to another country, because the question of pornography involves the attitudes of the individual as imposed by parents, religion, and society.

Danish society has long had a reputation as a sexually permissive society, and the State Lutheran Church, to which 90 percent of Danes belong, brought no effective pressures to bear against repeal of pornography laws. In other countries, society and organized religion impose a different set of attitudes upon the individual, and this influence would go into the mix of variables that could cause different media effects.

This has not been an attempt to set up communication research as a straw man to be knocked down. Each day, media are deriving benefit from the projects of communication researchers throughout the United States, and the major media are using the tools of communication research to understand their audience better and market their products more successfully. This chapter rather has been an attempt to urge those exposed to communication research to go beneath the surface. Understand the variables and the qualifications. Look at the factors the researcher was able to test, and those that defied examination.

If an editor schedules the report of a political poll, the editor should know—and should let the reader know: When was the poll conducted? How large was the sample? What was the location of the sample? What is the margin of error? What were the actual questions asked?

When mass murderer Theodore Bundy blamed his fate on his exposure as a young man to sex and violence in the mass media, few took him seriously, nor should they have. What kind of sex and what kind of violence was he exposed to? What kind of psychological baggage did he bring into the exposure? What kind of empirical evidence exists to support the blaming or not blaming of sex and violence in the media for effects on the individual?

First comes the reporter's or editor's understanding of the limits of any specific piece of communication research. Then comes transmission of that understanding to the reader, listener, or viewer.

AFTERTHOUGHTS

1. Is your choice of a television network news program determined in any way by the overall content of the program or by your favorable impression of the anchor? In what way is this choice influenced by "kinesics" (body language)?

2. Write down on a piece of paper the number of hours that you believe you watch television in an average day. Now keep a fairly accurate log of how much television you actually watch during the next seven days. How does the number of hours you watch compare with those of specific relatives? How do these answers and findings reflect the problem of interviewing people to determine media viewing habits?

3. Do you believe mass media can move the average adult to any action to which that person has a prior resistance? Can the mass media have harmful effects on the average child? If so, do you believe there should be stricter laws to reduce any harmful effects?

4. Assuming you wanted to check the effects of commercials on the average viewer, how would you go about doing so? Outline the factors you would want to examine and explain how you would go about investigating this in a scientific manner.

5. Assume that there is a local election in which there in only one race on the ballot. If at 2:00 P.M. you heard a credible prediction (based on valid exit polling) that the candidate you favored would lose the election by a landslide, would you go the polls at 6:00 P.M. as you had planned? If at 2:00 P.M. you heard a credible prediction that the candidate you favored was winning by a 2 to 1 margin, would you go to the polls at 6:00 P.M. as you had planned? What if, in the case mentioned above, there were two additional, less important races on the ballot? Would they make a difference in whether you went to the polls?

PART 3

Freedom and Responsibility

CHAPTER 12

Beyond Four Theories: Media and Government

By what other means may we analyze a media system so as to gain further understanding and insights about that system? Media systems are closely related to the kinds of governments in which they operate; they are, in essence, reflective and *supportive* of the governmental philosophy. For example, we have the Western model of a "free" press, which is based in a system that we call "political democracy." In fact, survey after survey has shown that there is a closer correlation between political democracy and "press freedom" than with any other factor in society except "free elections." When such correlation is not the case, some sort of quiet revolution is taking place that should be noted, because within a short while either the political system will change to conform to the media characteristics, or the press will soon change to conform to the existing govenmental philosophy.

The caveat for any person reading this chapter, however, should be that we are somewhat arrogantly judging other press systems (and thus other political systems) by our Western model. We can imagine two professors in the Soviet Union establishing *their* model, their yardstick by which to measure our media system. Undoubtedly, they would find our system less free (certainly less responsible) than theirs. They could hardly be faulted, because they are creatures of their political system, just as we are of ours. Or imagine the press minister of a Third World nation checking out the ideal of press libertarianism at a time when that minister's nation is beset by outside enemies, a tottering economy, internal dissension between peoples who speak a dozen languages, rampant illiteracy, vestiges of colonialism, and a simmering *coup d'état*. Could the minister be blamed for giving it a rather low priority?

So it is well to remember that media systems are *supportive,* not directive; they are to be considered more as *extensions* of a nation's political philosophy than as determiners of its philosophy. Obviously the media do have some impact on government but their impact will always be within the limitations of existing political philosophy. A realistic view of media systems would admit this ideological limitation on their freedom and emphasize the degree of freedom *practiced,* not simply permitted, in the various media systems. No press system is truly free, regardless of how freedom is defined. Restrictions of every kind are exerted, though to different degrees, on all press systems.

Press freedom exists on a continuum, and the only sensible way to talk about it in an international, comparative way is by using a systematic methodology that focuses on similarities and differences. Before surveying specific ways media systems have been, are, and may be classified and discussed, however, it might be useful to deal briefly with a basic, two-valued consideration underlying all relevant typologies and philosophical discussions. At the risk of offending those readers who feel an intellectual repulsion toward any kind of either-or conceptualization, we will submit a few generalizations about such an approach.

People, as well as nations, tend to be either *authoritarian* or *libertarian.* Of course, they are all somewhat schizophrenic, but basically they are disposed either toward a well-structured, disciplined world view with definite rules and an ordered society, or toward an open, experimental, nonrestrictive society with a minimum of rules and controls. We will examine these two broad concepts more closely under "The 'Four Theories' Concept" later in the chapter. Governments, too, are designed on the philosophical base of one of these two orientations. Of course, no person or government is quite so simple. Some authoritarians are more flexible and open than most would suspect, and many libertarians are more assured of the validity of their position and more dogmatic than most would suspect. The same is true of governments. But this does not mean that people and governments are not primarily or basically inclined in one of the two directions. A nation such as Albania, we may quite validly say, has an authoritarian press system, while a country like Denmark has a libertarian press system.

In light of what has been said, it is probably safe to divide the world's press systems, too, into two basic classes: "authoritarian-tending" and "libertarian-tending." In order really to determine whether a media system or government is primarily one or the other, one must look very carefully at that total system, observing not only the philosophical literature of the nation but the total cultural heritage that has manifested itself either in an open, competitive, laissez-faire national ethos or in a closed, noncompetitive, highly structured, directive, and paternalistic society.

Assuming, then, that this basic philosophical dichotomy exists among nations and press systems, it might be well to look briefly at the two orientations.

AWAY FROM DEMOCRACY

The philosophical basis for countries that subscribe to the authoritarian concept may be traced back at least to Plato, the first great proponent of "law and order" and advocate of rule by an aristocracy of the best. This is basically an elitist orientation, reflecting a suspicion of the masses—in Western terms, an antidemocratic stance. People in general are not intellectually capable, psychologically equipped, or educationally competent to make many decisions for themselves, say the elitists. The masses, in fact, are frightened and frustrated when they have power in their hands and, having it, pose a great danger to the whole society. They basically want to escape from the problems of decision making, especially as it relates to governing. Special people must rule—people interested and competent, people dedicated to accumulating and wielding power.

Many important writers and thinkers since Plato have contributed to the development of the totalitarian, elitist political philosophy; a few of them are Machiavelli, Hobbes, Hegel, Nietzsche, Treitschke, Fichte, and possibly even Rousseau. A desire for strong government, fear of the masses, a respect for power and hatred of anarchy, an inclination to personal arrogance based on a felt superiority and a desire to control— these are some of the natural proclivities of elitists and authoritarians.[1]

In an authoritarian society there are many things that the populace— the people in general—must not know; the mass media must keep these things secret. There are things that the people need to know; the mass media must publicize these things. The power elite will either encompass

---

[1] For excellent discussions of the authoritarian personality and the function of power, see Karl R. Popper, *The Open Society and Its Enemies* (Princeton, NJ: Princeton University Press, 1950); T. W. Adorno et al., *The Authoritarian Personality* (New York: Harper & Brothers, 1950); Erich Fromm, *Escape from Freedom* (New York: Rinehart, 1941); George Orwell, *1984* (New York: Signet Books, 1950); Bertrand Russell, *Power: A New Social Analysis* (New York: W. W. Norton, 1938); Niccolò Machiavelli, *The Prince* (many editions); Richard Hofstadter, *Social Darwinism in American Thought* (Boston: Beacon Press, 1955); Carl Friedrich and Zbigniew Brzezinski, *Totalitarian Dicatorship and Autocracy*, 2nd ed. revised by C. Friedrich (New York: Frederick A. Praeger, 1968); Robert Tucker, *Philosophy and Myth in Karl Marx* (London: Cambridge University Press, 1969).

the mass media or will control and dictate to them. The mass media will, in effect, be instruments of the governmental leadership. Their goal: maximizing political and social equilibrium and harmony. This is true whether the country is an authoritarian nation of the right or the left. Actually, as Friedrich Hayek demonstrates in *The Road to Serfdom* (1944), there is no real difference in the basic philosophy of rightists and leftists: both advocate statism and control. Plato may well be considered the grandfather of both fascism *and* communism, as Hegel is quite likely the father of both.

The basic characteristic of the authoritarian orientation, then, is political and intellectual arrogance on the part of a small elite group having a deep-rooted suspicion on the part of the masses. This orientation filters down into the media system in many ways, depending on the particular type of government the nation has. In theory, right meets left so far as basic philosophy is concerned, the emphasis being on control of the populace and the mass media being the instrument of control.

TRUSTING THE MASSES

The libertarian philosophical stance has many roots. "Freedom lovers" undoubtedly have always existed, but it was not until the seventeenth and eithteenth centuries that the libertarian philosophy began to infiltrate the press. John Locke with his insistence on "popular sovereignty" was one seventeenth-century pioneer. John Milton was another. In his *Areopagitica* (1644) he put forth a "self-righting" process that has been useful to students of media: "Let all with something to say be free to express themselves. The true and sound will survive, the false and unsound will be vanquished." Thomas Jefferson in eighteenth-century America supported the concept, and John Stuart Mill in nineteenth-century England added further theoretical foundations to the libertarian orientation.

All these men, and many others, propounded a philosophy that was quite different from that of the authoritarians. They basically trusted the "mass man"; they believed that all kinds of information and ideas should be made public; they despised secrecy and censorship; and they believed that free criticism was essential to happiness and growth. They were fundamentally "democrats" rather than autocrats or some other variety of aristocrats. Of course, there are certain paradoxes in this generalization, which are very well exemplified by Jefferson, the southern, slave-holding aristocrat who was also early America's leading libertarian.

A national libertarian orientation is one in which there is a basic trust of the masses, a belief that the majority can come closest to the truth and can make good decisions. This trust of the people relates to the function of mass media in that it is the media that must inform the people so they can know enough to intelligently elect their representatives, direct them, and change them when necessary. *In theory, the libertarian nation is one in which the people control their leadership instead of the other way around, as in an authoritarian nation.*

Two Libertarian Ideas

Two important ideas related to a libertarian press system have come to stand out and, in a sense, define such a system. They relate to (1) the press as "the fourth branch of government" and (2) "the people's right to know." Theoretically, at least in the United States, the media system serves as a check on the government Establishment, keeping it honest. And as theoretical rulers of their country, the people have a right to know what their government is doing. These two ideas have become generally accepted as foundation stones of media libertarianism.

Let us briefly consider the "fourth branch of government" concept. The phrase is an American adaptation of the English "fourth estate." The first two estates, or political bodies, were the nobles and clergy. To these were later added the third estate, the commoners (hence, House of Commons), and still later, in figurative terms, the press. The "fourth branch" concept is based on the assumption that the press is an integral part of government—that it theoretically supplements the executive, legislative, and judicial branches. This, of course, is really not the case at all. Another related assumption, heard very often, is that the press serves as a "check on government," This, of course, would locate the press *outside* of the government and would tend to contradict the fourth-branch idea.

Since the people do not elect the press to represent them in any way, it is quite probable that the press itself, rather than the people, has developed this fourth-branch concept. In effect, the press is a self-appointed part of government and a self-appointed check on government. Yet neither the U.S. Constitution nor the constitution of any other country gives the press the responsibility or obligation to watch the government and check on its actions.

Fourth-branch apologists will immediately say that traditional practices in American journalism plus "common sense" tell us that our mass media have this responsibility and obligation. And certainly these persons will insist, the press recognizes this obligation. But, does it, really? If so, why are there so many newspapers and other media that do not serve as watchdogs of government, or checks or critics? Obviously many segments of the press do not recognize this obligation.

If any conclusion can be drawn from the questions raised above, it might be that the press is simply not a fourth branch of government and has no reason to consider itself even a critic of, or check on, government. After all, does not freedom of the press include the freedom of the press *not* to be a fourth branch of government or a critic of or check on anything? So perhaps the mere setting up of a premise of what the libertarian press *is* automatically restricts its freedom and demolishes the whole concept of libertarianism.

Now let us turn briefly to the other assumed cornerstone of libertarianism in the mass media: the "people's right to know." If the source of this "right" is ever inquired into at all, it is generally assumed to be the "free press" clause of the First Amendment to the American Constitution. But is it really? The question might be asked if a free press should not have the freedom to *withhold* certain things from the people—the freedom, if you will, to keep the people from knowing.[2]

Even if we pass over this basic conceptual contradiction, many other puzzling questions arise. For instance, if there is a "right to know," then one might ask: the right to know *what?* (Surely the people *cannot* know, do not *need* to know, and do not *want* to know, everything.) If the answer to the above question is that the people have the right to know "public business," then we have the problem of defining "public business."

Let us look again at the basic concept: "the right to know." If we agree that it is basic and important, then the next question is *Who* must decide what is appropriate for the people to know? Somebody or some group must make this decision, since not all information can be disseminated.

This person (or institution), then, must serve as a gatekeeper or censor—a "definer" of what the people have a right or, perhaps more accurately, a need to know. If this is true, then the concept of the "right to know" is abridged; it simply means now the "right to know" *certain* things that *somebody* wants us to know. In effect, then, the "right" is not a right at all. If we really had a "right" to know government business, the media could *insist* (by law) that the government provide them with any or all of its information. And beyond that, we citizens could insist (by law) that the mass media provide us with any or all of the information they obtain. But if we were to insist that the press do that, we would be contradicting the concept of press freedom—which includes the freedom to make editorial decisions.

These two basic orientations—authoritarianism and libertarianism—

---

[2] This is a modern variation on the well-known "paradox of freedom," first pointed out by Plato. Free men, said Plato, may exercise their freedom by curtailing their state of freedom and deciding to live under a tyrant.

seem to us prime shapers of the world's media philosophies and structures. Now, from this rather simple, dichotomous approach, let us turn to a more discerning, discriminating, and complex method of describing and analyzing media concepts and systems.

THE "FOUR THEORIES" CONCEPT

Probably the best-known typology of press systems is the "four theories" concept. Although these theories had long been discussed singly, from time to time, by a large number of authors and speakers, it was not until 1956, when three professors of communication—Fred S. Siebert, Theodore Peterson, and Wilbur Schramm—brought out their *Four Theories of the Press,* that this kind of typology was taken seriously. Now the little volume (in paperback since 1963[3]) has become standard reading in journalism departments and schools and has implanted the "four theories" concept rather firmly in the minds of journalism students, faculty, and practitioners. Almost every article and book dealing with philosophical bases for journalism has alluded to this book, commented on it, or quoted from it. It has definitely made an impact.

Siebert, Peterson, and Schramm discuss journalism philosophy by presenting these four theories ("concepts" might have been a less pretentious term): (1) the authoritarian theory, (2) the libertarian theory, (3) the communist theory, and (4) the social responsibility theory.

Authoritarian

The highest expression of organizational structure, the state, supersedes the individual, and only with state domination is the individual able to acquire and develop the attributes of a civilized being. Mass communication, then, must support the state and the government in power so that the society may advance and the state may reach its objectives. The state (the "elite" that runs the state) directs the populace, which is not considered competent or interested enough to make political decisions. Rather, one person or a few persons are placed in a position to lead, and

---

[3] *Four Theories of the Press* (Urbana: University Chapter of Illinois Press, 1963). Cf. a good discussion of the four concepts by William L. Rivers in Chapter 2 of Rivers and Schramm, *Responsibility in Mass Communication,* rev. ed. (New York: Harper & Row, 1969). For a critique of these "four theories," see John C. Merrill, *The Imperative of Freedom* (New York: Hastings House, 1974), esp. Chapter 1.

part of their duty is to control the mass media, which must be used to build up the leadership and further its goals.

The media, then, under authoritarian theory, are "educational," directive, and propagandistic. They are instruments of *control,* not truly educational in the sense of enabling free and open information flow and discussion. Generally the media are privately owned, although the leader or his or her clique or party may own units in the media system. The authoritarian approach revolves around the idea that persons engaged in journalism are so engaged as a special privilege granted by the national leader; therefore they owe an obligation to the leader and the leader's government. This press philosophy has formed, and now forms, the basis for many press systems of the world; in each case such systems owe their existence to the state and operate to support and perpetuate the authority that permit them to survive. The mass media have only as much freedom as the national leadership will permit them to have at any time.

Libertarian

The concept of press "libertarianism" can be traced back to the seventeenth century, when it took roots in England and in the American colonies. The philosophy that looked upon man as a rational animal with inherent natural rights gave rise to the libertarian press theory. One of these natural rights was the right to pursue truth, and thus would-be interferers with the search for truth should be restrained. Exponents of this libertarian philosophy during the seventeenth, eighteenth, and nineteenth centuries included Milton, Locke, Erskine, Jefferson, and John Stuart Mill. Individual liberties were stressed by these philosophers, along with a trust in the people to make intelligent decisions, *if* there was freedom of expression.

Theoretically, "libertarian" press functions to uncover and present the truth, splintered though it may be in a pluralism of voices. It cannot do this if it is controlled by some authority outside itself. The press must serve as the informational link between government and people, and if this link is cut by governmental censorship or secrecy, the concept of freedom of information is largely invalidated. Today the libertarian press accepts (or claims to accept) the obligations of keeping the public abreast of government activities and of watching for and serving as a check on government improprieties. In theory at least, the libertarian press is a "fourth estate" or "fourth branch of government," supplementing the executive, legislative, and judicial branches. In addition, through its pluralism it represents the many aspects of society and serves as a "forum" of discussion for the people.

Communist

The first quarter of the twentieth century saw the birth of the communist theory of the press. Karl Marx was its father, drawing heavily on the philosophy of his fellow German, Georg W. F. Hegel. The functions of the mass media in a communist society, said Marx, were basically the same as those of the entire ruling apparatus—viz, the perpetuation and expansion of the socialist system. Means of communication then, exist to transmit social policy and not to aid in searching for the truth.

Under this theory, the mass media are instruments of government and are integral parts of the state. They must be owned and operated by the state and directed by the Communist party or its agencies. Self-criticism in the media is permitted (i.e., criticism of failure to live up to communist planning and goals); in fact, such criticism is actively encouraged. The communist theory, like the authoritarian, is based on the premise that the masses are too fickle and too ignorant and unconcerned with government to be told very much about the workings of government. Mass media must do what is best for the state and party; and what is best is what the leadership elite says is best—in line, of course, with Marxist theory. Whatever the media do to support and contribute to the achievement of communism is moral; whatever is done to hinder the achievement of communism is immoral. *Perestroika* and *Glasnost,* signs of liberalizing tendencies in Marxist societies, have not significantly altered this main premise.

Social Responsibility

This theory is a mid-twentieth-century-concept of the press as it is recognized in the Western world. It has its roots in the libertarian theory, say its proponents and explainers. It goes beyond the libertarian theory, however, in that it places a great many moral and ethical restrictions on the press; and it not only places restrictions on the press, but it proposes that the press do many things that it has not been doing.

The emphasis in the social responsibility theory is shifted from press *freedom* to press *responsibility.* The theory, named and systematized in *Four Theories of the Press,* has been drawn largely from a report published in 1947 by the Hutchins Commission.[4] It maintains that the importance of the press in modern society makes it absolutely necessary that an obligation of social responsibility be imposed on the communications media. To

---

[4] See Commission on Freedom of the Press, *A Free and Responsible Press* (Chicago: University of Chicago Press, 1947).

many persons, including the authors of the present volume, there are many problems with this theory, and these will be discussed in the next sections. A growing number of scholars, press critics, and even media practitioners, however, are becoming increasingly concerned with the performance of our "libertarian" press and are urging all manner of reforms. This would indicate that it may be, as the authors of *Four Theories of the Press* contend, that libertarianism as the ethos of this country's media system is evolving into social responsibility.

It may well be that through using different terms and structuring the typology to permit more flexibility, the objections that many have to the "four theories" concept—and especially to the social responsibility theory—can largely be overcome. Let us now look briefly at a new modification.

DEFINING THE SYSTEM

Attempting to fit a nation into one of the four theories, or vice versa, has been comparable to fitting the proverbial square peg into a round hole. What philosophy, for example, prevails in Kenya, Burma, Egypt, or a few dozen other Third World nations?

The "four theories" concept lacks the flexibility needed for proper description and analysis of all of today's press systems and therefore should be modified. The following is the gist of a new "two-tiered" typology which can be applied to both the *ownership* and the *philosophy* of a given press system:

Press Ownership
1. *Private*. Ownership by individuals or nongovernment corporations; supported primarily by advertising or subscriptions.
2. *Multiparty*. Ownership by competitive political parties; subsidized by party or party members.
3. *Government*. Owned by government of dominant government party; subsidized primarily by government funds or government-collected license fees.

Press Philosophies
1. *Authoritarian*. Government licensing and censorship to stifle criticism and thereby maintain the ruling elite.
2. *Social-Authoritarian*. Government and government-party ownership to harness the press in the service of national economic and philosophical goals.
3. *Libertarian*. Absence of governmental controls (except for mini-

mal libel and obscenity laws), ensuring a free marketplace of ideas and operation of the "self-righting" process.

4. *Social-Libertarian.* Minimal governmental controls to unclog channels of communication and ensure the operational spirit of the libertarian philosophy.

5. *Social-Centralist.* Government or public ownership of the limited channels of communication to ensure the operational spirit of the libertarian philosophy.

The three types of press ownership obviously consider the press from the point of view of sources of financial support. This is done for a purpose: The source of support will, in almost every case, point to important operational characteristics of the press. For example, to say that a press system is "privately owned" is to indicate that its chief source of revenue must come from advertising and/or subscriptions. It can be understood, then, that the system must be immediately responsive to the needs of the advertising community and/or its subscribing public.

Slighty different titles are given to two of the "four theories" basic press philosophies. Authoritarian and libertarian remain the same; the philosophies they represent *are clear,* and the terms themselves have behind them centuries of usage. "Communist," however, has been abandoned to make way for "social-authoritarian". The latter term admits a broad enough spectrum to include all the nations of the Eastern bloc, plus those centrally guided press systems in many developing countries. The social-authoritarian philosophy is a modern modification of the authoritarian philosophy as set forth in the "four theories" concept. The clear difference is that when this philosophy, in all its variations, governs, the press is controlled, not primarily to keep it from doing harm to the ruling elite, but to channel the power of the media in what the state sees as constructive educational, developmental, and political directions.

The term "social responsibility" has been discarded because the name itself is ambiguous. This category has now been split, with one new category being called "social-libertarian" and the other "social-centralist." Both these philosophies pay allegiance to the "spirit" of libertarianism, but each believes that modern society and modern technology have in some ways restricted the marketplace of ideas and that societal interference is necessary to unclog these choked channels. The social-libertarian philosophy utilizes outside regulation to ensure the operational spirit of the libertarian philosophy. That is, it recognizes the need for such regulatory groups as the Federal Communications Commission, self-regulatory bodies such as national press councils, and industry-wide code authorities. The social-centralist philosphy goes a step further and institutes government or public ownership of the limited channels of communication to ensure the operational spirit of libertarianism. The major difference between social-centralism and social-authoritarianism is that the former aims at providing a multitude of competing voices over limited channels, while the latter is interested in providing only the "right" voice—the voice of government.

It must be pointed out that mixed philosophies are possible within a given nation, and it is also quite likely—especially in the West and in developing nations—for a country to have mixed ownerships. One might find all three ownerships in the print media alone, or one type of ownership for the print media and another for the electronic media.

For example, England may be classified in the following manner under this two-tiered system:

Print media:
Ownership: Private
Philosophy: Social-libertarian

Television:
Ownership: Government
Philosophy: Social-centralist; social-libertarian

Radio:
Ownership: Government
Philosophy: Social-centralist

Classification of the media in a given country takes into account the overall pattern of that country's media, not the exceptions that exist in every medium. For example, a number of magazines in England are produced by governmental or publicly owned agencies (*The Listener,* published by the BBC, is one example), but these are exceptions to the general pattern in England. The classification of television, however, does take into account the dual programming system—BBC networks, on the one hand, and Independent Television (ITV) networks on the other. Government still owns the channels and broadcasting facilities of ITV, but programming is a private affair, partly dependent on advertising. ITV has therefore developed a different philosophy or rationale, which we can classify as social-libertarian.

We can also classify a state—Israel—whose media are not so well known in the United States. This example demonstrates that much can be said about the media of a specific country in a few words using this classification system:

Print media:
Ownership: Private, multiparty, government
Philosophy: Social-libertarian, social-centralist

Electronic media:
   Ownership: Government
   Philosophy: Social-centralist

The identification of these ownerships and philosophies in clearer terms also offers new insights into the historical development of press philosophies. In Figure 12.1 we delineate an "evolution of media" philosophy.

In an *authoritarian* press system, the media consumers (usually a literate elite) are in balance with the number of channels. The elite tends to be politically homogeneous rather than heterogeneous. There are relatively few press units, and they are easy to license and censor.

As literacy increases, the mass audience tends to become politically more heterogeneous and to desire more channels of information and opin-

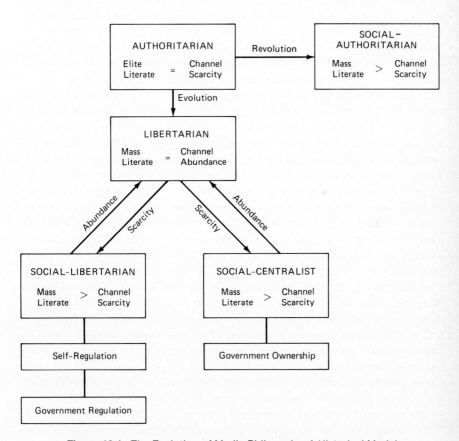

Figure 12.1. The Evolution of Media Philosophy: A Historical Model

ion. The authoritarian regime is unable to license and control the larger number of press units needed to satisfy the demand of the enlarged literacy pool, so it tries to restrict the growth of the press artificially. A volatile imbalance exists between demand (the mass literate) and supply (the number of media channels).

This situation usually evolves toward a balanced situation: abundant channels for the mass literate. We would then say that a *libertarian* philosophy governs.

This situation of channel abundance can change, however. Monopoly can limit the number of voices in society, if not the actual number of channels, and the boundaries of technology can limit the number of electronic channels available. When scarcity of channels causes a new imbalance between the literate masses and the number of channels, a country can move in one of two directions.

If it moves in the direction of *social-libertarianism,* it attempts to maintain the idea of a privately owned press but at the same time tries to ensure the operational spirit of libertarianism through self-regulation and government regulation. If if moves in the direction of *social-centralism,* it abandons the idea of a privately owned press and turns to government or public ownership to ensure the operational spirit of libertarianism.

The aim of both social-libertarianism and social-centralism is to ensure a pluralism of voices despite the limited number of channels. If the aim is not to ensure pluralism but to ensure governmental control of information and opinion, we have revolutionary (rather than evolutionary) change to *social-authoritarianism*. Theoretically, improvements in technology (e.g., offset printing, FM radio, cable television, satellite broadcasting) may provide a new abundance of channels, removing the rationale for either social-libertarianism or social-centralism. We may then see a reversal back in the direction of a *libertarian* philosophy. It is unlikely that this reversal would occur in the case of *social-authoritarianism;* rather, the imbalance between media consumers and the number of channels would be artificially maintained.

Obviously, other possibilities can occur that are not indicated by the diagram. Once technology makes possible an abundance of channels, a social-centralist philosophy may first move toward social-libertarianism before moving on toward unfettered libertarianism. Revolution can move a libertarian or social-libertarian philosophy directly to social-authoritarianism, and so forth.

The United States provides an excellent example of this sort of movement. Looking only at the electronic media, we would probably classify radio and television as having private ownership and a social-centralist philosophy. There was probably no time when the electronic media in this country were absolutely in the libertarian stage. The physical qualities of the medium called for government intervention from the very beginning as a "traffic cop" to assign frequencies and to ensure that existing frequencies would not impinge on each other or new licensees would not raise their power to hog that spot on the spectrum in an inordinately wide area. At some early point, government, with its foot already in the regulatory door, recognized that this new medium could (and probably did) veer from the libertarian philosophy in the following ways:

- The spectrum could support only a limited number of stations in any community.
- The few stations available could be (and were) bought by newspapers that already controlled one medium in the city, or by networks that could fill the programming day, coast to coast, with the same message.
- Those few stations might not (and frequently did not) provide the diversity that the community needed.

As a result, over a good number of years the government, mostly through the Federal Communications Commission, used regulatory practices for the following purposes:

- To limit the number of stations that could be owned by chains or networks.
- To limit cross-ownership of stations in the same community by newspapers.
- To keep station owners from providing the exact same program to two stations within range of each other.
- To ensure "fairness," so that a range of voices on controversial subjects could be heard.
- To ensure equal time, so a station could not favor one political candidate over another.

These were only some of the regulations, along with regular license renewal procedures, established to see that U.S. broadcasting stations operated in the "public interest, convenience, and necessity." The National Association of Broadcasters established its own Radio Code and Television Code largely to prevent even more government regulation. The codes established specific standards for advertising and programming, laying down general principles and statements of things that could not be done. Almost all stations adhered to the codes. The United States, then, was squarely in the social-libertarian framework of media philosophy. In addition, the government established and supported public broadcasting to ensure a wider variety of programming than that likely to be supported by advertisers. To this minor extent, the United States moved into the social-centralist philosophy.

Then the pendulum began to shift the other way, in a direction more conducive to unrestricted libertarianism. The popularization of FM (frequency modulation) doubled the radio spectrum. The development of ultra-high frequency television increased the television spectrum sixfold—and the introduction of low-power television, which could serve small communities and even neighborhoods in larger cities without causing signal interference problems, increased it even more. Cable television blossomed, providing more than 30 television channels and numerous new radio frequencies in a community; and direct broadcast satellites promised further to multiply the number of channels. During the Reagan administration, in the 1980s, an effort was made to deregulate broadcasting and move back to a libertarian philosophy. The number of stations that could be owned by chains was increased, license renewal was made less frequent and less stringent, and the fairness doctrine was eliminated. The NAB Television Code was all but ignored. With the increase in the number of channels, some specialized commercial channels are providing the programming that it was once thought only public broadcasting could produce: documentaries, children's programs, and arts programs. In broadcasting, accordingly, the United States is clearly moving away from a social-centralist philosophy and toward the direction of a libertarian philosophy.

A similar trend is taking place in England and undoubtedly in most of the Western European nations. Even in social-authoritarian nations, especially those in the Soviet bloc, the trend seems inexorable in the direction of the libertarian philosophy as the opening of new channels and the existence of less expensive printing processes make it almost impossible to maintain the strict control of even ten to twenty years ago.

An interesting sidelight to this trend toward libertarianism in the U.S. broadcasting industry is the history of resistance to the trend on the part of those who at one time agitated the loudest for less regulation. Over-the-air broadcasters, who traditionally complained that they did not have the same First Amendment freedoms as the print media, are urging the FCC and Congress to regulate cable so as to force cable to rebroadcast their channels; cable is seeking government regulation to keep telephone companies out of the cable television business; and newspapers are lobbying for government regulation to keep telephone companies out of the video-tex business.

Our new, two-tiered typology and the related model of media evolution are not without their handicaps. There will still be nations whose press systems defy simple classification. And to modify and expand an existing concept is also to complicate it in some ways. But the possibilities of more subtle understanding and clearer analysis will, we hope, compensate for these relatively minor problems.

There are reasons why the various media systems throughout the world are different from each other. By analyzing these systems through looking at the politcal environment in which they exist, and by considering the communications technologies available to them, one can predict with some accuracy their movement toward or away from libertarianism. Communications media are dynamic and in flux as we move into the twenty-first century, and this movement will undoubtedly have political and social effects.

AFTERTHOUGHTS

1. If you were classifying the print media in the United States according to our two-tiered typology, how would you identify them on the basis of "ownership" and "philosophy"?
2. The Hutchins Commission of 1947 expressed serious concern about monopoly in the mass media and considered this a distinct threat to the libertarian philosophy. Would you consider this a problem today?
3. "Political democracy" correlates more closely with "Press freedom" than it does with any factor other than "free elections." What other factors in society would you suppose also correlate closely with "political democracy"?
4. In a society that would like to think of itself as very close to libertarian, what are the arguments for regulating some of the aspects of (a) cable television, (b) radio and over-the-air television, (c) newspapers, and (d) telephone companies?
5. If there is a "right to know," how would you define it?

CHAPTER 13

Historical Perspectives on Liberty

When we concern ourselves with press freedom, we plunge immediately into the realm of ethics. The two are symbiotic, and a brief historical perspective will show how the two have impacted on one another through the years. Although they are closely related, they contain elements of paradox; philosophers have recognized this and have tried to reconcile them. And it has not been easy. Most journalists today appear to think more about freedom than about ethics—but this attitude may be changing, albeit slowly, and it is this change that we shall deal with in this chapter.

The basic question that prompts such a discussion is this: What is freedom and how can it be used to channel journalism into more productive, progressive, and moral directions?[1] To get some help with this question, let us go back some two centuries—to the Enlightenment.

Philosophers of the eighteenth century felt that they lived in the best of all possible times and worlds; nature seemed good and people rational. There was optimism, and progress seemed inevitable. Reason during this century was definitely on the throne while occultism and emotionalism cowered in the few remaining shadows. At least this was true in Europe, the home base of American journalism.

---

[1] For a recent in-depth discussion attempting to answer this question, see John C. Merrill, *The Dialectic in Journalism: Toward a Responsible Use of Press Freedom* (Baton Rouge: LSU Press, 1989).

THE SPIRIT OF REASON

Although the spirit of the Age of Reason did not last very long in the overall sweep of history, it did have a powerful impact. If nothing else, it reached into the early American colonies and the newly created American nation. It influenced Franklin, Jefferson, Hamilton, Madison, Jay, and others—Enlightenment men, all who valued rationalism and individualism and, most important of all for the press, freedom of expression. Let us consider some of the perspectives on freedom that were prominent in Europe during the Age of Reason.

In this time of rationalism in Europe full appreciation was given to the concept of freedom. And this concern with freedom did not remain on an intellectual level but spilled over into economics, politics, and the general social domain.

Since the British were staunch supporters of freedom, let us turn first to them. As we noted in Chapter 12, Milton proposed a "self-righting principle," which has stood through the centuries as a justification for a free press system, at least as it is understood under capitalism. His thesis was based on the assumption that men have reason and are wise enough to know right from wrong and good from bad. This being the case, they should be free from government control over their expression. And unless they have free choice in their communication activities, people cannot fully exercise their reason. Milton believed that, given a free and open encounter, truth will defeat error. This is the core of his well-known principle, which still prevails in the mass consciousness of the West, although it is questioned often by individual intellectuals.

John Locke, generally considered the leading philosopher of the Enlightenment, set the tone for the Enlightenment philosophers who followed. It was Locke, by and large, who had the greatest influence on the later development of the American republic. Liberty was very important to Locke. He saw it as a *natural* right, one that should not be abridged except when so doing might interfere with the liberty of another. He also saw government as being a creation of, and thereby a servant of, the people. Locke believed that power was given freely by the people to government—not surrendered by them, as Hobbes had maintained. The idea of majority rule and governmental responsibility to the people, so important in the new American government at the time, was largely borrowed from Locke. There is little doubt of the great influence of Locke on such thinkers as Jefferson and Paine in America and Rousseau and Montesquieu in France.

Locke also stressed the sanctity of the individual, the rule of law, checks and balances in government, the rule of reason in human affairs, and a belief that the mind is capable of finding the truth. He saw the need for maximum freedom for the individual if the mind were to be able to do its proper work. While Locke was enthroning Reason, there were important figures like George Berkeley who were planting seeds of mysticism in the philosophical terrain. Berkeley was opposed to Locke's theory of knowledge, which separated ideas from things. For Berkeley, the only things that were real were ideas. So the seeds of "idealism" were planted, and they would grow well in the late eighteenth and nineteenth centuries.

DISCORDANT VOICES

A danger sign for the Enlightenment emphasis on freedom was also appearing in France. Jean-Jacques Rousseau (1712–1778) was talking about liberty (coining the slogan "liberty, fraternity, and equality") while at the same time setting the stage for the terrorism of the French Revolution and the coming of tyranny to the country. According to Bertrand Russell, Rousseau was the father of the romantic movement and the precursor of modern authoritarianism: he led to Hitler, whereas Locke in England led to Franklin Roosevelt and Winston Churchill. For in spite of Rousseau's basic affinity for freedom, he came to the position that each person, for everyone's sake, must give up freedom and power to the state; the collective will must be obeyed. This French "democrat" would turn the clock back to Plato, with the Collective Will taking the place of the Philosopher King.

Unlike Plato, however, Rousseau was an egalitarian, probably the foremost such in the history of political thought. For him, the social contract was overriding. There must, he said, be "the total alienation of each associate, together with all his rights, to the whole community." He saw individuals as parts of a corporate whole, conforming to the general will. He actually defined freedom as "absolute power": a kind of forced obedience and conformity to the whole. Not the liberty of *individuals,* but the liberty of the corporate body, was paramount. It is easy to see how Rousseau strongly influenced authoritarians of all types—from a Hitler to Stalin—and how, especially, his concept of "freedom" as corporate freedom is reflected in contemporary Marxist societies such as the Soviet Union. It may also be noted that present-day "press freedom" in the United States reflects vestiges of Rousseau's thought: the newspaper, for example—the corporate entity, not the individual journalist—has the freedom.

Many philosophers of the eighteenth century added their variations to the idea of freedom. David Hume defined freedom in such a way as to combine the later idea of "positive" and "negative" freedom: it was an all-encompassing concept which saw liberty as the "power of acting or not acting according to the determinations of the will." Hume believed that the essence of freedom is this: "If we choose to remain at rest, we may; if we choose to move, we also may."

But the philosophers of eighteenth-century Britain, where liberty was stressed, did not conceive of freedom as absolute; they generally held that reason dictated moderation in its use. Thus Edmund Burke: "The *extreme* of liberty (which is its abstract perfection, but its real fault) obtains no-where, nor ought to obtain anywhere. . . . liberty must be limited to be possessed."

Beginning early in the nineteenth century, freedom of expression and the press began to be stressed by many philosophers. Jeremy Bentham (1748–1832) in England was acknowledging that the liberty of the press had its "inconveniences" but went on to say that the "evils which result from it are not to be compared to those of a censorship." Censorship was terrible to Bentham, and he called it "nothing less than the danger of stopping the whole progress of human kind in all its paths."

Lord Acton saw freedom as an end in itself, not merely as a means to an end. He said: "Now liberty and good government do not exclude each other; and there are excellent reasons why they should go together. Liberty is not a means to a higher political end. It is itself the highest political end."

In Germany, Hegel was also talking about freedom. This preeminent philosopher of the nineteenth century saw individual freedom going through stages or changing throughout history; this view, of course, was consistent with his philosophy of becoming, of growth, of progress. He shows how freedom diminishes through history: first (in its youth) there is the dominance of one individual, the ruler, who alone is free; then there is a second stage (adolescence), in which "individualities" are forming them-selves, and then a third stage (old age), which sees social aims absorbing all individual aims.

Offsetting the incipient statism of Hegel, Alexis de Tocqueville enters the scene—a kind of radical libertarian among more moderate ones. A Frenchman, whose *Democracy in America* is one of the most perceptive analyses of America ever written, de Tocqueville spoke of freedom in glowing terms and championed the individual against the state. De Toc-queville believed that freedom produces a recognition of the importance of individualism. He wrote that it gives people "an exalted idea of their own individual value, and a passionate love of independence." It also provides people with what de Tocqueville called "extraordinary energy and ardour [for the] pursuit of their own interests and passions." Individual freedom, according to de Tocqueville, has led to extraordinary actions, and adopted by an entire people—the Americans among others—"it has created the most energetic nations that have ever existed."

JOHN STUART MILL

Across the channel in England was the utilitarian philosopher John Stuart Mill, who is counted among the greatest champions of freedom, especially freedom of expression. Mill was not as convinced of the absolute nature of free expression, however, as was Locke. If such expression caused social harm, Mill believed, it should be circumscribed. Whereas Locke had seen freedom of the press as a God-given natural right, Mill saw it in utilitarian terms: what it could do in bringing about happiness or good in a society.

In his famous essay "On Liberty," Mill wrote: "If all mankind minus one were of one opinion, and only that person were of the contrary opinion, mankind would be no more justified in silencing that one person, than he, if he had the power, would be justified in silencing mankind." We might note, however, that Mill was talking about *opinions* and not about the gamut of information—including what is called "pornography"—that is available today. Mill believed that truth, if it has a fair chance, always triumphs over error in the end. This position of Mill's was evidently not very well planted in his mind, however, for we find that another time he called the "self-righting" process of Milton "one of those pleasant falsehoods which are repeated until they are taken for granted, but which all experience tends to repudiate." At any rate, we do know that Mill valued free discussion of serious matters; it was essential, he said, for good government. In fact, Mill believed it "equal in value to good government, because without it good government cannot exist."

Mill felt, though, that freedom was appropriate only in societies of relatively high educational standards, where people could *rationally* exercise such freedom. He did not project his freedom principle onto everyone. For example, he would exclude from his freedom principle all "backward states of society." For people of such states, Mill said, despotism would remain necessary until such time as social evolution would bring them to the level of modern Western civilization. Freedom, for Mill, was for those who could use it for the expanding of happiness and the social good. It was, in short, a utilitarian instrument. So we can see that John Stuart Mill was not really the freedom lover and absolutist he is often said to be. He was, in short, an early advocate of "responsible" freedom.

Be that as it may, Mill's basic tenets have been very influential and are generally accepted by journalists to this day, at least in the West. This does not mean, as is often pointed out, that everyone (especially government) puts Mill's philosophy into practice. Probably the greatest restraint on liberty in Western society, as many contemporary analysts are pointing out, is the increase in secrecy and in strictures on the free flow of information.

EARLY AMERICAN PERSPECTIVES

Having looked at some of the European Enlightenment's perspectives on freedom, let us now turn to the new American nation, where Enlightenment perspectives infused the minds of the Founding Fathers with a love of reason, individualism, and freedom.

The Enlightenment spirit sweeping into America in the eighteenth century was essentially Aristotelian. On many issues Aristotle had differed from the eighteenth-century philosophers, but in a broad way his thought was Enlightenment thought. At the center of his philosophy was the rejection of the notion of the ideal and affirmation of the reality of particulars and of individuals, and of lawfulness of nature. That is, form and matter together make up concrete, observable individual realities; there are no abstract forms unto themselves. The essence of a thing was in itself and thus we fulfill ourselves when we exercise that essentially human characteristic, rationality. Enthroned were the sovereignty of reason, belief in objectivity and absolutes, a positive view of man's potential, and the value of intellectual development, self-fulfillment, and personal happiness.

America's Founding Fathers were well educated, articulate, and imbued with the basic ideas of individualism, reason, and freedom. James Franklin, for instance, gave great stress to the Miltonic notion that controversy must be made public, that it is necessary for the self-righting process to take place so that truth and falsehood can fight it out in the public print. His brother, Benjamin, also proposed a free flow of information in the marketplace, but he, like so many others, envisioned limits to freedom; for instance, he would not approve of printing anything that might offend the Church or State, another reflection of Miltonic thought. Ben Franklin was one of the first to see the dilemma of a capitalistic press system, the paradoxical motives of public service versus private profit. was concerned about the conflict but offered no real answers.

Under the pseudonym of "Hortensius," George Hay of Virginia wrote perhaps the strongest polemic in defense of press freedom in early America. In "An Essay on Liberty of the Press," published in 1799, Hay came out for total exemption of the press from any kind of legislative control—an absolutist doctrine of press freedom. Hay advocated the press's "printing any thing without control."

Alexander Hamilton, although he argued (under the pen name "Publius") against a Bill of Rights for the Constitution, was a staunch believer in free expression. He saw no reason to put into the Bill of Rights anything about press freedom unless such a freedom was strictly defined. How could something be protected, Hamilton asked, unless we knew what that something was? It is a question that has challenged us ever since.

JEFFERSON AND MADISON

Thomas Jefferson, often considered Freedom's Founding Father, believed that human beings were rational and perfectible—but this perfectibility was contingent on their being exposed to a wide variety of information and ideas. In this belief he drew heavily on Milton, Locke, and Mill. And like them, Jefferson would put strings on freedom.

He believed, for example, that the press had an obligation to provide dependable, accurate, and comprehensive news and opinion. (He sounds like the Hutchins Commission in this respect.) He believed that if the press failed in its responsibility, the people should—as the ultimate check on the press—force the press into a more responsible mode. Jefferson had a "responsibility" view of press freedom. Liberty, he believed, was not doing as you please, but rather doing as you *ought*. This is, of course, a limited view of freedom, but it is a socially responsible one, the nature of which is determined by ethics and not by personal or institutional whim.

James Madison, another Founding Father, had a different concept of press freedom. He did not have a strong belief in the people's desire to seek the truth—feeling, as did Ben Franklin, that the people sought mainly to reinforce their own beliefs and to seek the company of those who shared these beliefs. Accordingly, Madison posited the existence of groups of like-minded people, called "factions." Factions sought social control, even at the expense of other freedoms, so as to maintain their own value systems. Madison was thereby led to a different view of press freedom and of journalism's role in society. He would have the press provide accurate, comprehensive information, but he believed that factions would seek to influence the press for their own advantage. So the press was in a sense in an adversarial relationship—not just with government, but with a multitude of factions or constituencies in the society.

The primary responsibility of the press, thought Madison, was to preserve its independence from any outside interference. The press should be free to be "responsible" *or* "irresponsible." There would obviously be some press abuse. Madison put it this way: "Some degree of abuse is inseparable from the proper use of everything; and in no instance is this more true, than in that of the press." Freedom was the ultimate responsibility for Madison. So we can see that it was really Madison, not Jefferson, who was the radical libertarian among the Founding Fathers. Madison did prize pluralism, in the sense of factions checking on one another. Press pluralism, which we hear so much about these days, really got into the lexicon of journalism on account of this Madisonian emphasis. It should be noted that the concept of "objectivity," so prominent in press discussions today, did not even come up in the thinking of the Founding Fathers, probably because press discourse was, by and large, practical and not theoretical.

Many other early American leaders could be quoted here, but the ones we have heard from well exemplify the Enlightenment values of freedom and reason that got our republic underway. It can also be seen that even in these early days, notions of moderation, of social responsibility, of limits on freedom—in short, a concern with ethics—was being injected into the discourse on freedom.

RECENT AMERICAN VOICES

By and large, recent American voices on press freedom (and freedom generally) are little more than footnotes to the classic statements of European and early American spokesmen from the Age of Reason. It is difficult indeed to say more about the subject than was said by Locke, Voltaire, Mill, Burke, Madison, and Jefferson. But the subject of freedom still intrigues modern intellectuals. Concern with freedom is continuous and arguments endless. Let us briefly look at some contemporary manifestations.

A professor of journalism at the University of Missouri, Ed Lambeth, in *Committed Journalism,* pays tribute to liberty as being indispensable to the idea of justice. But he cites Warren Breed, a sociologist who studied the workings of newsrooms in depth, as showing how reporters may lose "their potential as moral agents by a socialization process in which the reporter is taught to accept newsroom policies inimical to wider public needs."[2] The idea of loss of freedom by the individual journalist within the organization is an interesting one that has received very little attention in American journalism; most of the emphasis has been on freedom of the media *from government* and not on freedom of the individual journalist from social control in the workplace.

Robert H. Bork, professor of law at Yale, warns that journalists should look at press freedom as a "problem" and not just as a right. He implies that press freedom may actually be lost unless journalists use freedom more wisely and responsibly:

> If they [journalists] would preserve their freedoms, the members of the press might do well to realize that freedom is not merely a right, it is also a problem. Increasingly the press is perceived by many people as being a center of irresponsible power.[3]

---

[2] Quoted in Ed Lambeth, *Committed Journalism* (Bloomington: Indiana University Press, 1986), pp. 34–35.

[3] Robert Bork, "The First Amendment Does Not Give Greater Freedom to the Press Than to Speech," *The Center Magazine* (March–April, 1979), p. 31.

Mortimer Adler, a popular contemporary philosopher, believes in limited freedom, a freedom inhibited by moral concern. He speaks of *acquired freedom,* calling it "moral freedom," or "having a will habitually disposed by virtue to seek what it ought." This is the type of freedom, says Adler, associated with wisdom and moral virtue; it is possessed only by those who, in the course of their personal development, "have acquired some measure of virtue and wisdom." This acquired freedom is, for Adler, a kind of freedom to act virtuously. So we see that Adler, like Jefferson, Milton and others, would place limitations on freedom.

Many persons feel that the First Amendment should provide freedom to the broadcast media as well as to the print media in the United States. This has long been a bone of contention, for as some point out, if the principle of press freedom is valid for the print media, it is equally valid for the broadcast media. Bill Monroe of NBC News is one who has made a strong plea for First Amendment "protection" for broadcasters. Others have echoed his message.

Professor Murray Rothbard, writing from an anarchistic or radical libertarian perspective, agrees with Monroe about broadcasting's lack of freedom and draws sweeping conclusions about the current condition of broadcasting in the United States:

> There is one important area of American life where no effective freedom of speech of the press does or can exist under the present system. That is the entire field of radio and television. . . . The federal government, as the licensor of the airwaves, asserts the right and the power to regulate the stations minutely and continuously. Thus, over the head of each station is the club of the threat of nonrenewal, or even suspension, of its license. In consequence, the idea of freedom of speech in radio and television is no more than a mockery.[4]

Rothbard and other radical libertarians are, in a sense, throwbacks to James Madison and are not really in the mainstream of current intellectual concerns about "responsibility," media obligations to society, and what has become known as "positive freedom." Thus, Robert Nozick, a Harvard philosopher, takes a strong stand in favor of maximum freedom—for the individual as well as for the institution or group. With respect to government interference in press affairs, he takes a radical libertarian view: *government should keep hands off entirely.* Nozick believes in a "night watchman" role for the state, whereby the state would interfere in social affairs only as a protector of the safety and freedoms of the people. Nozick, like most libertarians, believes that freedom and any kind of

---

[4] Murray Rothbard, *For a New Liberty* (New York: Collier Books, 1978), p. 98.

forced redistribution of wealth—to say nothing of complete equality—are in radical opposition. In this he differs greatly from his distinguished colleague at Harvard John Rawls, who is vitally concerned both with egalitarianism and with the social responsibility (defined by the state, if necessary) of the press.

The extreme counterpoint to Nozick and the radical libertarians might be Herbert Marcuse, a Marxist philosopher in California, who has presented a formidable argument that free choice is *not* necessarily a good thing—that *what* is chosen is more important than simply having a wide range of choices. He would therefore, seem to oppose the capitalist world's avowed dedication to a pluralistic information system.

THE TREND TOWARD "RESPONSIBLE" FREEDOM

Far more in the mainstream of the trend toward ethical concern in any talk about freedom is John Phelan, a Fordham communications professor, for whom philosopher Isaiah Berlin's distinction between positive and negative freedom is instructive. *Positive freedom,* for Berlin, is an inner spiritual reality. It is the capacity to choose "the better thing, at times the best thing, according to some moral vision or religious ideal." It is the freedom to want what one should. Professor Marcuse would most likely agree but would stress that some outside authority usually determines the "should" instead of the person him or herself. *Negative freedom,* on the other hand, is simply the absence of external constraints on our behavior. One may, while restrained outwardly, have positive freedom: Mahatma Gandhi in jail, for example, enjoyed a high degree of positive freedom even while deprived of negative freedom. Berlin and others, riding the crest of social responsibility today, believe that positive freedom is the more noble concept. Negative freedom is merely a condition that can come to good only if positive freedom is also present. Using one's freedom well—ethically and responsibly—is the growing concern.

Professor Phelan, however, draws our attention to a danger in the concept of positive freedom: The censor extols it, for it provides a rationale for censorship. The censor wishes the state to guide citizens "to want what they should by shielding them from temptations to want what they should not," as Phelan puts it. Positive freedom does emphasize what we should *do* with freedom, whereas negative freedom simply protects one from restrictions that would *prevent* self-determination of what one will do—good or bad.

Clifford Christians of the University of Illinois, a leading voice on media ethics among journalism educators, feels that far too much attention is given to the press's negative freedom (from restraint) and not nearly enough to the press's positive freedom or responsibility. It is his desire that ethics be woven more thoroughly into the fabric of the press—and of journalism education.

> . . . In an environment where freedom is prized above all, accountability is not often understood clearly. Accounting, properly requested and unreservedly given, is alien territory. . . . Ethical principles concerning obligations and reckoning do not find a natural home within a journalism hewn from the rock of negative freedom.[5]

Professor Christians expresses a reasoned suspicion of freedom, especially of the "negative" kind. But he also seems to realize that it is this negative freedom—this freedom from outside restrictions—that forms the core of the journalist's concept of press freedom. Positive freedom may be noble, and tied closely to a concept of social responsibility, but at the same time it conjures up the danger of censorship. This is indeed one of the paradoxes of freedom. Professor Christians insists on more ethical concern in journalism—the tempering of freedom with virtue. This insistence does not really, it seems to us, endanger negative freedom. Rather, it places more and more responsibility on the individual journalist. At any rate, this concern with ethics exemplifies the increasing concern in America with a moral dimension whenever a discussion of freedom takes place.

This quick survey of perspectives on press freedom has, of course, neglected many interesting and important viewpoints, especially non-Western ones. We have, rather, concentrated on the values of the European Enlightenment, which have so significantly informed the Western World's understanding of liberty. We have seen that from the very early days of Western civilization, when the individualistic spirit of Aristotle merged with the more collectivistic spirit of Plato, the tendency among intellectuals generally has been toward a moderate, or "positive," view of freedom. Freedom, tempered with social concern and a respect for consequences, is becoming ever more the emphasis of Western journalism—or at least of Western journalism's rhetoric.

Positive freedom has become more important as the concept of the ethical use of freedom has come to the forefront in journalistic dialogue. Negative freedom is still important, but it appears to be looked upon generally as a kind of sterile freedom that is not progressive or self-

---

[5] C. G. Christians, Kim B. Rotzoll, and Mark Fackler, *Media Ethics* (White Plains, NY: Longman, 1983), p. 28. See also the second edition of this book (1987).

assertive in a socially concerned way. Jefferson, not Madison, appears to be the prophet of America's journalistic present and future. The freedom to be "irresponsible" is receding in serious discussions among Western journalists: Madison's contentiousness of factions is giving way to a kind of cooperative spirit and social harmony in the use of journalistic freedom.

And with all these developments in our conceptual understanding of freedom of expression, Aristotle still seems to be the spiritual guru. He stands as a force of rationalism, a symbol of moderation, a stalwart of personal self-realization, and a lover of freedom—but one who, we must remember, loved freedom *rationally*. And that does not mean blindly or selfishly. Aristotle's "social side" is getting more exposure these days—his concern for moderation and for the feelings and welfare of others.

Freedom. It is still a powerful force in American journalism, but it is being increasingly tempered by an ethical concern and a new, Aristotelian spirit of moderation—a redefinition, really, in the direction of "positive" freedom, whereby socially helpful or constructive journalism takes precedence over introverted and uncaring communication activities. Public criticism of the media tells us that such a trend has not gone nearly far enough, but it is underway and increasing numbers of voices are urging its continuance.

AFTERTHOUGHTS

1. The idea that truth will win out in a free marketplace of ideas is certainly as old as John Milton and has generally been accepted in the United States. Is there any evidence at all that this hypothesis is valid?

2. The philosophers of the Age of Reason, especially John Locke, stressed the individual and wanted to keep government to a minimum. How does this general philosophy bear on the development of the American concept of press freedom?

3. John Stuart Mill viewed freedom of expression in utilitarian terms, not in the natural rights terms of Locke. How does Mill's concept presage the modern concept of "positive freedom" and social responsibility? Is Locke's view more in keeping with absolute libertarianism, which sees press freedom even as the freedom to be irresponsible?

4. Explain why, if you believe it is the case, Madison was more of a press libertarian than Jefferson. If you were to compare Jefferson with Locke and Mill, with whom would he have the greater affinity?

5. If broadcasting in the United States were to enjoy the same degree of freedom as the print media, what would have to transpire? What would be your rationale for proposing such freedom for broadcasting? For opposing such freedom?

CHAPTER 14

Ethical Perspectives

In one sense this whole book deals with the ethics of mass communication and the mass media, for there is no way to divorce the problems and basic issues of mass communication from ethical considerations. What are the right activities for this or that medium? How do we balance the harm sometimes caused by our communications against their obvious benefits? What standards should media practitioners apply, and whence do they derive them? Should media people have definite, absolute ethical principles or should they adjust their actions to each situation as it comes up?

Media ethics may be defined as the branch of philosophy (or of mass communication) that helps media workers determine what is right to do—or what is best of several alternatives. It is, then, part of moral philosophy—a normative science of conduct—with voluntary, freely chosen behavior as the focus of concern. Thus journalistic ethics should set forth guidelines, rules, norms, codes, and principles that will lead—not force—journalists to make moral decisions. Ethics should give a journalist standards by which he or she can judge actions to be right or wrong, good or bad, responsible or irresponsible.

Although it has always been difficult to discuss ethics, it is especially so today, because the entire intellectual atmosphere is filled with voices insisting to be taken seriously in regard to ethical matters. This is indeed the day of egalitarianism, freedom, intuition, and relativity, even as the scientific method is extolled, and these emphases have projected themselves into the field of ethics.

It would be much easier to discuss law. Many actions are legal but not ethical, and in such cases no codebooks of ethics can be consulted in order to settle disputes. Even so-called codes of ethics adopted by various communication societies and associations give little or no specific, direct guidance. Ethics is primarily personal, and to be meaningful it must be internalized within the media practitioner; what some fuzzy and impersonal "code" may say is of no great importance to the individual facing a moral decision. Following such a code would obviate moral reasoning and make ethics a kind of mechanistic activity.

NEEDED: AN ETHICAL CONCERN

We have taken a big first step when we are *concerned* about being ethical. Whether we are talking about a TV reporter, a magazine publisher, a radio talk-show host, a movie producer, or a newspaper reporter, the important first principle in ethics is a sincere *desire* to do the right thing, the helpful thing, the responsible thing. Such concern for doing right, for being ethical, reflects respect for the public welfare and a sense of responsibility about personal action. It leads the media practitioner to a commitment to reasoned ethical decision making among alternatives.

Sometimes journalists are seen as lacking a coherent moral commitment and a consistent, predictable practice with respect to ethical matters. Or they are seen as arrogant and power-hungry Machiavellians (see Chapter 17) who are dedicated to their own self-interest and success and believe that the ends justify any means. If a media person is not concerned with being ethical, only through chance will he or she take a right turn in the maze of daily media practice. A real concern with being ethical imposes upon the actor a rational, systematic analysis of alternative actions in an attempt to choose the best, most moral one—the right thing, or at least the best thing.

A TUFF ETHICAL FORMULA

Being ethical is difficult. Devising a guideline or formula to help in the enterprise is also difficult, and perhaps impossible. But we are suggesting a rather simple device here:

T—Truthful
U—Unbiased
F—Full
F—Fair

Consider the semantic problems attached to each component. One can say that a journalist should be *truthful*. But what does that mean? Telling everything the journalist knows? Not protecting sources or not concealing the names of rape victims? And can a journalist really be *unbiased?* Every position we take, even the one to be unbiased, involves "sides." As for providing *full* or thorough reporting, we all know that this is more idealistic than practical. In fact, in the name of being "ethical," journalists often purposely omit certain information and quotations, thereby keeping the report from being "full."

Perhaps the *fairness* element is most troublesome of all. And it is, without a doubt, the element that keeps the TUFF formula from being internally consistent. For example, if a journalist tries to be fair in a certain story, the full or the unbiased elements may have to be sacrificed. So in a very real sense, trying to be fair will often compromise the truth or objectivity of the story.

TWO BASIC JOURNALISTIC ORIENTATIONS

Before getting into a discussion of ethics per se, let us consider two main tendencies or orientations.[1] These undoubtedly shape the kind of ethical outlook a journalist adopts.

1. *The people-oriented journalist.* Such journalists make most journalistic decisions on the basis of the way they think the decisions will affect people. They are either egoists or altruists, and sometimes a little of both. People's feelings and areas of sensitivity are taken into consideration when the story is being written. News determinations and decisions are made largely on the basis of perceived consequences. This might be called a "personal consequence" journalistic orientation; certainly it is very much a *subjective* one.

The people-oriented journalist, therefore, always places people at the center of journalism, not in the traditional sense of "names make news," but in a sense whereby the journalist considers the impact of journalistic actions on people. A certain story may be slanted because of the journalist's concern for a particular person, because of a certain bias for or against a participant in or on the periphery of a story. The journalist's sensitivity to, or bias toward, certain people will determine to a large degree what will be considered news in the first place; it will also determine the emphasis or

---

[1] For these and other basic journalistic orientations, see Merrill's *The Imperative of Freedom* (New York: Hastings House, 1974), *Existential Journalism* (New York: Hastings House, 1977), and *The Dialectic in Journalism* (Baton Rouge: Louisiana State University Press, 1989).

slant—what will be omitted or selected, played up or down. This is very much the "involved," subjective orientation.

2. *The event-oriented journalist.* This journalist is concerned with facts and events, with circumstances per se. Of course, he or she knows that people are important in news stories, but there is little concern about the consequences for the people in the stories; only the event is important. As aloof as possible, ever the neutralist, telling the story and letting the "chips fall where they may," this journalist is the paradigm of the *objective* reporter. Such journalists make constant efforts not to become involved with people and to keep their own feelings out of the story. They try to detach themselves from all personal opinions, attitudes, or biases. They seek to be dispassionate and objective in their news presentation. The important thing is to get the facts; if they are connected with persons (and they almost always are), then so be it. Facts, to the event-oriented journalist, are indeed sacred; they are essential to the account of what happened.

The person who is an egoist and/or an altruist will find that his or her ethics follows or supports that psychological orientation. The concern with ethics will be quite different from that of the person who is basically an objectivist or neutralist, who tries to keep aloof from journalism and who focuses on the events or facts rather than on the way journalistic practices may affect people.

REASON AND ETHICS

Ethics is truly a personal matter, personal in the sense that it arises from a rational concern for one's conduct. It is also personal in the sense that one's conduct is self-directed and self-enforced; a person voluntarily follows a code of conduct because he or she thinks it is the right thing to do. There are those who wish that ethical standards could be externally imposed and enforced, that people could be *made* to be ethical. This is of course contradictory to the concept of ethics, for ethics are unenforceable. When a person's conduct is enforced, he or she is then under legal control, with free will taken away. "Ethics," then, describes a code of conduct that is self-enforced and, in general, is considered to be rationally arrived at. Reason enforces one's ethics. It might be said that a person's ethics is *personal* in the sense discussed above, it is *predictive* in that it serves as a guide for conduct and indicates pretty well what one can be expected to do in a certain situation, and it is *rational* in that reason dictates its acceptance.

Regardless of the particular ethical decisions they make, the important thing for journalists is that they think about ethics. They should care about ethics; they should not be amoral or nonethical in their activities.

Personal codes are of course always evolving to some degree, but they should always be becoming more, not less, demanding on the individual— demanding in the sense that the standards become ever more difficult to achieve and that they become increasingly more rational. Ethics, or at least a concern for ethics, instills in journalists a continuing sensitivity to their every action, to their every decision; it integrates or blends with the total search for truth. It is the alpha and omega of public communication.

What about the person who uses the freedom *not* to accept an ethical position? He or she is simply playing semantic games with the concept of freedom when trying to live without rules. Immanuel Kant, the eighteenth-century German philosopher, commonly considered the "philosopher's philosopher," said that a person is free only by setting up rules to live by and that no person's conduct can be moral if there is any outside compulsion such as reward or punishment. He put these two aspects together in his famous Categorical Imperative, which said in effect that we are required (duty bound) to act in such a way that we would be willing to see our conduct become a universal law. Although ethics is indeed personal, a person acts ethically or morally only when identifying self with all humankind.

ETHICAL THEORIES

Like so many other important and complex subjects, ethics can be looked at from a number of perspectives. Moral philosophers have devised many systems for classifying theories of ethics; we will discuss briefly a few of the most prominent typologies.[2]

Absolute/Relative

The ethical absolutist believes that there is one universal and eternal ethical code that basically applies to everyone in all ages. Changing opinions, traditions, and conditions make no significant difference from the point of view of this absolute moral code. There are actions that are "right" and actions that are "wrong," regardless of the place, time, or special circumstance.

The ethical relativist, on the other hand, ties morality more closely to emotion, putting considerable faith in intuition, inclinations, and feelings. The relativist says, in effect, that we have no right to make judgments about the ethics of others, for these judgments only indicate a bias—a

---

[2] The terminology and typology used here are adapted from several sources, but largely from William Lillie, *An Introduction to Ethics* (London: Methuen, University Paperbacks, 1961).

prejudice—on our part. He or she sees no moral superiority on the part of one code over another—an idea that would, if carried far enough, indicate that no action (or person) is any better than another. The relativist also holds that moral standards vary with different circumstances, at different times, and in different cultures.

Objective/Subjective

The ethical objectivist is an advocate of absolute ethics, seeing all absolute standards in ethics as necessarily objective. Ethical standards are objective in the sense of being formed *outside* the person; they are rational, based on something other than feelings or opinions. Something is "right" or "wrong," then, independent of the way a person might subjectively *feel* about it.

The ethical subjectivist, taking the contrary view, looks at ethics as simply the opinion or preference of a person; ethics is seen as a form of relative morality that views variability in moral judgments as being caused purely and simply by the *mental state* of a particular person. For example, a "good" action for me is one that I like.

Attitudinal/Consequential

An attitudinal ethical theory, a type of subjectivism, defines a right action as one toward which a person feels well disposed. In other words, conduct is "right" if it is harmonious with one's attitude. A consequence theory is quite different: it is closer to the objective position in that it places standards of value *outside* the person, specifically *in the consequences* of the action. So it is a kind of hindsight theory, determining the goodness or badness of an action only after the consequences have been noted. Utilitarian ethics (as espoused by such men as Jeremy Bentham and John Stuart Mill), in which the benefits to the greatest number of persons would be taken as the moral yardstick, is an example of consequence ethics.

Deontological/Teleological

The deontological ethical theory states that the rightness or wrongness of an action is dependent on the action itself and not on the results or consequences it produces. The intuitionist or existential journalist would be an example of a person with a deontological orientation; there is a natural and spontaneous sense of what is right and wrong, and this sense or "conscience" will be a reliable guide.

The teleological ethical theory is similar to the consequence theory discussed above. For example, the journalistic *hedonist,* teleologically oriented, would say that the rightness or wrongness of a particular journalistic action would depend on the pleasure or displeasure it brings to the journalist. *Theoretically,* then, if one received pleasure from lying or misrepresenting in a news story, he or she would have done the right thing. So we see that the bringing of pleasure, for example, either to the person acting or to others, is one aspect of the consequence theory.

A DIALECTICAL TYPOLOGY

In addition to the several ways of classifying ethical theories mentioned above, another might well be discussed briefly. It is a ternary typology that seemingly has developed by a Hegelian dialectical process through which a kind of compromise (or synthesis) has grown out of a clash between two extreme theories (the thesis and antithesis, in Hegelian terms). The thesis, as it were, can be called *legalistic* (or code) ethics, the conflicting extreme or antithesis can be called *antinomian* ethics, and the synthesis or compromise theory may be called *situation* ethics.[3] There is reason to believe that all the many theories and systems of ethics can be accommodated in this typology.

Legalistic Ethics

This is an absolute or objective ethical system based largely on tradition, on social agreement, or on a firm religious moral code. It is partly—perhaps largely—rational, although many people insist that any kind of reliance on a rigid code of conduct cannot really be rational. The rationality of legalistic ethics stems from the fact that adherents to this morality have a good *reason* to follow it; they have determined through the years that there have emerged certain basic, objective, absolute principles of conduct that serve the society best and bring the greatest amount of pleasure to the most people. So, although it is traditional ethics, and quite rigid in most respects, the legalistic theory is rational in that it is pragmatic, socially beneficial, and personally comforting. It is also, we might add, very much consequence-oriented.

When a person breaks the code, doing so is considered *unethical* by the members of the society; morality, then, is defined by (the vast majority of)

---

[3] These three ethical theories have the best and fullest exposition in Joseph Fletcher, *Situation Ethics: The New Morality* (Philadelphia: Westminster Press, 1966). As far as we know, however, we are the first to view this ternary classification in the light of Hegelian dialectics.

a person's contemporaries. This kind of *consensus ethics* says that people are ethical or unethical to the degree that they conform to, or deviate from, the norms or codes of their society. If, for example, American journalism had a single code of ethics that was adopted by journalists throughout the country, and if a practitioner "broke" a part of the code, his or her action would (or could) be considered unethical, at least within the profession. Legalistic or code ethics implies a general agreement on basic ethical or moral precepts; if this agreement is lacking—as it seems to be in libertarian press systems—then there is little chance of legalistic ethics having any great impact.

So we see that a legalistic ethical system is an absolute one in which wrong is wrong and right is right, and judgments on personal conduct can be made relatively easily. It is only natural that a reaction should set in against it, and, as is true with most reactions, the reactionaries (or rebels) quickly equal or even outdistance the advocates of the old system in their extremism and rigidity. This is what has happened in the case of those who despise code ethics to such a degree that they, in effect, have repudiated *all* ethics and have rebelled against any kind of standard or law.

Antinomian Ethics

The constrictions and absolutes of code ethics, then, inspired what has been called *antinomian* ethics. The antinomians have desired to toss out all basic principles, precepts, standards, and laws. Whereas the legalists tend toward absolutist ethics, antinomians gravitate toward anarchy or nihilism in ethics.

Antinomians are against all standards, thinking they need no directions or rules. They "play it by ear," making decisions in the area of morality, intuitively, and spontaneously. They are in a sense existentialists[4] who have lost faith in reason so far as ethical decisions are concerned. They want no guide other than the senses and their own intuitions and instincts. In many ways, antinomians really do not subscribe to an ethical theory, for antinomianism is a kind of *un*ethics or *non*ethics that leads to behavior that is quite unpredictable, erratic, and spontaneous. Although antinomians claim to be the real *humanists,* their irrational and sensory inclinations resemble more those of lower animal orders, for instinctivism is hardly compatible with humanism.

---

[4] Of the many excellent books on existentialism, two we feel are especially good discussions: William Barrett, *Irrational Man: A Study in Existential Philosophy* (New York: Doubleday, 1958), and F. H. Heinemann, *Existentialism and the Modern Predicament* (New York: Harper Torchbook, 1958).

Antinomians make ethical decisions as they go, not even realizing that they are making them—not even really considering them ethical decisions. Rather, the decisions are just reflections of feelings, instincts, inclinations, and intuitions. This ethical (or nonethical) system might simply be referred to as "whim ethics."

Situation Ethics

Now we come to the "synthesis" theory of ethics, generally known as *situation ethics*. This is the middle ground between legalistic and antinomian ethics, although it must be admitted that it is often confused with the nonethics of antinomianism just discussed. This confusion is unfortunate, for situation ethics is rational, whereas antinomian ethics is irrational. The two have very little in common.

Situation ethics is a synthesis because it is a compromise between legalistic and antinomian ethics. Therefore, situation ethics does have *something* in common with each of the other two. It resembles antinomian ethics in that it is not tied to absolute principles. It resembles legalistic or code ethics in that it is rational and not intuitive, and it has not entirely forsaken traditional legalistic or absolutist moral principles. In fact, situation ethics begins with traditional code ethics.

But there the resemblance ends. Situationists are guided by traditional code ethics but are not rigidly bound by any ethical rules; they break them when they think it necessary to do so. They take the *situation* and relevant special circumstances into consideration; in this sense they are relativists, but rational relativists—who *think* before they depart from a basic ethical principle. They are rational because they have a *reason* for departing from an ethical principle.

Journalistic situationists may well be those who believe that it is all right to distort a particular story, or even to lie, if they foresee that the harm done to their newspaper or their country will be very great if they "play it straight" and tell the truth. There are times when it is *right* to play down—or leave out completely—certain stories or pictures; there are other times when it would be wrong. But the important thing here is that journalists *think* before taking a certain action; they are not acting on instinct or intuition.

It appears to us that today the majority of American journalists subscribe to the situation ethics position. There are some rigid legalists or code moralists in journalism, to be sure, but they do not seem to exert much influence. Increasingly one finds the antinomian in the mass media or in journalism schools, scorning rationalism and flaunting existential instinctivism, but the mass media—rather rigid institutions that they are—have not yet fallen under the spell of these ethical nihilists.

JOURNALISTIC ETHICS: A MIDDLE WAY?

Journalists would be wise, in trying to find a reasonable ethical ground upon which to stand, to consider combining deontology and teleology. They would start from the former approach, with basic principles or maxims to which they could reasonably pay allegiance, ones to which they feel a duty to follow. Some such journalistic maxims might be: never fail to give the source of your quotes in every story; never tamper with direct quotes; never purposely omit from a story any pertinent information you have in hand; never purposely quote out of context.

Such general principles should be very important to the journalist. But going a step further, the journalist must show a willingness to deviate from such principles when reason dictates another course, when projected or anticipated consequences warrant the desertion of these basic ethical maxims.

The important point is this: Journalists should not abandon *the idea of* basic principles or maxims of conduct; they should not abandon overriding guidelines for ethical action to which they are dedicated and which they feel a duty to (generally) uphold. These guidelines are what gives their ethics a sense of meaningfulness and considerable predictability. Having an allegiance to such maxims gives the journalists some concept of loyalty to principle, which most people need in order to consider ethics seriously as a guide to right actions.

But this having been said, it is important to stress that journalists must not blindly and unthinkingly follow maxims. Journalists must *consider* the ethics of particular situations; they must entertain some modification of these principles when their ethically conscious intellect deems such modification imperative. They must be flexible, in other words, willing to modify or moderate a basic ethical tenet in order to attain a *higher* ethical objective dictated by a reasoned analysis of the ethical situation. But it is important to stress that they should never capriciously break a rule or maxim. An exception must be made only after serious thought.

It is therefore incumbent on journalists who reason, who think, to bring anticipated or likely *consequences* into their analysis. When they do this, they begin shifting to a teleological orientation. To think ethically, they come to realize, is to be concerned with consequences. Journalists recognize that it is sound for them to graft teleology onto their basic sense of duty to certain ethical principles; in short, they merge teleology with deontology.

On the other hand, thinking too much about consequences carries its own dangers, such as the sort of expedient behavior against which Kant warned. And purely utilitarian decision making, on the basis of the greatest good for the greatest number, or some such principle, is questionable in journalism because acting on this principle can be tantamount to ignoring the desires, feelings, or fate of the minority—and can lead to making decisions on the basis of numbers alone.

So if not utilitarianism, nor ethical egoism, what then serves the journalist as a guide? The "something other" would include loyalty to some ethical principles above and beyond concern for consequences. As Kant never tired of stressing, thinking only of consequences before making an ethical decision is likely to lead to some kind of expedient action. Or said another way, seeking certain consequences from an action may well wash away any real ethical meaning in the action. This means that deontology and its recognition of the place of maxims is a very deep-seated consideration in journalistic ethics; when we talk of a "principled newsman" or a journalist as a "person of principle," we are implying a strong dedication to deontology. This position stresses that the journalist, like each of us, should accept the duty to do what is right *always,* even when he or she does not really feel inclined to do it.

What appears to be the best position for journalists is the middle way of ethics, that is, a synthesis of deontology and teleology. This is the reason we have worked our way through the aspects of ethical theory. We may conclude that the journalist can be a basic or principal deontologist but at the same time be a rational teleologist—willing to *depart from a basic loyalty to principle from time to time to achieve what he or she reasons is a higher moral decision.*

What are some of the practical ramifications of such an ethical synthesis? Let us consider a few:

- Journalists can in certain cases withhold information from their story, although they are basically dedicated to an ethics of full disclosure.
- They can, on occasion, act ethically by refraining from identifying a source and at the same time declare an allegiance to providing their audiences with the sources of their information.
- They can, at times, ethically justify some tampering with direct quotes in a story while retaining a sense of duty to the principle of accuracy in reporting.
- They can, from time to time ethically justify *not* "letting the people know" about some government document or policy that, although not released to the press and public, has somehow fallen into their hands.

Now, many persons will say that journalists are compromising their basic ethical principles when they rationally deviate from following them. No doubt they do compromise principles, but they compromise them in the name of, and for the sake of, a *higher ethics,* one that they arrive at *conscientiously, rationally,* and *in good faith.*

Even a strict deontologist could not seriously object to such a teleological departure from time to time. Why? Because it shows good will or an ethical motivation. And the deontologist puts great stock in good will and in the motives of a person taking an action. Besides, it might even be argued that this "middle way" ethicist is dedicated in reality to a basic principle or maxim. It might be worded this way:

> Accept a basic maxim and act on it out of duty, deviating from it when, and only when, using reason, you feel that probable consequences stemming from adherence will result in a less moral action.

By following the above maxim, the journalist is permitted to be fundamentally a deontologist; at the same time, he or she allows room for reason to intrude itself in the ethical situation and makes it possible for teleological readjustment in the cause of a higher morality. This synthesis of deontology and teleology—this "middle way of ethics"—seems a sound one for the journalist of today, who values commitment to principle yet desires a flexibility of action based on reason.

From our longtime observation of journalists making decisions that they hope are ethical, it has become clear that most of them have adopted, perhaps without realizing it, this synthesis of deontology and teleology which we will call *deontelic* ethics. Often they are apologetic or defensive about this position, however, for they feel they are in some way guilty of a watered-down or inauthentic ethics.

This attitude is unfortunate and should be abandoned. The middle position between deontology and teleology is *rational* and *ethical.* The fact that this ethical stance does not have a firmly established label in the history of philosophy is no reason why it is not a valid and sensible stance. The great impact of formal logic through the years has rendered such a synthesis stance unreliable, or at least suspicious. But for those who find great value in the logic of Hegelian dialectics, this synthesis ethics of deontology/teleology not only makes sense but also offers the soundest foundation for a journalistic ethics.

AFTERTHOUGHTS

1. In our society, where there is an expectation that media workers conform to the policies of media managers, is media ethics nothing more than the expectations of the institution for which someone works, those expectations being set by the boss?

2. If a newspaper reporter believes that the most ethical thing he or she can do is to provide a story as close to reality as possible—a "full-disclosure" report—should the reporter compromise this ethical principle by withholding verified facts from the story for whatever reason?

3. Which of the two types of journalists depicted in this chapter would have more trouble making ethical decisions: people-oriented journalists or event-oriented journalists? Why?

4. What makes us think that a rational ethical decision will be any better than an intuitive ethical decision? Cannot our "thinking" be as flawed as our "intuitions"?

5. If synthesis ethics—called in this chapter "deontelic" ethics—is sound ethics for media people, how will they ever know that it is?

CHAPTER 15

External Restraints

Like other freedoms in the United States, freedom of the press is constantly evolving. Many people look back nostalgically to a time in our early history when the press was supposedly more free. In fact, the press in the early days of the Republic was *less* free than it is today. The various state legislatures had inherited (and in many cases adopted into law) British restrictions on "seditious" writings, blasphemy, and press access to legislative assemblies.[1] The fight against prepublication restraints had ended for the most part with the Revolutionary War; the fight against *post*publication restraints, however, still had a long way to go.

Another misconception surrounds the First Amendment: "Congress shall make no law respecting an establishment of religion, or prohibiting the free exercise thereof; or abridging the freedom of speech, or of the press, or the right of the people peacefully to assemble, and to petition the government for redress of grievances." It was not, as many think, originally intended as a blanket guarantee of press freedom. Rather, there is reason to believe that the entire Bill of Rights was an effort by anti-federalists to prevent federal authority from superseding state authority. The First Amendment, if read with emphasis on the word "Congress," imposed limitations on national government only. The state legislatures

---

[1] In *Legacy of Suppression* (Cambridge, Mass.: Harvard University Press, 1960), Leonard W. Levy offers documentation to prove that America's founding fathers had no real understanding of freedom of speech and the press as we know it today. It was not until about 1800, according to Levy, that true libertarian thought began to emerge in America.

were still free to enact laws regarding the press, and most of them did. Not until much later was the First Amendment applied to the states as well as to the federal government.

The genius of the Founding Fathers lay in their locating the freedoms of speech and press in the same amendment with three other basic protections. There have been times in our history when a majority's desire to amend or abrogate the freedoms of speech and press was deterred only by a reluctance to tamper with the other three.

In any case, the press of the United States ranks today among the freest in the world. Its freedom is partly, but not entirely, due to the First Amendment. Every nation in the world with a written constitution "guarantees" press freedom. But having guaranteed it, most then pass restrictive legislation and engage in discriminatory practices against the press. The press in the United States is free because America is in fact a democracy with an independent, unintimidated judiciary. Otherwise, our own guarantee would be as meaningless as those in the constitutions of authoritarian countries.

Most persons would agree that the press plays a vital role in a democracy by serving as a watchdog over government, providing channels for popular participation in government decisions, and reevaluating the standards of society. However, we believe that no democracy, including the United States, can offer the press *complete* freedom; otherwise the nation would run the risk of abridging the freedom of all individuals or otherwise adversely affecting society as a whole. Few people would feel secure, for example, in a society that had no libel laws. Therefore, in many cases press controls are necessary, though in a democracy these are kept to a minimum by the press's vigorous appeal to the law and to public opinion.

Press controls are not always an obvious phenomenon. Governments in some countries manage to exert great pressure on the press by such devices as allocating newsprint, bribing—or licensing—newspeople, granting licenses for purchase of printing equipment abroad, or distributing all foreign news through government-owned wire services.

If we take a look at the press controls that exist in the United States, an acknowledged free-press country, we may have a better idea of the rationale for and potential dangers of press control. In approaching this subject, however, we must leave out all the contrivances of concealment exercised by individuals in government (ranging from the President down to the most insignificant municipal employee) and the activities of individual newspersons and press units to limit the flow of news. Excluding these two vast (and unchartable) areas, controls on information in the United States can be divided into three major categories: (1) punitive laws for harmful publication, (2) regulations that prevent access to information, and (3) pressures on publishers and broadcasters to restrict the flow of legally harmless information.

PUNISHING THE PRESS

A number of laws involving the press protect the reputation or property rights of individuals. More than this, however, the laws are also there to prevent breaches of the peace. When a person's honor or property rights have been damaged, society must offer some avenue for recompense or revenge other than a resort to violence. The laws affording this nonviolent avenue involve the following.

Libel

False reports adversely affecting reputations open the way to civil libel suits, although it must be remembered that there are 50 different sets of libel laws in the United States, one for every state.[2] In order to protect—and even encourage—freedom of speech and the press, the courts have sought to place strict limitations on the law of libel. The *New York Times* v. *Sullivan* ruling by the U.S. Supreme Court in 1964 greatly extended freedom of the press. The ruling essentially held that a public official could not recover libel damages, even for a false report, unless the official could prove that actual "malice" was involved. And malice, according to the Court, exists only if the plaintiff can prove that the defendant knew the material in question was false or had a "reckless disregard" for its truth or falsity. The Supreme Court declared that "debate on public issues should be robust and wide-open, and that it may well include vehement, caustic, and sometimes sharp attacks on government and public officials."

Since 1964 the ruling has been consistently broadened, primarily by liberally defining "public official" until it now includes "public figures"—persons in whom there is a public interest, and private citizens who engage voluntarily in public discussion of matters of "grave public concern and controversy." The courts have indeed searched for the outer limits of this First Amendment right. Libel law in the United States is considered by most observers to be among the most liberal in the world.

The media have been troubled, however, by suits involving large damages. In the 1980s entertainer Wayne Newton sued NBC for implying that he had connections with the Las Vegas underworld. The jury awarded Newton almost $20 million, which the judge reduced to $5,275,000. By the turn of the decade, the case was still moving through the appeal courts. In the early 1980s the media were also worried about the plethora of libel suits, but by the end of the 1980s the number of suits filed dropped sharply.

---

[2] "Criminal" libel suits, in which the state is the plaintiff, rarely occur in the United States. First, it is difficult to convince a public prosecutor to bring such charges; second, any fines assessed go to the state, not to the individual damaged. Such suits, when they do appear, are usually brought on behalf of a public official who believes he or she has been libeled.

This decrease was attributed to widely publicized libel suits in the mid-1980s that brought no significant monetary awards to the plaintiffs. These suits included those of General William Westmoreland against CBS, General Ariel Sharon (of Israel) against *Time* magazine, and William Tavoulareas, president of Mobil Oil, against the *Washington Post*. In the face of such a trend—with plaintiffs not winning, jury awards being reduced by the judge, or the cases being reversed on appeal—libel suits, and their attendant attorney fees and court costs, have apparently become less attractive to potential plaintiffs in recent years.

Privacy

The concept of privacy as a legal right is less than a hundred years old in the United States, one of the first countries ever to adopt it into law. In its broadest meaning, it entails the "right to be let alone." But insofar as publication or broadcasting is concerned, it involves unauthorized use of a person's name or likeness, putting a person into a false light (the portrayal in a distorted or fictionalized manner), publishing or broadcasting intimate details about an individual's life, or intruding or trespassing on a person's private property. In news stories, news features, or biography, "public figures" lose much of their right of privacy, under an extension of the *New York Times* v. *Sullivan* rule, and even a private citizen's name and picture can be used in television pieces, news stories, and feature articles without that person's consent, as long as the material was obtained in a public place. Supreme Court Justice William J. Brennan, Jr., has explained: "Exposure of the self to others in varying degrees is a concomitant of life in a civilized community. The risk of this exposure is an essential incident of life in a society which places a primary value on freedom of speech and of press." Even so, the public's "right to know," the courts have ruled, does not justify using identifiable photographs of people in humiliating acts or poses when the story can be told as well without so identifying the individuals.

Copyright

Copyright law, authorized in the Constitution of the United States, protects tangible creative works from infringement. For example, one may not make photocopies of significant portions of this book, especially for commercial use, without the authors' consent. However, there is a "fair use" provision in copyright law that permits small amounts of copying for educational and informational purposes. In a celebrated case in the mid-1980s the Supreme Court ruled that *Nation* magazine exceeded fair use by publishing unauthorized excerpts from former President Gerald Ford's memoirs prior to publication of the book itself. The court said that this publication infringed upon the publisher's right to first publication and right to market portions of the book to other magazines, and that this infringement outweighed the *Nation*'s contention that the material (which involved Ford's pardon of Nixon) had significant news value to the public.

Other laws are designed to protect society as a whole from what is considered to be harmful communication. Such laws involve the following.

Fraud

The U.S. Postal Service and the Federal Trade Commission are empowered to initiate action against advertisers and publications that seek to defraud the public, either through false advertisements or through stories that publicize fraudulent schemes. There is a gray area between "legitimate advertising puffery" and outright falsehood, however, and this often defies satisfactory solution by either regulatory or self-regulatory agencies.

Sedition

Every country can be expected to protect itself from violent overthrow, whether from external or internal enemies. In order to "advocate" violent overthrow of the government, one must speak or write; the government's right to self-defense is thereby placed in opposition to the individual's speech and press freedom. There is still one sedition act on the federal books in the United States, the Alien Registration Act of 1940 (usually referred to as the Smith Act), which makes advocacy of violent overthrow of the U.S. government a crime. It was the first peacetime sedition law enacted by Congress since the infamous Alien and Sedition Acts of 1798. Although two Supreme Court justices have referred to it as an abridgment of speech, press, and assembly in violation of the First Amendment, a Court majority found it constitutional in the *Dennis* case of 1951. In the 1957 *Yates* case, however, the Court effectively emasculated the act by ruling that lower courts had to distinguish between advocacy of forceful overthrow of the government as an "abstract doctrine" and advocacy of action to that end. Preaching an "abstract doctrine" of forceful overthrow is no crime, the Supreme Court implied, since this does not demonstrate a "clear and present danger" to the U.S. government.

Obscenity

The legal aspects of obscenity are affected by two questions: (1) Is pornography harmful in that it incites sexual offenses?[3] (2) To what degree is

---

[3] This question is considered in some detail in Chapter 11.

pornography protected by the free speech and free press guarantees of the First Amendment?

Some contend that obscenity is illegal not because it is harmful *per se,* but because it is offensive. It is a punishable offense, they say, not because it is a crime, but rather because it is a sin.

On the second question, it is best to give the answers of the Supreme Court justices themselves, from the landmark *Roth* case of 1957. First, the minority opinion of Justice William O. Douglas:

> . . . if the First Amendment guarantee of freedom of speech and press is to mean anything in this field, it must allow protests even against the moral code that the standard of the day sets for the community. In other words, literature should not be suppressed merely because it offends the moral code of the censor . . . the test that suppresses a cheap tract today can suppress a literary gem tomorrow. All it needs is to incite a lascivious thought or arouse a lustful desire. The list of books that judges or juries can place in that category is endless.
>
> I would give the broad sweep of the First Amendment full support. I have the same confidence in the ability of our people to reject noxious literature as I have in their capacity to sort out the true from the false in theology, economics, politics, or any other field.

But Justice Brennan, delivering the majority opinion, wrote that the Supreme Court had always assumed that obscenity is not within the area of constitutionally protected speech and press. He added:

> All ideas having even the slightest redeeming social importance—unorthodox ideas, controversial ideas, even ideas hateful to the prevailing climate of opinion—have the full protection of the guaranties, unless excludable because they encroach upon the limited area of more important interests. But implicit in the history of the First Amendment is the rejection of obscenity as utterly without redeeming social importance.

If obscenity was not protected by the First Amendment, it remained for the Supreme Court to set down guidelines for identifying obscene material. Anything *not* fitting the description would then be "protected." In *Miller* v. *California* (1973), the Supreme Court established the current guidelines:

1. Whether the average person, applying contemporary community standards, would find that the work, taken as a whole, appeals to the prurient interest of the average adult.
2. Whether the work depicts or describes, in a patently offensive

way, sexual conduct as specifically defined by the applicable state law.
3. Whether the work, taken as a whole, lacks serious literary, artistic, political, or scientific value.

To be found obscene, a publication must fail all three tests independently. In other words, if the material can pass only one test, it cannot be judged obscene, even if it fails the other two. In addition, the Court has established three other special situations in which "borderline" obscenity could bring convictions: (1) the sale of smut to minors, (2) the obtrusive presentation of titillating material—"publication in a manner so obtrusive as to make it impossible for an unwilling individual to avoid exposure to it," and (3) pandering promotion—advertising that emphasizes the sexually provocative aspects of the material.

Supreme Court rulings have qualified the identification of obscene material. The subsequent qualifications all serve to define something called *variable obscenity*, which means simply that what is obscene for one group may not be obscene for another, and what is obscene in one place may not be obscene in another place. For example, material not obscene for adults may be obscene for minors; material not obscene to the average person may be obscene for homosexuals—and would be adjudged obscene if it is directed at that group. Also, material that is subject to legal action if offered for "public distribution" may not be actionable if it remains in the privacy of one's home.

Recently there has been a move by a feminist group to ban as "obscene" certain publications that would pass at least two of the guidelines set down in *Miller* v. *California*. The group contends that "men's" magazines and even such classic erotic literature as *Lady Chatterley's Lover* promote the subordination of women. Two cities passed laws in line with such objections; the courts later struck down those laws as unconstitutional.

KEEPING THE PRESS OUT

By law and by tradition, many governmental meetings are out of bounds for all or part of the press. These include meetings convened by all levels of government, ranging from municipal bodies to the U.S. Congress. Although open-meetings laws exist in some form in all states, the laws provide for exceptions. In any case, committees and legislative bodies can avoid the technicality by moving into closed executive sessions or by simply holding informal premeeting conferences. A wide variety of reasons are offered for holding closed meetings, some of them legitimate.

Congressional committees, for example, may contend that they are discussing national security or foreign policy secrets. Municipal bodies may argue that newspaper reports may be embarrassing to personnel whose records are being discussed, or that the city may be put to greater expense if plans for new roads are publicized before rights-of-way can be purchased. Even so, information that the public has a right to know is often withheld under such camouflage. It is a problem for which there is no solution other than the establishment of strict guidelines for closed meetings, and continual prodding by newspeople to see that they are observed.

Most state legislatures now permit some form of television or photographic coverage of their general sessions. Those that do not allow such coverage argue that many legislators would be tempted to "perform" for the cameras, thereby lengthening the sessions. In 1979 the House of Representatives permitted television coverage of its sessions. The U.S. Senate held out but soon discovered that it was suffering a public relations disadvantage. Instead of being the "senior house," it was becoming the "junior house" as daily coverage flowed to the place where good footage was available. In 1986 the Senate followed suit and permitted radio and television coverage also. However, it should be noted that this is far from full or objective coverage. The production crews are employees of the government, and the cameras can aim only at the podium, not at the empty seats, sleeping solons, or faces buried in newspapers while debate rages.

The Canadian House of Commons opened its sessions to live television in 1977, with excellent results. Canadian TV camera operators are permitted to direct their cameras at any part of the chamber. Many cable companies carry the proceedings in their entirety.

Many of the reasons given for closing meetings are also given for closing public records to the public and the press. News organizations have been able, however, to get "open records" laws established in most, if not all states. The most ambitious open records law ever passed was the Freedom of Information Act of 1966, which made it mandatory for all federal agencies to make records available. The law gave citizens immediate recourse to the courts if they were denied access to records. However, the possible loopholes in even such a carefully drawn act as this one are apparent when one considers that there are nine major categories of information exempted from the provisions of the law. These include national defense and foreign policy secrets, interagency and intraagency memorandums, personnel and medical files, and investigatory files compiled for law enforcement purposes.

The courts—local, state, and federal—have increasingly placed obstacles in the path of media coverage of the judicial process. Restrictions on the press were intensified as a result of the Supreme Court's *Sheppard* ruling of 1966, but other shackles on the press had been in effect well before that date. Cameras had been barred from the courtroom, and juvenile cases in many states had been closed completely to the press. Guidelines established by the Department of Justice in 1965 limited the amount of pretrial information that could be released to the press. These rules were quickly adopted by state and local judiciaries and law enforcement officials. The justification offered for all these restrictions was concern for the rights of defendants, to ensure that they would receive a "speedy and public trial, by an impartial jury," as provided for in the Sixth Amendment. But the contradiction that exists between barring the press and ensuring the defendant a fair trial has been lost on many members of the legal profession. There is no doubt that a few individuals, involved in sensational trials, have not received justice, partly as a result of press irresponsibility. Even in such cases, however, defendants have always had certain safeguards against negative press influence. These include legal processes such as change of venue, challenging of jurors, requests for mistrial, and appeal.

But for every case of "trial by newspaper," there are dozens wherein the functions of a free press vis-à-vis the judicial system have been a boon to defendants and society. In a modern society, where few members of the concerned population can attend a trial itself, press coverage of pretrial, trial, and posttrial procedures fulfills the "public" trial provision of the Sixth Amendment by bringing trials and their related legal processes to the people. And this has often helped to ensure fair trials as well. The press has been able to expose abuses of police power; jurists are more likely to perform properly under the scrutiny of the press; witnesses are more inclined to tell the truth; and pretrial publicity is likely to bring forth witnesses who would not otherwise have known about the case. Pretrial and trial publicity benefits society by acquainting citizens with their rights under law, while the publicity attendant to a trial serves as a deterrent to further crime.

In *Richmond Newspapers* v. *Virginia* (1980), the Supreme Court ruled that press and the public have a constitutional right to attend trials and that judges may not prohibit their access unless there is an "overriding interest" in doing so. This and subsequent cases generated three guidelines for deciding to close a portion of a trial: (1) the court must be shown proof that the defendant's right to a fair trial will be impaired; (2) the judge must have found no other alternative to closure, such as sequestering the jury or changing the venue; and (3) the order must be narrowly tailored, so that, for example, only that portion of the trial is closed as is necessary to fair trial.

Most states now permit complete coverage of trials by still cameras and television. Perhaps the most ambitious effort in this area was that of Florida, which opened all courts to cameras in 1977. One celebrated case, the trial of teenager Ronnie Zamora (whose murderous nature, his attorneys argued, was caused by overexposure to violence on television), was telecast in its entirety by a Miami station. The Florida Supreme Court had set down very general guidelines for cameras in the court, and they are still being followed today: only one pool television camera operator and one pool still photographer are permitted in the courtroom at a time; they cannot use flash or bright lights; cameras have to be quiet; and photographers and camera operators are not allowed to move around. The U.S. Supreme Court upheld the legality of cameras in the courtroom in *Chandler* v. *Florida* (1980). Yet federal courts, including the U.S. Supreme Court, still do not allow coverage by radio or by still and television cameras.

Protecting Press Sources

The subpoena and contempt powers of the courts have also indirectly served to bar reporters from access to sources. Reporters and/or their notes have been subpoenaed for law enforcement purposes or for actual trial testimony. Reporters have been held in contempt if they do not reveal the names of their sources, information they may have been told in confidence, or their notes from specific stories. The effect of such legal action, though unintended, is to cut reporters off from their sources of information.

The answer to this problem might appear to be the establishment of "shield laws" granting reporters the same right of professional secrecy sometimes accorded doctors, lawyers, and clergy. It must be pointed out, however, that reporters, in their relationships with their sources, are in an entirely different position from that of doctors or priests. These other professionals normally keep to themselves the information given to them by patients, clients, and congregants; reporters gather their information precisely in order to make it public. In such cases, innocent individuals are often hurt by the resulting publicity. If shield laws absolved reporters from accountability for this damage, society as a whole could suffer. In addition, many attorneys and public officials argue that members of the press, like other citizens, have an obligation to disclose information that would further the cause of justice. Therefore, fewer than one-third of the states have enacted shield laws that would grant reporters an exemption from compelled testimony. And the courts have also been reluctant to extend this privilege.

Higher courts seem to be moving in the direction of a compromise solution to this problem. Without disallowing the government's right to compel reporters to testify, they have indicated that such subpoena power should be highly restricted where the press is concerned, utilized only when the government can demonstrate a compelling need for testimony that could not be obtained by any other investigatory process.

In an odd twist to the "protection of sources" question, a public relations practitioner in 1988 sued two newspapers in Minnesota (for breach of contract) because they *did* name him. The man contended that reporters from the two papers had promised him that he would not be named as a source for political information that he had given them but had subsequently reneged on the promise, causing him to lose his job, income, and reputation. A lower court and an appeals court ruled in his favor.

Where press freedom has been an issue, the Supreme Court at one time accorded First Amendment rights a *preferred position*. This meant that when the First Amendment seemed to be in conflict with other constitutional or human rights (especially rights protected by the Sixth Amendment), the Court ruled in favor of press freedom.[4] During the last few decades, however, the Supreme Court appears to have been applying a *balancing doctrine*, carefully weighing the First Amendment vis-à-vis the rights in conflict with it and no longer according it a preferred position in the struggle.

Two significant cases in 1978 indicated a judicial trend favoring the Sixth Amendment over the First Amendment. In a case involving a Stanford University newspaper, the U.S. Supreme Court ruled that judges could authorize the police to search for a reporter's notes in a newsroom. In a second case, the New Jersey Supreme Court upheld a contempt citation against *New York Times* reporter Myron Farber for refusing to turn his notes over to the defense in a murder trial. Farber was sent to jail, even though New Jersey had a shield law. (When the trial ended, Farber was released from jail because his notes were no longer relevant to the trial.)

CHILLING THE PRESS

In addition to laws punishing the press for harmful publication and laws and regulations limiting press access to the news, a number of subtle pressures exist in the United States to discourage the press from printing news that is legally harmless but discomfiting or embarrassing to governments, businesses, or individuals. The sources of some of these pressures have been mentioned in other chapters, but briefly discussed below are other factors, not always so obvious, that facilitate these pressures.

---

[4] See the majority decision in the 1941 *Bridges* v. *California* case for an example of a preferred position ruling.

Government Ownership of Media

The federal government is involved in media ownership to a greater extent than the average person realizes. Through the Government Printing Office, the United States is one of the major book publishers in the country. It owns two wire services (an agricultural service and a weather wire), produces hundreds of magazines through its federal agencies, publishes numerous military camp and service-wide newspapers, produces motion pictures for the United States Information Agency, and broadcasts throughout the world over armed forces radio and television networks and the Voice of America. Quite obviously, the government is a gatekeeper in each one of these wholly owned enterprises. For example, congressmen may alter so-called verbatim accounts of their speeches before they are published in the *Congressional Record*. There are recurrent charges of censorship in the armed forces broadcasting networks and in the publication *Stars and Stripes*. The Voice of America tells the truth in its news reports, but not necessarily certain aspects of the truth that one would hear on a network news program or on public or listener-sponsored radio.

Licensing

The power to license electronic media enabled the government to exert more pressure on broadcasting than it has ever been able to exert on print media. For example, it has always been understood that the First Amendment gave publishers the right to be one-sided, opinionated, and highly critical, without giving opponents a chance to reply. Broadcasters, under the theory that they are accountable to all of the people in return for the lease of an exclusive frequency or channel, had no such right, so long as the "fairness doctrine" was in effect. Even after the elimination of the fairness doctrine in 1987, the right was incomplete for broadcasters. They still had to adhere to the equal-time rule during political campaigns, and there remains uncertainty about how far they can go in criticism without receiving an inquiry from the FCC, or a threat by Congress to impose the fairness principle as law (before, it was simply a doctrine promulgated by the FCC). Broadcasting, after all, is still a licensed medium and still, according to law, must act in the public "interest, convenience, and necessity."

Government Advertising

Advertising from state, county, and township governments is an important source of income for weekly newspapers. For many of them, such advertising may well determine profit or loss. Therefore, the ability of governments to withhold these legal notices, or perhaps give them to one favored newspaper, discourages papers in some areas from being too critical of their local government. In most states, adequate safeguards against this form of pressure have been written into statute. But such statutes are subject to change.

Tax Powers

Although few newspapers and broadcasting stations are cowed by this hidden threat, the power to tax can be a potent weapon in the hands of county and municipal governments. This threat takes the form, primarily, of assessed valuation of plant and equipment, rather than a tax on the product (the newspaper, advertisements, etc.). If press units are given favored treatment (that is, assessed at a lower level than equivalent business plants), then they already operate under the knowledge that they owe a return favor to the taxing authority.

Economic Marginality

The American tradition holds that competition is a good thing. In the case of newspapers and broadcasting stations, too much competition may be a bad thing. Press units that are not economically strong are subject to all sorts of pressures—from subscribers, from advertisers, and even from themselves. The threat of a canceled subscription or canceled advertisement is more dangerous when one is on the borderline of profit than when one is well into the black. And the temptation not to antagonize, not to be too critical—in short, to exercise more "self-censorship"—accompanies economic insecurity. Commercial media operate in a marketplace of ideas and an economic marketplace at the same time. One marketplace frequently has an adverse effect on the other.

Press Councils

Experiments with local press councils were conducted in Oregon, California, Colorado, and Illinois in the late 1960s. In 1973 the National News Council was founded, with headquarters in New York City and funding coming primarily from foundation grants. In 1984 it was dissolved, bringing to an end the only "national" news council ever to operate in the United States. It attributed its demise to "a general lack of news media acceptance of the concept of a news council" (see Chapter 12 for the *New York Times'* stand against the council).

A national press council can take one of two forms. It can be a commission that observes and reports on the performance of the press each year, or a council that hears individual complaints about press units and passes down specific judgments. The National News Council fit the latter description. Those who argue in favor of a press council have emphasized that it does more to extend press freedom than to abridge it. A press council can improve the image of the press by clearing up false accusations against the press in general and by using its influence (and, presumably, credibility) to oppose restrictive legislation. At the same time, it can improve society by using its moral pressure to improve press responsibility.

Even if the motives are good and the results beneficial, however, a press council is a potential control on the press. Although it is "self-regulatory," it serves a purpose similar to that of libel laws. Few people would like to live in a country that had no libel laws, but most newspersons would agree that libel laws restrict the press, even though the restrictions may be necessary. There has been concern by many newspersons that the press council concept, even if completely shorn of enforcement provisions, would result in gradual erosion of press freedom. In the words of J. Russell Wiggins, former editor of the *Washington Post,* "It is one of the virtues of a good newspaper that it does not have to give way to every transient majority. It does not have to please or persuade a jury every day."

THE POSITIVE APPROACH

We have mentioned in this chapter three broad areas of press restrictions. But it must be noted that there are those who believe government should interfere in a *positive* way to *encourage* publication of certain information.

This is not a new attitude in the United States. The early mail acts prior to 1800 set ridiculously cheap rates for newspapers in order to promote the diffusion of political information to those living on farms as well as in towns. But whereas the old attitude favored government intervention to bring the press to the people, the latest plea is for government intervention to bring the people into the press. Certainly the equal-time and fairness doctrines of the Federal Communications Commission supported this idea.

Some media critics argued that these concepts should be extended to the print media as well, giving citizens a "right of access" and a "right of reply." They contend that protecting newspapers' rights of free expression is not the same as *providing* the right of free expression, because the press practices its own repression of ideas and opinions.

The U.S. Supreme Court rejected this call for a "right of access" to the print media in the *Miami Herald* v. *Tornillo* case (1974). The Court ruled that (1) the Constitution does not require a publication to be "responsible''; (2) the First Amendment implies that a newspaper and a newspaper alone will have control over what is selected for publication; and (3) editors might publish less criticism about public officials if they had to provide free space for any rebuttal.

According to those who generally support a right of access to the press, the monopolistic nature of mass media and their dependence on advertising have meant that they reflect the opinions of, and exist to serve, only the mainstream majority. This means that intellectual minorities, ethnic minorities, political minorities, and nonconsumer minorities (preschool-age children) are left out in the cold. In theory, the government could alter this situation in one of two ways: (1) by using its coercive powers to force publication or transmission of minority information and opinions in the mass media, or (2) by using government funds to subsidize or wholly sponsor publications and programming that commercial enterprises would find unprofitable.

In the 1980s the government moved away from the first alternative in a process of deregulation. The FCC eliminated the fairness doctrine, although the equal-time rule stayed on the books. However, the second alternative was still being fully utilized, even in this atmosphere of government noninterference. The United States subsidizes special-audience programming—for children, seniors, and ethnic minorities, for example—through money made available to the Corporation for Public Broadcasting. The government is also involved in other media operations that commercial media would find unprofitable—the *Congressional Record,* military publications, and the Voice of America, to name only a few. Even so, *Stars and Stripes* is a direct competitor to commercial, military-oriented newspapers such as the *Army Times*. The government can justify this seeming conflict on the grounds that *Stars and Stripes* is intended for its own employees and no one else. The government has also given preference with respect to new broadcasting licenses to minorities and women, partly to bring new points of view into radio and television.

Compared with other countries, however, there is little government ownership or control of the mass media in the United States. In large measure, this freedom is due to a vigilant press, and a commitment by Congress and the courts to the underlying principles of the First Amendment.

AFTERTHOUGHTS

1. Observe a day's coverage of the House or Senate floor as transmitted by C-SPAN, or network excerpts from this feed. What changes would there be if the networks could send their own crews to cover these proceedings, and what benefits and disadvantages would accrue as a result?

2. It is said that the Constitution allocates no rights or privileges to the press as an institution that are not allocated to any individual citizen. Discuss whether you believe this is true or false.

3. Why should a "public official" have a more difficult time recovering damages in a libel action than any ordinary citizen?

4. Does it make sense to support a theory of variable obscenity? If something is "obscene," why should it not be obscene at any time or in any place?

5. Do you believe that there should be complete freedom of the press to cover all court proceedings, without exception? Explain why.

CHAPTER 16

"Marketplace" Media:
An Appraisal

Critics abound who snipe at the edges of the "marketplace model" of media functioning and accountability. But in spite of frequent thrusts and jibes at this market theory, at least in the United States such a model is believed to be most compatible with the American dedication to both media freedom and media responsibility. There are many, however, who would disagree with that assertion, insisting that this traditional American theory does not adequately synthesize freedom and ethical practice. These critics agree that the marketplace may ensure maximum freedom *to the media managers* but believe that it fails to provide any real freedom for, or accountability of the media to, the people.

Just who is right in this debate? Could it be that both apologists and critics have something valid to say? We need to look a little closer at this important controversy. Market forces may not work perfectly in ensuring maximum pluralism and accountability, but they do, at least to some extent, bring the public into the ultimate process of accountability through a kind of economic (or "public") determinism which goes a considerable distance toward injecting audience values and preferences into the thinking and products of the media elite.

Certainly other systems of media accountability can be suggested. The normal array of pressures on the media, such as media councils, ethical codes, and litigation, do have an impact on media activities and serve as important mechanisms of accountability. These systems just mentioned are seen by "marketplace" advocates as supplemental—certainly not contradictory—to marketplace or *laissez-faire* accountability.

SOURCES OF THE MARKETPLACE MODEL

Out of a synthesis of bits and pieces of the philosophies of Locke, Voltaire, Rousseau, Milton, John Stuart Mill, Adam Smith, and Oliver Wendell Holmes, the "marketplace model" (or market model) of communication in society has emerged. Although a broad spectrum of influential persons and movements have had their impact on the market model, five historical ideas have notably advanced and perpetuated the model:

1. The philosophy of freedom and individualism originating in the Age of Reason in Europe
2. The hard-work-and-competition values of the Protestant Ethic (well explicated by Max Weber in *The Protestant Ethic and the Spirit of Capitalism*)
3. The influence of Social Darwinism, with its concepts of "natural selection" and "survival of the fittest" as applied to business competition
4. Adam Smith's theory of capitalism, built on a *laissez-faire*, free-market approach wherein the laws of supply and demand determine the flow of goods and services
5. Oliver Wendell Holmes's notion of a "marketplace of ideas" (updating Milton's self-righting process of three centuries earlier), which he saw as based on the "power of thought to get itself accepted in the open competition of the market"

The media, in this model, become the market—or serve on the informational and opinion level of society as the main foundation of the market. That this marketplace of ideas be as free (from outside control) as possible and as open (to diverse content) as possible is considered essential, for according to this model, the availability of a full range of ideas, information, and opinions ensures the greatest possible chance of reaching the truth.

ASSUMPTIONS OF THE MODEL

The *market model* is predicated on the assumption that audiences can ultimately control the media and keep them accountable for their actions. The model postulates that media are accountable to their publics in the sense that they will be rewarded (gain circulation or viewership, and thereby profits) or punished (lose circulations or viewership, and possibly go out of business) as they satisfy or fail to satisfy the desires and expectations of their audiences. As Herbert Altschull has written in his *Agents of Power*,[1] "If the reader reacts negatively to the content of his newspaper, he will cease to buy it, and the newspaper will be forced to modify its behavior in order to survive in the marketplace." This is how audience members participate in the formulation of news, according to Altschull. And this is the essence of the marketplace theory of mass communication. Media that provide desired services in the competitive market will survive and thrive, and those that fail to do so will languish and possibly die.

If public support of a certain medium declines, this decline is a warning signal to management that things need to be changed and policy altered, that editorial content is not what it should be. If public support *increases,* this increase is a signal that the basic policy is all right, that editorial content is at least adequate, and that changes—at least major ones—are unnecessary. Thus media managers (like elected government officials in this respect) must please and represent their constituencies.

A potential problem with the model is that it assumes not only a competitive marketplace, with all media seeking to gain and keep audience members and to be economically sound, but a highly knowledgeable and concerned audience. Seemingly built into such a model is a Platonic assumption that when people know the good, they will do good.

But the market model goes even further and assumes that the people, if they know the good, will see to it that others (in this case, media managers) know and do the good. The acquisition of knowledge via education is critical here. Through education people will know the good; they will also pursue the good. An obvious question arises at this point: Does such a degree of knowledge and education really exist in the marketplace of mass communication?

Consider for a moment the concept of *caveat emptor* (let the buyer beware), which is often brought up in connection with the market model. Certainly the consumer or "buyer" of mass media messages must beware—must, if you will, take his or her chances in the communication marketplace. For in the market there is information that is misleading, untruthful, incomplete, biased, inaccurate, and in some cases quite deleterious to personal, social and national well-being and progress. Consumers take their chances. They decide which messages to expose themselves to, which to retain and take seriously, and which to reject.

It is through precisely this process of turning to the mass media for

---

[1] White Plains, NY: Longman, 1984.

information, opinion, and analysis that audience members exercise their personal freedom. In theory, audience members also understand the importance of checking one medium against another, of seeking information from a variety of sources and perspectives—in short, of becoming more intelligent and better informed individuals. The alternative: being taken advantage of by the media in the marketplace.

As consumers of information become more skeptical and better informed about the media and the world about them, the media will, says the marketplace theory, become more responsible, more pluralistic, and more concerned with fulfilling the ever-rising expectations of their audiences. At least that is the theory.

PROBLEMS WITH THE MODEL

The market model posits that there is an interactive relationship between audiences and media: What the people want, the media will provide. If the people demand higher quality, the media will give it to them. As to a possible demand by the public for *lower* quality, the model has little to say, for the assumption is that people will become ever more demanding of better information as they themselves achieve higher levels of education and moral consciousness. Of course, the market model could accommodate a lowering of public taste; if such a situation developed, the media in the marketplace would still be accountable by virtue of adjusting to the lower expectations of their audiences. This is not to say that there would be a *moral* benefit in such an adjustment, however.

Marketplace advocates see the market model as a truly democratic one. The people, speaking clearly through the market, determine to a great degree the content of the media. But the question might be raised whether or not the people really *do* speak clearly through the market. Certainly we know that some people are able to speak much more loudly than others through the market. It is fair to wonder if inequalities of wealth and power do not limit the democratizing potential of the market.

Another weakness of the marketplace approach to accountability is that individual audience members do not have authority or power in their attempts to pressure the media. The individual audience member is essentially impotent. It is only when individuals band together to form powerful pressure groups that "the people" have enough authority to insist that the media be accountable to them. For example, church groups, political activists (both left and right), and professional associations all may influence the way a publication or a station performs.

Consider the changes that have come about on "women's pages" in newspapers; they are now quite different from the older, home-related "society pages" that dominated the newspaper scene into the 1950s. Consider also the increased coverage of black Americans in the news media. Women and blacks, as they have organized and become more outspoken—and as they have had increasing access to dollars to use in the marketplace—have had a larger and larger impact on the policies of the mass media.

Another problem is that in the real world the "people" (even those who have maximum access to the media) seem to be largely passive or unconcerned about the routine affairs of the media—and the world. Feedback of any significant kind from the people to the media is episodic and splintered. It offers little or no real guidance with respect to media policies and behavior. The media in a capitalistic society, we can say, are dependent on the marketplace for financial support but are relatively unaffected, at least in the short term, so far as professional and moral guidance is concerned.

Market accountability, at least on a moral level, implies that audience groups will want or demand a more responsible communication system and will insist that the media be more ethical in their practices. In reality, we know that, by and large, audiences know little or nothing about the moral quandaries of the media and care little about them. The media are "mixed bags" anyway, with some "irresponsible" as well as some "responsible" aspects. The public has learned to accept the good with the bad and, in the great expanse of public ignorance, to take on faith the mass of information that lies in the neutral area between responsible and irresponsible mass communication.

It is very difficult, in any case, for a mass audience to respond adequately to perceived irresponsibility in a communication medium. The mass audience is too heterogeneous, too scattered, and too anonymous to constitute a potent force for accountability. Some members of the audience may cancel their subscriptions to a newspaper because of perceived media weaknesses—but other members will either condone such behavior or be unconcerned about it. So the circulation of the newspaper varies very little, if at all, because of editorial decisions. Newspapers do pass away, but there is no substantial empirical evidence that they do so because of editorial practices.

If a newspaper were really accountable in the marketplace—or to the marketplace—it could, and would, rather regularly be punished for irresponsible journalism and rewarded for responsible journalism. But too often this is not the case. Take the passing away of the *Washington Star* in the early 1980s, for example. It was, in the opinion of media critics, at the zenith of its quality. Was it being punished for its editorial activities? Nobody really believes that it was. And take the *National Enquirer* as another example. If it is punished today for its gossipy, sensational manner of playing loosely with the truth, it is through the legal system, not through the marketplace. Readers of this publication get what they want, regardless of the often fraudulent journalism that this paper may actually contain. There is, in other words, a large enough segment in the marketplace to sustain this kind of publication.

There is really little accountability at work here, except perhaps in an ethically negative sense. What *is* operative, and influential, is audience acceptance—and a desire on the part of editors to provide what they have determined that their audience likes. If this is considered "accountability" in any kind of ethical sense, then it is a very vague and broad concept. In fact, this sort of marketplace approval may actually lead to more unethical and irresponsible journalistic behavior in order to expand audiences and garner larger profits. Therefore the sanctioning of media in a financial way by the public is not the same thing as ensuring moral media behavior. To that end, the market needs supplementation both from internal restraints—voluntary self-regulation—and from external reinforcement—via the legal system and strict codes of ethics with teeth in them.

In fact, the marketplace by itself cannot ensure, in the short term, either quality or ethical practice. It can, however, ensure considerable freedom for media managers, and to a lesser extent it can ensure diversity or pluralism in media content. It may result in some accountability for some media with respect to some members of some audiences, but it is not reliable when it is acting alone—without legal restraints, peer pressure, and the like. In fact, it may be even less reliable than the individual moral consciousness of media managers. And certainly it is less reliable than the legal system. The sad fact is that in too many cases the marketplace and the profit motive tend to corrupt or displace the moral sensitivity of media managers.

The suggestion that market forces are the best means of media accountability is one that has been supported by many economists and social and political philosophers. Taking such a position, at least to a considerable degree, have been such disparate modern intellectuals as Friederich Hayek, Milton Friedman, Russell Kirk, Ludwig von Mises, Eric Voegelin, and Ayn Rand. But notably missing from such a list are the *moral* philosophers. Where there is one Robert Nozick speaking out in favor of the marketplace, there are no less than ten John Rawlses taking the other side.

QUESTIONS FOR THE MARKETPLACE MODEL

The marketplace model postulates, as we have seen, that the market will control the media and cause them to eliminate irresponsible or unethical activities. It also assumes, among other things, that people can freely exchange ideas and information that will promote the public interest. But

Robert Picard, in *The Press and the Decline of Democracy* (1985), questions this tenet. John Milton and his truth-will-win-out concept to the contrary, there is considerable doubt that in the so-called free marketplace, where falsehood and truth are grappling, truth will actually prevail. Picard finds no empirical evidence to support this assumption. And aside from its inherent philosophical plausibility or lack of it, there is the question of a restriction-free marketplace. As Picard documents very systematically, restrictions of many kinds tend to corrupt the marketplace.

Many other recent authors—Herbert Schiller, Dallas Smythe, Theodore Glasser, Herbert Altschull—have contended that choices in the marketplace may be, and have been, removed by any number of factors and that the possibility of truth emerging in the marketplace of ideas and information has been subverted—if, indeed, it were ever possible.

One other warning should be given. Since the market model relies to a large degree on media pluralism, the increasing development of huge newspaper groups and multimedia conglomerates poses a threat to the underpinnings of the marketplace system. People may change from one newspaper to another if choices really exist in the marketplace, but in fewer and fewer cities are such choices available.

It is true, as marketplace defenders point out, that we need to consider more than just the number of media in a community, or even the number of separate owners. The fact that the number of discrete media or ownerships may be diminishing does not in itself spell gloom and doom. We need to bring into a discussion of pluralism the very important consideration of discrete *messages,* and it is possible that more messages will reach audience members in a city with one newspaper than will reach the audience in a city with three newspapers.

All such negative commentary aside, it may be that in the long run a medium that is grossly insensitive to its audiences will suffer, even to the extent of going out of business. And this economic punishment—or potential punishment—in the marketplace is evidently what many mean when they say that the media are accountable to an outside force, in this case the marketplace.

As we think about mass communication, it is well that we take criticisms of the marketplace theory seriously. Does the marketplace actually determine the ethics of the media? We can understand the reasons why market apologists contend that it does. But there is that lingering question: Might certain media find that their unethical practices are actually *ratified* or *supported* by their particular audiences, a situation precluding any desire to change these practices? Certainly we know that this is true in some cases. Therefore, might we not conclude that audience impact on media is beyond ethics, that it is not a moral but a pragmatic effect that the audience has on the media?

In a country such as the United States, where the general public is splintered or segmented into myriads of specialized audiences wanting different things from their media, can we not say that specialized audiences do indeed have an influence on their specialized media, impelling them to give them basically what they want? But is not this type of accountability simply expedient accountability, devoid of any real moral or ethical meaning?

"Megalomedia" (mass-mass media), in their desire to provide a cafeteria choice for everyone, are largely immune to the moral dictates of their gigantic, heterogeneous audiences, for a very simple reason. Some of what they provide will not be liked by some audience members but will be liked by others. The dissatisfied segments are typically so small and powerless that they cannot really have a moral impact on the media. So again we might ask: What real impact do audience members have on the moral tone of the megalomedia?

Undoubtedly, if the media go too far, get too far ahead of the expectations and cultural limits of their audiences, they will encounter trouble. But, then, even from a capitalistic viewpoint, doing so would be media madness. An important part of editing for the media is paying attention to proper proportion.

The market model assumes that people have some *power*. And of course, economically, in a general sense, this is a reasonable assumption. But is not this people's power related largely to people *getting what they want?* It assumes a certain degree of pluralism, no doubt, but does pluralism equate with *morality?* Whether we have one or two thousand lies in a newspaper fails to come to grips with the question of the ethics of lying.

Now the question arises: Even if some media are not *morally* accountable to the people, are not others so accountable? In other words, purposely unethical practices may be sanctioned in some media by their audiences, but are not there other media (of a more serious, responsible, "elite" sort) whose audience-feedback thermostat keeps them within the bounds of a high level of morality and integrity? Undoubtedly this is so. For example, a newspaper such as the *New York Times* cannot afford to take the kind of liberties taken by a publication such as the *National Enquirer*.

One audience member wants half-truths, fictionalized news, sensation, and sex; he or she tolerates or even expects that from Medium A. Another audience member wants carefully reported, verified, fact-oriented news from Medium B and has no tolerance for ribald, sloppy, distorted, or fictionalized news. The first person may impact on his or her medium but does not hold it *morally* responsible. The second person, however, does indeed hold Medium B morally responsible. One can suppose that if Medium A's audience member finds that its messages are getting *too serious* (and thereby uninteresting), he or she might exert some influence in bringing the medium back into line with its former practices. But this is not *moral* accountability; rather, it is a kind of *immoral* accountability.

But then, can we not at least say that all audience members serve as part of an accountability mechanism, whether for good or for ill? This is, of course, to some degree true, at least in a capitalistic society, with a media system governed by a competitive, marketplace philosophy.

Those who put much faith in the marketplace concept base their rationale mainly on people's participation in, or impact on, the media. But isn't such impact extremely passive? Isn't such participation nothing more than the belief that a medium will become more responsible if I stop exposing myself to it? Is not such a belief extremely naive, given the fact that we're dealing with a *mass* audience? I stop subscribing to a newspaper; another person begins—or maybe three others. So? In a mass medium–mass audience situation, an individual with high moral standards—or even sizable numbers of people with such standards—gets lost in the extremely weak (maybe nonexistent) interaction between the megalomedia and the pluralistic values and wishes of their splintered audience.

Let us conclude with this question: Is not the marketplace model of media accountability nothing more than an uncritical rationale built into the fabric of the capitalistic system, purporting to give it a moral foundation when really it is no more than an essential and pragmatic part of a business or market economy?

AFTERTHOUGHTS

1. The marketplace model of media responsibility is often said to be *ethically* based. What are your thoughts on this?
2. How does the idea of a kind of "media Darwinism" (the strong will survive) relate to the marketplace model in the United States? Is such an idea consistent or inconsistent with the American ideal of democracy and of "giving the people what they want"?
3. If the people know "the good," they will do "the good," said Plato. Do you think this is true as related to the marketplace model of media accountability? In other words, will people support media that they know are not doing "the good"?
4. Is the marketplace model of accountability consistent or inconsistent with the American concept of press freedom, with its emphasis on editorial self-determination by the media?
5. Why do you think there is so much skepticism about the market directing or controlling media responsibility? Do these doubts about the system evidence a fatal flaw in the American capitalistic ideology?

CHAPTER 17

Are the Media Machiavellian?

The chapters of this book have presented philosophies, theories, practitioners, models, attitudes. This one goes back in time to visit a man who at one time provided a model, a body of thought, and a journalistic contribution. There are media critics foreign and domestic who have seen Niccolò Machiavelli (1469–1527) as the patron saint of modern American macromedia. Certainly Machiavelli had much to say, especially in *The Prince* (1513) and *Discourses* (1519), about tactics of power and success. In Chapter 18 of *The Prince* he makes his boldest suggestions for the means used by an "ideal" prince to increase his sway. Interpretations of Machiavelli's real intent—prescription? description? satire?—are ongoing but this remains the most quoted of his writings, what one usually refers to when the term "Mahiavellian" is used.

The term presents itself as a possible model for today's media ethics dilemma. Machiavelli was writing about power politics; the prototype for his Prince was his fellow Florentine, Cesare Borgia, whose political tricks and blunt cynicism he knew firsthand. What does this have to do with modern journalism? Well, cynics and realists alike often see media leaders as exhibiting a kind of coldness and arrogance, with a heavy dash of pragmatism and power grasping that places a Machiavellian stamp upon them.

Let's start with the man behind the label—or at least those aspects that led to the label. Walter Lippmann (in *Public Opinion*) has said that Machiavelli is one of the most reviled men in history but that he probably has the greatest number of followers.

SUCCEED BY ANY MEANS

Machiavelli was a good reporter, although he didn't work for any newspaper. (He also wrote some significant history, plays and poems.) He was a keen observer and traveled widely, analyzing political conditions in Europe, especially France and Germany, during the first decade of the sixteenth century. His reports have been preserved, and they show a keen understanding of political institutions and politics. He was definitely one of the first "watchdogs on government," as his writing at the onset of the modern age clearly show.

He was also a political philosopher and historian. In addition he was an amateur ethicist, or better, amoralist; he developed the idea that morality differs from and is not bounded by the usual ethical norms. He also introduced the important concept that power is the decisive factor in political (read: journalistic) life.

He was a believer in success, in pragmatics. In many ways he influenced the thought of such Enlightenment thinkers as John Locke and Voltaire, who influenced Thomas Jefferson and other early American leaders who had a significant impact on the country's journalism. He also had an impact on statists or authoritarians, such as Rousseau, Hegel, Marx, and Hitler. He stressed the importance of power, which is the common denominator of global libertarians *and* global statists.

How did Machiavelli influence a person like John Locke? By stressing the benefits of competition while championing the powerful competitor over the weaker one. He certainly believed in meritocracy and the rule of the elite. He definitely believed in *freedom*—freedom for the elite (the press elite, for example). And, since the press has the freedom, it also has the power. The modern American press owes much to Machiavelli.

And how did he influence a person like Karl Marx? According to *The Prince,* the power elite are justified, however noble or ignoble their ends, in using any means (even immoral ones) to achieve them. Often, wrote Machiavelli, a leader must use an immoral means to achieve what is considered a moral end. In fact, in *The Communist Manifesto* we can see an example of the position that the ends justify the means when one is dealing with the basic problem of social justice.

Marx maintains that one fact is common to all past ages: the exploitation of one part of society by another. Only when a society is purged of such class exploitation can genuine justice emerge. And note this conclusion by Marx: *To achieve this end, violence and revolution are justified in forcibly sweeping away old conditions.* This was picked from the mind of Machiavelli himself.

Those critical of today's publishers and editors find that , Machiavelli, in his day, was very much like them.[1] He was goal-oriented; he believed in advising and directing the government; he was arrogant; he was an agenda setter; he was a pragmatist; he was confident of his expertise in almost every area; he believed he was above and beyond accountability; he had an answer to practically all questions; he believed in having objectives and pursuing them vigorously and by any means.

AN AMORAL PHILOSOPHY

In ethical theory terms Machiavelli was a deontological teleologist. Meaning: He had an overriding Kantian maxim, which combined both duty and consequences: "Do those things which will maximize personal success." To duty to such a principle (deontology) he would bind today's journalists, and at the same time he would exhort them to effect the consequences (teleology) that would most benefit them. Certainly this is not a course of action for the altruistic journalist.

If Machiavelli were talking to today's journalists, he would give them this one-word ethical imperative: *Succeed.* By all means—or by *any* means—achieve your objective, he would say. Get that story. That is, if getting it serves your purpose. Don't get that story, if it harms in any way your purpose. So, for Machiavelli, journalistic tactics are to be considered as effective or ineffective, not as moral or immoral.

Now, we don't want to misunderstand Machiavelli. He was not absolutely against social ethical principles. What he would say is this: Be ethical (follow social norms) if it does not harm your objective; but don't let ethics get in the way of success.

Machiavelli in the modern city room might well advise a young reporter to report the story fully and as truthfully as possible. In most cases, let the people know. But in some cases, where full-disclosure reporting might endanger the editor's or the newspaper's editorial position or other *ends,* he might advise the reporter to tamper with the story in some way. Ethics, then, is fine for Machiavelli if there are no unfavorable consequences to the editor or the newspaper.

The Machiavellian model promotes information control. His Prince

---

[1] Many readers will hold a comparison of such a man with contemporary American journalists invalid—and thus take exception to the whole thrust of this chapter. But we feel that Machiavelli's basic persona closely resembles quite a number of American media practitioners. He was, like most journalists, a Renaissance person: interested in all sorts of things; striving for wordly acclaim, influence, rewards; mindful of the importance of pragmatics. Such a man was Machiavelli. At least in this sense are journalists not largely Machiavellian?

should not communicate anything to the people that might undermine their confidence and respect for the regime. If the people are ethical, they will have to adapt their beliefs, values, and actions to those of the Prince. (Shades of Plato, Rousseau, Hegel, and Marx!)

The Press is the modern Prince, destined to lead, to set standards, to create the valid vision of the world for the people, to keep all institutions honest, to be a "fourth branch of government" (or in statist societies "the most important instrument of government"). The Princely Press must never get on the defensive, must never admit error (except when it is expedient), and must never apologize or appear weak or indecisive. Machiavelli does not trust the masses, although from a journalistic perspective the Press need the masses—but as means to an end: the power and wealth of the Press.

ARROGANCE AND EXPEDIENCY

In other words, the Machiavellian Press is arrogant. It gets its arrogance from its Power.[2] And it gets its Power from constitutions (e.g., the U.S.) or from authoritarian leaders or parties that, because they need the Press, permit the Press to share power with them (e.g., the U.S.S.R. or Paraguay). The journalist absorbs the power of the institutions: the Press's power becomes the journalist's power. Institutional arrogance becomes the journalist's arrogance.

What are some of the common manifestations of Machiavellian journalism in the United States? Let us note just a few:

1. A reporter passes himself off as a mental patient in order to write an exposé of a state mental hospital.
2. An editor gives excessive coverage to a candidate whom she wants to see elected.

---

[2] The concept of "press power" is looming ever larger in contemporary communications literature. Most articles and books assign tremendous power to the media, especially television. Several books dealing with media power follow: Robert Stein, *Media Power: Who Is Shaping the Picture of The World* (Englewood Cliffs, NJ: Prentice-Hall, 1970); J. C. Merrill, *The Imperative of Freedom* (New York: Hastings House, 1974); Donald Shaw and Maxwell McCombs, *The Emergence of American Political Issues: The Agenda-Setting Function of the Press* (St. Paul: West, 1977); David L. Paletz and R. M. Entman, *Media Power Politics* (New York: Free Press, 1981); J. Herbert Altschull, *Agents of Power: The Role of the News Media in Human Affairs* (New York: Longman, 1984); William A. Rusher, *The Coming Battle for the Media* (New York: William Morrow, 1988); and S. R. Lichter, S. Rothman, and L. S. Lichter, *The Media Elite: America's Power Brokers* (Bethesda, MD: Adler and Adler, 1986).

3. A reporter surreptitiously records a conversation or interview with a news source.
4. A reporter fabricates information for a story or attributes a fictitious—but believable—quote to a nonexistent source.
5. A reporter gives more attention to statements from a source that agrees with his own perspectives than to another that disagrees— *unless the second source comes across as a fool.*
6. An editor gives the name of the rape victim in a story, rationalizing it by saying that he believes in truthful or full-disclosure reporting.
7. A reporter tells one interviewee that she has some information from another source that she really does not have; she wants the second source to make a response out of fear of what the first person may have told the reporter.

Examples abound in all the media. For the Machiavellian journalist any action is justified if it achieves the purposes, the objectives, the ends desired. Machiavelli's stance is a very pragmatic one and is in keeping with the hard-nosed, competitive American spirit of journalism. For Machiavelli, the journalist must do what is expedient. In addition, the journalist's stance is consistent with the press power (often called the press freedom) clause of the First Amendment. And the Machiavellian position is that, after all, press responsibility is a relative concept. Who's to tell a journalist that his or her action is irresponsible? Machiavelli tells us that self-interest and self-perpetuation *are* the responsible course. Why then should journalists be irresponsible and do something that might be against their best interest? Such action would be foolish journalism, not good journalism.

Machiavellianism appeals to a sense of individualism. It appeals to a desire for power. It appeals to an inclination to succeed. It can provide journalists with the wherewithall for a pleasurable ego trip. Machiavellian journalism is not the journalism of a "wimp"; rather it is the journalism of vision, of dedication, of self-interest, of pride, of social transcendence.

Machiavelli, according to a sizable group of critics, said about all there is to say about the hard-nosed "American Way" of doing journalism. In many respects he was, indeed, the father of the practical, success-oriented, competitive, bottom-line, winner-take-all spirit of the national tradition. After all, American journalism is indeed a Prince that legitimately lords it over other institutions and strikes fear even in the hearts of elected officials.

This Prince is not always understood—or loved—but is the guiding light of the people, the conscience and royal spokesperson for the nation. It is protected by the Royal Charter's very first amendment. What else is there to say? Machiavellian journalism may not be the kind of journalism many think it *ought* to be, but many others think it is very close to journalism as it is. The Princely Press marches forward into the future of social responsibility, defining it every step of the way.

AN INTERVIEW WITH MACHIAVELLI

Machiavelli was at his home in the suburbs of Florence on August 2, 1520, when the interviewers, Lowenstein and Merrill (cited below as L&M), arrived with quills and pads. They tried very hard to be "friendly" (or at least neutral) although they were really not.

    L & M: Thank you very much for sparing some of your valuable time. Can you say a few words about your qualifications to advise journalists?

    NM: You know I'm just a friendly man who wants to right wrongs and create a better society based on the Roman Republic. But I'm a true journalist at heart: I am therefore *per se* qualified to discourse on anything. Beyond that, I know that journalism is power. Journalists need advice from someone like me to keep them connected with power. Too many journalists are soft and have muddled brains due to too much concern with ethics.[3]

    L & M: Do you know many journalists?

    NM: Not really. As you know, there are few such persons around today, but politicians are everywhere trying to change the world to conform to their concepts. And when the so-called journalists arrive, they will not be significantly different from the political scribes and rhetoricians who inform and persuade the people on the streets, in the parks, and in the palaces and schools.

    L & M: You finished your book, *Il Principe* (we call it *The Prince*) recently. Do you have a publisher for it?

    NM: Not yet, but I'm talking with some publishers here in Florence, and then there is a possibility down in Rome. It's a good book, and it will be published.[4] Lorenzo di Medici needs it very badly. I really wrote it for him, you know. What's so good about it is that it is in accord with human nature. The world is full of people who want to succeed, to gain power, to direct others. My book will give them the proper *tactics* to achieve their goal. It's based, you know, on the actual

---

[3] Machiavelli's replies in this fictitious interview are believed to be quite in line with beliefs presented in *The Prince* and in his larger work, *The Discourses* (both written between 1512 and his death in 1527).

[4] *The Prince* was finally published in 1532, five years after Machiavelli's death.

practices of my old acquaintance, Cesare Borgia. If you don't know him, you will. He was successful . . . not always liked, you know, but he was effective in achieving his purposes. But unfortunately he doesn't write well, so I will share his concepts with my fellow Florentines and with posterity.

L & M: How will *The Prince* help journalism?

NM: Well, what is good for the politician is good for *any* power-hungry person. And if you can't be one of them, write about them, affect them, frustrate them, or help them. It's fun being the power behind the throne, you know. *The Prince* gives the recipe for personal success. The journalist will find it very useful.

L & M: But, many journalists don't agree with your ideas about succeeding by any means. They want to be ethical. If they succeed, good; if not, that's all right too. Don't you think that's the proper way to do journalism?

NM: Maybe in 10,000 years. But not now, nor any time soon. People are just not ready for morality. Pragmatics is the name of the game. Succeed. And success breeds success. If deceit is needed in journalism, it must be used. One must do what is necessary. Fight trickery with trickery, not with goodwill and honesty. If you don't, you'll lose every time.

L & M: But you are talking about authoritarianism. What we're hearing is more talk about democratization of the newspaper. Journalists, some say, should put the public welfare ahead of their own interests. Isn't that a good, responsible idea?

NM: No, no. You have the mistaken idea that democracy is good. It is bad for everybody—at least in the real world we live in. People need authority. They want to be told. They want to escape from freedom; it's too traumatic for most of them. A newspaper (or a State) should be run by an absolute despot. Civic freedom may be injured, of course, but most citizens don't really want it. Think of what your newspaper would look like if all the journalists had a hand in determining its appearance and policy. Chaos. Utter chaos. No, democracy just won't do the job—in a State or in a newspaper. As I've said, maybe democracy's day will come, but it will be a long, long time.

L & M: But it worked in Greece, didn't it?

NM: Not really. Do you call the system of sexism and slavery that existed in the time of Socrates democracy? I don't. And remember that Plato and other thinkers were certainly not sold on democracy. A good dictator, strong and intelligent, is preferable any day.

L & M: But shouldn't the editor or publisher want to be highly thought of by his colleagues?

NM: No. Remember what I have written: To be feared gives more security than to be loved. Workers like a strong leader. Respect is better than love, and respect comes from power, not from sentimental gestures.

L & M: But can a person be virtuous by being powerful?

NM: Virtue is strength. Virtue is harmony with the natural law. Power seeking is the natural law. A weak person can never be virtuous. Weakness makes a person timid and afraid to take chances, to use what freedom he has. When a person takes chances, he may make mistakes—in the sense of not accomplishing his objectives—but even there mistakes, if admitted, will lead to a strength of resolve and character.

L & M: You mention freedom. How can a journalist have freedom in a system such as you propose?

NM: Many journalists cannot, of course. They are basically robots, functionaries, slaves. And that's all they want to be. But others, of stronger will, can garner some freedom, and with it power. But actually the publishers and editors have the freedom. And so they have the real power. The two go together. If I want freedom, I seek power. That is the secret. Unfortunately . . . or fortunately . . . most people don't understand this principle.

L & M: Should not journalists try to give the people more access to their media? It seems to some of us that media ethics requires media to expand the public's voice, to champion people power, to enlarge the field of discourse.

NM: Absolutely not. Why should journalists want to sap their own power? Why should the Press forsake its power position in society by sharing it with the people—the great majority of whom wouldn't know what to do with it? The Press should not want "people power" substituted for Press Power. That's insane in the kind of world we live in. Journalists must write, editors must edit, and publisher must publish . . .

L & M: But what about the ethics of Editorial Tyranny—or Press autonomy?

NM: There you go again with ethics. You never hear me talk about ethics. That's something weaklings get agitated about. The Princely Press need not worry about being merciful, kind, humane, and democratic—and should never get ethics all mixed up with the need to succeed. If journalists think too much about ethics, it will actually be dangerous for it will limit their range of actions. Remember: the virtuous journalist, the courageous journalist is one who prizes "editorial tyranny," as you call it. And when he gives it up, he is nothing more than a frail reed under the foot of the vulgar masses.

L & M: But you are expressing a very conservative or elitist position. Journalists in our country are basically liberal and have a "populist" orientation. Justice, they feel, is achieved through egalitarianism and through journalistic expansion of communication opportunity rather than through self-interested editorial determinism.

NM: Then your journalists are wrong. And, if I may say so, many liberals talk like populists but they don't act that way. If they are to retain their power and their capacity to determine what journalism is, they must be "conservatives"—in the sense of conserving their prerogatives and rights; they must be elitists in the sense of believing they know what is the best journalism for the people. I consider myself an amoral scientist (although some Florentines call me an "artist") and I think journalists must so consider themselves. Meet the world as it is, not as some may think it ought to be. Journalism is the political nation of the journalist, in effect the playing field for him in the game of life. And the rules are clear: Play to win. It seems to me that journalists, if they are to retain any self-respect and power, must follow such rules.

L & M: But you are known far and wide as believing in government of Princely authority and power. How do you reconcile that with the advice you are giving us about journalism?

NM: Well, you asked about journalism, not government. Your country claims to be a liberal democracy and your press theory is libertarianism. Within your special context the Press is the Prince—you even call it the fourth branch of the Prince's realm. So when I talk about Press Power and not about Government Power, I am simply proposing that in your system the Press is very much a Power Elite and must keep and expand its power.

L & M: Well, Machiavelli, time's up for us, and I know you must be on your way to the city. We appreciate your taking time to talk with us. But one last question: Is not *The Prince* really no more than a handbook for tyrants?

NM: That's right. You have hit the proverbial nail on its head. Tyrants of all kinds—effective ones, at least—need good handbooks. I have given them one of the very best.

AFTERTHOUGHTS

1. If you believe that the main responsibility of a mass medium in American society is to exist—to stay in business in order to serve some constituency—would you say that Machiavellianism is a natural philosophy to embrace?

2. Pragmatism, the "bottom line," achievement, competition, and success being the cornerstones of American society (if you believe they are), would you think Machiavelli's concepts are compatible or incompatible with such a society? If you feel they are not, what would be your main arguments?

3. Would you say that American "liberals" would be more prone to Machiavellianism than American "conservatives"? If so, why? If not, why?

4. Machiavelli was interested in power. How do you think the concept of "power" relates to the media's relationship to (a) government and (b) the people? How does power impinge on "journalistic freedom" in respect to a reporter's freedom as against the publisher's freedom?

5. Do you feel it is unfair to characterize the American press as "Machiavellian"? If so, how would you describe the press? If not, why not?

PART 4
Media and Society

CHAPTER 18

Credibility:
A State of Mind

Many years ago, the editor of a major British newspaper walked out into his newsroom and said something like this: "The unfortunate truth, gentlemen, is that when we read in our newspaper a story about an incident in which we ourselves have been involved, the story is more often wrong than right." A news story can represent only a fraction of what has actually occurred—because of limited space or time, because of what the reporter has not seen, or because of what the reporter has not been told or has not found out.

The barriers to complete and accurate coverage have, seemingly, always been there. Yet in recent years there has been a heightened disaffection on the part of readers and viewers. Editors and news directors have been concerned about a *credibility* problem. In the short term, the problem partially explains the plateauing of daily newspaper circulation during a period when the American population is increasing. In the long term, it could result in limited support by the public for press rights, including those guaranteed by the First Amendment.

In 1985 the American Society of Newspaper Editors published the results of a nationwide survey on credibility.[1] One of the startling findings: Some three-fourths of all American adults have *some* problem with the credibility of the mass media, and one-fifth are deeply distrustful of the press. Some editors argue that the credibility problem is the price that one

---

[1] *Newspaper Credibility: Building Reader Trust*, ASNE.

has to pay for doing a good job as a journalist. But David Lawrence, Jr., then publisher of the *Detroit Free Press* and head of the committee that arranged the survey, said that there is a difference "between newspapers being loved (impossible, really) and being respected as people who work very hard to get at the truth (surely worthwhile)."

One editor, Baxter Omohundro of the Columbus (Georgia) *Ledger and Enquirer,* wrote to Lawrence that "we constantly impress upon our staff that a credibility gap is created like the Grand Canyon—not just by the Colorado River but by the erosive effect of every drop of water that makes up the river." Another, A. M. Rosenthal of the *New York Times,* asked if editors themselves are satisfied "that we are giving people enough space to have at us in letters, not just in one section, but throughout the paper, or through Op-Ed pieces, or other kinds of outside contributions? Are we willing to acknowledge our own errors, not simply to satisfy the record, but to satisfy ourselves as well? Are we printing enough corrections, and are we printing them prominently enough?"[2]

As far as credibility is concerned, there was little difference between newspapers and television, according to the survey. However, the respondents found television to be a more "reliable" medium than newspapers, basically because "seeing is believing."

Complaints about the press are certainly not a new phenomenon in press history. However, there are a number of relatively new factors that have exacerbated the problem for the press. First let's look at the traditional reasons for the credibility problem. Then we'll examine those of more recent vintage.

TRADITIONAL CREDIBILITY PROBLEMS

Belief that the Media Invade Privacy. In order to cover a great number of stories, reporters must "invade" areas where the subjects of stories would rather not see them. Unfortunately for the subject, these usually turn out to be public meetings, or public property, or public records. The other kind of "privacy invasion" involves probing into the personal life of a public figure, an exercise resented not only by the person in the public eye but by many ordinary citizens as well. In the case of such stories, editors must frequently choose between the interests of the public and the interests of the individual. Will the rather gory photo of a prominent citizen being extricated from a wrecked car educate readers about traffic safety more than it will embarrass the wreck victim? Will the photo of a policeman's widow at a funeral service remind viewers of the sacri-

---

[2] The Lawrence, Omohundro, and Rosenthal statements appeared in *Newspaper Credibility: 206 Practical Approaches to Heighten Reader Trust,* ASNE, 1986.

fices made by officers of the law, or will it simply intrude on a family's grief?

Cynics will say that the question is, "Will it sell newspapers or get TV ratings?" But even if that is the primary motivation of the editor or news director, and it rarely is, the consequence is still a public good versus an individual's desire for privacy. One publisher in Virginia routinely prints the names of rape victims, believing that the potential protection this affords the accused is more important than the privacy of the victim. In Sweden, newspapers do not print the name of any person accused or even convicted of a crime, except in the most sensational cases, believing that such publication would result in a diminished ability on the part of the accused or convicted person to be rehabilitated into society.

Confusion between News and Opinion. Although it might appear obvious to a communications student or a member of the press, the difference between news and opinion is frequently lost on the average reader or viewer. One-fourth of the people surveyed in the ASNE report said that the front page of a newspaper contains more opinion than the rest of the newspaper. Many Americans do not realize that the *National Enquirer* is not a newspaper, in the traditional sense. They do not know the difference between an editorial and a straight news story, between the evening news and *60 Minutes*, between a documentary and a "tabloid TV" show, or between an editorial cartoon and a front-page graphic. Considering this failure on the part of so many to grasp what newspeople would consider to be obvious, one wonders how many readers understand the nuance of moving "Doonesbury" from the comic page to the Op-Ed page, as many newspapers have done.

Belief that Newspapers Emphasize Bad News. Bad news brings pain rather than pleasure to most. However, no one is interested in the ordinary—and fortunately for society, good news is usually ordinary and bad news is usually extraordinary. Allen H. Neuharth, former chairman of the Gannett Co. and founder of *USA TODAY,* called upon the press to emphasize "news of hope." Even if newspapers and broadcasting stations made that effort, they would still have to disseminate the bad news along with the "news of hope," or else abandon all traditional yardsticks for measuring news value.

Belief that Newspapers Are Controlled by Large Advertisers. Most newspapers and broadcasting stations maintain a solid separation between their business and news operations. However, this separation is not recognized, or not seen as credible, by most media consumers.

Errors of Fact, Grammar, and Spelling. As the Columbus editor said, these are the drops that ultimately help dig the canyon. The reader or

viewer cannot determine whether a given error was caused by carelessness or ignorance. On the newscasts of two different television stations in
the same city recently, this item was read by the anchor: "The agency
reported 289 cases of AIDs this year compared to 139 last year, an increase
of more than 200 per cent." An entire string of people who prepared and
finally read this news item apparently could not recognize the error.

Erroneous Image in Movies and TV Dramas. From the days of *The Front
Page* and perhaps earlier, reporters have been depicted as drunks, individually, or howling mobs, collectively. Watch any relevant present-day
movie or television drama for the following scenario: the celebrity, the
accused, or either one's attorney steps out of a building and is immediately
mobbed by a crushing horde of reporters and photographers. This image of
undiscipline, reinforced by continual repetition, must play some role in the
credibility picture.

RECENT FACTORS DIMINISHING CREDIBILITY

Credibility has been diminished as a result of technical, socioeconomic,
and competitive factors in American society. Following are some of these
factors.

The Changing Nature of Readers and Viewers. Media audiences, especially for print, are better educated and more sophisticated than ever
before in our history. Some 50 percent of all high school graduates go on to
some form of college education. One in ten families moves every year,
exposing the population to a broader national experience. The minority
population as a percentage of total population is growing every year,
because of immigration and birth rate. This new type of population expects
a higher degree of accuracy, less parochialism, and less ethnic and racial
stereotyping than were found in the media in the past.

The Mismatch in Age between Journalists and Audience. The Weaver-
Wilhoit book *The American Journalist,* referred to in Chapter 8, pointed
out that journalists, as a group, are younger now than when the profession
was surveyed ten years earlier, and strikingly younger than the audience
for which they are writing. In 1982–1983, when the Weaver-Wilhoit survey
was taken, 44.9 percent of journalists were 25 to 34 years of age. (A similar
survey in 1971 recorded only 33.3 percent in that age group.) Only 28
percent of the U.S. civilian labor force was in that age group in 1981.
Weaver and Wilhoit found that the typical reporter was 31 years old, the
typical desk editor or news producer 35 (compared with 42 in the survey
taken ten years earlier), and the typical managing editor 39 (compared with

49 ten years earlier). TV news directors had a median age of 35 and radio news directors a median age of 30.

One can only imagine the subtle effects of this age gap in influencing what gets presented and how in newspaper and TV reports and how an older audience perceives the results. One example: 15 rainless days in the summer mean great recreation weather for a young reporter living in an apartment; they mean parched lawns and gardens for an older family living in a suburban home. Which vision will the young reporter refer to in any given story relating to weather?

Chain Ownership and Monopoly Newspapers. Very few daily newspapers are home-owned any longer, and the two-newspaper town is an anomaly. Only 20 cities in the United States now have two independent dailies, and 143 newspaper chains now own 1,212 of the 1,650 daily newspapers, accounting for 74 percent of the total number of papers and 82 percent of total daily circulation in the United States. Readers view this as absentee ownership. There is also the concomitant phenomenon of the "corporate publisher" and "corporate editor," people who move up and down in the chain, making their mark or otherwise, but in any case moving on to the next waystation after four or five years in a city. Many editors, publishers, news directors, and reporters are never rooted in a community long enough to become known, and hence credible, there. There are exceptions, fortunately, but the overall result is not good for credibility. There are many advantages to group ownership (economic strength, outbreeding, editorial resources), but the truth is that familiarity breeds credibility much more than it does contempt.

New Competition. Although monopoly is a factor on the local scene, the (typically) one remaining newspaper has plenty of competition for audience. National newspapers, published with the help of satellites, are available in every city; radio and television stations have increased, because of FM and UHF; and cable channels are making possible large numbers of new news programs. Readers and viewers are able to read, hear, and view competing presentations of the same event, and they frequently find them quite different from each other. This does not help credibility. In addition, there is the alienation syndrome. Persons dissatisfied with a newspaper or television station no longer have to adapt themselves to it. They can simply turn off the spigot of local news by reading a national newspaper or listening to a distant telecast.

"Fast Food" Information. A perception of the audience as busy viewers with a short attention span encouraged television stations to reduce the length of stories, already measured in seconds. Radio newscasts were also shortened, to stay in tune with listeners who, it was thought, did not really want their musical reveries interrupted anyway. (The longer news programs from public broadcasting are largely Washington oriented and appeal to only a small segment of the U.S. public, less than 5 percent.) As newspapers found it necessary to compete with television news, they changed their formats to include more illustrations and shorter stories. Whatever the medium, news abbreviated is news that is obviously incomplete and thus more subject to misinterpretation.

Scarcity of Minority Journalists. Very few big-city newspapers have staffs representative of the ethnic and racial populations they serve, and minority groups recognize this imbalance. The Weaver and Wilhoit survey found that in 1982–1983 only 2.9 percent of journalists working in broadcasting and print journalism were black, compared with 3.9 percent ten years earlier, and with *12* percent in the U.S. population, according to the 1980 census. Only about half of one percent of journalists were Hispanic in 1982–1983, compared with 6.5 percent Hispanic in the 1980 population.

Changes in News Formats. As was discussed in an earlier chapter, the format of the television news story is chronological, more like that of a feature story, and frequently including a subjective conclusion. In recent years, as the newspaper has become less immediate and more of an all-day paper, the traditional inverted pyramid format of the news story has given way to a feature lead and a feature ending. The style of such stories is inherently subjective. The ASNE survey results, in which one-fourth of the respondents said there was more opinion on the front page than in any other place in the newspaper, is not so surprising if one examines these changes in format and writing style. Add to these the fact that most newspapers now subscribe to news services in addition to AP or UPI, and that these services provide material that is very subjective when compared with the AP standard. Documentaries have devolved into ambiguous "docudramas," and there is a thin line, at least in the viewer's mind, between television news and the "Inside Edition" or "Unsolved Mysteries" genre. These rather sensational crime shows, proliferating in prime and nonprime time, purport to be factual but "re-create" scenes using people who play the role of the victim, witness, or assailant. Television news has now borrowed this fictional device, euphemistically calling it "simulation" (rather than dramatization, which is what it actually is). In the summer of 1989 a running network story centered around Felix Bloch, an American diplomat under investigation for spying for Russia. On one evening ABC news carried a "simulation" of Bloch passing a briefcase to a Russian agent. Cross hairs were superimposed on the screen to make it look as though it were photographed surreptitiously. Viewers were not immediately notified that it was a "simulation."

Investigative Reporting. The development of investigative reporting enhanced the power of newspapers and television to bring hidden information into the sunlight. But there was also a credibility problem associated with this development. Investigative reporting is perceived by many as oppressive, intrusive, and unrelenting and as being directed, on occasion, against innocent people.

The Changing Editorial Page. Opinion dwells on the editorial and Op-Ed pages. Traditionally, this opinion has been not only forthright but frequently one-sided, provocative, and even "irresponsible," all perfectly within the umbrella of the First Amendment. In the era of the monopoly newspaper the opinion page is expected to be more balanced, yet it is fraught with *im*balance. An editorial page editor has a large number of means at his or her disposal to make the page supersubjective, from the selection of syndicated columnists, cartoons, and letters to the editor to the placement of letters and the headlines over letters and columns. Many newspapers excercise minimum supervision over this department, which carries a heavier responsibility for fairness than any other in the paper.

The Power of Cartoonists. In a visual age, talented cartoonists have unusual power. When this talent is applied to politics, the power can be greater than many editors recognize. Cartoonists, who once simply existed to reinforce editorial positions, have now become the tail wagging the editorial-page dog. Their positions can be one-dimensional, penetrating, and unfairly one-sided because by their very nature they aim to make a forceful, single-image statement. "Comics page" cartoonists can also become a credibility problem when they become political, as did "Doonesbury" and "Bloom County." Does one move them onto the Op-Ed page so they are clearly labeled "opinion" and won't "contaminate" the comics? Does one move them off the Op-Ed page when they go through a nonpolitical stage? And what kind of "balance" can one offer in cartoons, similar to the balance attempted with syndicated columns and letters?

CLOSING THE CREDIBILITY GAP

Ideas abound for improving the credibility of newspapers and broadcasting stations. Here are some of them:

- Work harder to retain staff who will be rooted in the community, and assign reporters with the greatest knowledge of the community to the more sensitive beats, such as government and business.

- Conduct accuracy checks. Go back in a random fashion to news sources and ask them if the stories in which they appeared or were quoted were accurate.
- Hire an *ombudsman:* a person who can read the newspaper like a reader (or view a news program like a viewer) rather than like an insider, and who can offer daily feedback—while also serving as a conduit for reader and viewer feedback. This does not have to be a full-time position, nor need the ombudsman have a chilling effect on the paper. Ideally, this ombudsman should be the publisher or editor, but given the duties of these two individuals, an outside person is usually needed.
- Pay special attention in the editing process to news stories written in a feature style.
- Clearly distinguish news from "news analysis" or interpretation. Don't assume that a reader or viewer will know the difference.
- Print corrections prominently in a set place or places each day in the newspaper. Don't be reluctant to correct errors made in broadcast reports.
- Bend over backward to maintain fairness in coverage during political campaigns.
- Insist that everyone who represents the newspaper or broadcasting station look professional. Sloppy-looking reporters and photographers give readers, listeners, and viewers the impression that they will produce sloppy stories. If the public is permitted into the newsroom, make certain that the newsroom looks professional. Political or philosophical slogans pasted on terminals or doors may express the unbridled individuality of reporters and editors; they also send a message—usually the wrong message—to visitors.
- Decide whether, as a goal, the editorial page should achieve balance. If so, examine the selection of cartoons and syndicated columnists, and review whatever policy governs letters selection. Try to get local columnists outside the newspaper who hold opinions different from those of the editorial board, or at the very least, seek out aggressive, locally written Op-Ed pieces that express opinions different from those in the paper's editorials.
- Work within the community and with local academic institutions to build a staff representative of the racial and ethnic groups served by the newspaper or broadcasting station.
- Take time each year to educate the audience, in a nondidactic fashion, about the role of mass communications in the community and how the various media function. There are few newspapers and broadcasting stations that do not get visits from kindergarten classes

in the course of the year. It would be better if the visits came from ninth- and tenth-graders and if their guides and discussion leaders were general managers, publishers, editors, and news directors.

AFTERTHOUGHTS

1. Wilhoit and Weaver found American journalists as a group to be significantly younger in 1982–1983 than in 1971. To what do you attribute this change, and do you believe it resulted in any appreciable difference in the way the news was reported?
2. Do you believe that "Doonesbury" belongs on the editorial page? Is it necessary to achieve balance in political cartoons?
3. Should a newspaper try to seek "balance" in its editorial endorsements during a political campaign?
4. Is it better for a failing newspaper to go out of business, thus strengthening the suburban press and reducing advertising costs, or is it better for the failing newspaper to be permitted to enter a "joint operating agreement" with the stronger newspaper, thus preserving two independent editorial operations in the community?
5. Does a person accused of rape suffer any disadvantage when the name of the rape victim is not published? Should the names of victims of other crimes also be withheld?

CHAPTER 19

Media and Propaganda

Someone said to us recently that "thinking about the mass media is a good thing, but thinking about media people as propagandists is harmful, for it undermines media work for the many students wishing to make it their careers." Although this statement came from a public relations teacher and virtually the same sentiment was expressed by an advertising professor, there is no doubt that a wide assortment of media people feel the same way.

We plead guilty to often expressing the idea, in lectures and conversations, that media practitioners—even journalists—not only cooperate in the spread of propaganda but often initiate it themselves. Again, of course, the semantic problem rears its head: Just what is propaganda?

For many years John Merrill, in his classes, has suggested an acronym which encapsulates the essence of "propaganda," stressing those ingredients prominently mentioned by a wide variety of scholars. The acronym is: PASID. We believe that essentially propaganda is Persuasive, Action-oriented, Selfish, Intentional, and Devious.

People who think about such things will find faults—minor, and maybe even major—with this essential characterization of propaganda. Can you pose any valid objections to one or more of its components? Certainly propaganda is trying, more forcefully than other forms of communication, to persuade somebody to believe a certain thing or think a certain way and to take a certain action—vote a certain way, buy a certain product, or send a child to a certain university. Propaganda is selfish since the propagandist has a vested interest in propagandizing; he or she wants to "sell" something or achieve some end that is related to self-interest or group or institutional interest. Furthermore, propaganda is intentional. It is not an accident that the ad appeared, or the editorial took a certain position, or the talk-show host loaded his panel with conservatives. Propaganda is a *planned* activity. Finally, a quite common characteristic of propaganda is that it is devious. In other words, in some way the persons receiving the propaganda are having the "wool pulled over their eyes." At least, they are not getting a balanced (or factually oriented) version; in short, they are getting a biased message.

In this chapter we shall give something of an extended definition of the term "propaganda," but regardless of what definition is given, many will still think of it as a negative and unworthy endeavor—something that media people, with few exceptions, rise above.

MEDIA-RELATED PROPAGANDA

Probably the best justification for the inclusion of this subject is our belief that propaganda is tied very closely to the mass media: it is almost impossible to think about mass media in the modern world *without* considering propaganda. We contend, then, that the mass media are (1) filled with a wide variety of propaganda, and (2) filled with a wide variety of propagandists. Media are both transmitters and formulators of propaganda.

Propaganda loses any kind of meaningful significance if it is defined too broadly, if (as some writers propose) it becomes synonymous with the organized dissemination of messages. Then, of course, every kind of communication might be considered propaganda, admittedly depending on the connotations of the word "organized." Propaganda in the context of journalism, or in the context of the mass media, must be understood to be something more limited, more specific; otherwise, we might as well scrap the word altogether. It has been said that the term *propaganda* has a negative or evil connotation in a journalistic context. This is undoubtedly true, especially in that part of journalism that purports to be objective, reliable, balanced, thorough, and credible—the *news* aspects.

On the other hand, many journalists and other toilers in the vineyards of the mass media embrace propaganda as a very necessary part of media output. Propaganda, even in its most negative aspects, has chiseled out a niche for itself in the most highly respected of the mass media. Columnists and news commentators accept it as a valid aspect of their journalistic endeavors. Editorial writers could not operate without it. Even many so-called interpretive or analytical writers and speakers call on propaganda techniques to explain, interpret, analyze, discuss, and persuade.

The "straight" newscast on radio and television or the news story in the press is about the only mass media sector still resisting the label of propaganda. At least this is the case in theory. In practice, many students of propaganda recognize that the very best propaganda vehicle is the so-called objective, neutral, dispassionate news report. We contend that journalism today is spilling over with propaganda, not only in advertising, where one would expect it, but in the voice inflections and facial expressions, in headlines, photographs, and captions—everywhere. In fact, many cynics suggest that *journalism is propaganda*. Although we also feel that propaganda manifests itself in journalism to a very great degree, we do not want to go so far as to propose that there is no journalism that cannot be considered free of propaganda. The distinction between propaganda and nonpropaganda must be preserved in journalism if the credibility gap we hear so much about does not become so broad as to become total disbelief.

TOWARD A DEFINITION OF PROPAGANDA

One of the main problems in talking about propaganda, of course, is that so many concepts or definitions of the term exist. What is the core meaning of "propaganda"? Are there any common denominators of meaning associated with the term? We believe there are. And although the semantic tangle which has grown up around the term is sticky and dense, we believe that the whole subject of propaganda is important to the journalist and should be considered seriously. Why? Because any extended discussion of propaganda brings the concerned person into an area of discourse when certain basic issues of journalism have their roots. When one considers propaganda in the context of journalism he or she becomes forced to look directly at many of the "first principles" or foundation stones of journalistic endeavor.

Regardless of which of the many definitions is being examined, one finds certain core ideas about propaganda: "manipulation," "purposeful management," "preconceived plan," "creation of desires," "reinforcement of biases," "arousal of preexisting attitudes," "irrational appeal," "specific objective," "arousal to action," "predetermined end," "suggestion," and "creation of dispositions." Out of all these terms one may gather a certain impression about propaganda. It seems that propaganda is related to an attempt (implying an *intent*) on the part of somebody to manipulate somebody else. By manipulate we mean *to control*—to control not only the attitudes of others but also, sometimes, their actions. Somebody (or some group)—the *propagandist*—is predisposed to cause others to think a certain way, in some cases so that they may take a certain action. Propaganda, then, is the effort or activity by which an initiating communicator intends to control the attitudes and actions of others through playing on their preexisting biases with messages designed largely to appeal to their emotions and/or irrationality.

The propagandist does not want the audience to analyze or think seriously about the message and does not want to be questioned or forced to deal in specifics or to present evidence, having what Harold Lasswell has referred to as a noneducational orientation; this means that the ends or solutions had already been determined before the search for truth began. Contrasted to this is what in Lasswellian terms may be the "deliberative attitude," the nonpropagandistic orientation that implies an unprejudiced and open search for the truth.[1] Lasswell uses the term "deliberative attitude" to refer to education as distinct from propaganda. Propaganda is not an invitation to the audience to deliberate, to contemplate, to analyze, to think, or to question. It is an invitation to come to rather quick conclusions or to reinforce existing ones. It is an invitation to change or strengthen one's attitude and perhaps to involve oneself in an action of some type.

Another way to say this might be: propaganda is dependent on the *intention* of the communicator to use the message so as to affect the attitude of the audience, so as to achieve an end or goal in keeping with the communicator's desires. This emphasizes the *deliberate* nature of propaganda, the *desire* of the communicator to achieve a preconceived purpose.

So the propagandist (1) is *not* disinterested; (2) is *not* neutral; (3) *has* a plan, a purpose, a goal; (4) *wants* to influence, to persuade, to affect attitudes and action; and (5) is not interested in the audience members making up their own minds on the basis of a fair and balanced presentation of information.

JOURNALISM AND PROPAGANDA

The journalist may well ask: Am I a propagandist? Quite likely the answer will be yes. At least, he or she is probably propagandistic at many times and in many circumstances. Some journalists, of course, are almost pure

---

[1] H. D. Lasswell, "The Theory of Political Propaganda," *American Political Science Review*, 21 (1927); for other good discussions of propaganda, see Hadley Cantril, *The Psychology of Social Movements* (New York: John Wiley & Sons, 1941); L. W. Doob, *Propaganda: Its Psychology and Technique* (New York: Henry Holt, 1935); A. M. and E. B. Lee, *The Fine Art of Propaganda* (New York: Harcourt, Brace, 1939); P. M. Linebarger, *Psychological Warfare* (New York: Duell, Sloan & Pearce, 1954); F. E. Lumley, *The Propaganda Menace* (New York: Century, 1933); William McDougall, *The Group Mind* (New York: G. P. Putnam's Sons, 1920), Graham Wallas, *The Great Society* (New York: Macmillan, 1914); and Jacques Ellul, *Propaganda* (New York: Vintage, 1973).

propagandists. Others have very little of the propagandist in them. It depends on many factors, but two stand out as most significant:

1. The type of journalistic work the particular journalist performs
2. The basic ethical, ideological, and psychological "character" of the particular journalist

Editorial writers, for example, deal in propaganda far more often than does the writer of sports stories or obituaries. And generally speaking, a by-lined columnist is more of a propagandist than is an anonymous "straight" news writer. The television analyst or commentator is more likely to propagandize than is the reporter in London or the anchor in Washington. But, as we have already pointed out, there are exceptions to these generalizations. In fact, *news* writers are potentially in a more favorable spot to propagandize than are editorial writers: editorial writers are *expected* by their readers to propagandize (to try to affect attitudes and action), while news writers are expected simply to present the facts. The facts, of course, may be carefully selected, juggled, and twisted; certain facts may be played up or down, or omitted altogether, and the reader will never know it. So the idea that propaganda is only on the editorial page is a myth; propaganda is on every page of a newspaper and on every radio or television news show.

The fundamental journalistic orientation of a person engaged in disseminating information and interpretation has much to do with the amount of propaganda contained in his or her effort. What are his ideological and political commitments? In other words, is she *inclined* by personality, political commitment, ethical standards, and the like to want to be *informational* (dispassionate, neutral, balanced) rather than *persuasive* (involved, passionate, concerned, subjective)?

If a journalist is inclined to be persuasive, even one who writes only anonymous news stories, he or she *will* be persuasive as a general rule. On the other hand, there are editorial writers who are inclined to be balanced, dispassionate, and neutral; their editorials reflect this orientation. Therefore, it may well be that mass media audiences need to revise their old stereotypes concerning propaganda and subscribe to a new one: don't analyze the particular *article* to determine the presence of propaganda; rather, analyze *the writer* of the article.

The question arises, of course, as to how a reader, listener, or viewer can detect propaganda in the mass media. Certainly not every member of the audience could analyze the communicator even if every audience member were a trained psychiatrist. Clues as to propaganda in a message must come largely from the message itself. Of course, in the case of television, the viewer may suspect the propagandistic nature of a message by watching the facial expressions of the speaker very carefully. However, inferences drawn from smiles, raised eyebrows, voice inflections, and general demeanor can be quite misleading.

The only way to check on propaganda or the lack of it in a newspaper or some other medium is to be in a position to verify the information, the quotations, and the total context of the communication being considered.[2] By and large, this is impossible. Audience members must accept most of what they get from the media on faith—or, of course, disregard or suspect it. Certainly most of us are not well enough informed about all of the complex events reported to us and analyzed for us every day to know when we are being misled. In some cases, especially when a story relates to us or to some event we witnessed, we are able to detect bias in a story, but this does not happen very often.

If we know a great deal about a particular writer or commentator, we may be able to detect propaganda in his or her message—*especially if we are not in the same ideological camp.* We are more suspicious of, and hence more critical of, reporters or commentators who are known to be of a different political persuasion from ourselves. Either we tune them out altogether or we constantly look for flaws and contradictions in their message. On the other hand, when we are listening to an ideological or political sympathizer, we are prone to accept most of what we hear as rational and truthful.

We are also more prone to have faith in a message if it is compatible with our own cultural and national interests. Egyptians believe *Al Ahram* because it reinforces their own beliefs—and what they want to believe. *Ma'ariv* has the same credibility value for (like-minded) Israelis for the same reason. Given this basic proclivity to believe what one wants to believe, what kind of credibility can an *outside,* supposedly disinterested voice have for a specific country or its citizens? Undoubtedly, the more a citizen is convinced of the disinterestedness of the outside voice, the more credible the message is likely to be. The BBC, for instance, is likely to be considered far more credible in Southeast Asia because it is politically disinterested in the area and because it has a tradition of objectivity. Iranian radio perhaps *reinforces* opinions in that country, but the BBC is *believed.* It is quite possible that reinforcement and belief are two entirely different news objectives.

Propaganda in a closed society (a dictatorship) obviously serves a fundamentally different purpose than it does in an open society (a democracy). In a closed society it serves mainly to confirm and reinforce atti-

---

[2] By the same token, communicators themselves are often unable to determine whether their facts are themselves products of propaganda if they and their staff are barred by government from the sources of news.

tudes created by the restrictive environment so as to minimize social disharmony and friction; on the other hand, in a democracy or open society propaganda is pluralistic and competitive and provides the information and ideas necessary for political argument and the formation of public opinion.

PROPAGANDA TECHNIQUES

Techniques of propaganda abound. Skilled propagandists are like artists as they blend them, change them, obscure them, and generally use them carefully depending on the particular audience and the specific occasion. They generally subscribe to the belief that the end justifies *any kind of propaganda technique*. Propagandists are pragmatists, using what will work. Therefore, they must constantly study people, techniques, and results. They are practicing psychologists, using everything at their command to manipulate, to persuade, to cause action. Technique—tactic and strategy—is their weapon. Therefore, they take it very seriously.

A main strategical technique is a constant concern with passionate rhetoric and advocacy. The propagandist has little or no use for dispassionate argument, trying to avoid open discussion and questions. The Socratic method is out of the question; propagandists *already* have their answers determined, so their main technique is *the avoidance of rational dialogue*.

In line with this overriding strategical objective is a wide variety of tactical techniques, which are used singly or in clusters to achieve specific objectives in different situations with various audiences. Many persons are led to believe that if they can only learn these techniques and condition themselves to recognize them, they can defend themselves against them. Often propaganda devices are taught for this reason—so that people can defend themselves against them. The only thing wrong with this idea is that people may know something of the nature of these techniques—enough to recognize and even label them—but still be unable to become immune to their effects. The propagandist knows this and is aware that some propaganda will get through and accomplish its purpose even if it is recognized for what it is. Also they keep a step ahead of the general level of propaganda sophistication in their audience, thus keeping the audience guessing, off-balance, and uncertain. Some techniques of propaganda are wasted on some people in some situations. The propagandist is aware of this fact and simply makes his or her campaigns broad enough and flexible enough to reach people of various temperaments, personalties, and circumstances. Techniques are constantly revamped and blended.

Seven basic propaganda devices, defined by the Institute for Propaganda Analysis during World War II, are usually presented in textbooks and discussion of propaganda. Since they are found in so many source materials and are generally well known, we shall only name them here, without discussing them. They are name-calling, testimonials, glittering generalities, bandwagon, transfer, plain folks, and card stacking.[3] Although these seven are important, and are used regularly by propagandists of all kinds, they by no means exhaust all possible techniques. For example, *repetition* is a basic one; another type is *faulty analogy* along with its first cousin, *unfair association.*[4]

THE PROPAGANDISTIC JOURNALIST

Few people like to think of journalists as propagandists. Journalism is to be believed, trusted, respected: this is the traditional concept. Even though opinion has always been accepted as an important part of journalism, the basic image of journalism is one of reliability, factualness, and trust. At any rate, it does not seem quite right to go around referring to journalists as propagandists. For if the traditional image changes and journalists are looked upon as propagandists, what would happen to the libertarian idea that a free people must remain free by being informed by the press so that they might make rational decisions? Do we really want to receive our important political information, with which we make our "popular sovereignty" work, from a propagandistic press?

It would be rather presumptuous to say that all journalists are propagandists, but it is probably safe to say that most of them are. We may not like to think of them in this way, but a careful observation and analysis of journalists will indicate that they reveal the traits and characteristics of propagandists, at least in many of their activities.

We are not talking here about journalists as propagandists in that they "propagate" or spread information. We are talking about journalists as propagandists in that they "propagate" or spread their own prejudices, biases, and opinions—trying to affect the attitudes of their audiences. Without a doubt, there are journalists who are machinelike in their work or who have the kinds of duties not involving them in potentially propagan-

---

[3] See Alfred McClung Lee, "The Analysis of Propaganda: A Clinical Summary," *American Journal of Sociology,* September 1945. Cf. Jacques Ellul, *Propaganda,* for probably the best discussion of all aspects of propaganda, including techniques. This is an original, catalytic communications-oriented book.

[4] This is not simply "guilt by association" but also "virtue by association." The association tactic is perhaps the most useful of all propaganda techniques.

distic situations, but these are probably a minority. Large numbers of journalists, even among those involved in "straight" news reporting, are propagandists in that they purposely intend to mislead or at least influence their audiences in specific ways.

What are some of the techniques used by journalists who participate in such propaganda efforts? There are, of course, dozens of them, but the following are a few of the most notable.

Use of Stereotypes. The mass media, in their news and interpretation, regularly simplify the reality of events. They present people and events as one-dimensional and static. They not only create stereotypes but perpetuate and spread them through repetition and emphasis. The journalist who wants to propagandize finds this an easy and effective tactic.

Opinion as Fact. Even a casual analysis of the mass media will show that a favorite technique is to present opinion disguised as fact. "The audience gave the speaker an enthusiastic welcome." "There was no doubt in anyone's mind that Mr. X was criticizing the President out of a desire for revenge." So much reporting of this type exists in the mass media—in almost every story—that a whole book could be written on this technique.

Biased Attribution. How do the media attribute information to a source? What kind of language is used? An attribution verb such as "said" is neutral (not opinionated and evokes no emotional response); an attribution verb such as "snapped" (negatively affective) is designed to appeal to the reader's emotions. A verb such as "smiled" is a favorable term, for it is positively affective. A journalist's—or an editor's—bias for or against some person in the news can be ascertained by analyzing his or her method of attributing statements to the person.

Information Selection. What will a journalist choose to say about a person or an event? Is there a pattern in his or her choices? Does he or she stack the message by presenting *only* "bad" or *only* "good" information? What is the nature of what is ignored as contrasted with what is included? Of course, every reporter must select, but the message becomes propagandistic when a *pattern* of selection becomes evident. Quoting out of context is, of course, a form of this technique. It is impossible for an audience member of the mass media to detect this type of propaganda. There is no standard for comparison.

Misleading Headlines. The headline writer can propagandize effectively, knowing that, by and large, people come away from stories with the substance of the headline—not the story—in their minds. In fact, many see the headline but do not read the story underneath it. So many headlines are twisted, biased, and distorted that one is led to believe that headlines bear about as much resemblance to their stories as the stories bear to the reality they purport to report.

Biased Photographs. Present your heroes from the best perspective, smiling, positive, calm. Show your enemies from the worst possible perspective, frowning, negative, nervous. Photographs may not lie, but they can mislead. Like facts and quotations in a story, they can be selected for a purpose. Anyone who has ever taken news photographs or shot television footage knows that the potential for propaganda is extremely great. And anyone who analyzes photographs in newspapers and magazines and film on television can observe the practical tactics of photographic propaganda.

Censorship. Usually we do not think of the mass media indulging in censorship; that is something for government officials to do. But the media do censor, even if they might call it exercising their editorial or news prerogatives. They leave this story or this picture out; they delete part of this quotation; they throw that entire story into the wastebasket; they chop away two-thirds of this story. They censor, all right, and anyone who thinks it is all perfectly innocent and that journalists restrict information only out of the purest of motives simply has not faced the realities of a journalistic medium. Those who would say that the journalist or the medium has the right under press freedom to censor may well be right; here we are stating only that censorship *by the media themselves* is a very real propagandistic tactic. Two main forms of censorship exist, and the mass media use them both. They are (1) selective control of information so as to favor a particular viewpoint or editorial position and (2) deliberate doctoring of information in order to create a certain impression.

Repetition. Look at a newspaper that you know to have a particular bias, political or otherwise. You will see that certain themes, persons, ideas, and slogans appear on its pages again and again, day to day, week to week. Readers of a "liberal" newspaper such as the *Washington Post* or the *St. Louis Post-Dispatch* get caught up in the newspaper's repetitive pattern of news presentation and editorial stances until they can predict exactly what line the paper will take on almost any event or issue that arises. A reader of the "conservative" *Chicago Tribune* or *Washington Times* can do the same. Television network documentaries and newscasts with certain rather obvious biases are also predictable as to their repetitive positions, themes, and issues.

Negativism. This is a very potent (and observable) tactic of propaganda in journalism. In its news and interpretation, a mass medium should not just be *for* something or somebody. It should emphasize the negative; it should spotlight the "enemy"; it should be *against* something or somebody. Mass media often appear to find it much more exciting, for example, to be against an American President than to be *for* him. They likewise seem to relish the idea of blasting away at established institutions and lending support to the forces in society that are violent, emotional, irrational, atypical, and destructive. Emphasize the negative: this is an important journalistic propaganda tactic. Focus on an enemy, selecting targets in line with preexisting disposition of the audience.

Appeal to Authority. This tactic is closely related to the common "testimonial" technique in that it relies heavily on support from well-known and reputable sources and persons. The journalist may attribute a statement to a veiled or vague authority or may selectively quote a prominent person.[5] In many news stories there are "leading educators" or "prominent theologians" who say or believe this or that. There is some Pentagon spokesman saying something, or some "source close to the President" who is taking a certain stand. If commentators want to make a point for their television audience on a controversial subject, they may find it advantageous to quote some prominent person (who is in agreement) relative to the subject rather than present their own positions directly.

Fictionalizing. A mass medium may present mere fiction, camouflaging it, of course, as fact. Most often, journalists do not totally fictionalize; they simply mix some fiction (or conjecture) into their fact skeleton. They do not have everything needed to make a good, complete, compelling story, so they splice in a little fiction—what might well have happened. They "creatively" fill the gaps in the story, even dreaming up certain direct quotations to put in the mouth of the source. Nobody, after all, will ever know any better—except perhaps the source, and what will that matter in the long run? For, after all, is there not a "core of truth" in the story, and, as the old saying goes, you cannot be completely objective in a story, anyway.

Journalists undoubtedly use many techniques other than those mentioned above. They propagandize every time they slant the news, and as Tamotsu Shibutani correctly points out, slanting the news is a very old and

---

[5] A journalist may quote a suspicious or discredited source, also, depending on the effect he or she wishes to achieve.

extremely widespread practice.[6] Among techniques used to color the picture are misrepresentation of facts, omission of certain items tending to favor an ideological "foe," giving undue prominence to one side of an issue, selectively quoting from a speech or interview to make a person look good or bad, and arousing strong negative feelings against scapegoats to take attention away from main issues. Propagandistic journalists do not simply tell lies; whenever possible they tell the truth (or at least a portion of it), but this "truthful" slice-of-reality reporting can be propaganda. Shibutani talks of true or factual propaganda, which is very difficult to distinguish from news.

What does all of this mean? Does it imply that consumers of mass media messages should look upon these messages as basically propagandistic? It is difficult to answer such a question, for different persons would respond variously, depending on their sophistication, knowledge, and experience with the media as well as on their cynicism. But it is probably safe to say that the mass media and their functionaries generate propaganda and spread the propaganda of others to a far greater extent than most citizens believe.

Is it possible for the receiver of mass media messages to detect bias and propaganda in them? Probably not, in most cases. The audience member, seldom in a position to check on the factual accuracy, balance, and thoroughness of press reports, is largely at the mercy of media reporters and editors. He or she is also in a "detached" position from the communicator so that there is no real knowledge of the intent and motivation—or the standard of ethics—of the person designing the message. He or she can assume, of course, that most media messages are misleading or biased, can be skeptical and even cynical, can disbelieve *everything* read in the newspapers or seen on television; then he or she will, of course, be safe from journalistic propaganda. But, if one takes such a drastic position, one will also be ignorant of major events and trends going on in the world.

So what should sensible audience members do? They must accept some information and opinion and reject some. They must expose themselves to as diverse a sample of media matter as possible. They will find discrepancies among sources as to factual statements and will find contradictions among the opinions and observations of columnists and commentators and they will never know just which source is most reliable, but they will develop some ways to make decisions and preserve sanity amid the frustrating welter of information. They will build up their own complex

---

[6] *Improvised News* (Indianapolis: Bobbs-Merrill, 1966), pp. 188–89.

safety mechanism for screening incoming information; they will see less and less that does not agree with their dominant dispositions (selective exposure) and will then select from these selected media only those messages that are compatible with their own biases (selective perception); finally, will they remember or be affected by only those parts of the message that give comfort or mental pleasure (selective retention). This whole selectivity process permits audience members to largely protect themselves against hostile propaganda; at any rate, they use propaganda simply to reinforce—not challenge—their basic attitudes and predispositions. If they did not do this, they would quickly fly into a million emotional pieces in the face of unverifiable and disharmonic information and opinion that surround them every day.

It may well be, then, that propaganda is really not very potent after all. At least it does not seem extremely powerful in changing opinions; a study of newspaper support of candidates vis-à-vis election outcomes in American history would indicate that this is the case. But journalistic propaganda undoubtedly provides comfort and reinforcement for the receiver if it is compatible with his or her basic needs. In a pluralistic media system this function of propaganda may work very well; the danger arises when the press begins to contract in its pluralism and the propaganda becomes more and more standardized, preventing increasing numbers of persons from finding self-supporting and satisfying propaganda.

Strange as it may seem, then, one of the principal reasons for maintaining a pluralistic press is so that we can provide a wide variety of propaganda, suitable for a multitude of needs.

AFTERTHOUGHTS

1. What do you think would be the impact of propaganda on society if there were no mass media? What do you think would be the nature of mass media if there were no propaganda?

2. Can a reporter be a good reporter if he or she never indulges in propagandistic (basically persuasive) activities?

3. Is it possible for a mass medium's audience member to elude propaganda? Totally? Partially? How might such persons protect themselves against being successfully propagandized?

4. Would it be a salutary thing for audience members to be free from the effects of propaganda? How would you argue that propaganda is *necessary* in a free society?

5. If propaganda's key characteristic is *persuasive intent,* what are the principal mass media that would be *least* susceptible to serve as propaganda vehicles? What kinds of journalistic messages would be *most* likely to contain propaganda?

CHAPTER 20

Letting the
People Know

A basic premise of the reportorial mode of mass communication is that the people should know the truth. In fact, it is usually said that they have a *right* to know.[1] In a sense, such a belief forms the very foundation of American journalism. A belief in full disclosure and a dedication to objective reporting are normally pounded into the minds of prospective and practicing journalists quite early in their education or careers.

We need to think about this whole business of "neutral" journalism and the people's right to know. Too often such concepts are presented as givens, as necessities for the responsible practice of journalism. In short, the basic premises of objective reporting and the people's right to know are solidly entrenched in our journalism. Are such ideas simply platitudes, or are they meaningful? Are these premises valid? Or are they nothing more than myths?

FULL-DISCLOSURE REPORTING

Students of communication, especially those in journalism, will recall that in their basic newswriting classes, they were bombarded with heavy doses of "objectivity" training. They should keep themselves and their ideas and

---

[1] Many books and articles have propagated the concept of the people's right to know. Three of the standard or basic books of this type have been Harold Cross's *The People's Right to Know* (New York: Columbia University Press, 1953), Kent Cooper's *The Right to Know* (New York: Farrar, Strauss, and Cudahy, 1956), and Charles Whalen's *Your Right to Know* (New York: Vintage Books, 1973). The term has made its way into general parlance and is heard regularly in conversations and speeches.

opinions out of the story. They should be neutral, dispassionate, thorough. They should disclose the facts (verified, of course) as fully as possible. This is what was meant by "full-disclosure" reporting. Facts were sacred, and the reporter should report, not tamper in any way with the story.

Someone will object: But we all know that it is *impossible* to completely or fully disclose the facts of a story. *Everything* cannot be said about anything. True. But does not traditional American reporting philosophy insist that reporters should disclose everything *of significance* that has been gathered and verified? Obviously a reporter cannot report everything, but a reporter *can* report everything that he or she has that is of significance.

Of course, the conscientious reporter immediately runs into a quandary: how to report objectively, neutrally, and dispassionately while facing the necessity to make decisions, to act out of personal values, and to follow hunches. How can the reporter be *objective* in a job that requires subjectivity from beginning to end?[2]

This, it seems, is the basic question. The reporter usually resolves such a dilemma by caving in on the side of personal involvement, editorial intrusion, and rationalized subjectivity. Out the window goes the concept of keeping oneself out of the story, of full disclosure, of being truthful (in the sense of disclosing verified information). Enter the new justification (hidden, of course, from the public): *What the people don't know won't hurt them.*

WHAT ABOUT "FAIRNESS"?

Standing alongside the concept of full disclosure is another supreme journalistic value: that of *fairness*. The reporter is taught to present the unvarnished truth and at the same time is admonished to be "fair." Another quandary. How can the reporter provide the untampered-with facts in an unbiased manner and be fair at the same time? Does not fairness imply

---

[2] Two excellent articles among the myriads written on the subject of journalistic objectivity are Gaye Tuchman's "Objectivity as Strategic Ritual: An Examination of Newsmen's Notions of Objectivity," *American Journal of Sociology,* 4 (January 1972), and Arnold Hadwin's "Objectivity Is Crucial—But Is It Possible to be Objective?" *Journalism Studies Review* (Cardiff, U. K., July 1980). Cf. Chapter 8 ("Journalistic Objectivity") in Everette Dennis and J. C. Merrill, *Basic Issues in Mass Communication* (New York: Macmillan, 1984). The Society of Professional Journalists, Sigma Delta Chi, considers objectivity possible and important, for its Code of Ethics says that objectivity "serves as the mark of an experienced professional" and that the Society honors "those who achieve it."

tampering with the facts, leaving out certain things, playing up certain things, using this quote instead of that one, and so on?

Not necessarily, some would say. There is no conflict between fairness and full-disclosure reporting, they would argue. Being thorough, accurate, and unbiased *is* being fair. Those who take this position conceive of the object of fairness as being the *integrity* of the story, or the "truth." The question here is not "fair to whom?" Rather it is "fair to what?" The answer: fair to the basic essence of the story so far as the reporter knows it.

But it is a different matter for the reporter who conceives of fairness as having a *personal* object or referent. This reporter must try to think of the consequences of the story to some person (or persons), must try to write the story and report only those facts that result in fair treatment to those thought deserving of it. This concept of fairness immediately gets the reporter into the fact-tampering or censorship business—though no journalist would want to describe it that way. At any rate, such a concept influences the reporter *in decisions about which facts to put in and which ones to leave out,* in short, purposely to "subjectivize" the story. The key word here is "purposely," for it implies that the reporter has a self-determined reason or motive for such censorship. And quite likely this reason is thought of by the reporter as a moral or ethical reason. In other words, the reporter's ethics is put ahead of the dedication to report fully. The reporter settles for partial reporting or a flawed report, all in the name of avoiding some possible or anticipated consequences. One question often ignored by such a reporter, however, is the question of *fairness to the audience member.* Is the reader or viewer treated fairly by the reporter if the story is intentionially modified to fit the subjective biases of the reporter?[3]

AND WHAT ABOUT THE "RIGHT TO KNOW"?

It might be well also to think about reportorial *gatekeeping* as being in conflict with the journalistic belief in the people's right to know. Reporters would be the first to condemn the government for withholding facts from them, thus ultimately keeping the people from knowing. But these same reporters see no problem in doing exactly what they criticize government officials for doing: managing information. Of course, journalists call it

---

[3] Most media ethics books (see bibliography) give short shrift to "fairness." Nobody has really dealt with this complex problem from either a semantic or a techniques perspective.

"exercising their journalistic prerogatives" or "performing their editorial function," or something like that. If the government does it, journalists call it "secrecy," "censorship," or "news management."

But is it not true that, if the people do have a right to know, such a right can be abridged by parties other than the government? If Mr. Doe does not know something about Senator Klean, he doesn't know it regardless of who is keeping that something from him. Often, in their self-adulation and self-righteousness, journalists fail to realize that *they* may play as great a part in keeping the people from knowing as does the government.

But, say the journalists, *we* are supposed to make informational decisions about what the public knows and doesn't know; the government is not. Is that right? Where do journalists get any such right that is denied to government? Certainly not from the Constitution. Well, some journalists may say, that's not true. The First Amendment gives me the right to tamper with the news if I want to! Correct, but doesn't the government have the same right? Cannot a government official, as well as a journalist, feel morally inclined to keep certain information from the public?

Of course, journalists can retreat from their usual litany and *deny* that the people do have a right to know. And this attitude would, obviously, justify any tampering, managing, and "editing" that they would want to do. In spite of the fact that such journalists would be on solid philosophical ground, not many would make such a denial. That would fly in the face of years of the press's extolling the people's right in order to justify its desire to get the government to open up.

So it looks as if this "right to know" (whence we get it, we never learn) will be a continuing shibboleth of journalism. And this in spite of the fact that it contradicts an even more precious concept: the press's right of editorial self-determination, a right that *does* have a constitutional basis.

THE STORY'S INTEGRITY

Most reporters know almost instinctively that letting their own values impact on a story—distorting, changing, adding, subtracting—does damage to the story's basic integrity. This does not mean that a reporter does not indulge in such tampering for one reason or another, but usually this is done with the knowledge that the integrity of the study is compromised. In other words, most reporters recognize that the duty of a reporter *is to report:* to present the facts of the case as fully and truthfully as possible, attempting to make the report conform to reality as closely as the reporter's acquired facts and perceptions permit.

Because of personal biases—political, religious, or other—reporters are tempted to deviate from basic reportorial principles because of consequences that might ensue if full-disclosure reporting were done. The motivation for such deviation may be egoistic or altruistic; it matters little, for the damage to the integrity of the story is done when the reporter steps out of the reportorial mode into a moralistic or subjective one or tampers with the facts. The reporter has taken this step, for example, when he or she has a rape victim's name but chooses to leave it out of the story.

All kinds of reasons can be invoked to justify such an action, but these are subjective, opinion-based justifications having to do with possible consequences, not with reportorial integrity. If the head of a government department were to invoke some similar justification (e.g., anticipated negative consequences) for not releasing some facts of a story to the press, the press would be outraged.

Remember the Gary Hart "story" in the winter of 1987?[4] Many critics of the *Miami Herald's* account of the Hart affair found fault in the fact that the reporters did not do a sufficiently careful, thorough job (not watching the *rear* entrance of the building, for example, from which, theoretically, Hart's lady friend might have left the previous evening)—in other words, they thought that the principal defect of the story was the lack of really good reporting. Other critics, of course, questioned the wisdom of publishing such a story at all, arguing that it was irrelevant to a presidential candidate's campaign and qualifications for public office and constituted an invasion of privacy.

This case seems rather inconsequential, perhaps, but it is typical of the reportorial problems that face journalists every single day. Should the reporter attempt to be as thorough as possible, or should he or she be satisfied with an obviously incomplete account? And with any given subject, an even more important question might be this: Should the reporter even try to report the story at all?

What is involved here? The people's right to know? Objective reporting? Fairness? Reportorial integrity? Freedom of the press? All of these, of course. The problem comes from the fact that there is such a wide disagreement among journalists (and others) about the meaning of each of these concepts. Everyone likes to play the game, "Some Antics with Semantics." Did the people have a right to know about the amorous activities of a candidate for the country's highest office? This question gets

---

[4] While a leading candidate for the Democratic nomination for President in 1987, Gary Hart and a young lady were observed coming out of Hart's apartment in the morning, by *Miami Herald* reporters, who broke the story and, in a very real sense, knocked Hart out of the presidential race. The case caused quite a stir among journalists and others, some thinking that the public did not need to know about such things—which were in the realm of a person's *private* life—and others thinking that it was the duty of the press to inform the people fully about the lives of public figures.

the journalist into the problem of deciding not only what a "public right" is, but whether it applies to every situation and person.

How does one objectively report a story that is largely hidden from reporters' perceptions? Was it fair to Hart and his lady friend to have had such an "incomplete" story printed? Or should *any* kind of story have been printed? Did the *Miami Herald* have the right to print the story? Possible answers to the above questions: One can't report such a story objectively. It may not have been fair to Hart to publish the story, but it may have been fair to the public. It is debatable whether any kind of story should have been printed. The *Miami Herald* did, indeed, have the right to print such a story.

One thing is certain—or should be certain: *If* a reporter decides to write such a story (or any story), there should be a determination to protect its integrity. In other words, once the die is cast and the decision to report is made, the reporter should concentrate on making the report as accurate and thorough as possible. A report is not an editorial; it is a report, and as such it must have integrity—accuracy, thoroughness, and proper proportion.

No reporter *has* to write a given story. But if he or she decides to do so, then what is the reporter's duty or obligation? Many would say that it is *to report: to provide as complete and accurate an account as possible.* In other words, once the reporter begins reporting, he or she should report— that is, provide the fullest, most accurate disclosure of the event *without intentional distortion.* That is what is meant by story integrity.

REPORTER OR MORALIST?

Not every reporter would agree with the "integrity of the report" hypothesis presented above. Some would say that they should publish the story with some tampering of the facts, with intentional distortions; these reporters obviously believe that accuracy, or at least completeness, is not of prime importance. What is more important to them? Ethical considerations. Does not a reporter show good intentions when he or she considers the consequences of publishing certain information in a story? Yes. But is the reporter showing respect for the report itself? No. Or at least maybe not.

Here is something to think about: Is the journalist a reporter or a moralist? Should the reporter report and "let the chips fall where they may," or should he or she modify the story in view of the possible consequences to somebody? Is not the answer to these questions an indication as to whether the journalist is a *reporter* or a *distorter?* And it is not enough to reply that "all reporters are distorters" since no reporter's report can perfectly match reality. That is too obvious. We are talking about *intentional* distortion, not natural distortion.

If a reporter slides too far over into a moralist's mode and takes possible consequences too much into consideration in writing a story, does he or she not deprive the story of significant substance? We could end up with an ethically safe story that is a reportorial disaster. Much of our reporting might resemble this: "A presidential candidate (who preferred not to be named because of possible harm to his campaign and his familial harmony) was host last night to a comely model (whose emotional state might deteriorate if her identity were made known) at an apartment somewhere in the Washington, D.C. area."

This kind of reporting may be ethical in one sense, but how does it help the people "to know"? They know *something,* of course, but not much. The names of the principals in a story *are* important. The locations of events *are* (sometimes) important. Few reporters would deny that. But when they decide they want to, they intentionally omit such facts from their stories. And, of course, they justify such omissions by appealing to morality. They have, in effect, ceased being reporters and have become moralists.

REMAINING QUESTIONS

One might think that, in journalism, full-disclosure reporting would be considered the ethical position to take. But this is not so generally. One is therefore led to believe that most journalists, even those who make noises about objectivity, the people's right to know, and the sanctity of truth, are really more concerned with manipulating facts, hiding biases, projecting an ideology, "cleaning up quotes" (unless they don't like the speaker), concealing sources, and editorializing through emphasis, deemphasis, and omission. It often seems that editorial self-determination (journalistic freedom of a negative kind) is more sacred in journalism than either full-disclosure reporting *or* journalistic integrity.

Why can't the reporter use press freedom to be objective? The idea that full-disclosure, untampered-with reporting is ethical *per se* is not a new idea. Reporters, editors, and especially journalism teachers have made such assertions many times. But when ethicists and theoreticians come into the picture with visions of full-fledged media ethics courses dancing in their heads, the notion of reportorial purity as itself ethical begins to blur. The moralists of news reporting enter; they look about for all sorts of exceptions to full disclosure, and they manifest concern and moral anguish for the feelings of the principals in a story.

What about the old, basic question posed by countless editors in newsrooms and by teachers in the classroom: Am I a good reporter if I fail to be truthful, balanced, and complete in the story?

The question we *do* hear goes something like this: Am I a good reporter if I simply report accurately the facts of a story without first thinking about all the emotional, psychological, and sociological ramifications of my reporting them and then adjusting the story to fit my conclusions about the possible consequences?

Another question that we perhaps should hear, but don't, is this: Am I a good reporter when I, for *any* reason, purposely keep the people from knowing some salient facts of the story if I have them?

The answers to such questions will vary, of course, but they only show that among journalists there is no real dedication or loyalty to the integrity of the story itself, but rather to the journalist's right to "play with" the facts for any reason deemed important. Objectivity goes down the drain. Subjectivity is enthroned. And there are rationalizations galore for departing from straight, full-disclosure reporting. There are many things more important, it seems, than to be accurate, full, and balanced in a report.

And thus comes this interesting point, which many of us refuse to face: Reporting may well be one thing, and editorial manipulation of the facts another. Take the case of the reporter who decides (maybe because of ethical considerations) not to print the name of a rape victim. The report is then flawed. It is incomplete. Verified and pertinent information is purposely omitted from the story. It is a partial report in every journalistic sense. Reporting is suffering at the hands of ethics—or the reporter's perception of ethics. But it is better, says the reporter, that the reporting suffer than the rape victim suffer through being named. Maybe. But if the reporter can justify this stand, can he or she really be called a reporter?

Perhaps we should admit, if we are honest, that reporters' ad hoc values are more important to them than is their dedication to truth, even-handedness, verisimilitude, and dispassionate neutralism in reporting. So is it possible to be a good ethicist but not a good reporter? Take the rape story again: Reporters may worry about the victim and thereby omit her name, while at the same time having no qualms about printing the name of the accused rapist. In other words, the report contains the name of the *suspected* attacker (who may well be innocent) but omits the name of the confirmed victim.

And, of course, there are innumerable cases in which the reporter decides that the people will not know the sources of quotations and information. The reporter knows that *who* says something is important—often more important than *what* is said. But again, the decision is made on the basis of possible consequences, either to the source or to the reporter's future access to that source. Expediency or self-interest, perhaps coupled with some vague sense of ethics, thereby takes precedence over letting the people know the salient facts of the story.

Good reporting? Fulfilling the people's right to know? It's worth thinking about.

AFTERTHOUGHTS

1. Do you agree with the statement that a basic premise of mass communication is that the people should know the truth?
2. Is the idea that the people *should* or *ought to* know the truth the same thing as the people's having *a right* to know the truth?
3. In American journalism who is it that decides what the people know? Is journalistic news management consistent with the people's "right to know"?
4. If the people do have a right to know, whence do they get such a right? How can they be assured that they are receiving the fruits of such a right?
5. Which is more important in reporting—the integrity of the story or the impinging of ethical considerations that distort the story? How does such a question relate to the people's "right to know"?

CHAPTER 21

Semantics and Objectivity

Basic to mass communication are the problems of semantics—the *meaning* of the symbolic message—and of objectivity. How closely does the symbolic message represented by the story correspond to the actuality? How detached from the subjectivity of the communicator is the substance of the story?

Of all the perspectives on mass communication, of all the threads taken up in this book, these two—the semantic and the epistemological (encompassing the nature of knowledge) are critical to the whole realm of language, knowledge, thought, and truth. In this chapter we want to look at this two-pronged problem and to think about certain implications for the journalist and other mass communicators. We will focus on the concept of objectivity, and to do so we begin by examining certain principles of general semantics.

THE GENERAL SEMANTICS PERSPECTIVE

Alfred Korzybski[1] and the many general semanticists who have followed him have been, and are, vitally interested in the matter of objectivity—in trying to develop an orientation in language users that will make their

---

[1] Korzybski, a Polish immigrant to the United States who died in 1950, is known as the "father of general semantics." His classic work in this area was *Science and Sanity* (Lancaster, PA: Science Press, 1933). Many writers have translated his rather abstruse ideas into lay terminology; among the best known are Stuart Chase, S. I. Hayakawa,

writing and talking more scientific, precise, balanced, and accurate. The general semanticists have much to say to journalists and other mass communicators about how to become more objective, how to make their language "map" better resemble the "territory" it describes, which is what journalistic objectivity is all about.

No attempt will be made in this chapter to go into all (or most of) the teachings of general semantics. Rather, we shall deal here with a few of the most important principles as they relate to objective reporting. And we shall discard some of the traditional labels common in the writings of Korzybskians, using only those that we feel are the most useful.

1. *There is need for a multivalued orientation.* Journalists must realize that people and events are multifaceted and extremely complex. Simple descriptive "tags" will not do; a person is far more than a "liberal" or a "conservative," a "professor" or a "legislator." Journalists must lose their good–bad, black–white, this-side–that-side orientation and get into the habit of thinking on a continuum, avoiding hard-and-fast classification. Describing in detail what a person thinks is better than simply labeling the person a "fundamentalist" or a "progressive," a Democrat or a Republican.

2. *Events and persons have unlimited characteristics.* A habit of thinking about this principle is a good first step in the direction of becoming more objective. The journalist who recognizes this truth will consciously attempt to provide as many of the characteristics of people and events as can possibly be given. Of course, much of the story will be lost in the editing process, but the reporter can at least know that he or she did all that could be done to make the story objective. Keeping the "etc." (always more can be said) concept in mind will help.

3. *One must go beyond the "Is" of Identity.* Reporters, like most of us, overuse what the general semanticists call the "is of identity." Michael Dukakis *is* a man experienced in government, we say. But Dukakis is *much more than that.* This "is of identity" is a simplification of the man; it identifies him inadequately. It often characterizes a person in a way that displaces many far more important descriptors. If nothing else, this principle will alert the reporter to the fact that gaps need filling in and will force the reporter to ask, "What *else* 'is' he?"

4. *Every person and everything constantly changes.* Reporters often treat persons, institutions, and the like as if they were what they had been and as if they will be what they seem to be at present. We must remember,

---

Wendell Johnson, Irving J. Lee, Samuel Bois, and Bess Selzer Sondel. Korzybski drew on a number of fields, and his general semantics is a very eclectic orientation. Many academic areas have proposed similar ideas, notably the linguistic philosophers, the cultural anthropologists, and the deconstructionists.

say the general semanticists, that George Bush 1930 is not George Bush 1980, is not George Bush 1990. He is, in reality, constantly changing, although he keeps the same name or label. Reporters should always report as if they recognize that people change. There is a natural tendency to dredge up old descriptive phrases from the past to attach to a person in the news today; much of this is unfair and biasing, for it ties the person to old actions, thoughts, and places and causes the reader, listener, or viewer to think in static terms, in old images. Harvard 1940 is certainly not Harvard 1990, nor will it be Harvard 1999; the good reporter will not treat *Harvard as Harvard,* but as an ever new institution carrying the same old name.

5. *Members of the same class or group are quite different.* The recognition of this basic principle will help the reporter avoid stereotypes. Generalized tags will be shunned. Democrat$_1$ is not Democrat$_2$, and Sandinista$_1$ is not Sandinista$_2$, as the general semanticists would put it. The journalist may say that this in only "common sense," but a continuing analysis of journalism indicates that in practice many reporters do not write or speak as if they gave much thought to the principle. Individual differences must be stressed by the reporter if objectivity is to be approached.

6. *Highly abstract terms are subjective.* The reporter should realize that abstract terms such as "patriotism," "radical," "freedom fighter," "terrorist," "socialist," and "liberal" are subjective in that they are colored by the *meaning* the reporter (and the audience) associates with them as well as the *feelings* toward them. Therefore the objective reporter, or the one who wishes to be as objective as possible, will be careful to use such terms sparingly. If they must be used, they should be objectified, externalized, or exemplified, by associating the person's *actions and thought* with them. In other words, don't say the man is a "liberal"; tell us what he believes, how he acts, how he votes, what he says. Then we may come a little closer to understanding him.

7. *Descriptive adjectives are often subjective.* Many journalists will describe persons, places, and things with adjectives that they feel add to the objectivity of their story. However, many adjectives—probably most adjectives—really tell far more about the reporter (the use of the adjectives) than about what is being described. For example, the reporter refers to Mrs. John Jones as "lovely" or "elegantly dressed," but nothing is being said *about Mrs. Jones.* The reporter's language is simply self-reflexive; we are learning something about *the reporter's concepts* of feminine loveliness and his or her clothing preferences. The reporter must even be careful of using phrases such as "enthusiastic audience," for often what we have is nothing more than the reporter's personal feelings projected onto the audience. A basic question touching an "objectivity": How does the reporter judge (or measure) enthusiasm?

8. *A natural tendency exists toward bias through selection.* Journalists should recognize a tendency to select (or abstract) from reality those portions that are appealing, that coincide with biases, and that give pleasure. The reporter seeking to be objective must constantly be on guard against this egoistic proclivity. Journalists must force themselves to include information that is unpleasant to them and with which they disagree —information that they would normally be disposed to leave out. If journalists get into the habit of doing this (difficult as it is), they will find that their stories will be better balanced and fairer.

Many other principles of general semantics could be adapted to the requirements of reportorial objectivity, but these are especially important. Journalists can greatly profit from a general semantics orientation if it is not taken too far. If they become too preoccupied with the subject, they will become bogged down in their own language sophistication and will harm their ability to communicate. (In addition, they will likely become linguistic eccentrics and social boors.) A little general semantics orientation, then, is healthy and helpful; too much emphasis on the subject is dangerous.[2]

A small dose of general semantics should help journalists become more tolerant and less dogmatic, better able to see the many sides of what is going on and to appreciate the complex, dynamic personalities who people news stories. Such an orientation should also make a reporter more scientific or objective in that he or she becomes more and more of a neutral observer, a careful selector and arranger of data.

OBJECTIVITY REVISITED

For the sake of simplification and discussion, we propose that there are two main ways of looking at journalistic objectivity:

1. As a "myth," purely and simply—an impossible goal to achieve.
2. As a largely reachable ideal or goal, which forces the journalist to try to be fair, accurate, balanced, dispassionate, uninvolved, unbiased, and unprejudiced.

---

[2] One of the best critiques of general semantics, and especially of its misreading of Aristotle, is Lionel Ruby, *The Art of Making Sense: A Guide to Logical Thinking* (Philadelphia: Lippincott, 1954), especially Chapter 12.

The first of these perspectives is interesting to comtemplate, but it ultimately relegates the whole concept of objectivity to the trash can. It concludes that there is really no distinction between objectivity and non-objectivity. However sophisticated this idea may be from the viewpoint of the Korzybskian semanticist, it denies the evidence of our critical senses and judgment: to wit, that there really *is* a difference between a story that can be considered "objective" and one that can be considered "subjective."

The second of these perspectives is the more traditional one; it is based on the assumption that reporters can, to significant extent, objectify their stories by demanding of themselves as much balance, accuracy, and thoroughness (correspondence to reality) as is humanly possible. It is thus the reporter's *attitude* that basically determines his or her objectivity.

To be quite realistic, one must admit that a reporter—wrapped in the constricting net of language, reality, and personal psychological and ideological conditioning—cannot be perfectly objective in communication. The reporter strains reality through his or her perceptual filter and journalistic voice, and it comes out distorted. So in a sense, the anti-objectivists are correct. But those who contend that a reporter *can* be objective are not thinking in absolutes; they say that a reporter with a proper *attitude* toward objectivity can go very far along the objectivity continuum. They consider objective reporting as a goal toward which to strive; they are proposing that a reporter sincerely trying to achieve objectivity (or dedicated neutrality) can at least come rather close to it.

It seems that the first perspective, objectivity as a myth, is growing in popularity. Existentialism and its first cousin in the media world, "advocacy journalism," appear to be "in" today and gaining converts each year. The traditional idea that a reporter can be objective tends to be losing ground; since the reporter cannot possibly get everything into the story, why not just admit subjectivity and forget the concept of objectivity?

A certain danger exists in being tied too tightly to either one of these perspectives. The person who says that objectivity is impossible is one who may be simply building a rationale for his or her own forays into biased, polemical, propagandistic communication. On the other hand, the traditionalist who believes without doubt that he or she can be objective is living in a fool's paradise and may well get to the point of believing that the story—*the whole story*—really has been told in a given piece of journalism.

It might be worthwhile to consider these two basic perspectives more closely. Undoubtedly each journalist is inclined toward one or the other of these two positions.

THE SUBJECTIVIST OR ADVOCACY POSITION

Those subscribing to this position believe that objectivity in journalism is no more than a myth: objective reporting simply does not exist. Not *everyone* who believes this is also in favor of advocacy journalism, however. The subjectivist is often amenable to taking positions and biasing his or her journalisitic production. We do believe, though, that subjectivism and advocacy are highly correlated in a journalist. The journalist who has little concern for, or faith in, objective reporting is quite likely to be a person who is eager to become involved, to take sides, to want to persuade, to slant stories, and to advocate what is believed to be the proper stance for others to take. Anyone who watched the TV extravaganzas of the 1988 presidential campaign and saw the intrusion of network anchors and reporters into the activities, with their biases showing, cannot but accept the existence of the subjectivity–advocacy hypothesis.[3]

The subjectivist feels that objectivists cling unrealistically to a myth. It is time, says the subjectivist, for these believers in objective reporting to be intellectually honest and admit that it is impossible to be objective. Let us look for a moment at the concept of objective reporting from the subjectivists' viewpoint.

The objective report would be detached, unprejudiced, balanced, fair, dispassionate, impersonal, uninvolved, and unbiased. It would, in effect, match reality: it would tell the truth, the whole truth, and nothing but the truth. Where, the subjectivist asks, do we find this kind of report in the mass media? No reporter knows the truth; no reporter can write a story that can match reality, for as the general semanticists say, "the map is not the territory." It is "impossible to say everything about anything." The story is never what it purports to report.

Perhaps truly objective reporting might be called "sponge reporting" with the reporter acting like a sponge, soaking up everything while remaining unfeeling, completely neutral, and intent only on absorbing, and reflecting reality. Of course, this is not really the way it is with reporters, the

---

[3] For a more detailed discussion of the passionate, committed, persuasive, and "subjective" nature of the American journalist, see John C. Merrill, *Existential Journalism* (New York: Hastings House, 1977), especially Chapter 5. And for recent books dealing with the proclivity of journalists (especially at the elite media level) to bias their reporting and involve themselves in the actual events, see S. Robert Lichter, Stanley Rothman, and Linda S. Lichter, *The Media Elite: America's New Power Brokers* (Bethesda, MD: Adler & Adler, Publishers, 1986); William Rusher, *The Coming Battle for the Media: Curbing the Power of the Media Elite* (New York: William Morrow and Co., 1988) and J. C. Merrill, *The Dialectic in Journalism* (Baton Rouge, LA: Louisiana State University Press, 1989).

subjectivists point our; reporters are persons and persons cannot be objective. So the whole idea of journalistic objectivity is a myth and nothing more.

Questionable Assumptions of Objectivists

When we talk of objective reporting, we must make several assumptions. One is that the communicator is *free* to *be* objective. This is not really true, however, for the reporter is conditioned—by experience, intelligence, circumstances, environment, education, and a host of other factors. This conditioning is often completely unconscious. The reporter is in a sense destined to bring to the report his or her own perspectives, slants, and emphases. The reporter is, in effect, conditioned to be *non*objective and can be nothing else.

Another assumption is that the reporter can be objective in the sense of being able to *present the whole story*. This, too, is false. Every reporter *must* be selective. This selectivity works in any of several ways: according to what is most easily obtainable; what the reporter is exposed to personally; is "pushed" most forcefully and cleverly upon the reporter; what appears to be the most interesting or colorful; what reinforces existing biases and ideological values; and what the reporter has been taught constitutes "news."

At any rate, the reporter selects, and the selection of what to put in a story automatically *subjectivizes* it, in a sense biasing and distorting the reality that the reporter is claiming to objectify in the report.

Another assumption is that the reporter can be *detached*. This is really impossible , say the subjectivists. Any reporter, in order to try to get at the meaning of a story, must become involved in the story; he or she must become concerned, make judgments, and take positions with regard to the persons and viewpoints in the story. There are many meanings of "detachment," of course, but it would seem that in any case a stance of detachment will not ensure objectivity. In fact, many subjectivists insist that the degree to which a person is detached indicates the degree to which he or she is *subjective,* not objective.

Another assumption is that a reporter can be *unprejudiced*. Prejudice is difficult to define but is usually understood to mean an opinion for or against anything held without adequate basis. The key word in the preceding sentence is, of course, "adequate." One wonders if the basis for or against almost any opinion is adequate, in the sense of being valid, complete, or true. Is not all reporting, ask the subjectivists, based on at least some degree of prejudice, or inconclusive evidence? Try to imagine a reporter operating in a context wherein he or she would have no prejudices. Of course, the more complex and controversial the reportorial context, the more prejudice becomes operative. Is not every reporter, then, a victim of prejudices?

A final assumption is that a reporter can *keep his or opinions out* of the story. The subjectivists deny that this can be done. They raise the following questions: How can reporters select certain things to include, or make determinations as to their order and emphasis, without acting on their own opinions? How, indeed, can an editor or reporter even decide to cover a certain event in the first place without acting on opinions? A reporter's opinions determine his or her entire reportorial output, say the subjectivists; it is impossible to report without opining, and when one opines he or she is subjective.

A French sociologist, Armand Mattelart, writing from a Marxist perspective, refers to objectivity as "the golden rule of journalistic practice, the cornerstone of its professional deontology, and the equivalent of the Hippocratic oath."[4] However, he does not believe it exists. He points out:

1. The concept presupposes on the part of the journalist certain perceptive powers capable of penetrating reality and determining what is important and what is not.
2. The concept postulates that the description of facts (which purports to be what they are *in themselves* and not what the journalist sees them to be) goes no further than the facts themselves.
3. Facts are *isolated* by objectivity-oriented journalism, "cut off from their roots, deprived of the conditions which would explain their occurrence and detached from the social system which endows them with meaning and in which they possess an intelligible place."

Is it not reasonable in light of these overpowering doubts, ask the subjectivists, to state categorically that a reporter *must* be subjective and that objective reporting is but a myth?

THE OBJECTIVIST OR NEUTRALIST POSITION

No, answer the objectivists; it is not necessary to refer to objective reporting as a myth. But enter the semantic problem again. Objectivists have their own definition of objective reporting. Perhaps they would admit that there is no such thing as objectivity as the subjectivist defines the term; but

---

[4] Armand Mattelart, *Mass Media, Ideologies, and the Revolutionary Movement* (Atlantic Highlands, NJ: Humanities Press, 1980), p. 39.

they say that the concept should be considered not as requiring a pure or perfect state, but pragmatically. They say that objectivity is a goal—an approachable goal—that a reporter should constantly strive for; and although he or she may never reach it in the perfect state that the subjectivist talks about, he or she can attain it to such a degree that it is a meaningful term, not a myth at all.

The Objective Attitude

The objectivist believes that the way to achieve objectivity in a story is to *desire* to achieve it and *make an effort* to achieve it. If a reporter sincerely *wants* to be fair, unbiased, balanced, and factual, he or she can be so at least to the extent that the term "objectivity" has any usable validity and meaning.

So the key question is this: What is the reporter's *attitude* toward the story and the audience? Is the reportorial attitude *neutralist* or *engaged?* Objectivity, if grounded in an attitude of neutralism, is a realistic concept in journalism, say the objectivists.

Objectivity is related to an attitude favoring—a bias toward—accuracy, comprehensiveness, balance, truth and verifiability. Objectivity is a show of good faith. It is the conscious attempt on the part of a reporter to be objective. It reflects a desire, an ideal, on the part of the reporter. And, objectivists insist, if reporters do not keep *trying* to be objective, they will slip quickly and deeply into the slough of pure opinion, carelessness, imbalance, and polemic.

Pitfalls Aplenty

Although the objectivist sees reportorial objectivity as a realistic and valuable goal in journalism, there is a recognition that there are innumerable obstacles to be overcome. The objectivist reporter knows just as well as the subjectivist that language restricts full and accurate reporting, that reporting is colored by biases and prejudices, that value judgments must be made, that journalistic behavior is largely conditioned, and that full detachment is virtually impossible.

But the objectivist reporter looks upon these facts of language and existence as obstacles to be overcome, as one of journalism's greatest challenges. The fact that a reporter cannot be *fully* objective does not mean that the battle to surmount these obstacles should be given up. A recognition of human weaknesses does not mean that a reporter must forsake the goal of objectivity; it only imposes greater challenge and calls for more effort. Such a reporter at least desires to present a full, unbiased, balanced, and reliable account—and believes that this determined effort will make it possible to achieve objectivity to a far greater degree than can be achieved by the person who scoffs at the concept of objectivity and plunges head-long into opinionated, biased, or advocacy journalism.

Trying is better than not trying, say the objectivists, and the reporter who *tries* will in the long run be more credible and more objective that will the reporter who does not try. In other words, the objectivist believes that the attitude of the reporter—the attitude *toward* objectivity—will deter-mine how objective journalism can be.

WHAT DOES IT ALL MEAN?

Epistemologically, objectivity in communication signifies a relationship between symbol and reality, with virtual correspondence or harmonizing being the ideal. Semantically, objectivity may conjure up cognitive com-pleteness or it may suggest natural knowledge limitations kept to a mini-mum by attitudinal determination.

Now what does all that mean? It means communicators and communi-cation students are concerned with the spread of knowledge, and that the want the knowledge to be as thorough and accurate as possible. It also means that some of them think of objectivity as being defined by the thoroughness and accuracy of the story while others consider the attitude or motive of the *communicator* as the touchstone.

How do we *know* something? Where do we get our knowledge? To whom do we turn for our view of the world and what is happening in it? How do we know that what we get is correct? Such questions reflect our concern with epistemology.

What does that commentator *mean* by his or her statement about Palestinians on the West Bank? I'm getting a lot of news about the intra-national frictions in Nicaragua, but what does it all mean? We learn that the United States will spend billions of dollars on "Star Wars" technology, but what does it mean insofar as protecting the United States is concerned? Such questions reflect our deep concern for semantics.

The bottom line is that it is hard to separate epistemology and seman-tics; they have a symbiotic relationship. Knowledge is impossible without meaning. And meaning is extremely complex—and certainly relative. If I don't know what some message means, I really can derive no knowledge from it. In short, I cannot *know*. If we have as our purpose to impart truth through our communication, we are necessarily concerned with both epis-temology and semantics. We must get the real facts, the real story, and we must present this story so that it will be correctly understood.

This is the goal toward which communicators strive. And as commu-nicators take this symbiosis seriously and they conscientiously pursue the intricacies of knowing and understanding, they will learn to contend with problems of objectivity.

AFTERTHOUGHTS

1. What would the general semantics orientation imply for the reporter who tries to be "objective" (in any sense of the term)? Would the idea of *flux* (or constant change) as first explicated by the pre-Socratic philosopher Heraclitus demolish any journalistic objectivity? (If you say it would, explain.)

2. If President Bush, for example, is constantly changing, as the general semanticists say, how can the people know at any time just what he thinks on a particular subject? How could he ever be held responsible for anything?

3. What do you think a reporter means when he or she talks about an "objective" news story? Do you feel this is an adequate or helpful concept of objectivity in reporting?

4. Is there any contradiction or tension in the idea of reportorial objectivity and the idea of press freedom? If so, explain, and show how the two could be reconciled.

5. Sometimes objectivity in journalism is considered to be full-disclosure reporting. Is this a reasonable way of looking at it? If so, how would journalistic ethics compromise or contradict such a perspective?

CHAPTER 22

For the Mass Media, the Future Is Now

The thrust of modern civilization has made many of the tools of the traditional workplace equally available in the home. The telephone, the computer, the photocopier, and the facsimile machine now permit a great number of white-collar workers to operate out of their homes with almost the same facility that they enjoy in the office. The mass media will play an essential role in delivering the vast amount of specialized information and programming into this home-office and entertainment center.

Gutenberg provided the means for "multiplying the message" on a universal scale. Message multiplication is no longer a challenge for modern technology. The same message can be delivered instantaneously today to every home with a television set in any country in the world. The challenge tomorrow is to deliver any piece of information for which there is a need to any place in the world at the command of the individual. That challenge will bring us out of the twentieth century, the era of mass communications, into the twenty-first century, the era of personal retrieval.

The first steps toward this new era have already been taken. Although they will seem primitive one hundred years from now, national newspapers, cable television, communication satellites, videocassette recorders, videotex, and the burgeoning specialized magazine industry provide a blurred image of what we can expect well into the twenty-first century.

The specter of the Hutchins Commission report stands before anyone trying to foretell the future of mass communications. That report, issued in 1947, correctly predicted that FM would soon supplant AM radio, but incorrectly forecast the early success of a facsimile newspaper, noted only briefly the possible impact of television, and did not foresee at all the transistor radio, cable television, the computer, and communication satellites. It may well be that remarkable new inventions, as yet undreamed of, will revolutionize journalism in the twenty-first century. In the authors' opinion, however, most communications inventions that will affect our lives and the lives of our grandchildren have already been devised in at least prototype form or they are technically possible if not yet developed.

THE WORD IS "DIGITIZE"

In the classic movie *The Graduate,* the young protagonist, just out of college, was advised at a cocktail party to get into "plastics." Today he or she would be told to get into "digital equipment." Everything we deal with in the twenty-first century is going to be associated with some sort of digital device, a one-or-zero coding that is the communication language of computers. The old analog technology (signals in the form of waves) used in telephone transmission, radio and television signals, and videocassette recorders will be relegated to the junk heap. Here are some of the pieces of hardware that will affect the speed, quality, and storage of information in the twenty-first century:

Cellular Telephones. We will be able to accept and send voice or data messages from any point on earth without benefit of a telephonic umbilical cord.

Fiber Optics. A single strand of wire into our home or office will provide thousands of channels for telephone, video, computer storage, and data transmission.

Videocassette Recorders. Already in 62 percent of American homes by 1988, they will hit almost 100 percent by the turn of the century. When equipped with digital recording and storage devices, they will be able to store unlimited hours of digitized video signals and will serve as a vast video library for home and office.

Flat Antennae. Lying flat on the roof and only 15 inches square, these antennae will be able to bring in signals from direct broadcast satellites.

Flat Screen Monitors. With the use of digitalization, these screens will eliminate the traditional picture tube and provide thin but very large high-definition television screens for the walls of our homes and offices.

Filmless/Tapeless Cameras. These cameras will store moving images in digital form; the product can then be presented as normal television footage or still photographs. A still photograph can be shown on a home television screen or immediately printed on a color copier. For newspaper and magazine purposes, a digital photograph can be transferred directly to the computer for sizing, separation instructions, and pagination.

TWENTY-FIRST-CENTURY MEDIA

What will media be like in the twenty-first century? On the basis of what we now know about the possibilities afforded by computer technology, we can predict the following.

Books. The problem with books was never production, but distribution. The growth of mall bookstores and the development of paperbacks have been two successful attempts to address the distribution problem. Books were among the first of the mass media to enter the specialized stage of media development. The revolution in books will be not in the bookstores, but in the library. Here rarely used books, journals, and newspapers will be reduced to digital storage, probably directly from the computers of publishers. The effect will be to save money in new library construction and make any item in the library immediately available in the home or office via data transmission.

Magazines. Magazines also were early arrivals into the specialized stage. The change to expect here is in production. The entire production process, except for printing, will take place in the editorial offices of the magazine (or in the editor and staff's own homes), where desktop computers with extensive typeface and graphic software will permit sophisticated production. Magazines will continue to increase in number, and the most highly specialized, designed for the smallest audiences, will be delivered directly by color fax into subscribers' homes.

Newspapers. The newspaper has proved to be a more durable and more adaptable medium than anyone would have guessed fifty years ago, and the authors are optimistic that it will be around in the twenty-first century in much the same form as today. As Joe Urschel, a television news consultant, has observed: "Compared to a newspaper, TV is still a primitive thing. Viewers have to take their information at the pace you deliver it, in the order you deliver it, and at the hour you deliver it." He added that newspaper stories are "all there for the reader to pick and choose. Newspapers are old technology, but very modern in their way. A newspaper is like a randomly accessible portable computer.'' Computer technology will enable newspapers to deliver to homes desiring them specialized inserts reflecting a wide variety of interests and needs. Cellular telephones, film-less cameras, and desktop publishing will allow newspapers a later deadline and eventually eliminate all backshop workers other than the press crew and delivery drivers.

Videotex. Videotex as a supplemental newspaper and vast information source will be available to most American homes early in the twenty-first century. Several million Minitel videotex devices have already been installed in France, the only country where it has been a success. Videotex will essentially make the output of any newspaper, magazine, or other information source accessible to the home or office. Using this device, along with a home computer or specialized monitor and keyboard, one can retrieve weather information, financial data, library archives, news stories, or children's games. The device can also be used for messaging and electronic mail.

Compuserve and Dow Jones News Retrieval are already successful videotex services in the United States, but their success is primarily with business customers, not in the home. The barrier to videotex in America is political, not technological. (This problem is discussed later in this chapter.)

Videotex now requires a telephonic connection to the special monitor or computer receiver. Commuters of the future will be able to read video-tex news and information on small flat screen monitors in their commuter trains (via cellular telephone) or by storing the information on their portable computers before they leave in the morning.

Radio. Radio signals will change from analog to digital. This means that all sound will be transmitted as 0-or-1 digits, and digitized radio receivers will take these data and retranslate them to sound within the receiving set. This concept will ensure that sound in the home, car, or office is of the exact fidelity as when it left the microphone or recording. Since there will no longer be any difference between AM and FM sound, we can expect to find AM radio in a competitive position once again. Digitalization will permit the FCC to assign a virtually unlimited number of stations to any local area, since there would be little chance of signal interference.

Recordings. All recordings will be digital, like the current compact disks. And the perfect fidelity of the disk will now be transmitted over the air via radio receivers.

Movies and Television. In the twenty-first century there will cease to be any real difference between the two media. With the development of high-definition television, many movies will be taped rather than filmed, and the "movie" itself will be delivered in completed form to either movie houses or television stations via satellite. Television signals will be delivered in digital form, and television receivers will translate this signal into a video picture of perfect fidelity in sound and color. Through the use of either flat antennae or fiber optics, viewers will be able to order a vast number of programs or movies, store them as digital signals within their VCRs, then call them up in perfect fidelity at a time of their choosing. Pay TV in various forms will put video stores out of business, since all material will be deliverable directly into the home. It is quite likely that there will be fierce competition between the local telephone company and the local cable company, each offering hundreds of video channels.

THE QUANDARY OF REGULATION

Nothing can stop the tide of technology—except regulation. The entity best equipped to bring the new communications technology into homes and offices is the telephone company, but court regulation is now preventing the "telcos" from moving the nation's communications into the twenty-first century. This regulation is a vestige of the divestiture (or breakup) of the American Telephone and Telegraph Company in the early 1980s.

In fairness to newspapers, television stations, and cable companies, one must look at the situation from their point of view. The telephone company as an information provider can be an awesome competitor for each. Using videotex, the phone company could quickly take at least classified advertising away from newspapers, if not more. As a cable operator, the telephone company could choose not to carry the local television signals, or it could provide so many channels into so many homes that the audience (and advertising income) for local stations would be greatly diminished. Using fiber optics and taking advantage of its access to many more homes, the phone company could provide more channels at less money than the local cable operator. It is feared that the telcos could also use the capital strength derived from regular telephone services to undercut prices charged by existing communications competitors.

From the point of view of effectiveness and efficiency, however, the phone company is into 93 percent of U.S. homes, compared with 54 percent (in 1988) for cable. Its head start in fiber optics would allow it to offer a full range of cable, data, videotex, telephone, and computer services. Access to many of these services will be delayed for decades if telcos are prevented from providing them.

Videotex has been a success in France because the government owns the telephone company and moved ahead to install inexpensive videotex receivers in homes throughout the nation. In the United States, Knight-Ridder attempted to provide a videotex service to the general public in the mid-1980s and failed. Without a telephone company as a major operator, general videotex services are probably doomed.

What is needed is some kind of careful regulation that prevents the telcos from competing unfairly, that provides "must carry" guarantees for all area television stations, and that gives newspapers a fair chance to compete as an information provider for telco information services.

The twenty-first century will mark an age when all knowledge known to human beings will be available to every person at the touch of a keyboard. Digital storage and digital transmission will make knowledge inexpensive and universal. Each person will be his or her own editor, choosing from material aimed at the individual rather than at the mass.

This transformation from mass communications to personal communications will not be without its disadvantages to society. There is something to be said for true mass communications that exposes a large number of people to a limited number of channels. Individuals in such an environment come into contact with a wide spectrum of cultures, ideas, and opinions, including those that they would normally reject. The era of personal retrieval communications will offer such a vast number of choices that individuals are likely to wrap themselves in isolated political, social, and educational cocoons. To the extent that this occurs, society will suffer, since it is likely to be divided into highly polarized, and probably uncommunicating, segments. To some extent, this is already happening in America.

Despite this drawback, nothing can stop the inevitable transposition of our society into this digital, personal retrieval age. It will still be left to the human spirit in this great new age to determine whether these media developments will serve primarily to educate and inform society or simply to entertain it.

AFTERTHOUGHTS

1. Once all information comes through one source, say the computer or a specialized terminal in our homes, will it be easier for an authoritarian government to control what we read, hear, and see? What safeguards would we need in order to prevent this?

2. Is the cocoon effect—the act of exposing ourselves only to political and social

information with which we agree—likely in the twenty-first century? Is it already evident in present-day life?

3. Why is videotex, which is nothing more than a newspaper, magazine, or book available by computer, unlikely to supplant the printed page as we know it today?

4. Is there any social or business disadvantage to utilizing the new forms of communication to conduct all business from our homes instead of from our offices?

5. Would it be better to have strict regulation of telephone company involvement in information distribution, as is now in effect, or no regulation, as is sought by the telcos?

Selected Annotated
Bibliography

Altschull, J. Herbert. *Agents of Power: The Role of the News Media in Human Affairs*. White Plains, NY: Longman, 1984.
The author deals with the role of news media in modern society, in the United States and abroad. He criticizes traditional press theories and long-standing myths surrounding the mass media. He compares and contrasts Marxist and capitalist press systems and provides insights into the complexities of global communication.

————. *From Milton to McLuhan: Ideas and American Journalism*. White Plains, NY: Longman, 1990.
The author presents a wealth of information interspersed in a history of journalistic ideas from the seventeenth century to modern times. This is a readable and important journalistic intellectual history.

Anderson, James A., and Timothy P. Meyer. *Mediated Communication: A Social Action Perspective*. Newbury Park, CA: Sage Publications, 1988.
The authors argue that old theories locating the site of media effects in the individual and the source of the effects in the content are inappropriate for modern society. They propose "accommodation theory" which deals with the interpenetration of three elements: media, texts, and our daily lives.

Barrett, William. *Irrational Man: A Study in Existential Philosophy*. New York: Doubleday & Co., 1958 (paperback edition, Doubleday Anchor, 1962).
Probably the finest definition of existentialism ever written. The heart of the book is composed of four long chapters explaining the views of existentialism's foremost spokesmen—Kierkegaard, Nietzsche, Heidegger, and Sartre.

Barron, Jerome A. *Freedom of the Press for Whom? The Rise of Access to the Mass Media*. Bloomington: University of Indiana Press, 1973.

The author, a lawyer, repeats and elaborates on his contention that press freedom belongs to the people and not to the press and that citizens and minority groups should have a legal right to have their positions, information, and views aired in the press.

Becker, Lee, et al. *The Training and Hiring of Journalists*. Norwood, NJ: Ablex, 1984.

This book examines the system used to produce professional communicators in the United States and compares this system with that of other countries.

Becker, Jorg, et al., eds. *Communication and Domination: Essays to Honor Herbert I. Schiller*. Norwood, NJ: Ablex, 1986.

Deals with some of Dr. Schiller's favorite topics: the influence of American advertising on the Third World; the militarization of our schools; the cooperation between the military–CIA complex and American media; the homogenization of national cultures as a result of Western media; and the dominating force of opinion research.

Berns, Walter F. *Freedom, Virtue and the First Amendment*. Baton Rouge: Louisiana State University Press, 1957 (paperback edition, Chicago: Henry Regnery Co., 1965).

An interesting book that contends that freedom is not justice and that some limitation on freedom is required for the maintenance of the common good. One of the best defenses of limited censorship and restraint in the name of "virtue" written in this country.

Boorstin, Daniel J. *The Image: A Guide to Pseudo-Events in America*. New York: Harper & Row, Harper Colophon Books, 1964.

A fascinating discussion of the growing art of self-deception, of how we hide reality from ourselves. Chapter 1 ("From News Gathering to News Making: A Flood of Pseudo-Events") is certainly the most interesting for the journalist, but the entire book is easily adapted to the concerns and problems of mass communication.

Bower, Robert T. *Television and the Public*. New York: Holt, Rinehart & Winston, 1973.

A resurvey, ten years later, of the classic study of the American television audience conducted earlier by Gary A. Steiner. Bower finds that the audience still goes to television primarily for entertainment but there is increasing movement toward news and information.

Brogan, Patrick. *Spiked: The Short Life and Death of the National News Council*. New York, NY: Priority Press Publications, 1985.

This book was underwritten by the Twentieth Century Fund, which provided the initial grant to create the National News Council. Brogan follows the NNC through its eleven years of existence, and blames lack of media support for its ultimate demise.

Brown, J. A. C. *Techniques of Persuasion: From Propaganda to Brainwashing*. Baltimore: Penguin Books, 1963.

A clear and concise discussion of the process of persuasion and the related concept of personality itself. This survey ranges from political propaganda, religious conversion, and advertising, through an appraisal of the mass media of communication and their roles in indoctrination and persuasion.

Brucker, Herbert. *Freedom of Information*. New York: Macmillan Co., 1949.

This book provides an excellent discussion of the entire problem of government–press relations as they revolve around freedom and censorship. Especially insightful are the chapters on the concept of the press as the "fourth estate" (Chapters 5 and 6), the chapter on objective reporting (Chapter 18), and the final chapter (Chapter 19) on freedom of information.

Carey, James W. *Communication in Culture: Essays on Media and Society.* Winchester, MA: Unwin Hyman, 1988.

This seminal book provides useful thought in such dichotomous areas as administrative versus critical theories, positivist versus Marxist theories, and cultural versus power-oriented theories. Many leading theoreticians in communication studies are introduced and evaluated.

Chilton, Paul. *Orwellian Language and the Media.* Winchester, MA: Unwin Hyman, 1988.

This book deals with language and politics of the nuclear age, showing how language through the media provides a powerful control-mechanism. Provides suggestions as to how we can minimize the harm such language can do.

Commission on Freedom of the Press. *A Free and Responsible Press.* Chicago: University of Chicago Press, 1947.

A basic criticism of the U.S. press by a self-appointed "commission" headed by Robert Hutchins. Criteria for a responsible press are set up and the American press is held up to these criteria—and it is found deficient. One of the most controversial and catalytic books published in this century in the field of journalism, it is probably the main stimulant to the current concern about "social responsibility" of the press.

Cooper, Kent. *The Right to Know.* New York: Farrar, Straus & Cudahy, 1956.

A former chief executive of the Associated Press exposes the evils of government news suppression and propaganda and contends that press freedom in this country is the same as the right of the people to know.

Cooper, Thomas W., Clifford G. Christians, Frances Forde Plude, and Robert A. White. *Communication Ethics and Global Change.* White Plains, NY: Longman, 1989.

This book, the first in English to deal extensively with media ethics in the international context, provides an excellent theoretical base for the subsequent discussion of ethical problems in more than a dozen countries. In addition to essays dealing with the problems and possibilities of internationalizing media ethics, the book presents (in appendices) many national and global codes of ethics.

De Fleur, Melvin L., and S. Ball-Rokeach. *Theories of Mass Communication,* rev. ed. New York: Longman, 1989.

A study of the processes and phenomena of mass communication within a sociological perspective. De Fleur's chapters on the development of newspapers, motion pictures, radio, and television provide a particularly good background for the Elite-Popular-Specialized (EPS) curve of media progression discussed in this text.

Dennis, Everette E., and John C. Merrill. *Debates: Issues in Mass Communication,* rev. ed. White Plains, NY: Longman, 1990.

This book, presented in the form of a series of debates on basic journalistic issues, gives the main arguments pro and con for such topics as the public's right to know, the professional status of journalism, the dominating power of the American press abroad, the benefits of advertising and public relations, and the propagandistic nature of journalism.

Ellul, Jacques. *Propaganda*. New York: Alfred A. Knopf, 1965.
In this seminal book (translated by Konrad Kellen and Jean Lerner), a Frenchman who does not like propaganda decries the inescapable necessity of propaganda in the modern world and curses its effects on mankind. The book is a fresh discussion of the mechanisms, categories, and effects of propaganda. Especially interesting is the discussion of how propaganda tends to splinter or partition society and how it is necessary to a democratic society.

Ewing, A. C. *Ethics*. New York: Macmillan Co., 1953 (A Free Press Paperback, 1965).
A leading British philosopher presents what is one of the clearest, most readable general discussions of ethics, in which he focuses on the two main considerations of ethics (What is good? What is one's duty?). The book provides especially analyses of egoistic hedonism, utilitarianism, and Kant's ethics of "duty for duty's sake."

Final Report of the Attorney General's Commission on Pornography. Washington, DC: United States Government Printing Office, 1986.
This is the report of an official commission that met in 1985 and 1986 as a follow-up to the 1970 Commission on Obscenity and Pornography. Like the earlier commission, this one could find no compelling evidence on the causal effect of pornography, but asked for stronger enforcement of existing laws, and called upon states to pass stronger child pornography laws.

Fisher, Glen. *American Communication in a Global Society*. Norwood, NJ: Ablex, 1987.
The author looks at the effect of U.S. communications internationally and shows how new trends will impact American foreign policy. He deals with such issues as information flow among nations, educational exchange, and the role of national images in global affairs.

Fisher, Paul L., and Ralph L. Lowenstein, eds. *Race and the News Media*. New York: Frederick A. Praeger, 1967 (paperback ed., New York: Anti-Defamation League of B'nai B'rith, 1967).
Newspaper personnel, broadcasters, advertising executives, and black leaders offer comment on the performance of the press in racial coverage, with recommendations for improvement. Among the contributors are representatives of the *New York Times, New York Post, Los Angeles Times, Chicago Daily News, St. Louis Post-Dispatch, Life,* ABC, CBS, NBC, the U.S. Community Relations Service, and the National Association for the Advancement of Colored People.

Fletcher, Joseph. *Situation Ethics: The New Morality*. Philadelphia: Westminster Press, 1966.
This little paperback by a professor of social ethics at Episcopal Theological School, Cambridge, Mass., deals mainly with the love ethic of *agape* and is oriented specifically to the Christian context, but its principles are easily applicable to human morality and conduct generally. The author contends that any act—even lying, adultery, and murder—may be right, depending on the circumstances.

Friedrich, Carl J., and Z. K. Brzezinski. *Totalitarian Dictatorship and Autocracy*.

2nd ed., revised by C. J. Friedrich. New York: Frederick A. Praeger, 1965.
An excellent general discussion of the historical roots of totalitarian ideology, the general characteristics of totalitarian dictatorship, and a look at the future of totalitarianism–both Left and Right. Especially interesting to the journalism student and journalist are Chapters 11 and 12, dealing with propaganda and the monopoly of mass communication and with education as indoctrination and training.

Friendly, Fred W. *Due to Circumstances Beyond Our Control . . .* New York: Random House, Vintage Books, 1967.
A readable and compelling analysis of how commercial television works, what is wrong with it, and how it got that way. An "outsider" now who was an important "insider" at CBS offers important and constructive criticism of perhaps the most influential news and opinion medium in modern society.

Fromm, Erich. *Escape from Freedom.* New York: Holt, Rinehart & Winston, 1941 (paperback ed., Avon Library, 1965).
Using the insights of psychoanalysis, Dr. Fromm discusses the inclinations of people to "escape from freedom" to some kind of institutionalized situation where they will not feel so isolated, anxious, and powerless. The flight from individuality and freedom to some form of authoritarianism and control is analyzed in a very interesting and readable manner.

Gartner, Michael. *Advertising and the First Amendment.* Winchester, MA: Unwin Hyman, 1988.
The author, a lawyer and newspaper owner, examines the creeping censorship which results from major court decisions in recent years.

Goldstein, Tom. *The News at Any Cost: How Journalists Compromise Their Ethics to Shape the News.* New York: Simon & Schuster, 1985.
Goldstein, a former reporter for AP, the *Wall Street Journal,* and *The New York Times,* gives dozens of examples of lapses between ethics as preached by the media and ethics as practiced. Goldstein is now dean of the Graduate School of Journalism, University of California at Berkeley.

Hall, Edward T. *The Silent Language.* New York: Doubleday & Co., 1959.
An exciting look at nonverbal communication—our manners, behavior, customs, etc.—and how they often communicate more plainly than our words. The important part that culture patterns play in international communication is discussed.

Haselden, Kyle. *Morality and the Mass Media.* Nashville: Broadman Press, 1968.
This book, out in a paperback edition, is one of the very few books that has dealt with the ethics of the mass media in a systematic way. Lucid in style and provocative throughout, it approaches journalistic ethics mainly from a Christian perspective.

Hayakawa, S. I. *Language in Thought and Action.* New York: Harcourt, Brace & World, 1964.
An excellent survey book pointing out the relationship among language, thinking, and acting, and showing how we might improve our communication and our emotional stability through a more sophisticated orientation (general semantics) to language. One of the most readable "translations" of the ideas of Alfred Korzybski into layman's terminology by one of the foremost contemporary proponents of a more scientific use of language.

Hertsgaard, Mark. *On Bended Knee: The Press and the Reagan Presidency*. New York: Farrar Straus Giroux, 1988.

This book presents a history and indictment of the relationship between the Reagan administration and the American press. The author contends that the media abdicated their responsibility to report what was really happening.

Hocking, William Ernest. *Freedom of the Press: A Framework of Principle*. Chicago: University of Chicago Press, 1947.

This book, by one of the members of the Commission of Freedom of the Press (Hutchins Comission), is one of the best philosophic discussions of press freedom to be found anywhere. It discusses the problems of press freedom , the development of the concept, the conflicting interests of those concerned with press freedom, and the various impediments to such freedom.

Hoffer, Eric. *The True Believer*. New York: Harper, 1951.

This little paperback provides one of the most readable discussions of mass movements and the people who lead them and make them up that has been written. In memorable epigrammatic language, Hoffer reports on the psychology behind mass movements and analyzes the motives and responses, and the potential power, of the true believer, and shows how propaganda is used in the process.

Hughes, Frank. *Prejudice and the Press*. New York: Devin-Adair Co., 1950.

A Chicago journalist, obviously disgusted with the 1947 report on the American Press by the Commission of Freedom of the Press, presents a well-documented albeit somewhat emotional and biased criticism of the Commission chaired by Robert Hutchins and of its main report, *A Free and Responsible Press*. Undoubtedly the most thorough of the many criticisms of the Hutchins Commission.

Joyce, Ed. *Prime Times Bad Times: A Personal Drama of Network Television*. New York: Doubleday, 1988.

Joyce, a former president of CBS News, tells what it was like to be at the top through four crucial years, 1981–1985. He gives the real flavor of the struggle between news and entertainment and the reasons why news frequently loses.

Jung, C. G. *The Undiscovered Self*. Boston: Little, Brown & Co., 1957. Translated from German by F. F. C. Hull (paperback edition, Mentor, 1958).

One of the greatest of modern psychiatrists pleads that we abandon the concept of the organization man, which he sees as leading to loss of individual freedom. He urges that we bring to light the true nature of the individual human being, "the undiscovered self," and points out the dangers in mass thinking and conformity.

Kendrick, Alexander. *Prime Time: The Life of Edward R. Murrow*. Boston: Little, Brown & Co., 1969.

A biography of a man whose life was inextricably bound up with the early history of news and public affairs broadcasting in both radio and television. In the first chapter the author reviews the strengths and weaknesses of commercial broadcasting.

Key, Wilson Bryan. *Subliminal Seduction*. Englewood Cliffs, NJ: Prentice-Hall, 1972.

Key charges, with the support of illustrations, that disguised images in advertisements are intended to be noticed by the subconscious mind and associated at

Freudian level with the product advertised. This was the first of a number of books by Key on this same theme. (See also his *Media Sexploitation*, New York: New American Library, 1977.)

Klaidman, Stephen, and Tom L. Beauchamp. *The Virtuous Journalist*. New York: Oxford University Press, 1987.

This book, by a journalist and a philosophy professor, serves as a guide to journalistic ethics, staying close to concrete examples. The authors provide a good mix of practical case-centered ethics and more theoretical meta-ethical concerns.

Klapper, Joseph T. *The Effects of Mass Communication*. Glencoe, IL: Free Press, 1960.

A basic book for those interested in the research done (up until 1960) on the effects of the mass media on society. Although the book leaves much to be desired so far as coming up with definite "conclusions," it does shed much light on many of the most significant effects of mass communication and points out many areas needing further study.

Kozol, Jonathan. *Illiterate America*. New York: Doubleday, 1985.

Kozol shocked America with his contention that 60 million people—one-third of the adults in the U.S.—are functionally illiterate. His book tells the ultimate danger of this situation to America, and suggests ways of reducing the number by half.

Lambeth, Edmund B. *Committed Journalism: An Ethic for the Profession*. Bloomington: Indiana University Press, 1986.

The author deals with enduring ethical principles appropriate for the practicing journalist. He gives emphasis to basic philosophical ethical concerns without abandoning the reader in abstract theoretical swamps. The book provides the journalist and student with helpful moral guides in the practice of journalism.

Le Bon, Gustave. *The Crowd: A Study of the Popular Mind*. New York: Ballantine Books, 1969.

This is a paperback edition of Le Bon's long-out-of-print classic work on crowd behavior written in 1895. Although dated in some repects, this book still provides one of the clearest and most perceptive discussions available of the nature of crowds and the psychological dispositions of those who compose them.

Levy, Leonard W. *Legacy of Suppression*. Cambridge, MA: Harvard University Press, 1960.

One of the most original investigation into the evolution of press freedom in America, supported by solid scholarship. Levy reveals that the founding fathers had a concept of press freedom far more restrictive than the one now associated with the First Amendment. Passage of the Alien and Sedition Acts was a trauma that caused press law to move in a more liberal direction.

Lichter, S. Robert, Stanley Rothman, and Linda Lichter. *The Media Elite: America's New Powerbrokers*. Bethesda, MD: Adler & Adler, 1986.

The authors provide a look at the backgrounds of people who comprise what they call the "media elite," persons who work in editorial capacities for the *big* media such as *Time, The Washington Post,* the *New York Times,* CBS, NBC, and PBS. Interviews were held with 240 journalists, getting at their backgrounds, their voting habits, and their attitudes on a wide range of social issues.

Liebling, A. J. *The Press*. New York: Ballantine Books, 1961.
Liebling is dead, but the insights of this newspaper reporter live on—although a number of the newspapers he mentions do not. Surprisingly, publishers generally accepted with good humor Liebling's barbs, many of which originally appeared in the columns of the *New Yorker*.

McLuhan, Marshall. *Understanding Media: The Extensions of Man*. New York: McGraw-Hill, 1965.
Those who like to quote McLuhan should plow through this source book first. Hot, cool, and "the medium is the message" are all here. McLuhan shoots forth several hundred communication ideas in this book, now a classic, although most of the ideas are open to different interpretations.

Mayer, Martin. *About Television*. New York: Harper & Row, 1972.
This could be called a "vertical" look at American television. Mayer produces a mass of information about the television industry as it now exists in this country. Nevertheless, he could have given a better picture of the forest had he not included so many trees.

Merrill, John C. *The Dialectic in Journalism: Toward a Responsible Use of Press Freedom*. Baton Rouge: Louisiana State University Press, 1989.
Primarily a book on journalistic ethics, this book shows how Hegelian dialectics can be applied usefully to many areas of journalism. A "synthesis-oriented" book which proposes that the dialectic is an important journalistic stance, especially as it relates to press freedom–press responsibility.

———. *Existential Journalism*. New York: Hastings House, 1977.
Presents the existentialist stance or orientation in journalism, relating to the press some of the basic ideas of such men as Kierkegaard, Nietzsche, Camus, Sartre, and Jaspers, especially stressing journalistic freedom on the level of the individual journalist.

———. *The Imperative of Freedom: A Philosophy of Journalistic Autonomy*. New York: Hastings House, 1974.
A book that intends to provoke an intense analysis of modern journalism in the open societies, pointing out roots and philosophical validity of a libertarian press while warning against the current drift toward a "theory of social responsibility" that tends toward press controls and journalistic conformity.

Meyrowitz, Joshua. *No Sense of Place: The Impact of Electronic Media on Social Behavior*. New York: Oxford University Press, 1985.
This communications professor at the University of New Hampshire, in this seminal book, shows how radio and television—especially the latter—alter our "sense of place" as they put us in new social situations unshaped by physical location. Mystified roles and barriers which once kept things and people in their place have now been shattered by the electronic media.

Middleton, Kent R., and Bill F. Chamberlin. *The Law of Public Communication*. White Plains, NY: Longman, 1988.
The authors present the First Amendment perspective in this comprehensive book as they present the law not only as it affects reporters and editors, but also as it affects the new technologies, public relations, and advertising.

Mill, John Stuart. *On Liberty*. Chicago: Henry Regnery Co.,1955.
First published in 1859, *On Liberty* is one of the most important tracts on which the libertarian press system is based. This paperback edition, with an introduc-

tion by Russell Kirk, is perhaps the best-known defense of liberty versus authority, of the individual versus the community.

Moore, G. E. *Principia Ethica*. London: Cambridge University Press, 1966.
This paperback edition of Moore's classic (1903) book on ethics is essential reading for those interested in the basic principles of ethical reasoning. It is concerned basically with these two questions: what kinds of things are intrinsically good; and what kinds of actions ought we to perform?

Murray, George. *The Press and the Public: The Story of the British Press Council*. Carbondale: Southern Illinois University Press, 1972.
Suggestions for a press council in the United States force one to look at the experience abroad. This book gives a thorough, yet concise, history of the British Press Council, with a good discussion of the philosophical dilemmas posed by its establishment and operation.

Neuman, Susan B. *Literacy in the Television Age*. Norwood, NJ: Ablex, 1989.
This book deals mainly with the impact of television on the decline in literary skills. Special focus is put on these questions: Does TV take time away from other leisure activities? Does TV influence the way people learn? Does TV affect school-related behavior? What effect does TV have on incidental learning?

Ortega y Gasset, José. *The Revolt of the Masses*. New York: W. W. Norton & Co., 1932.
This classic book by one of the greatest of Spanish philosophers is perhaps one of the truly relevant for twentieth-century person. In the last one hundred years in Europe and America the population has more than tripled, and out of this growth has risen the "mass man." Ortega poses, among others, these questions: Can Western culture survive the encroachments of the mass man? Can republican institutions survive this chaotic democracy?

Picard, Robert G. *The Press and the Decline of Democracy: The Democratic Socialist Response in Public Policy*. Westport, CT: Greenwood Press, 1985.
Stressing the importance of public participation in media matters, this book champions what the author calls the "democratic socialist" theory of the press. It provides an excellent critique of the capitalist (or libertarian) press and offers a "more democratic" path for press development.

Planning for Curricular Change in Journalism Education, Second Edition. Eugene, OR: School of Journalism, University of Oregon, 1987.
Now known as the "Oregon Report," this paperback is the product of a two-year study called "Project on the Future of Journalism and Mass Communication Education." The report called the state of journalism education "dismal," and suggested the development of generic courses that would serve both journalism and non-journalism students.

Prichard, Peter. *The Making of McPaper: The Inside Story of USA TODAY*. Kansas City, MO: Andrews, McMeel & Parker, 1987.
Prichard was managing editor of *USA TODAY* at the time the book was written. It is a seemingly no-holds-barred inside look at the creation of *USA TODAY*, from idea through the first four years of production.

Qualter, Terence H. *Propaganda and Psychological Warfare*. New York: Random House, 1962.
A small paperback with an excellent bibliography, this discussion of propaganda by a Canadian professor is one of the most useful available to the person

interested in propaganda. It takes up the theory of propaganda, its development, and how it is used in war, and it provides a stimulating discussion of the techniques of propaganda.

Rand, Ayn. *For the New Intellectual.* New York: Random House, Signet Books, 1961.

This book, as well as the author's *The Virtue of Selfishness* and *Capitalism: The Unknown Ideal* (by the same publisher), presents Ayn Rand's "objectivist ethics" of rational self-interest. These are excellent books for the journalism student or journalist who would like to divorce his or her activities from the ethics of altruism and self-sacrifice.

Real, Michael R. *Mass-Mediated Culture.* Englewood Cliffs, NJ: Prentice-Hall, 1977.

Book that explains how popular media of America dominate the culture of the United States and many other nations. It draws on scholarship from many fields to provide an in-depth summary of interaction among media, popular culture, and life in modern society.

Riesman, David. *The Lonely Crowd.* New Haven, CT: Yale University Press, 1950.

An interesting analysis of the growth of a mass society with the concomitant deemphasis of the individual. This discussion of depersonalization of society is well worth reading, in spite of its heavy dose of sociological jargon.

Rist, Ray C. *The Pornography Controversy.* New Brunswick, NJ: Transaction Books, 1975.

A book of readings presenting opposing viewpoints on the morality, legality, and effects of pornography in our society.

Rubin, Bernard. *Media, Politics, and Democracy.* New York: Oxford University Press, 1977.

A book from the political science perspective, discussing mainly communication objectivity and political reality, media and community values, media freedom and criticism, public participation in the media, and media and elections.

Rucker, Bryce W. *The First Freedom.* Carbondale: Southern Illinois University Press, 1968.

An updated version of the 1946 book by the same title by Morris Ernst; it traces the development of newspaper monopolies in the United States and pushes the thesis that there is an abandonment of the competition of ideas. A controversial book attempting to make a case for the proposition that press pluralism is disappearing in this country.

Rush, Ramona R., et al., eds. *Communications at the Crossroads: The Gender Gap Connection.* Norwood, NJ: Ablex, 1988.

The authors, all women, contend that communications is at an important crossroad because of, rather than in spite of, women. They further contend that there is evidence that women's language, orientations, and experiences are different from those of men. They probe the reasons behind the exclusion of women from mainstream communications channels.

Rusher, William A. *The Coming Battle for the Media: Curbing the Power of the Media Elite.* New York: William Morrow and Company, 1988.

Taking the position that there is a media elite in the United States and that it is "leftist" in its inclination, this book provides a conservative critique of the powerful American media and their influential "stars."

Russell, Bertrand. *Human Society in Ethics and Politics*. New York: Simon & Schuster, Mentor Books, 1962.

A noted philosopher redefines some traditional ethical terms as he subjects a whole series of conventional assumptions about moral codes, authority, and politics to vigorous rational investigation. Many ideas are easily adaptable to journalistic ethics in the modern world.

———. *Power*. New York: W. W. Norton & Co., 1938 (paperback edition, New York: Norton Library, 1969).

An excellent general discussion of the impulse to power, the types of persons involved in a power struggle, and the different forms of power. Chapter 11 ("The Biology of Organizations") is of particular interest to the student of mass media of communication as institutions and their potential as power wielders. Here is presented an analysis of the trend toward organizing, toward institutionalizing— a process to which the "average man submits because much more can be achieved co-operatively than singly."

Schiller, Daniel. *Telematics and Government*. Norwood, NJ: Ablex, 1982.

The author assesses the role of government in the computerization of American and global society. Stress is given to the importance of computers in modern mass media society.

Schiller, Herbert I. *Mass Communications and American Empire*. New York: Augustus M. Kelley, 1969.

A book very critical of the mass media system of the United States for cooperating with the capitalist economic system's endeavors to subjugate other nations. In short, this book, which is very heavy reading with its sociological jargon, discusses one of the author's favorite themes: American media imperialism.

Schramm, Wilbur, ed. *The Process and Effects of Mass Communication*. Urbana: University of Illinois Press, 1954.

A very valuable anthology on communication, with a wide variety of readings of leading scholars in the field, dealing with the process of communication, the audiences, channels, and effects. See especially the first article in the volume by Schramm ("How Communication Works") for an excellent survey of the communication process illustrated with helpful diagrams. See also these other books edited by Schramm: *Communication in Modern Society* (Urbana: University of Illinois Press, 1948), and *Mass Communications* (Urbana: University of Illinois Press, 1960).

———. *The Story of Human Communication: Cave Painting to Microchip*. New York: Harper & Row, 1988.

The late Dr. Schramm's last book provides a historical communications journey, providing many insights into the evolution of language, writing, printing, and the mass media. In the process, the author deals in a lively manner with a whole host of media-related issues.

Servan-Schreiber, Jean-Louis. *The Power to Inform*. New York: McGraw-Hill, 1974.

A French journalist looks at changing trends in the mass media and sees specialization as the wave of the future.

Shannon, Claude E., and Warren Weaver. *The Mathematical Theory of Communication*. Urbana: University of Illinois Press, 1949.
   Shannon deals with the communication process in mathematical terms, while Weaver discusses many of the theoretical implications in layman's language.
Shibutani, Tamotsu. *Improvised News: A Sociological Study of Rumor*. Indianapolis: Bobbs-Merrill Co., 1966.
   An interesting look at rumor and its relationship to news, with some insights into the nature of news. The paperback also provides the person interested in journalism with pertinent observations about news story "objectivity" and documents some of the principal ways of biasing and slanting news (See especially Chapter 2, "The Failure of Formal News Channels.")
Siebert, Fred S, Theodore Peterson, and Wilbur Schramm. *Four Theories of the Press*. Urbana: University of Illinois Press, 1956 (paperback edition, Illini, 1963).
   The four "theories"—authoritarian, libertarian, social responsibility, and Soviet Communist—are analyzed and interpreted by three journalism professors. One of the most widely used, and useful, books available in the area of press systems and concepts.
Singh, Indu B., and Vic Mishra. *Dynamics of Information Management*. Norwood, NJ: Ablex, 1987.
   The authors shed light on such topics as bilateral trade, international communication policy, telematic reindustrialization, transborder data flow, and the strategy for telecommunications development in the Third World.
Smith, Alfred G., ed. *Communication and Culture*. New York: Holt, Rinehart & Winston, 1966.
   This excellent book of readings, broad in scope, first deals with the theory of human communication (from three approaches: mathematics, social psychology, and linguistic anthropology) and then in the following three main parts it uses this theory to analyze the three dimensions of human communication (syntactics, semantics, and pragmatics).
Smith, F. Leslie. *Perspectives on Radio and Television: Telecommunication in the United States,* Second Edition. New York: Harper & Row, 1985.
   Smith provides virtually an encyclopedia of broadcasting, covering telecommunication history and every aspect of programming, production, regulation, and technology. The book has an excellent index and bibliography.
Sorensen, Thomas C. *The Word War: The Story of American Propaganda*. New York: Harper & Row, 1968.
   An even history of the United States Information Agency by one of its former deputy directors. The book considers all aspects of a central dilemma of the USIA: Is it possible to present information truthfully while efficiently fulfilling a propaganda function?
Spinoza, Baruch. *The Ethics: The Road to Inner Freedom*. New York: Philosophical Library, 1957.
   This paperback edition of Spinoza's influential work on "the road to inner freedom" is a valuable guide to the person who wishes to be master of his or her passions and emotions. It is probably one of the most profound and basic works in all philosophical literature.

Steiner, Gary A. *The People Look at Television*. New York: Alfred A. Knopf, 1963.

A report of perhaps the most thorough television viewing survey ever made in the United States. In essence, it is still not dated, because the same patterns of viewing among economic and educational levels of the population undoubtedly exist today. Intellectuals will be disappointed in Steiner's finding that they tend to avoid "cultural" programming almost as much as do the less educated.

Stevenson, Charles L. *Ethics and Language*. New Haven, CT: Yale University Press, 1944.

An American philosopher relates ethics to a sound scientific attitude and presents an analysis of the meaning of ethical judgments and the methods by which these judgments can be supported. One of the very best ethical discussions from the perspective afforded by studies of language and its impact on morality.

Swanberg, W. A. *Luce and His Empire*. New York: Charles Scribner's Sons, 1972.

Swanberg resorts to diatribe in this book, so no one should expect to get good biography or good history here. But it does give an interesting picture of Henry Luce's opinion of "objectivity" in the news, and it shows that there is virtually no difference between the Luce philosophy and the philosophy of the "new journalists" who followed 40 years later.

Toulmin, Stephen. *The Place of Reason in Ethics*. London: Cambridge University Press, 1968.

This paperback edition of Toulmin's book, first published in 1950, is designed to answer questions such as: How can we decide which ethical arguments are to be accepted, and which denied? What kinds of reasons for moral decisions constitute *good* reasons? And, how far—if at all—can we rely on *reason* in making moral decisions?

Turner, E. S. *The Shocking History of Advertising*. London: Michael Joseph Ltd., 1952.

An amusing, and frequently pointed, commentary on the history of advertising in England and America. The author is an Englishman, so the British perspective prevails. Turner has a lot to say about the ethics of the profession; he also recounts the efforts of advertising to dominate broadcasting in America (successful) and England (unsuccessful).

Turnstall, Jeremy. *The Media Are American: Anglo-American Media in the World*. London: Constable, 1977.

This book, by a professor of sociology at London's City University, discusses the complex problem of American media impact on other nations of the world; he rejects the simplistic "media imperialism" thesis, contending that most countries import American media messages as a "least worst" solution to a continuing problem: how to have modern media without paying the enormous price of making all the materials at home.

Weaver, David, and G. Cleveland Wilhoit. *The American Journalist; A Portrait of U.S. News People and Their Work*. Bloomington, IN: Indiana University Press, 1986.

Two respected Indiana University researchers give results of the most thorough survey ever made of American print and electronic journalists, their backgrounds and attitudes toward the roles, values, and ethics of their profession.

Whale, John. *The Half-Shut Eye: Television and Politics in Britain and America.* New York: St. Martin's Press, 1969.

By comparing the British and American experiences, this book places in better perspective the problems of both countries in achieving television fairness during political campaigns.

Whitaker, Urban G., Jr., ed. *Propaganda and International Relations.* San Francisco: Howard Chandler, Publisher, 1960.

A fascinating little paperback of readings relative to propaganda and psychological warfare. It looks at the nature of propaganda, discusses propaganda agencies of the leading nations, and presents proposals for government action in psychological warfare.

Whyte, William H., Jr. *The Organization Man.* New York: Simon & Schuster, 1956.

One of the most widely read and discussed books dealing with the change American society is undergoing—from a society emphasizing the individual to one that is group oriented. Certainly what Mr. Whyte says about business organizations in general can be related to the mass media of communication as institutions. He gives interesting insights into the group-related person and he sees mass education as a stimulator toward organizing as it increasingly trains people for group activity.

Wiener, Norbert. *The Human Use of Human Beings: Cybernetics and Society.* Boston: Houghton Mifflin Co., 1950 (paperback edition, Avon Books, 1967).

The founder of the science of cybernetics discusses important principles of communication in layman's language and provides a fascinating case for the need for better communicators (helped by manufactured machines) to fight against the powerful, disintegrating forces at work on our world.

Wober, Mallory, and Barrie Gunter. *Television and Social Control.* Aldershot, England: Avebury, 1988.

These prominent British communication researchers provide a clear summary and evaluation of the TV effects studies of George Gerbner and associates at the University of Pennsylvania. They also present some of their own findings of TV impact (especially of violent programming) on audiences, as well as summarizing similar research results from other countries, especially from Australia, the Netherlands, and Sweden.

Wright, Charles R. *Mass Communication: A Sociological Perspective,* 2nd ed. New York: Random House, 1975.

A well-organized, readable little book about the sociology of mass communication, exploring the characteristics that distinguish mass communication from other forms. Considers mass communication as to aims and functions, giving attention to the communicator, the audiences, and the effects.

Index

Abortion, 79, 106–107
Absolutism, in ethics, 190
Abstract terms, subjectivity of, 268
Academic groups, newspapers' reputations in, 136
Accountability
  of journalists, 107–109, 186–190, 193
  marketplace model of, 215–223
Accuracy
  of messages, 143, 145
  of newspaper reportage, 135, 242, 262
Acquired freedom, 182
Acton, Lord, 177
Adjectives, subjectivity of, 268
Adler, Mortimer, 182
Advertising, 4, 23, 24, 24n, 25, 73–75, 126, 213, 281
  audience reaction to, 76–77
  content, influence on, 77–79, 237
  costs of, 75–76
  false, laws against, 203
  by government agencies, 210–211
  and political views, 79–80
  in print media, 43, 53, 56, 75, 77, 78, 81, 82, 237
  regulation of, 80–83
  on television, 64, 65–66, 75, 76, 78–81
Advocacy journalism, 137, 270, 271–272
Affluence, 35, 56
Africa, 33, 52
Age mismatch, between journalists and audiences, 238–239
Agents of Power (Altschull), 217
Age of Reason, 174–175, 216. *See also* Enlightenment philosophy
Aggression, and TV violence, 143–44

Al Ahram (newspaper), 249
Albania, 158
Alien and Sedition Acts of 1798, 203
Alien Registration Act of 1940, 203
Alienation syndrome, 239
Allusion, frequency of, and newspaper evaluation, 135
Altschull, Herbert, 221; *Agents of Power,* 217
Ambiguous orientation, in journalism, 97
American Journalist, The (Weaver and Wilhoit), 104–105, 110, 238–239, 240
American Society of Newspaper Editors (ASNE), 108
  credibility survey, 235–236, 237, 240
American Telephone and Telegraph Company (AT&T), 281
Analog technology, 278
Anchorpersons, on television news, 66, 67, 69, 102, 271
Annenberg family, 102
Antinomian ethics, 192, 193–194
Appeal to authority, 254
Aranguren, José, 6, 9
Areopagitica (Milton), 160
Aristotle, 179, 184, 185, 197, 269n
Army Times, 213
Asahi Shimbun (newspaper), 136
Asia, 33
Associated Press (AP), 48–49, 240
Associated Press v. *United States* (1945), 49
Association, as propaganda technique, 251, 251n
Atlantic, The (magazine), 120
Attitude
  of audiences, 116–121
  of reporters, 270, 274
Attitudinal ethical theory, 191

Audiences, 6, 112–113, 242–243
  age of, 238–239
  attitudinal subgroups, 116–121
  behavior and motivation, 121–123
  characteristics, 115–116, 238
  fairness to, 259
  general public, 113–114
  and the marketplace model, 217–219
  and message, awareness of, 142
  and propaganda, detection of, 255–256
  proximity and participation of, 21–22
  specialized, 114–115, 221–222
Australia, 34
Authoritarian governments, 61, 67–68, 158–60,
  225, 227
  organization and press functions, 163–64, 166,
  169–70
  and propaganda, 249–250
Authority, appeal to, 254

Bad news, newspapers' emphasis on, 237
Bagdikian, Ben H., 105
Bakker, Jim and Tammy, 126
Balance, in editorial and news material, 134–35,
  248
Balancing doctrine, in court rulings, 209
"Bandwagon" effect, of political polls, 148
Belgium, 38, 50
Bennett, James Gordon, 101
Bentham, Jeremy, 177, 191
Berkeley, George, 176
Berlin, Isaiah, 183
Bias, 188, 249, 252, 253, 255, 259, 261, 269
Bild Zeitung (newspaper), 55
Bill of Rights, 179, 199. *See also* First
  Amendment rights; Sixth Amendment rights
Black Americans, 104, 219, 240
Block, Felix, 240
"Bloom County" (cartoon), 241
Bonfils, Frederick G., 108
Book publishing, 21, 43
  and distribution, 279
  paperback, 20, 48, 54
  single sales in, 24
  specialization in, 36, 53–54
Books, digital storage of, 279
Borgia, Cesare, 224, 230
Bork, Robert H., 181
Breed, Warren, 181
Brennan, Justice William J., 202, 204
Brinkley, David, 66
Brisbane, Arthur, 102
British Broadcasting Corporation (BBC), 23–24,
  168, 249
Brokaw, Tom, 66
Bundy, Theodore, 152–153
Burger, Justice Warren, 62
Burke, Edmund, 177, 181
Bush, President George, 268

Cable News Network (CNN), 44, 87
Cable television, 25, 29, 36, 37, 44, 46, 65, 69,
  170, 172, 206, 239, 277, 278, 281

California, 211
Canada, 45, 58, 62, 206
Canadian Broadcasting Corporation, 62*n*
Canons of Journalism (ASNE), 108
Capitalism, capitalistic societies, 89, 95, 175, 179,
  216, 219, 223
Cartoons, 241. *See also* Political cartoons
Categorical Imperative, 190
Catharsis effect, of media violence, 144
Caveat emptor concept, 217
Cellular telephones, 278, 280
Censorship, 93, 147, 151, 160, 162, 177, 259,
  259–260
  by advertisers, 77–78
  in government-owned media, 210
  by mass media, 253
  and positive freedom, 183
Chain ownership, of newspapers, 239
  See also Conglomerates; Monopoly ownership
Chandler publishing group, 102
Chandler v. *Florida* (1980), 208
Changes, in people, situations, 267–268
Channel noise, 12
Channels, 6, 7, 16, 17 *fig.,* 21
  flexibility of, 27
  literacy and demand for, 169–170
  number of, 25, 62, 65, 69–70
Chemical weapons ban, 71
Cherry Colin, *On Human Communication,* 6, 7
Chicago Tribune, 253
Children
  and mass-media violence, 143–148
  and pornography, 148
China, 53, 108*n*
Christian Leaders for Responsible Television, 79
Christians, Clifford, 183–184
Churchill, Sir Winston, 176
Cigarette advertising, 82
Circulation, 17 *fig.,* 19–20
Cities, and regional newspapers, 57–58
Closed meetings, 205–206
Codes of ethics, 108–109, 215. *See also* Ethics
Collective societies, 89–90
Color, in reproduction of media, 18, 28
Colorado, 211
Columbia Broadcasting System (CBS), 202
Commission on Obscenity and Pornography
  (1970), 147, 151*n*
Commission on Pornography (1985), 147
Committed Journalism (Lambeth), 181
Communication gaps, 14
Communication, 5–6
  barriers to, 11–13
  elements of, 6–8
  objectivity in, 275–276
  process of, 3–4, 6
  types of, 8–9
Communications Act of 1934, 68
Communications research, 141–143
Communist countries, 52, 52*n*, 95, 165
Communist Manifesto (Marx and Engels), 225
Compact disk recordings, 280
Competition, 44, 126, 211, 225, 228, 239, 281
Compuserve Videotex service, 280

Computers, computer technology, 18, 277, 278, 279, 280
Conglomerates, 47, 48, 58, 221. *See also* Monopoly ownership
Congress, 206, 210
Congressional Record, 210, 213
Consensus ethics, 193
Consequence ethics, 191
Conservatives, conservatism, 88–89, 104, 105, 114, 126, 232
Constitution of the United States, 161, 202, 260. *See also* Bill of Rights; First Amendment rights; Sixth Amendment rights
Contempt of court, 208
Content analyses, 141–142
Context, and the evaluation of media, 131–133
Contributing editors, 101
Control groups, representative, 145–146
"Controlled" newspapers, 138–139
Conveyer persons, 10
Cooperation, between media systems, 138
Copyright law, 202–203
Corporate editors, 239
Corporate publishers, 239
Corporation for Public Broadcasting (CPB), 24, 213
Corrections, printing of, 242
Corriere della Sera (newspaper), 136
Court trials, media coverage of, 206–208
Credibility, 135, 143, 235–236
   factors diminishing, 238–241
   traditional problems, 236–238
Credibility gaps, 5, 14, 236, 241–243, 246
Critics, criticism, 125–131
   and context, 131–133
   evaluative criteria, 133–139
Cronkite, Walter, 66
Curiosity, as motivational factor, 122–23

Daily Mirror (London), 52
Davis, Richard Harding, 102
Day, Benjamin, 101
Day, Robin, 66–67
Decoders, 7
Delayed feedback, 8
Delinquency, 144, 147
Democracy in America (de Tocqueville), 177
Democratic governments, 68, 93, 157, 160
   Machiavellian view of, 230
   and the marketplace model, 218
   press controls in, 200
   and propaganda, 250
Denmark, 151–152, 158
Dennis case (1951), 203
Deontelic ethics, 197
Deontological ethical theory, 191, 195, 196, 197, 226
Deregulation, of electronic media, 63, 68, 172, 213
Desktop publishing, 279, 280
Destination, in communication, 7
Detachment, in reporting, 272
Detroit Free Press, 236
Dewey, Thomas, 149

Dialectical typology, of ethics, 192–195
Digital technology, 18, 278–281
Discourses (Machiavelli), 224, 229n
Distribution process, 26, 279
Documentaries, television, 240, 253
Donaldson, Sam, 66
"Doonesbury" (cartoon), 241
Douglas, Justice William O., 204
Dow Jones News Retrieval service, 280
Downie, Leonard, Jr., 106–107
Dukakis, Michael, 267

Economic stability, of media, 138, 211
Editing (newspaper)
   audience response to, 219
   balance in, 134–135
   care in, 134, 237–238
   and credibility problems, 237–238
   freedom in, 137
Editorial fades, in TV reporting, 67
Editorializing, 263
   in newspapers, 137
   on television news, 68–71
Editorial pages, 101, 102, 105, 135
   and credibility problems, 236, 237, 241
   and propaganda, 245, 248
Editorial self-determination, right of, 260, 263
Editors (newspaper)
   age of, 238–239
   institutional, 100, 101–102, 103
Education, 101, 242–243
   of audiences, 217, 238, 242–243
   of journalists, 109–111
   and propaganda, 247
   of racial, ethnic minorities, 104
   and specialized media, 34–35
   and the tabloid press, 55–56
Egypt, 63, 249
El Nuevo Herald (Miami), 55
Electronic media, 11, 48, 60–61. *See also* Radio; Television
   advertising in, 78
   entertainment versus news in, 63–64
   government versus private control, 61–63
Elite-popular-specialized (EPS) curve of media progression, 31, 32 *fig.*
Elitist stage of media development, 31–33, 40
Emergencies, flexibility of media during, 27
Encoders, 7
England. *See* Great Britain
English language, 33, 38–40, 54, 103–104
Enlightenment philosophy, 174–181, 184, 225
Entertainment, 11, 28, 63–64, 76
Entropy, 13–15
Epistemology, 275
Equal-time doctrine, 68–69, 171, 210, 212, 213
Erskine, Thomas, 164
"Essay on Liberty of the Press, An" (Hay), 179
Ethics, 107–109, 174, 180, 181, 184
   basic maxim of, 197
   codes of, 108–109, 186–187, 193
   defined, 186
   dialectical typology, 192–195
   Machiavellian, 226–232

Ethics (*continued*)
  middle way in, 195–197
  and propaganda, 248, 255
  and the right-to-know doctrine, 259, 262–264
  theories, 190–192
  "TUFF" formula, 187–188
  two orientations, 188–189
Ethnic minorities, 238. *See also* Black
    Americans; Hispanic Americans
  education of, 104
  journalists, 240, 242
  on newspaper staffs, 103–104
  opinions of, 213
Evaluative critera, for mass media, 133–39
Event-oriented journalists, 189
Existentialism, 11, 193, 270
Exit polls, 150
Expository journalism, 118
Exposure cohesion, of mass audiences, 115–16
Express, L' (newsmagazine), 39, 49

Facsimile machines, 277, 279
Fact. *See also* Censorship; Full-disclosure
    reporting
  errors of, in newspapers, 237–238
  and objectivity in reporting, 273
  versus opinion, 252
  withholding of, 259, 260
Factions, 180, 185
Fairness
  to the audience member, 258–259
  in reporting, 92, 105, 188, 242, 258–259
Fairness doctrine (FCC ruling, 1949), 68–69, 171
    172, 210, 212, 213
Falwell, Rev. Jerry, 126
Farber, Myron, 209
Faulty analogies, 251
Feature news stories, 240
Federal Communications Commission (FCC), 63,
    167, 210, 212, 213, 280
  equal-time doctrine, 68–69, 171, 210, 212, 213
  fairness doctrine, 68–69, 171, 172, 210, 212,
    213
  indecent materials ban (1988), 147–48
  regulatory practices, 171, 172. *See also*
    Deregulation
Federal Trade Commission (FTC), 81, 203
Feedback, 7–8, 21–23, 242
Feminist groups, 205
Fiber optic technology, 278, 281
Fichte, Johann Gottlieb, 159
Fictionalizing, 254
Fiduciary principle, 62, 62*n*
Filmless cameras, 279
Finland, 50–51
First Amendment rights, 63, 68, 69, 108, 110,
    147, 172, 210, 213, 235, 241
  and the broadcast media, 182
  "free press" clause, 162, 199–200, 201, 204
  and obscenity laws, 204
  preferred position of, 209
  press freedom clause, 228
Flat antennae, 278, 281

Flat screen monitors, 278
Flemish language, 50
Florida, 207–208
Food and Drug Administration, 81
For the New Intellectual (Rand), 119*n*
Ford, President Gerald, 202–203
Foreign languages
  borrowing of, 38–40
  and circulation factors, 50–51
  and newspapers, 55
Forum for the people, press as, 93–94
Founding Fathers, 179–180, 199*n,* 200
"Four theories" concept, of press systems,
    163–166
Four Theories of the Press (Siebert, Peterson,
    Schramm), 163–166
Fourth-branch-of-government concept, 161, 164
France, 36, 136
  Enlightenment philosophers in, 175, 176, 177
  Videotex service in, 280, 282
Franchise principle, 62
Frankfurter, Justice Felix, 49
Franklin, Benjamin, 108, 175, 179
Franklin, James, 179
Fraud, laws against, 203
Freedom of Information Act of 1966, 206
Freedom seeking, defending, 93–94
"Free" newspapers, criteria for, 136–38, 139
Free press concept, 157, 158. *See also*
    Libertarian press
  and the Enlightenment, 174–178
  in the United States, 181–183
French language, 38, 50, 58
French Revolution, 176
Frequencies, for radio and television, 25, 62, 69.
    See also Channels
Frequency modulation (FM) broadcasting, 25,
    46, 170, 172, 239, 277, 278
Friedman, Milton, 220
Full-disclosure reporting, 258, 263, 264

Galbraith, John Kenneth, 73, 74
Gandhi, Mahatma, 183
Gannett Co. Inc., 47, 102, 237
Gatekeeping function, of the press, 70, 105–107,
    260
General public, 113–114
General semantics, 266–269, 271, 275
Geneva conference (1989), 71
Geographical factors, and print media, 51, 56–57
German language, 38
Germany, 177. *See also* West Germany
Glasnost, 139, 165
Glasser, Theodore, 221
Goldwater, Senator Barry, 80
Gossage, Howard L., 77, 78
Gould, Chester, 20
Government. *See also* Authoritarian
    governments; Democratic governments;
    Libertarianism
  advertising by, 210–11
  Enlightenment concept of, 175
  exclusion of press from meetings, 205–209

media ownership, 166–167, 210
press as supporter of versus watchdog over, 93–95, 137, 158, 161–62, 164
newspapers' reputations in, 136
taxation, powers of, 211
Graduate, The (film), 278
Grammar, in newspapers, 134, 237–238
Great Britain, 23–24, 36, 51–52, 55, 164
  Enlightenment philosophers in, 175–177
  media ownership, press philosophies, 168, 172, 235
  parliamentary elections (1970), 149
Greece, ancient, 230
Greeley, Horace, 101
Guardian (newspaper), 136
Gutenberg Bible, 18, 42, 277

Halftone engraving, 42
Hall, Edward T., *Silent Language, The,* 6
Hamilton, Alexander, 175, 179
Harding, President Warren, 108
Harper's (magazine), 120
Hart, Gary, 261, 261n, 262
Hay, George, "Essay on Liberty of the Press, An," 179
Hayek, Friedrich, 220; *Road to Serfdom, The,* 160
Headlines, of newspapers, 128, 128n, 137, 246, 252–253
Hearst, William Randolph, 101
Hedonism, in journalistic ethics, 191–192
Hegel, G. W. F., 159, 160, 165, 177, 225, 227
  dialectical process, 192, 197
High-definition television, 278, 281
Hill, A. Ross, 109
Hispanic Americans, 240
Historians, 136
Hitler, Adolf, 176, 225
Hobbes, Thomas, 159, 175
Holmes, Oliver Wendell, 216
Homogeneity, in mass audiences, 115
House of Commons (Canada), 206
Hume, David, 176–177
Hutchins Commission (Commission on Freedom of the Press), 125, 127–128, 129, 165–166, 180, 277–278

Idealism, 176
Ideologues, 120–121
Illinois, 211
Illiterate audiences, 116–117
Immediate feedback, 7, 9
Independent broadcasting, 69
Independent Television (ITV) networks, 168
India, 33, 33n, 50
Indices, to newspapers, 28–29
Individualism, 175, 177, 179, 216, 228
Individuals, laws protecting, 200, 201–205
Inferential feedback, 7
Information. *See also* Censorship; Information sources; Quotations; Videotex
  digital storage, transmission of, 278–282
  "fast food," 239–240
  personal retrieval of, 277, 282

restrictions on flow of, 200, 209–212, 226–227
  selection of, 252, 253
Information sources
  and biased attribution, 252
  confusion of, 144
  protection of, 208–209
  versus the right-to-know doctrine, 265
"Inside Edition" (TV program), 240
Institute for Propaganda Analysis, 250–251
Institutional editors, 100, 101–102, 103
Institutional equilibrium, 90
Institutionalization, 88. *See also* Social institutions
Integrity, of a story, 259, 260–262
Intellectuals, 119–121
Intelligence, 117
Internal specialization, 36–37, 53
Interpersonal communication, 8–9
Interpretive reporting, 137
Intrapersonal communication, 8
Investigative reporting, 241
Iran, 138, 249
"Is of identity," 267
Israel, 24n, 34, 39n, 50, 51, 168–169, 249
Italy, 136
Izvestia (Moscow), 51n

Jackson, President Andrew, 142
Jackson, Miss., 62
Jamieson, Dr. Kathleen Hall, 80
Japan, 34, 36, 50, 95, 136
Jay, Justice John, 175
Jefferson, President Thomas, 142, 160, 164, 175, 181, 182, 185, 225
  view of press freedom, 180
Jennings, Peter, 66
Jet transportation, 49
Johnson, President Lyndon B., 80
Journalism, 95–96, 118. *See also* Press concept
  advocacy, 137, 270, 271–272
  education for, 109–111, 184
  entropy in, 13–14
  fairness and objectivity in, 92, 96, 97, 137. *See also* Fairness; Objectivity
  four ages of, 100–103
  Machiavellian, 227–229
  orientations, 96–98
  professional standards in, 130–131
  regulation of, 107–109
  schools of, 91, 109–110
  and social responsibility, 129–130
Journalists, 103–105
  age of, 238–239
  attitudes and objectivity of, 270, 274
  ethics and accountability of, 107–109, 186–190, 193
  ethnic minority, 240, 242
  image of, in media, 238
  and liberalism, 104–105, 231–232
  and partisan causes, 106–107
  people- versus event-oriented, 188–189
  as personalities, 100, 102
  subpoenas of, 208–209

Kant, Immanuel, 190, 195, 196, 226
Kendrick, Alexander, 79
Kennan, George F., 74
Kennedy, President John F., 142
Kennedy, Robert, 146
Kinesic communication, 6, 65, 141. *See also*
    Nonverbal communication
King, Cecil, 78
King, Martin Luther, Jr., 146
Kirk, Russell, 220
Knight-Ridder publishing group, 102, 282
Koppel, Ted, 66
Korzybski, Alfred, 266, 266n, 267, 267n, 270
Kozol, Jonathan, *Literate America*, 45
Krock, Arthur, 102

Lady Chatterley's Lover (Lawrence), 205
Lambeth, Ed, *Committed Journalism*, 181
Large-group communication, 8, 9
Lasswell, Harold, 6, 11, 247
Lawrence, D. H., *Lady Chatterley's Lover*, 205
Lawrence, David, Jr., 236
Le Bon, Gustave, 114
Leadership function
    of journalism, 97–98
    of mass media, 92–93
Ledger and Enquirer (Columbus, Ga.), 236
Legacy of Suppression (Levy), 199n
Legalistic ethics, 192–193
Leisure time, and specialized media, 35
Letters to the editor, 241
Levy, Leonard, W., *Legacy of Suppression*,
    199n
Libel laws, 200, 201–202, 212
Liberals, liberalism, 104–105, 114, 231–232
Libertarian press, 137, 138, 164, 166–67, 170–72
Libertarianism, 158, 160–163, 199n, 232, 251
Liberty, Enlightenment concept of, 175
Libraries, 135–136, 279
Licensing, 62, 107–108, 171, 182, 200, 210
Life magazine, 36, 36n, 53
Lincoln, President Abraham, 142
Lippmann, Walter, 102, 224
Listener, The (magazine), 168
Literacy, illiteracy, 32, 33, 42, 43–44, 50, 53, 60
    and channels, demand for, 169–170
    as mass audience factor, 116–117
Literate America (Kozol), 45
Locke, John, 160, 164, 175–176, 178, 180, 181,
    216, 225
"Lone man" theme, of media dramas, 146
Loneliness, as motivational factor, 122
Long-range effects, of media messages, 146
Longevity, of mass audiences, 115–116
Look magazine, 53
Low-power television, 172
Lutheran Church, 152

Ma'ariv (newspaper), 249
Machiavelli, Niccolò, 159, 187, 224–226
    interview with, 229–232
    philosophy, 226–227
    Discourses, 224, 229n
    Prince, The, 224, 227, 229–230, 232

Machiavellian Press, 227–229, 231–232
Macrogroups, 9
Madison, President James, 175, 180, 181, 182,
    185
Magazines, 24, 25, 43–44, 46, 50, 51. *See also*
    Newsmagazines
    advertising in, 75
    frequency of publication, 26–27
    future of, 279
    government-owned, 210
    as mass media channel, 17 *fig.*
    specialization of, 36, 36n, 37, 53, 277, 279
Mail acts, 212
Majority rule, 175
Malayala Manorama (newspaper), 33n
Marcuse, Herbert, 183
Marketplace model, of media functioning,
    accountability, 215–223
"Married . . . with Children" (TV series), 79
Marx, Marxism, 95, 165, 176, 183, 225, 227, 273
    Communist Manifesto, 225
Mass audience, 10, 11, 113–15. *See also*
    Audiences
Mass communication, 8–11, 277–282
Mass hysteria, 9
Mass-mass media, 33, 36, 37, 53
Mass media. *See also* Credibility; Megalomedia
    censorship by, 253
    characteristics of, 16–30
    cooperation between, 138
    criticism of, 126–30
    growth patterns, 31–38
    as institutions, 90–91
    as opinion leaders, 92–93
    and political philosophy, 157–158
    and propaganda, 245–246
    social responsibilities, 127–128
    versus specialization, 37–38.
Mattelart, Armand, 273
McKelway, Benjamin M., 109
McLuhan, Marshall, 16, 16n
Mechanical noise, 12, 15
Media conglomerates, 47
Media for the Millions (O'Hara), 113n
Medici, Lorenzo di, 229
Megalomedia, 222, 223
Meritocracies, 225
Merrill, John, 244
Message choice, 46–47
Message saturation, 60
Messages, 4–5, 6. *See also* Entropy
    as cause versus effect, 146–147
    long-range effects of, 146
    multiplication of, 277
    and number of media, 221
    and personality of receiver, 143–144
    selection of, 121–122
Metacommunication, 3
Metalanguage, 3
Mexico, 51, 55, 58
Mexico City, 51
Miami Herald, 55, 261, 261n, 262
Miami Herald v. *Tornillo* (1974), 212–13
Microgroups, 9

Mill, John Stuart, 160, 164, 180, 181, 191, 216,
  "On Liberty," 178
Miller v. *California* (1973), 204–205
Milton, John, 164, 175, 179, 180, 182, 216, 221,
  Areopagitica, 160
Minitel Videotex service, 280
Minnesota, 209
Mises, Ludwig von, 220
Monde, Le (Paris), 136
Monopoly ownership
  by governments, 166–167, 210
  of mass media, 126, 170, 213
  of newspapers, 47–48, 56, 58, 102, 105–106,
    239
Monroe, Bill, 182
Montesquieu, 175
Moral philosophy, 186, 220
Morning newspapers, 57
Motion pictures, 11, 17 *fig.,* 20, 34, 281
  circulation of, 20
  dubbing of, 40
  specialization in, 37
Motivational factors, of audiences, 122–23
Movable type, invention of, 42
Multiparty ownership, of the press, 166
Multivalued orientation, of journalists, 267
Murphy, Reg, 45
Murrow, Edward R., 64, 102

Nasser, Gamal Abdel, 61
Nation, The (magazine), 114, 202
National Advertising Review Board, 81
National Association of Broadcasters (NAB),
  codes, 171, 172
National Enquirer, 219–220, 222, 237
National News Council, 109, 211–212
National Observer, 56
National Public Radio (NPR), 24
Negative freedom, 183–185
Negativism, as propaganda technique, 254
Neo-Marxist critics, criticism, 126
Networks, broadcasting, 69, 70, 71, 149–50
Neue Zürcher Zeitung, 136
Neuharth, Allen H., 237
Neutral orientation, in journalism, 97, 257
New Jersey Supreme Court, 209
New York Times, 28–29, 49, 57, 97, 101, 103,
  109, 136, 139, 222, 236
New York Times v. *Sullivan* (1964), 201
New Zealand, 34, 38
Newhouse family, 102
News Election Service, 149
Newsmagazines, 38–39, 48, 49–50, 102
Newspaper groups, 221. *See also* Monopoly
  ownership
Newspapers, 17 *fig.,* 53–59, 64
  accountability of, 219–220, 222–223
  and advertising, 25, 56, 75, 77, 78, 81, 82, 128,
    128*n,* 237, 281
  circulation, 44–45, 54–55
  credibility of, 236
  criticisms of, 128
  and the elitist stage of media development, 33,
    33*n*

evaluative criteria, 133, 134–39
future of, 277, 279–280, 282
gatekeeping function of, 70, 105–107, 260
government advertising in, 210–211
headlines, 128, 128*n*
internal specialization in, 37, 45, 47–48
monopoly ownership of, 47–48, 56, 58, 102,
  105–106, 239
national, 239
and the press concept, 91–92
previewability of, 28–29
and reader feedback, 22–23
regular publication, 26–27
self-regulation, self-evaluation of, 80–81, 135,
  138
staff quality, 135, 138, 139
women's pages in, 218–219
Newsweek magazine, 39, 39*n,* 49
Newton, Wayne, 201
Nietzsche, Friedrich, 159
Nixon, President Richard M., 203
Noise, 12–13, 14
Nonverbal communication, 6, 141, 246, 249
Nonverbal feedback, 21, 22
Norway, 51
Nozick, Robert, 182–183, 220

O'Hara, Robert C., *Media for the Millions,* 113*n*
Objectivity
  in ethical standards, 191
  in reporting, 92, 97, 180, 189, 257, 258, 264
  as myth versus reachable ideal, 269–273
  questionable assumptions about, 272–273
  and reporter's attitude, 274
  semantics perspective on, 266–269
Obscenity laws, 203–205. *See also* Pornography
Ochs, Adolf, 101
Offset printing, 103, 170
Ombudsmen, 242
Omohundro, Baxter, 236
On Human Communication (Cherry), 6, 7
"On Liberty" (Mill), 178
Open-meetings laws, 205
Open records laws, 206
Operating expenses, 26
Opinion leaders, 10, 31, 92–93, 135
Opinion, confusion between news and, 237, 251,
  252, 273
Oregon, 211
Ortega y Gasset, José, *Revolt of the Masses,
  The,* 118*n*
Ownership, of media. *See* Monopoly ownership;
  Private ownership

Page makeup, of newspapers, 128, 134
Paine, Thomas, 175
Paradox of freedom, 162*n*
Paraguay, 138
Participation, in verbal feedback, 21
Partisan causes, journalists' involvement in,
  106–107
Party papers, 47, 51
PASID (ingredients of propaganda), 244
Pay TV, 281

People, The (newspaper), 55
People Look at Television, (Steiner), 63–64
People-oriented journalists, 188–189
Perestroika, 139, 165
Person-to-person communication, 8–9
Personal retrieval communications, 277, 282
Personality factors, and message reception,
    143–144
Peterson, Theodore, *Four Theories of the Press,*
    163–166
Phelan, John, 183
Photography, 131
  digital, 279
  and propaganda, 246, 253
Physical noise, 12
Picard, Robert, *Press and the Decline of
    Democracy, The,* 221
Picture reproduction, in newspapers, 134
Picture symbols, 18
Plato, 159, 160, 162*n,* 176, 184, 217, 227, 230
Pluralism
  and the marketplace model, 218, 221, 222, 223
  in the press concept, 91, 93–96, 137, 164, 170,
    180
  and propaganda, 250, 256
Political cartoons, 241, 242
Political influence
  and advertising, 79–80
  of electronic media, 61, 68–69
  and newspapers, 47, 51–52, 58, 104–105
Political parties, rise of, 101
Political polls, 148–151
Politico-economic systems, 51–52
Popular stage, of media development, 31, 33–34
Population size
  and print media, 50–51, 54–55
  and specialized media, 35–36
  and technological languages, 38–40
Pornography, 147–48, 151, 151*n,* 152–153, 178,
    204
Portability, of media, 19
Positive freedom, 182, 183–184
Posner, Richard A., 73–74
Poverty, 32, 33, 117
Power elites, 159–160, 225, 232
Pragmatic audiences, 118–119
Pravda (Moscow), 51*n,* 136, 139
Prejudice, in reporting, 272–273
Presidential election campaigns, 80, 142
  and objectivity, 271
  and political polls, 148–151
  and the right-to-know doctrine, 260–262
Press and the Decline of Democracy, The
    (Picard), 221
Press concept. *See also* Free press concept
  in foreign countries, 94–95
  four theories, 163–166
  Machiavellian, 227–229, 231–232
  and pluralism, 91, 93–94, 95–96
  philosophies, 166–169, 169 *fig.*
  in the United States, 91–94.
Press controls, 199–200
  exclusion of press, 205–209
  individuals, laws protecting, 200, 201–205

restrictions on flow of information, 200,
    209–212
Press councils, 211–212
Press ownership, types of, 166–167. *See also*
    Conglomerates; Monopoly ownership
Press power, 227, 227*n,* 228, 232
Previewability, 28, 29–30
Prince, The (Machiavelli), 224, 227, 229–230, 232
Printing quality, of newspapers, 134
Print media, 11, 18, 25, 122. *See also* Book
    publishing; Magazines; Newspapers
  advantages of, 45–47
  advertising in, 43, 53, 56, 77, 78, 81, 82
  frequency of publication, 26–27
  and international communication, 49–50
  national factors, 50–52
  regulation of, 48–49
  right of access to, 212–213
  technical development, 42–43
  and television, 43–44
  world trends, 47–50
Privacy
  invasion of, 127, 236–237
  as legal right, 202
Private ownership. *See also* Monopoly
    ownership
  of electronic media, 61–64, 69
  of newspapers, 47–48, 56, 58
  of the press, 166
Progress, idea of, 174, 177
Proofreading, of newspapers, 134
Propaganda, 95, 98, 121, 164, 244–245
  definitions of, 244–247
  and journalism, 245–250
  techniques, 250–255
Protection, of sources, 208–209
Protestant Ethic, 216
Proximity, in verbal feedback, 21
Psychology, 141
Public Broadcasting Service (PBS), 24
Public broadcasting, 23–24, 171–172, 240
Public figures, 201
Public service, and newspapers, 137
Publication, frequency of, 26–27
Publisher-editor era, of journalism, 100, 101, 103
Publisher-printer era, of journalism, 100–101, 103
Publishing families, 102
Pulitzer, Joseph, 101
Punctuation, in newspapers, 134

Quotations
  ethical guidelines for, 195
  frequency of, and newspaper evaluation, 135
  and propaganda techniques, 254, 255
  versus the right-to-know doctrine, 264–265

Racial groups. *See* Ethnic minorities
Radio, 11, 16, 19, 20, 60, 61, 141, 239–240. *See
    also* Electronic media; Frequencies
  digitalization of, 280
  government-owned stations, 210
  government versus private control, 61–64
  as mass-media channel, 17 fig.
  talk shows, 21

and television, impact of, 43
transistor, 34, 60, 278
in underdeveloped countries, 32, 34
unit specialization in, 37
Radio Act of 1927, 62
Radio Cairo, 63
Radio Code (NAB), 171
Rakolta, Terry, 79
Rand, Ayn, 220, *For the New Intellectual,* 119*n*
Rape victims, 237, 261, 264–265
Rather, Dan, 66
Rating points, and advertisers, 78–79
Rationalism, rationality, 175, 179, 185
and ethical philosophies, 189, 192, 194, 197
and propaganda, 250
Rawls, John, 183, 220
Reader's Digest, 37, 53, 120
Reagan, President Ronald, 63, 66, 107, 172
Receiver, in communication, 6, 123, 143–145
Recordings, 11, 16, 17 *fig.,* 24, 37, 280
Red Lion, Pa., 62
Regulation, 48–49, 281–282. *See also*
    Deregulation; Federal Communications
    Commission; Press controls
of advertising, 80–83
of journalists, 107–109
of print media, 48–49
Relativism, in ethics, 190–191, 194
Reliability, of newspaper reportage, 135
Repetition, as propaganda technique, 251, 253
Reporters. *See* Journalists
Reproduction, in mass media, 17 *fig.,* 18–19
Resource persons, on newspapers, 139
Response, in communication, 6
Reviewability, of media, 19, 20, 28–29, 45–46
Revolt of the Masses, The (Ortega y Gasset),
    118*n*
Revolutionary War, 199
Richmond Newspapers v. *Virginia* (1980), 207
Right of access, reply, in print media, 212–213
"Right-to-know" concept, 161, 162, 257–258
and ethics, 261–263
and fairness, 258–259
full-disclosure reporting, 257–258
versus gatekeeping, 259–260
and integrity of story, 261–262
Road to Serfdom, The (Hayek), 160
"Roe v. Wade" (TV movie), 79
Romantic movement, 176
Roosevelt, President Franklin D., 142, 176
Roper Research Associates, 144–145
Rosenthal, A. M., 236
Rosten, Leo, 27
Rotary press, invention of, 101
Roth case (1957), 204
Rothbard, Murray, 182
Rotzoll, Kim B., 81
Rousseau, Jean-Jacques, 159, 175, 176, 216, 226,
    227
Russell, Bertrand, 176
Russian language, 38

St. Louis Post-Dispatch, 253
Satellite broadcasting, 37, 170, 172, 277, 278

"Saturday Night Live" (TV program), 79
Schiller, Herbert, 221
Schramm, Wilbur: *Four Theories of the Press,*
    163–166
Scripps-Howard newspapers, 102
Secrecy, 178, 260. *See also* Shield laws
Sedition laws, 199, 203
Selective perception, 46, 122, 256
Selective retention, 256
Selectivity, in reporting, 269, 272
Self-aggrandizement, as motivational factor, 123
Self-righting principle, 160, 175, 178, 179, 216
Semantic noise, 12–13, 14
Semantics, 266–269, 271, 275
Sender, in communication, 6, 123
Sensationalism. *See also* Tabloid press
    in the press, 55–56
    in television, 67
Sex crimes, and pornography, 151, 151*n,* 152–153
Sharon, General Ariel, 202
Sheppard case (1966), 206
Shibutani, Tamotsu, 254–255
Shield laws, 208–209
Shortwave broadcasting, 25
Siebert, Fred S.; *Four Theories of the Press,*
    163–166
Silent Language, The (Hall), 6
Simulation, in television news, 240
Simultaneity, of media, 19, 20
Singapore, 39
Single sales, of print media, 23, 24
Sirhan, Sirhan, 146
Situation ethics, 192, 194
Sixth Amendment rights, 207, 209
Small-group communication, 8, 9
Smith, Adam, 216
Smith Act, 203
Smythe, Dallas, 221
Social-authoritarian press philosophy, 166, 167,
    170–172
Social centralist press philosophy, 167–168, 170
Social classes, differences within, 268
Social contract, 176
Social darwinism, 216
Social institutions, 87
    as collectivizing bodies, 89–90
    common features, 88–89
    concept and structure of, 90–92
Social-libertarian press philosophy, 167, 170
Social responsibility, of mass media, 127–128,
    129, 138–139
    18th-century theories of, 180, 181
    as press theory, 165–166, 167, 170, 183
Socialistic countries, 51, 95
Socrates, Socratic method, 230, 250
Source, in communication, 6, 7
Sources of information. *See* Information sources
Soviet Union (U.S.S.R.), 51*n,* 58–59, 136, 138,
    139, 157, 165, 176, 227
Spanish-language communities (U.S.), 104
Spanish-language press (U.S.), 55, 58
Specialized audiences, 114–115
Specialized media, 31, 34–40, 45, 53
Speculative indefinite, in televion reporting, 67

Speech, freedom of, 199, 200. *See also* First
  Amendment rights
Spelling errors, in newspapers, 134, 237–238
Spiegel, Der (newsmagazine), 39, 49
Staff, of newspapers, 135, 138, 139
Stalin, Joseph, 176
Stanford University, 209
Stanley, Henry M., 102
Stars and Stripes (newspaper), 210, 213
Star system, and television news, 65–66
State legislatures, 199–200
"Stay-away" effect, of political polls, 148, 149,
  150
Steiner, Gary A., *People Look at Television,
  The,* 63–64
Stereotyping, as propaganda technique, 252
Structure, of social institutions, 90, 91
Subjectivism, in ethics, 191
Subjectivity
  of abstract terms, 268
  of adjectives, 268
  in reporting, 270–273
Subpoenas, of press sources, 208–209
Subscriptions, 23, 24
Subsidies, 23, 23*n*
Suburban newspapers (weeklies), 103
Suburbs, suburbanization, 55
Sulzberger, Arthur O., 109
Sulzberger family, 102
Supreme Court (U.S.)
  pornography and obscenity rulings, 147,
    204–205
  press rulings, 201, 207–209, 212–13
  sedition rulings, 203
Sustaining audiences, 21–22
Swaggart, Reverend Jimmy, 126
Sweden, 237
Switzerland, 38, 39, 136
Symbols, 18, 275
Syndicated columnists, 102, 105, 107, 241, 242

Tabloid journalism, 43, 55–56, 67, 237
Talese, Gay, 103, 104
Talk shows, 21–22
Tapeless cameras, 279
Tavoulareas, William, 202
Tax powers, of government, 211
Teapot Dome scandal, 108
Technological languages, 38–40
Technology, 170
Teleological ethical theory, 191–192, 195, 197,
  226
Telephone companies, 281–282
Television, 17 *fig.,* 19, 20, 34, 60, 122, 141, 239,
  277, 278. *See also* Channels; Electronic
  media; Television news
  advertising on, 64, 65–66, 75, 76, 78–81
  and audience proximity, participation, 21–22
  credibility of, 236
  daily watching of, 144
  government-owned stations, 210
  government versus private control, 61–64
  high-definition, 278, 281
  identity of, 64–65

and the print media, 43–44, 57
  previewing of programs, 29
  specialization in, 36, 37
Television Code (NAB), 171, 172
Television news, 57, 65–71, 133, 145. *See also*
  Anchorpersons
  format changes and simulation on, 240
  length of stories on, 239–240
  and propaganda, 245–246, 248
  reporter-personalities, 102, 107
Television sets, portable, 19–20
Ten Commandments, The (motion picture), 77
Textbooks, university, 53–54
Thatcher, Margaret, 24
Third World countries, 88, 95, 157–158, 166
Time Inc./Warner, 47
Time magazine, 39, 39*n,* 49, 202
Times, The (London), 51
Tobacco industry, 82
Tocqueville, Alexis de, *Democracy in America,*
  177
Transistor radios, 34, 60, 278
Treitschke, Heinrich von, 159
Truman, President Harry S., 142, 149
"TUFF" formula, of ethics, 187–188
Turner, Ted, 87
TV Guide, 29, 43*n,* 53
Typography, in newspapers, 128, 134

Ultrahigh-frequency (UHF) television, 25, 37, 46,
  65, 172, 239
Underdeveloped countries. *See* Third World
  countries
"Underdog" effect, of political polls, 148–49
Unfair association, as propaganda technique,
  251, 251*n*
Unit specialization, 36, 37, 53
United Press International (UPI), 240
United States, 36, 43, 53, 95
  Enlightenment philosophy in, 175, 179–80
  newspapers in, 54–59
  population, geography, politico-economic
    system, 52, 54–59
  press concept in, 91–94
  press controls in the, 200
  press freedom, theories of, 181–183
  social libertarian philosophy in, 170–172
  specialized audiences in, 221–222
University of Missouri, 109
Unlimited characteristics, of events, persons, 267
"Unsolved Mysteries" (TV program), 240
Urbanization, 55
Urschel, Joe, 279
Uruguay, 227
USA Today, 49, 56–57, 237
U.S. Department of Justice, 207
U.S. Government Printing Office, 210
U.S. Information Agency (USIA), 210
U.S. News & World Report, 49
U.S.S.R. *See* Soviet Union
Utilitarian philosophy, 178, 191, 195–196

Variable obscenity, 205
Verbal feedback, 21

Verbal symbols, 18, 19
Very-high-frequency (VHF) broadcasting, 65
Videocassette recorders (VCRs), 10, 20, 65, 277, 278, 281
Videotex, 16, 17 *fig.*, 18, 28, 29–30, 172, 277, 280, 281
Violence, on mass media, 143–148
Voegelin, Eric, 220
Voice of America, 210, 213
Voltaire, 181, 216, 225

Wall Street Journal, 56, 114, 120
"War of the Worlds" (radio broadcast, Orson Welles), 142
Washington, D. C., 240
Washington Post, 106–107, 202, 253
Washington Star, 219
Washington Times, 253
Weaver, David H., *American Journalist, The*, 104–105, 110, 238–239, 240

Weber, Max, *Protestant Ethic and the Spirit of Capitalism, The*, 216
Wiener, Norbert, 13
West Germany, 36, 55, 95, 136. *See also* Germany
Westmoreland, General William, 202
White, Justice Byron, 62–63
Wiggins, J. Russell, 212
Wilhoit, G. Cleveland, *American Journalist, The*, 104–105, 110, 238–239, 240
Will, George, 107
Wilson, President Woodrow, 142
Wire services, 200, 210, 240
Women's pages, in newpapers, 218–219

Yates case (1957), 203
Yugoslavia, 52*n*

Zamora, Ronnie, 208
Zeit, Die (newspaper), 136